HANDBOOK: PEGGY GUGGENHEIM COLLECTION

HANDBOOK

Peggy Guggenheim Collection

TEXTS BY LUCY FLINT AND
ELIZABETH C. CHILDS

CONCEPTION AND SELECTION
THOMAS M. MESSER

THE SOLOMON R. GUGGENHEIM FOUNDATION

Library of Congress Cataloging-in-Publication Data
Peggy Guggenheim Collection.
    Handbook, the Peggy Guggenheim Collection.
    Includes index.
    1. Art, Modern–20th century–Catalogs. 2. Peggy
Guggenheim Collection–Catalogs. I. Flint, Lucy.
II. Childs, Elizabeth C. III. Messer, Thomas M.
IV. Title.
N6488.18V46 1986   709'.04'00740531   85-19646
ISBN 0-89207-053-6

Illustrations © The Solomon R. Guggenheim Foundation,
    New York, 1986
Published by The Solomon R. Guggenheim Foundation,
    New York, 1986
Printed in Italy by Arnoldo Mondadori Editore
All rights reserved. No part of the contents of this book
    may be reproduced without the written permission
    of the Foundation.

CONTENTS

PREFACE

The Peggy Guggenheim Collection, as exemplified in the selected works surveyed in this Handbook, evokes the outlines of the history of art within the twentieth century. The main strengths of the collection are concentrated upon the form language of the French Cubists and its subsequent transformations in the hands of the Dutch Neo-Plasticists, the Russian Constructivists and the Italian Futurists; the transition from the pioneers of abstraction to the more recent abstract sensibilities that emerged between the two world wars; the imagery of Dada and Surrealism; and, finally, upon the early creative intuitions of the postwar European and American generation. None of these areas is explored exhaustively in this volume, and the collection itself does not raise claims to comprehensiveness. Frequently one or two well-chosen paintings or sculptures in the collection serve to carry the attentive viewer across sequential gaps. The sense of completeness, which, nonetheless, is one of the collection's attributes, therefore arises not from the presentation of large numbers of works but from their sheer intensity.

But the collection that Peggy Guggenheim brought together has meaning beyond the strength and value of individual works and even beyond the quality and intensity of the ensemble. During the first opening of her gallery Art of This Century, Mrs. Guggenheim received her guests wearing one earring by Yves Tanguy and another by Alexander Calder. She explained on this occasion and subsequently that she did so to demonstrate her neutrality regarding the warring parties of abstractionists and Surrealists. Later, in her publications and in her installations at the Palazzo Venier dei Leoni, she carefully separated "Surrealism" from "Abstract" art, mentioning repeatedly that Marcel Duchamp taught her the difference between the two.

With the hindsight now at our disposal, it may perhaps be permissible to translate the stylistic opposition perceived at the time into a more deeply rooted polarity between form and image. Obviously, the two are not separable, but varying degrees of emphasis surely can be felt in styles relying primarily upon structural elements—line, color, shape, plane, texture—for the projection of their content and in others that allow imagery —whether figurative or not—to articulate their meaning. Viewed from this perspective, Peggy Guggenheim's great accomplishment as a collector was to gather, with much intuitive perception and freedom from dogmatic assumptions, works that reveal the wide range and the ultimate unity of modern art.

Beyond such formal considerations, the Peggy Guggenheim Collection may be viewed as possessing two kinds of identity, depending upon one's viewpoint: first, as the now completed accomplishment of its creator, who spent forty years of her distinguished life in acquiring and in animating it; second, as part of the continuing, open-ended development of the collection of The Solomon R. Guggenheim Foundation, to which Peggy Guggenheim's former possessions now belong.

With respect to the first identity, the following by now well-known facts should be reiterated here for the record and for the information of the uninitiated. Converted to the pursuit of modern art sometime in the 1930s, Mrs. Guggenheim proceeded to acquire painting and sculpture under the informed guidance of, among others, Sir Herbert Read, Marcel Duchamp and Nellie van Doesburg. Her collecting of the European masters of modern art reached a decisive stage just as World War II spread across the Continent, so that she benefitted from a buyer's market *par excellence*. Returning to her native country and marrying Max Ernst, Peggy Guggenheim founded Art of This Century, a quasi-commercial gallery that functioned in New York from 1942 to 1947. It was then that she added to her collection works by American Abstract Expressionists (as many of her favorite artists eventually came to be known). Other works primarily from the postwar period were acquired after she returned to Europe to settle with her collection at the Palazzo Venier dei Leoni, but the mainspring of her passion for art collecting had loosened by this time, providing only sporadic impetus in the late years of her life. When Peggy Guggenheim died on December 23, 1979, she had become a legend and her influence upon modern art, particularly upon the formative stages of Abstract Expressionism, was firmly established.

The relationship of the Peggy Guggenheim Collection in Venice to The Solomon R. Guggenheim Foundation in New York is dependent on the extant legal structure. Within it, two museums, the Solomon R. Guggenheim Museum in New York and the Peggy Guggenheim Collection in Venice, function as analogous, operative branches of The Solomon R. Guggenheim Foundation. The two collections, therefore, are ultimately one, their different domiciles notwithstanding. It is for this reason that the exhibition *Guggenheim: Venezia-New York*, which consisted of sixty works selected from both collections and was presented on the Campidoglio in Rome in 1982, assumes such importance in the institutional history of the Guggenheim Foundation.

Because the New York museum must be viewed as the larger and older institutional sister of the Peggy Guggenheim Collection, its history as a collection should be described briefly here. The New York story started when Hilla Rebay, a German baroness, arrived in the United States in the late 1920s and acquainted Peggy Guggenheim's uncle Solomon with modern art. By 1937, when Mrs. Guggenheim was on the verge of opening a gallery in London, Miss Rebay persuaded Solomon R. Guggenheim to create the Museum of Non-Objective Painting in New York, later to become the Solomon R. Guggenheim Museum and to be housed from 1959 in Frank Lloyd Wright's famous spiral structure on Fifth Avenue.

Hilla Rebay's attitudes toward collecting were dogmatic. She believed in the intrinsic superiority of painting that does not depict recognizable objects, unlike Peggy Guggenheim who cherished nonobjective abstraction and figurative Surrealism equally. Fortunately, however, Miss Rebay's collecting practices did not always follow her theoretical bias, so that, to the detriment of semantic consistency, many marvelous representational works entered the holdings of the Museum of Non-Objective Painting. In any case, Miss Rebay effectively directed the New York museum from 1937 to 1952, relinquishing this post three years after Solomon Guggenheim died.

In 1952 James Johnson Sweeney assumed the directorship and obtained the approval of the Foundation's trustees to change the name of the Museum of Non-Objective Painting to the stylistically neutral Solomon R. Guggenheim Museum. This change of name, incidentally, allowed for an extension of the scope of the collection to include sculpture. What had been essentially a private American collection in public quarters during Hilla Rebay's time now became a functioning, fully professional museum with high critical and art-historical standards. But it was only upon completion of the Frank Lloyd Wright building at the end of 1959 that the museum in New York became wholly public in the sense that the now much expanded institution addressed itself to a large, worldwide audience. This phase in the institution's development coincided with my own appointment as the Museum's third director.

Thus, when the Peggy Guggenheim Collection is seen in its entirety and alone, it remains primarily a testimony to the sensibility and acumen of an extraordinary collector. When considered together with the works collected contemporaneously and subsequently by others for the Solomon R. Guggenheim Museum, it contributes decisively to a broader, less personally oriented view of twentieth-century art. The latter perspective will assume increasing importance in time, when the precedent of the Campidoglio exhibition is followed by other presentations that join works from both museums, whether in New York, Venice or elsewhere. However, for the visitor to her former home, Lorenzo Boschetti's uncompleted but lovely Palazzo Venier dei Leoni, Peggy Guggenheim's richly rewarding collection, still imbued with the spirit of her powerful personality, remains above all the unique achievement of a legendary individual.

THOMAS M. MESSER, *Director*
The Solomon R. Guggenheim Foundation
October 1985

ACKNOWLEDGEMENTS

This Handbook of the Peggy Guggenheim Collection has had precursors and is meant to have successors, although no book in either category is quite comparable to the current publication. Peggy Guggenheim first published her own illustrated and annotated checklist of all works in her collection in 1967 and issued several revised editions, the last shortly before her death in 1979. This large format contained brief biographies of the artists and equally condensed stylistic commentaries about each work, many of which were originally prepared by Ronald Alley, then Deputy Keeper at the Tate Gallery, London, for the catalogue of an exhibition of the collection at the Tate in 1964-65.

In 1982, when the last edition of the annotated checklist was sold out, The Solomon R. Guggenheim Foundation, which had by that time assumed charge of the palazzo and the collection, issued a picture book with a brief introductory text, *100 Works: The Peggy Guggenheim Collection*. Each of the one hundred selected works was reproduced in color, and a checklist of the entire modern collection, numbering 294 items, was included for the record.

The first Handbook, issued in 1982, substantially retained the selection of one hundred works made for the picture book, but enlarged the size and contents of that publication. The small souvenir format of the picture book has given way to a medium-sized format, identical with that used for the current sister publication of the Solomon R. Guggenheim Museum by Vivian Endicott Barnett, which surveys the holdings of the Foundation in New York. In keeping with the New York publication, biographical and critical entries have been included for each of the selected artists and works. The primary purpose of these publications is to orient the viewer by providing condensed information and interpretative texts best used in the presence of the original works of art.

This revised and enlarged edition of the Handbook is based on texts written by two scholars. The texts are therefore marked to indicate such separate authorship.

Lucy Flint has revised her original commentaries and Elizabeth C. Childs has added to these fifty new entries, thereby extending the scope of the new edition to one hundred and fifty works. Carol Fuerstein, the Guggenheim's Editor since the series of Handbooks was initiated, has again made her valuable contributions in terms of the current publication. Diana Murphy assisted with the production of the book, and Bia Papadapoulou researched material for artists' biographies.

At the Peggy Guggenheim Collection in Venice, Philip Rylands, Administrator, has effectively supervised many technical undertakings related to this volume. All of these individuals, as well as others who must remain anonymous, are entitled to our gratitude. Our sincere thanks are extended also to the Veneto Regional Government and in particular to its President Prof. Carlo Bernini for the annual subsidies so essential to the effective operation of the Peggy Guggenheim Collection.

By contrast with this and other Guggenheim Foundation Handbooks, the catalogue of the Peggy Guggenheim Collection by Angelica Zander Rudenstine deals with the substance of Peggy Guggenheim's legacy in terms of its individual works *in extenso*. Whereas the Handbooks are organized chronologically, the catalogue is arranged alphabetically by artist and focuses on each work as a separate achievement, illuminated by documentation that is as complete as current research on the subject. Much of the new factual information presented here derives from the extensive research for the catalogue, and is fully discussed in that publication.

T.M.M.

CATALOGUE

Titles, dates, mediums and dimensions listed in the headings in the following catalogue, as well as certain material in the entries, are based on information in Angelica Zander Rudenstine, *Peggy Guggenheim Collection, Venice: The Solomon R. Guggenheim Foundation,* New York, 1985. References to this publication appear in parentheses within the texts or in footnotes and are abbreviated "Rudenstine, p. 000." Changes in title, date or other factual information made in the entries that appeared in the first edition of this Handbook are based on research by Rudenstine.

Measurements are given in inches followed by centimeters and height precedes width followed by depth, where relevant.

The numbers listed after the mediums and dimensions (76.2553 PG 000; PG coll. cat. 000) are The Solomon R. Guggenheim Foundation number assigned to the work followed by the catalogue number given in Rudenstine.

Pablo Picasso 1881-1973

Pablo Ruiz y Picasso was born on October 25, 1881, in Málaga, Andalusia, Spain. The son of an academic painter, José Ruiz Blanco, he began to draw at an early age. In 1895 the family moved to Barcelona, and Picasso studied there at La Lonja, the academy of fine arts. His visit to Horta de Ebro of 1898-99 and his association with the group at the café Els Quatre Gats about 1899 were crucial to his early artistic development. In 1900 Picasso's first exhibition took place in Barcelona, and that autumn he went to Paris for the first of several stays during the early years of the century. Picasso settled in Paris in April 1904 and soon his circle of friends included Max Jacob, Guillaume Apollinaire, Gertrude and Leo Stein as well as two dealers, Ambroise Vollard and Berthe Weill.

His style developed from the Blue Period (1901 to 1904) to the Rose Period (1905) to the pivotal work *Les Demoiselles d'Avignon*, 1907, and the subsequent evolution of Cubism from 1909 into 1911. Picasso's collaboration on ballet and theatrical productions began in 1916. Soon thereafter his work was characterized by neoclassicism and a renewed interest in drawing and figural representation. In the 1920s the artist and his wife Olga (whom he had married in 1918) continued to live in Paris, travel frequently and spend their summers at the beach. From 1925 into the 1930s Picasso was involved to a certain degree with the Surrealists and from the autumn of 1931 he was especially interested in making sculpture. With the large exhibitions at the Galeries Georges Petit in Paris and the Kunsthaus Zürich in 1932 and the publication of the first volume of Zervos's catalogue raisonné the same year, Picasso's fame increased markedly.

By 1936 the Spanish Civil War had a profound effect on Picasso, the expression of which culminated in his painting *Guernica*, 1937. He was also deeply moved by World War II and stayed primarily in Paris during those years. Picasso's association with the Communist party began in 1944. From the late 1940s he lived in the south of France at Vallauris, Cannes and then Vauvenargues. Among the enormous number of Picasso exhibitions that were held during the artist's lifetime, those at The Museum of Modern Art in New York in 1939 and the Musée des Arts Décoratifs in Paris in 1955 have been most significant. In 1961 the artist married Jacqueline Roque and they moved to Mougins. There Picasso continued his prolific work in painting, drawing, prints, ceramics and sculpture until his death on April 8, 1973.

1 **The Poet.** August 1911

Oil on canvas, 51⅝ x 35¼" (131.2 x 89.5 cm.)
76.2553 PG 1; PG coll. cat. 137

Like *The Accordionist* in the collection of the Solomon R. Guggenheim Museum, New York, *The Poet* was painted during the summer of 1911 when Picasso was working in close association with Braque in the French Pyrenees town of Céret. Similar in style and composition to Braque's contemporaneous *Man with a Guitar* (Collection The Museum of Modern Art, New York), this canvas epitomizes a moment in the development of Analytical Cubism when the degree of abstraction was so extreme that objects in the painting are almost unrecognizable.

As the title indicates, it is the human form that has been visually dissected and reconstructed as an architecture of rectilinear and curvilinear elements. Despite the elusiveness of the visual clues, the viewer can detect a densely articulated central pyramidal figure fused coloristically and texturally with the less detailed ground. The small circle at the upper center of the canvas penetrated by the acme of a triangular plane becomes an eye when associated with the longer, broader plane of a possible nose and the crescents of a probable moustache. Once this recognition occurs, a complete image can be reconstituted by the inference of chin, pipe, neck, attenuated torso, elbows, chair arms.

Picasso presents multiple views of each object, as if he had moved around it, and synthesizes them into a single compound image. The fragmentation of the image encourages a reading of abstract rather than representational form. The imagined volumes of figure and object dissolve into nonobjective organizations of line, plane, light and color. Interpenetrating facets of forms floating in a shallow, indeterminate space are defined and shaded by luminous, hatched, almost Neo-Impressionist brushstrokes. The continuity of certain lines through these facets creates an illusion of a system of larger planes that also float in this indefinite space yet are securely anchored within an architectonic structure. The chromatic sobriety characteristic of works by Picasso and Braque in this period corresponds with the cerebral nature of the issues they address.

L.F.

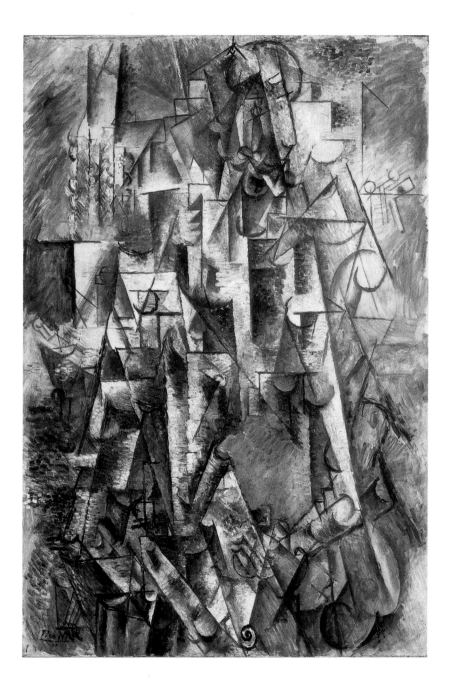

2 Pipe, Glass, Bottle of Vieux Marc. Spring 1914

Paper collage, charcoal, India ink, printer's ink, graphite and gouache on canvas, 28¹³⁄₁₆ x 23⅜" (73.2 x 59.4 cm.)
76.2553 PG 2; PG coll. cat. 138

After fragmenting representational form almost to the point of extinction in 1911 (see cat. no. 1), the following year Picasso and Braque reintroduced more legible imagery, usually derived from the environment of studio or café. Without abandoning all devices of Analytical Cubism, they developed a new idiom, referred to as Synthetic Cubism, in which they built their compositions with broader, flatter and chromatically more varied planes. In the summer of 1912 Braque produced the first *papier collé,* in which cut paper is glued to the support and used as a compositional element. In the present example Picasso's pasted papers include printed material—a piece of wallpaper and the January 1, 1914, issue of *Lacerba,* a Futurist magazine founded in Florence in 1913. These elements mimic their functions in the external world and therefore introduce a new level of reality into the picture. The printed papers appear to be integrated into the pictorial space rather than lying flat on the surface. A transparent plane outlined in chalk appears to penetrate the newspaper and the guitar seems to cast a shadow on it; the actual physical presence of the wallpaper is similarly contradicted by the addition of drawing.

The treatment of other collaged papers multiplies meaning. In the case of the pipe or table leg, the cutout itself defines the contour of the object and is modeled accordingly with chalk. Penciled indications of other objects, such as the guitar or glass, ignore the shape of the pasted paper, which acts as both a support and a compositional element. The opacity of the collage materials is refuted and the transparency of the object depicted is upheld when Picasso discloses parts of the guitar behind the glass. On the other hand, a piece of *Lacerba* remains visible through the guitar, which in reality is opaque. Not only does each object have a multiple nature, but its relations in space to other objects are changeable and contradictory. The table assuredly occupies a space between the wall and the picture plane; its collaged corner overlaps a portion of wallpaper and its visible leg obscures part of a baseboard molding. Yet the depth of this space is indeterminate, as the tabletop has reared up so that it is parallel to the picture plane. The respective situations in space of the still-life subjects it displays are equally equivocal—the silhouette of the bottle of Vieux Marc simultaneously obscures and is obscured by the guitar.

L.F.

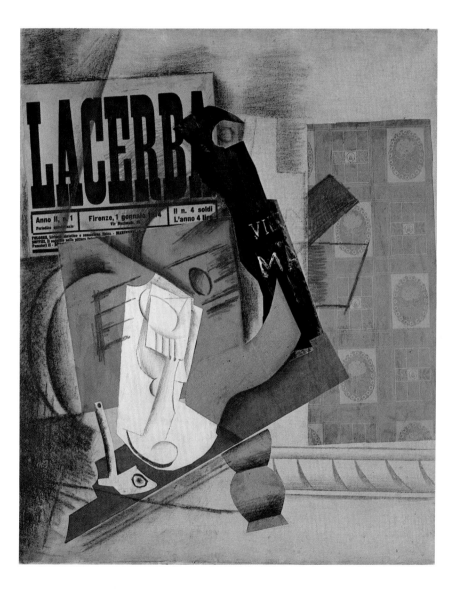

3 The Studio. 1928

Oil and crayon on canvas, 63⅝ x 51⅛" (161.6 x 129.9 cm.)
76.2553 PG3; PG coll. cat. 139

From 1927 to 1929 Picasso elaborated a complex discourse on the activity of the artist through the theme of the studio. Among the variations in the series, the closest to the present example is *The Studio* of 1927-28 (Collection The Museum of Modern Art, New York; repr. Rudenstine, p. 620, fig. c). Both works share the vivid palette of Synthetic Cubism, limited to draw attention to a conspicuous and authoritative facture in planar areas. This painterliness contrasts with the geometricized, wirelike contours that define the figures in the manner of Picasso's contemporaneous wire sculpture.

The figures in the Guggenheim *The Studio* can be identified as a sculptured bust (at the left) and a full-length painted portrait (to the right). By depicting artistic representations of humans in a highly schematized form, Picasso places the figures at several removes from the world of living beings. He relies on the viewer's willingness to believe in the reality of depicted objects, however abstract, and to imagine a human exchange or relationship between the male and female forms. Like the artist in The Museum of Modern Art version, the bust has three eyes; this may reflect Picasso's personal identification with the work of art.

Picasso's development of the theme of the artist's perception of himself and his subjects can be traced from his etching of 1927, *Painter with a Model Knitting,* in which a realistically drawn artist paints a fantastic and abstract portrait of a very ordinary woman. The artist becomes an abstract sign in *The Studio* at The Museum of Modern Art and disappears, or is at least submerged, in *The Studio* in the Peggy Guggenheim Collection. He reappears in *Painter and Model,* also of 1928 (Collection The Museum of Modern Art, New York), as a figure that is even more difficult to detect, yet nonetheless is engaged in painting a relatively realistic profile. The theme of the interaction of reality and illusion explored here was a central concern for Picasso throughout his life.

L.F.

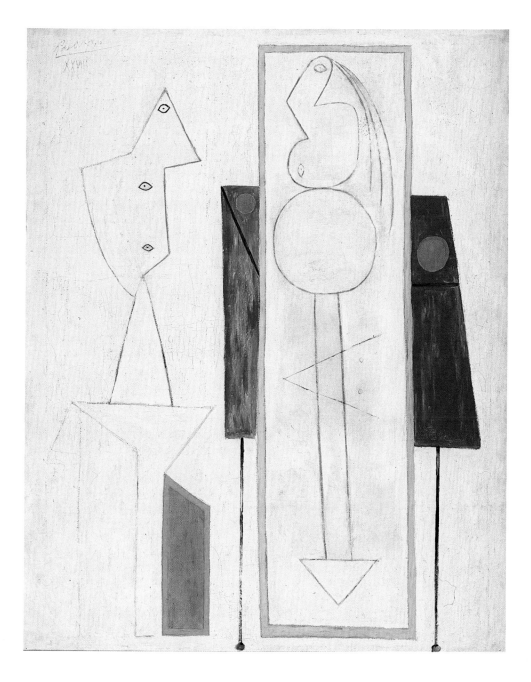

4 On the Beach. February 12, 1937

Oil, conté crayon and chalk on canvas, $50^{13}/_{16}$ x $76^{3}/_{8}$"
(129.1 x 194 cm.)
76.2553 PG 5; PG coll. cat. 140

During the early months of 1937 Picasso was responding powerfully to the Spanish Civil War with the preparatory drawings for *Guernica* (Collection Museo Nacional del Prado, Madrid) and with etchings such as *The Dream and Lie of Franco*, an example of which is in the Peggy Guggenheim Collection. However, in this period he also executed a group of works that do not betray this preoccupation with political events. The subject of *On the Beach*, also known as *Girls with a Toy Boat*, specifically recalls Picasso's *Three Bathers* of 1920 (Collection Stephen Hahn, New York). Painted at Le Tremblay-sur-Mauldre near Versailles, *On the Beach* is one of several paintings in which he returns to the ossified, volumetric forms in beach environments that appeared in his works of the late 1920s and early 1930s. *On the Beach* can be compared with Matisse's *Le Luxe, II,* ca. 1907-08 (Collection Statens Museum for Kunst, Copenhagen), in its simplified, planar style and in the poses of the foreground figures. It is plausible that the arcadian themes of his friendly rival Matisse would appeal to Picasso as an alternative to the violent images of war he was conceiving at the time.

At least two preparatory drawings have been identified for this work. In one (Collection Musée Picasso, Paris; repr. Rudenstine, p. 625), the male figure looming on the horizon has a sinister appearance. In the other drawing (present whereabouts unknown),* as in the finished version, his mien is softened and neutralized to correspond with the features of the two female figures. The sense of impotent voyeurism conveyed as he gazes at the fertile, exaggeratedly sexual "girls" calls to mind the myth of Diana caught unawares at her bath.

* Reproduced in C. Zervos, *Pablo Picasso,* Paris, 1957, vol. 8, no. 343.

L.F.

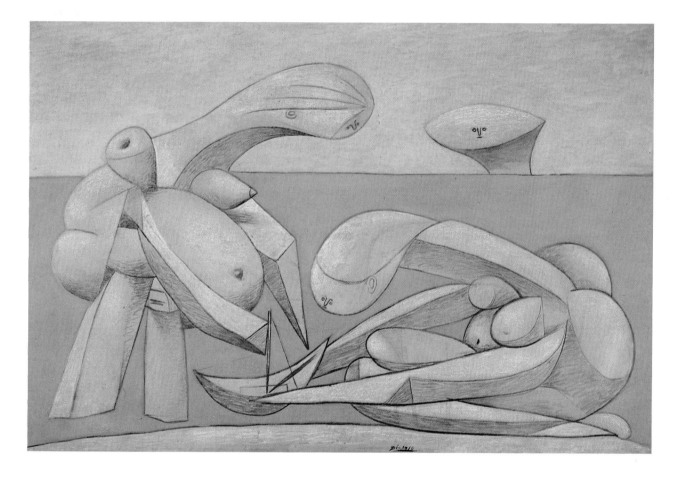

Georges Braque 1882-1963

Georges Braque was born in Argenteuil-sur-Seine on May 13, 1882. He grew up in Le Havre and studied evenings at the Ecole des Beaux-Arts there from about 1897 to 1899. He left for Paris to study under a master-decorator to receive his craftsman certificate in 1901. From 1902 to 1904 he painted at the Académie Humbert in Paris where he met Marie Laurencin and Picabia. By 1906 Braque's work was no longer Impressionist but Fauve in style; after spending that summer in Antwerp with Othon Friesz, he showed his Fauve work the following year in the Salon des Indépendants in Paris. His first one-man show was at D.-H. Kahnweiler's gallery in Paris in 1908. From 1909 Picasso and Braque worked together in developing Cubism; by 1911 their styles were extremely similar. In 1912 they started to incorporate collage elements into their painting and experiment with the *papier collé* (pasted paper) technique. Their artistic collaboration lasted until 1914. Braque was wounded during World War I; upon his recovery in 1917 he began a close friendship with Gris.

After World War I his work became freer and less schematic. His fame grew in 1922 as a result of a major exhibition at the Salon d'Automne in Paris. In the mid-twenties Braque designed the decor for two Sergei Diaghilev ballets. By the end of the decade he had returned to a more realistic interpretation of nature, although certain aspects of Cubism always remained present in his work. In 1931 Braque made his first engraved plasters and began to portray mythological subjects. His first important retrospective took place in 1933 at the Kunsthalle Basel. He won First Prize at the Carnegie International in Pittsburgh in 1937.

During World War II Braque remained in Paris. His paintings at that time, primarily still lifes and interiors, became more somber. In addition to painting Braque also made lithographs, engravings and sculpture. From the late 1940s Braque treated various recurring themes such as birds, ateliers, landscapes and seascapes. In 1953 he designed stained-glass windows for the church of Varengeville. During the last few years of his life Braque's ill health prevented him from undertaking further large-scale commissions but he continued to paint and make lithographs and jewelry designs. He died in Paris on August 31, 1963.

5 The Clarinet. Summer-fall 1912

Oil with sand on oval canvas, 36 x 25⅜" (91.4 x 64.5 cm.)
76.2553 PG 7; PG coll. cat. 19

The Clarinet was probably executed in the late summer of 1912, during the waning moments of Analytical Cubism. Characteristic of this period are the oval format, which frees the canvas from the stringencies of corners, the appearance of letters within the image and the use of imitation wood grain as trompe l'oeil (a technique Braque introduced into the Cubist repertory). The image is paler and less strongly articulated than that of Picasso's *The Poet* of the previous summer (cat. no. 1); the structure of planes is more compact and produces a shallower picture space. The planes, because they are more consistently parallel to the picture plane than before, suggest the flat surfaces of *papier collé*. Braque's incorporation of sand into certain areas of his pigment, an innovation of this transitional period, enhances the differentiation of surfaces created by the variations of brushstrokes and increases the subtleties of coloration. The use of sand accords with Braque's conviction that tactile qualities define space. Despite this emphasis on materiality the image remains evanescent. The paradoxical combination of tangible presence and elusive, palpitating abstraction is embodied in the contrasting handling of clarinet and guitar: the clarinet is shown almost complete, the guitar is fragmented into pieces that emerge here and there throughout the composition.

L.F.

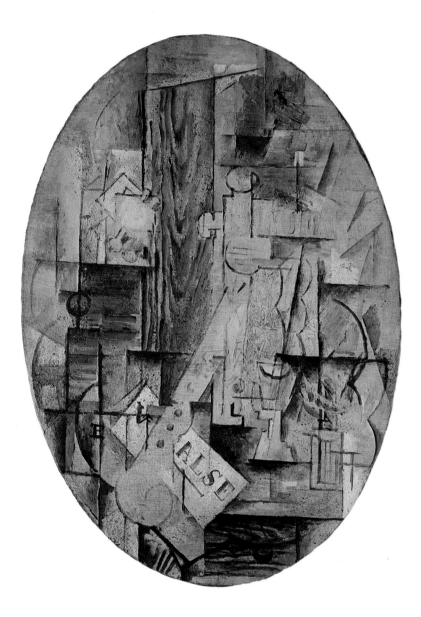

6 The Bowl of Grapes. 1926

Oil with pebbles and sand on canvas, 39⅜ x 31¼″
(100 x 80.8 cm.)
76.2553 PG 8; PG coll. cat. 20

After his return from military service in 1917, Braque, working independently of Picasso, developed the subjects and style of his prewar period. His use of collage in the teens provided formal innovations in paintings of the twenties. In still lifes such as the present example, he constructed objects with broad, frontal planes that remain discrete and are often vividly colored or decoratively patterned.

In subject matter, *The Bowl of Grapes* belongs to Braque's guéridon (round pedestal table) and mantelpiece series of about 1918 to 1929. It displays a rigorous and complex organization of shape and line combined with the sensuous appeal of rich color (three greens contrasted with chalky white and tan) and a masterful handling of paint. The structuring grid is softened by broad curves and clusters of circular forms, and in peripheral areas enriched by the textural variation provided by the addition of sand to pigment.

Formal rather than illusionistic needs govern the treatment of objects. The white drapery does not cascade down from the tabletop in foreshortened, shadowed folds, but rigidly asserts itself parallel to the picture plane. The distinction between lit and shadowed sides of the pitcher is artificially sharp. Reminiscent of Cézanne's still lifes are the heavy contours and voluminous presence of the objects, the tilted planes, inconsistent perspective and discontinuous background lines.

L.F.

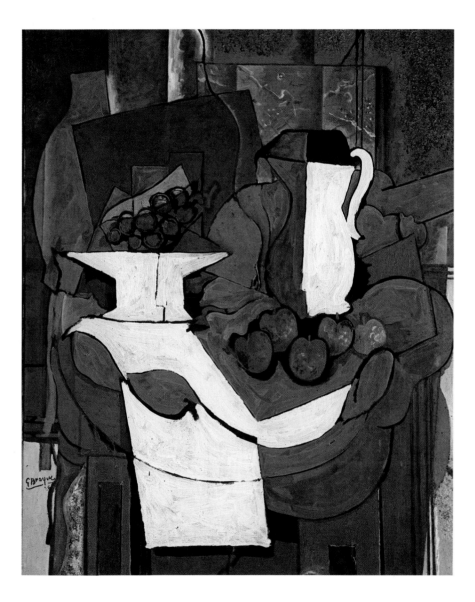

Fernand Léger 1881-1955

Jules Fernand Henri Léger was born February 4, 1881, at Argentan in Normandy. After apprenticing with an architect in Caen from 1897 to 1899, Léger settled in Paris in 1900 and supported himself as an architectural draftsman. He was refused entrance to the Ecole des Beaux-Arts, but nevertheless attended classes there; he also studied at the Académie Julian. Léger's earliest known works, which date from 1905, were primarily influenced by Impressionism. The experience of seeing the Cézanne retrospective at the Salon d'Automne in 1907 and his contact with the early Cubism of Picasso and Braque had a significant impact on the development of his personal style. In 1910 he exhibited with Braque and Picasso at D.-H. Kahnweiler's gallery, where he was given his first one-man show in 1912. From 1911 to 1914 Léger's work became increasingly abstract, and he started to limit his color to the primaries and black and white.

Léger served in the military from 1914 to 1917. His "mechanical" period, in which figures and objects are characterized by tubular, machinelike forms, began in 1917. During the early 1920s he collaborated with the writer Blaise Cendrars on films and designed sets and costumes for Rolf de Maré's *Ballet suédois*; in 1923-24 he made his first film without a plot, *Ballet mécanique*. Léger opened an atelier with Ozenfant in 1924 and in 1925, at the *Exposition Internationale des Arts Décoratifs*, presented his first murals at Le Corbusier's Pavillon de l'Esprit Nouveau. In 1931 he visited the United States for the first time; in 1935 The Museum of Modern Art, New York, and The Art Institute of Chicago presented exhibitions of his work. Léger lived in the United States from 1940 to 1945 but returned to France after the war. In the decade before his death Léger's wide-ranging projects included book illustrations, monumental figure paintings and murals, stained-glass windows, mosaics, polychrome ceramic sculptures and set and costume designs. In 1955 he won the Grand Prize at the São Paulo Bienal. Léger died August 17, 1955, at his home at Gif-sur-Yvette, France.

7 Study of a Nude. Winter 1912-13

Oil on paper, 25 x 19¹⁄₁₆″ (63.6 x 48.5 cm.)
76.2553 PG 19; PG coll. cat. 96

Study of a Nude is one of a group of drawings of a nude model seated by a table that Léger executed during late 1912 and early 1913. The series was followed by the painting *Nude Model in the Studio* of 1912-13 (Collection Solomon R. Guggenheim Museum, New York). The drawing, like the Cubist work of Picasso and Braque in 1911 and 1912 (see cat. nos. 1, 5), is made of interpenetrating planes and volumes that remotely correspond with recognizable imagery. Comparison with more naturalistic drawings in the group clarifies the subject matter of this example and enables the viewer to hypothesize the existence of objects and human body. Gradually and vaguely one makes out a hand in a lap, another perhaps raised to the cheek, a torso, buttock and legs, chair and table. However, the representational subject matter has virtually no importance, being almost entirely obscured by the vigorous interaction of line and form.

The modeled billows that constitute the curves of the nude's body are ultimately derived from Léger's images of smoke in works such as *The Smokers* of December 1911–January 1912 (Collection Solomon R. Guggenheim Museum, New York); here they have been solidified into nonspecific shapes that are at once volumes and two-dimensional motifs in a shallow Cubistic space. These curves are contrasted with the sharp angles of neighboring shapes. The treatment is more violent and dynamic, the contour lines thicker and more emphatic than in the austere, serene Analytical Cubism of Picasso and Braque.

L.F.

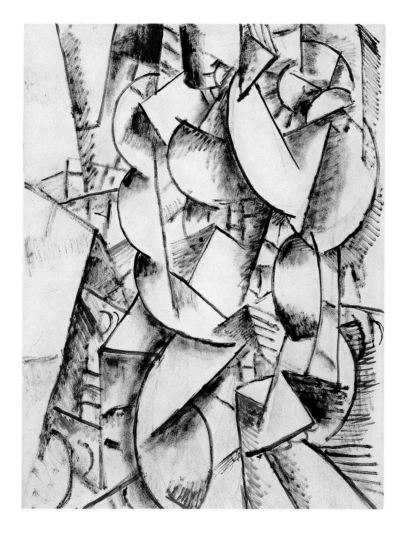

8 Men in the City. 1919

Oil on canvas, 57⅜ x 44¹¹/₁₆″ (145.7 x 113.5 cm.)
76.2553 PG 21; PG coll. cat. 97

Léger temporarily abandoned representational depiction in his *Contrast of Forms* series of 1913-14, begun a few months after he completed *Nude Model in the Studio* (see cat. no. 7). When he returned from the front in 1917 and resumed painting, he reintroduced recognizable imagery in his work. Responsive to the technological advances and assertive advertising that followed World War I, he embarked on his "mechanical" period with works such as *Men in the City* and the related *The City* of 1919-29 (Collection Philadelphia Museum of Art).

In the urban themes of this period the human figure becomes as de-individualized and mechanized as the environment it occupies. Léger is able to express the rhythmic energy of contemporary life by finding its pictorial equivalent. Form, color and shape are considered primarily for their plastic values and are given equal emphasis. They confront one another in a multitude of relations creating single images that capture simultaneous sensations. Confusion of parts does not result, because Léger distributes planes evenly and builds his compositions with blocky areas of flat, easily read, unmixed color and clear and incisive outline. He conveys a sense of depth through overlapping planes and changes in scale rather than with modeling. Léger's simple, varied and clear pictorial elements, like ideal machines, efficiently produce effects of maximum power.

L.F.

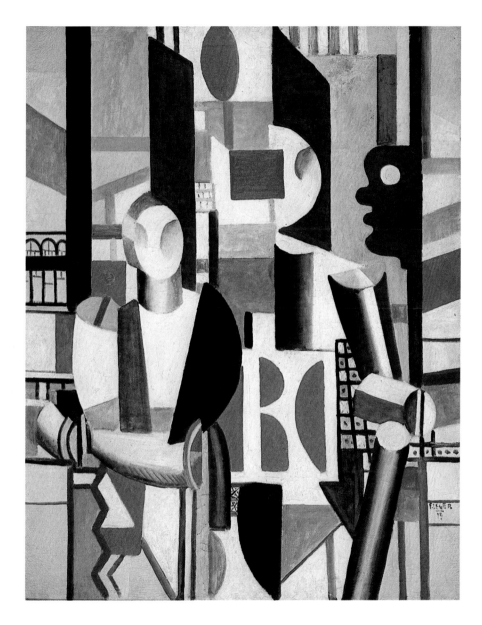

Juan Gris 1887-1927

Juan Gris was born José Victoriano Carmelo Carlos González-Pérez in Madrid on March 23, 1887. He studied mechanical drawing at the Escuela de Artes y Manufacturas in Madrid from 1902 to 1904, during which time he contributed drawings to local periodicals. From 1904 to 1905 he studied painting with the academic artist José Maria Carbonero. In 1906 he moved to Paris, where he lived for most of the remainder of his life. His friends in Paris included Picasso, Braque, Léger and the writers Max Jacob, Guillaume Apollinaire and Maurice Raynal. Although he continued to submit humorous illustrations to journals such as *L'Assiette au Beurre, Le Charivari* and *Le Cri de Paris,* Gris began to paint seriously in 1910. By 1912 he had developed a personal Cubist style.

He exhibited for the first time in 1912: at the Salon des Indépendants in Paris, the Galeries Dalmau in Barcelona, the gallery of Der Sturm in Berlin, the Salon de la Société Normande de Peinture Moderne in Rouen and the Salon de la Section d'Or in Paris. That same year D.-H. Kahnweiler signed Gris to a contract that gave him exclusive rights to the artist's work. Gris became a good friend of Henri Matisse in 1914 and over the next several years formed close relationships with Lipchitz and Metzinger. After Kahnweiler fled Paris at the outbreak of World War I, Gris signed a contract with Léonce Rosenberg in 1916. His first major one-man show was held at Rosenberg's Galerie l'Effort Moderne in Paris in 1919. The following year Kahnweiler returned and once again became Gris's dealer.

In 1922 the painter first designed ballet sets and costumes for Sergei Diaghilev. Gris articulated most of his aesthetic theories during 1924 and 1925. He delivered his definitive lecture, "Des Possibilités de la peinture," at the Sorbonne in 1924. Major Gris exhibitions took place at the Galerie Simon in Paris and the Galerie Flechtheim in Berlin in 1923 and at the Galerie Flechtheim in Düsseldorf in 1925. As his health declined, Gris made frequent visits to the south of France. Gris died in Boulogne-sur-Seine on May 11, 1927, at age forty.

9 Bottle of Rum and Newspaper. June 1914

Paper collage, gouache, conté crayon and pencil on newspaper mounted on canvas, 21⅝ x 18¼″ (54.8 x 46.2 cm.)
76.2553 PG 11; PG coll. cat. 74

In 1913 Gris began using the technique of *papier collé* developed by Braque and Picasso, with whom he had been working in close contact since 1911. By 1914 Gris's handling of the technique was personal and sophisticated, as evidenced by works such as *Bottle of Rum and Newspaper,* executed in Paris shortly before he left for Collioure at the end of June. Here the pasted elements overlap and intermesh with one another in relationships calculated with mathematical rigor. These collaged papers cover the entire surface of the canvas, simultaneously forming an abstract composition and serving as a multilayered support for naturalistic details.

The dynamism of the picture derives from the tension between horizontals, verticals and thrusting diagonals. Gris presents the table as if it were viewed from several vantage points at once, demonstrating that a diagonal can be understood as a horizontal perceived from an oblique angle and also suggesting the movement of the observer or artist around objects. The telescoping of a number of viewpoints in a single image produces the illusion of a spatial dislocation of the objects themselves. Dissected parts of the bottle of rum, recognizable by correspondence of shape or by labeling, float beside, below or above the drawing of the complete bottle. These paper cutouts, at once more tangible and more fragmented than the shadowy outline, confuse one's perceptions of the bottle's presence.

Gris confounds expectations of the nature of materials. He usually depicts the glass objects as transparent and the others as opaque but does not hesitate to betray this faithfulness to the properties of objects when formal demands intercede.

L.F.

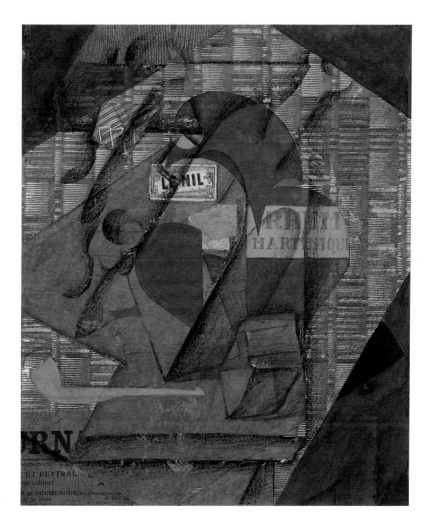

Jean Metzinger 1883-1956

Jean Metzinger was born in Nantes, France, on June 24, 1883. At the age of twenty he moved to Paris to pursue a career as a painter. One of his early friends in Paris was Robert Delaunay. About 1908 he met the writer Max Jacob, who introduced him to Apollinaire and his circle, which included Braque and Picasso. Picasso was to have a significant influence on Metzinger from this time to about 1923. In 1910 Metzinger exhibited for the first time at the Salon des Indépendants. In 1910 and 1911 he published several articles on contemporary painting and afterwards periodically contributed to the literature on modern art. Metzinger was the first to note in print that Picasso and Braque had dismissed traditional perspective and merged multiple views of an object in a single image; his article on this subject appeared in *Pan* in 1910.

In 1911, with Robert Delaunay, Gleizes and Léger, Metzinger participated in the controversial Salle 41 at the Salon des Indépendants, the first formal group exhibition of Cubist painters. His work was represented at the Salon d'Automne in Paris that same year. Metzinger collaborated with Gleizes in 1912 on *Du Cubisme*, in which a theoretical foundation for Cubism was proposed. During that year he was a founder of the *Section d'Or* and exhibited at the Galerie de la Boétie in Paris with other members of the group, including Gleizes, Gris, Roger de La Fresnaye, Archipenko, Marcoussis and Léger. In 1913 Metzinger's work was again shown at the Salon d'Automne, and he continued to exhibit in the principal salons of Paris thereafter. This same year he took part in an exhibition at the gallery of Der Sturm in Berlin and shared a show at the Galerie Berthe Weill in Paris with Gleizes and Léger. In 1916 Metzinger showed with Duchamp, Gleizes and Jean Crotti at the Montross Gallery in New York. After army service during World War I Metzinger returned in 1919 to Paris, where he lived for the remainder of his life. Among his one-man exhibitions were those at the Leicester Galleries in London in 1930, the Hanover Gallery in London in 1932 and The Arts Club of Chicago in 1953. The artist died in Paris on November 3, 1956.

10 **At the Cycle-Race Track.** ca. 1914 (?)

Oil and collage on canvas, 51⅜ x 38¼" (130.4 x 97.1 cm.)
76.2553 PG 18; PG coll. cat. 115

Metzinger, a sensitive and intelligent theoretician of Cubism, sought to communicate the principles of this movement through his paintings as well as his writings. Devices of Cubism and Futurism appear in *At the Cycle-Race Track*, though they are superimposed on an image that is essentially naturalistic. Cubist elements include printed-paper collage, the incorporation of a granular surface and the use of transparent planes to define space. The choice of a subject in motion, the suggestion of velocity and the fusing of forms find parallels in Futurist painting. Though these devices are handled with some awkwardness and the influence of Impressionism persists, particularly in the use of dots of color to represent the crowd in the background, this work represents Metzinger's attempt to come to terms with a new pictorial language.

L.F.

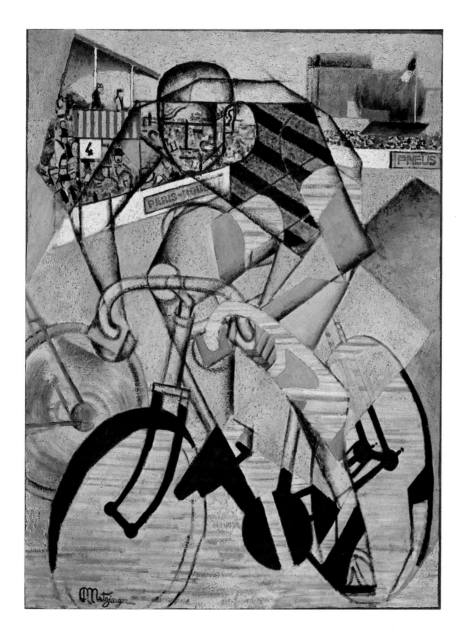

Albert Gleizes 1881-1953

Albert Gleizes was born in Paris on December 8, 1881. He worked in his father's fabric design studio after completing secondary school. While serving in the army from 1901 to 1905, Gleizes began to paint seriously. He exhibited for the first time at the Société Nationale des Beaux-Arts, Paris, in 1902, and participated in the Salon d'Automne in 1903 and 1904.

With several friends, including the writer René Arcos, Gleizes founded the Abbaye de Créteil outside Paris in 1906. This utopian community of artists and writers sought to create a nonallegorical, epic art based on modern themes. The Abbaye closed due to financial difficulties in 1908. In 1909 and 1910 Gleizes met Henri Le Fauconnier, Léger, Robert Delaunay and Metzinger. In 1910 he exhibited at the Salon des Indépendants, Paris, and in the *Jack of Diamonds* in Moscow; the following year he wrote the first of many articles. In collaboration with Metzinger, Gleizes wrote *Du Cubisme*, published in 1912. That same year Gleizes helped found the *Section d'Or*.

In 1914 the artist again saw military service. His paintings had become abstract by 1915. Travels to New York, Barcelona and Bermuda during the next four years influenced his stylistic evolution. His first one-man show was held at the Galeries Dalmau, Barcelona, in 1916. Beginning in 1918 Gleizes became involved with spiritual values, as reflected in his painting and writing. In 1927 he founded Moly-Sabata, another utopian community of artists and craftsmen, in Sablons. His book *La Forme et l'histoire,* published in 1932, examines Romanesque, Celtic and Oriental art. In the thirties Gleizes participated in the *Abstraction-Création* group. Later in his career he executed several large commissions, including the murals for the Paris World's Fair of 1937. In 1947 a major Gleizes retrospective took place in Lyon at the Chapelle du Lycée Ampère. From 1949 to 1950 Gleizes worked on illustrations for Pascal's *Pensées.* He executed a fresco, *Eucharist,* for the chapel Les Fontaines at Chantilly in 1952. Gleizes died in Avignon on June 23, 1953.

11 **Woman with Animals (Madame Raymond Duchamp-Villon).** Completed by February 1914

Oil on canvas, 77⅝₆ x 45¹⁵⁄₁₆″ (196.4 x 114.1 cm.) 76.2553 PG 17; PG coll. cat. 71

As in a number of his other paintings of this period, Gleizes depicts a domestic interior scene in a self-consciously "modern" style. Here the seated woman is the wife of Duchamp-Villon, the sculptor who took part in the discussions of the Cubist group at Puteaux during the early teens. She is portrayed as the epitome of bourgeois complacency, in a large armchair, with her dog and two cats, sensible tie shoe, wedding band and string of beads. Typically Cubist elements are the fusion of figure and ground, the frontal, centralized pose, the multiple views of the sitter's face, the choppy brushstrokes defining and shading planes and the patterning of areas to resemble collage. Futurist devices are the repetition of form to describe movement (the dog's wagging tail) and planar intersections and force lines meant to express notions of the dynamic interpenetration of matter and atmosphere.

L.F.

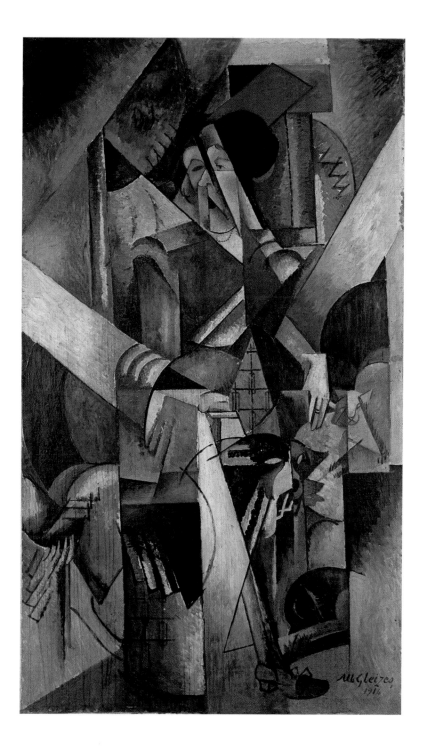

Louis Marcoussis 1878-1941

Louis Marcoussis was born Ludwig Casimir Ladislas Markus in Warsaw, on November 14, 1878. In 1901 he entered the Academy of Fine Arts of Cracow to study painting with Jan Grzegorz Stanislawski. In 1903 Markus moved to Paris, where he worked briefly under Jules Lefebvre at the Académie Julian and became a friend of La Fresnaye and Robert Lotiron. He exhibited for the first time at the Salon d'Automne in 1905 and at the Salon des Indépendants in 1906, and was often represented in both salons in subsequent years.

In Paris he made his living by selling caricatures to satirical periodicals, including *La Vie parisienne* and *Le Journal*. He frequented the cafés, such as the Rotonde, Cirque Médrano and the Ermitage, where he met Edgar Degas about 1906 and Braque, Picasso and Apollinaire in 1910. In 1907 Markus abandoned painting; when he began to paint again in 1910, he discarded his earlier Impressionist style to adopt the new Cubist idiom. About 1911, at the suggestion of Apollinaire, he began calling himself Marcoussis, the name of a village near Monthéry. In 1912 the artist participated in the Salon de la Section d'Or at the Galerie de la Boétie in Paris. By this time his circle included Gris, Léger, Picabia, Metzinger and Max Jacob. He served in the army from 1914 to 1919, returning to Poland for a visit after his demobilization.

Marcoussis exhibited in 1921 at the gallery of Der Sturm in Berlin with Gleizes, Villon and others. He was given his first one-man show at Galerie Pierre, Paris, in 1925. This was followed by solo exhibitions in 1928 at the Galerie Le Centaure in Brussels, a city he visited on that occasion, and at the Galerie Georges Bernheim in Paris in 1929. In 1930 the artist made the first of many trips to England and met Helena Rubinstein, who became his supporter. In 1934-35 he stayed for several months in the United States, where one-man shows of his prints opened at The Arts Club of Chicago in 1934 and M. Knoedler and Co. in New York in 1935. Marcoussis worked almost exclusively in graphics from 1930 to 1937; a retrospective of his prints took place at the Palais des Beaux-Arts in Brussels in 1936. The artist traveled to England and Italy in 1938, and during the following year was given a solo exhibition at the London Gallery in London. In 1940, as the German army advanced, Marcoussis left Paris for Cusset, near Vichy, where he died on October 22, 1941.

12 The Regular. 1920

Oil with sand and pebbles on canvas, 63¾ x 38³⁄₁₆"
(161.9 x 97 cm.)
76.2553 PG 22; PG coll. cat. 108

In this Synthetic Cubist work of 1920, Marcoussis presents a hieratic figure immobilized by habit, so much a part of his environment that he is barely distinguishable from it. Familiar Cubist motifs and effects are integrated in a strong, complex composition in which abstract and representational elements are harmonized. Sand, stippled paint and imitation wood grain lend texture to the broad, angular planes that organize the picture space. The large proportions of the canvas increase the impact of the architectonic structure of planes. Blocks of color echo and respond to one another to establish balanced relationships over the entire surface.

The limits of abstraction are tested in the treatment of the figure, which would not be recognizable without the humanizing details indicating face and head—the schematic eyes, nose, moustache, furrowed brow, cigar, hat. The right hand is merely a strip of modulated cylinders, the left only slightly more articulated with fingernails. The only naturalistically described objects are the dominoes on the table, which, unlike the human form, would be unidentifiable if they were distorted. Like letters, they are signs with unchangeable meanings that can be combined in various ways to produce larger meanings. Similarly, parts of a Cubist picture have an intrinsic, independent significance that is expanded and complicated when they are related within an ordered composition.

L.F.

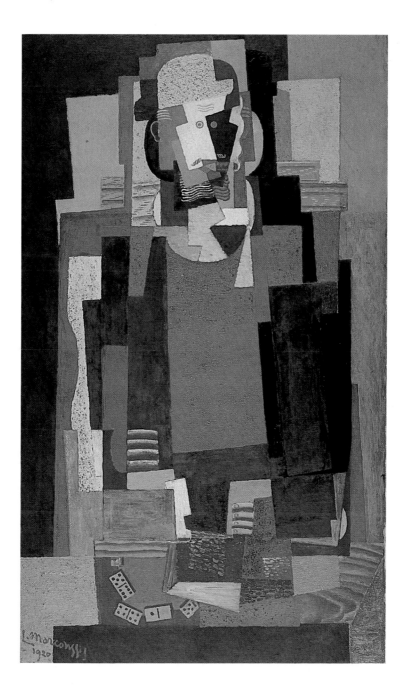

Marcel Duchamp 1887-1968

Henri-Robert-Marcel Duchamp was born July 28, 1887, near Blainville, France. In 1904 he joined his artist brothers, Jacques Villon and Raymond Duchamp-Villon, in Paris, where he studied painting at the Académie Julian until 1905. Duchamp's early works were Post-Impressionist in style. He exhibited for the first time in 1909 at the Salon des Indépendants and the Salon d'Automne in Paris. His paintings of 1911 were directly related to Cubism but emphasized successive images of a single body in motion. In 1912 he painted the definitive version of *Nude Descending a Staircase*; this was shown at the Salon de la Section d'Or of that same year and subsequently created great controversy at the Armory Show in New York in 1913. The Futurist show at Galerie Bernheim-Jeune, Paris, in 1912 impressed him profoundly.

Duchamp's radical and iconoclastic ideas predated the founding of the Dada movement in Zürich in 1916. By 1913 he had abandoned traditional painting and drawing for various experimental forms including mechanical drawings, studies and notations that would be incorporated in a major work, *The Bride Stripped Bare by Her Bachelors, Even* of 1915-23. In 1914 Duchamp introduced his *Readymades*—common objects, sometimes altered, presented as works of art—which had a revolutionary impact upon many painters and sculptors. In 1915 Duchamp came to New York where his circle included Katherine Dreier and Man Ray, with whom he founded the Société Anonyme, as well as Louise and Walter Arensberg, Picabia and other avant-garde figures.

After playing chess avidly for nine months in Buenos Aires, Duchamp returned to France in the summer of 1919 and associated with the Dada group in Paris. In New York in 1920 he made his first motor-driven constructions and invented Rrose Sélavy, his feminine alter-ego. Duchamp moved back to Paris in 1923 and seemed to have abandoned art for chess but in fact continued his artistic experiments. From the mid-1930s he collaborated with the Surrealists and participated in their exhibitions. Duchamp settled permanently in New York in 1942 and became a United States citizen in 1955. During the 1940s he associated and exhibited with the Surrealist emigrés in New York, and in 1946 began *Etant donnés*, a major assemblage on which he worked secretly for the next twenty years. Duchamp directly influenced a generation of young Americans. He died in the Paris suburb of Neuilly-sur-Seine on October 2, 1968.

13 Nude (Study), Sad Young Man on a Train. 1911-12

Oil on cardboard, 39⅜ x 28¾" (100 x 73 cm.)
76.2553 PG 9; PG coll. cat. 49

This painting, which Duchamp identified as a self-portrait, was probably begun during December of 1911 in Neuilly, while he was exploring ideas for the controversial *Nude Descending a Staircase, No. 2* of 1912 (Collection Philadelphia Museum of Art; see Rudenstine, pp. 265-266). In *Nude (Study), Sad Young Man on a Train* his transitory though acute interest in Cubism is manifested in the subdued palette, emphasis on the flat surface of the picture plane and in the subordination of representational fidelity to the demands of the abstract composition.

Duchamp's primary concern in this painting is the depiction of two movements, that of the train in which we observe the young man smoking, and that of the lurching figure itself. The forward motion of the train is suggested by the multiplication of the lines and volumes of the figure, a semitransparent form through which we can see windows, themselves transparent and presumably presenting a blurred, "moving" landscape. The independent sideways motion of the figure is represented by a directionally contrary series of repetitions. These two series of replications suggest the multiple images of chronophotography, which Duchamp acknowledged as an influence, and the related ideas of the Italian Futurists, of which he was at least aware by this time. Here he uses the device not only to illustrate movement, but also to integrate the young man with his murky surroundings, which with his swaying, drooping pose contribute to the air of melancholy. Shortly after the execution of this and similar works, Duchamp lost interest in Cubism and developed his eccentric vocabulary of mechanomorphic elements that foreshadowed aspects of Dada.

L.F.

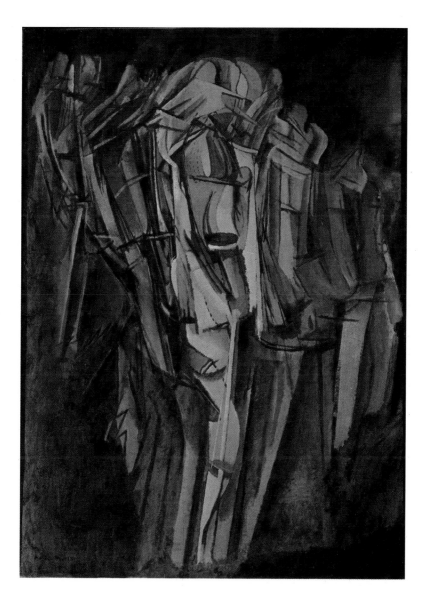

Jacques Villon 1875-1963

Jacques Villon was born Gaston Duchamp on July 31, 1875, in Damville, Normandy. While still a lycée student in Rouen he began his artistic training under his grandfather, Emile Nicolle, who taught him engraving. In 1894 he began to study law at the University of Paris; that same summer he entered the Ecole des Beaux-Arts in Rouen and shortly thereafter started to send his drawings to local illustrated newspapers. After securing his father's reluctant permission to study art on the condition that he continue his law studies, he returned to Paris where he attended the Atelier Cormon. He adopted the name Jacques Villon in 1895.

For almost ten years the artist worked largely in graphic media, contributing drawings to Parisian illustrated papers and making color prints and posters. In 1903 he helped organize the drawing section of the first Salon d'Automne. In 1904-05 he studied at the Académie Julian in Paris, painting in a Neo-Impressionist style. Villon's first gallery exhibition, shared with his brother Raymond Duchamp-Villon, took place at Galerie Legrip, Rouen, in 1905. He began to spend more time painting about 1906-07 and from 1910 devoted himself primarily to it. In 1906 he settled in Puteaux. There, in 1911, he and Duchamp-Villon started to meet with the Puteaux group, which included their brother Marcel Duchamp, Kupka, Picabia, Gleizes, Robert Delaunay, Léger and others. That same year Villon named and helped found the *Section d'Or*. He exhibited nine paintings at the 1913 New York Armory Show and sold them all.

Villon's first one-man show in America was held at the Société Anonyme, New York, in 1921; by the thirties he was better known in the United States than in Europe. In 1932, he joined the *Abstraction-Création* group and exhibited with them. An important exhibition of Villon's work was held in Paris in 1944 at the Galerie Louis Carré, from that time his exclusive representative. Villon received honors at a number of international exhibitions, including First Prize, Carnegie International, Pittsburgh, 1950, and Grand Prize for Painting, Venice Biennale, 1956. He designed stained-glass windows for the cathedral at Metz in 1955. Villon died on June 9, 1963, in Puteaux, at the age of eighty-seven.

14 Spaces. 1920

Oil on canvas, 28¾ x 36¹⁄₁₆" (73 x 91.6 cm.)
76.2553 PG 23; PG coll. cat. 177

This painting, dating from Villon's first abstract period of about 1919 to 1923, demonstrates his modification of the Cubist analysis of objects. Like the Cubists, he dissects natural forms and then reconstructs them as organizations of planes. However, his deeper interest in scientific method results in planes that are regularized and finite, arranged in a sequence within a methodically composed field. This rational approach led to his frequent use of a grid system in drawings for paintings. Principles of color theory govern his selection and juxtaposition of hues. Though the drawings for each work become progressively more abstract, the object often endures in disguised form. The persistence of the object in many of Villon's other works prompts one to attempt to identify the spherical forms and the piers of rectangles intersecting them in *Spaces*. Though no preparatory drawings have come to light to confirm the suggestion, the circles may represent the globes Villon owned, one of which had a relief contour.* This interpretation is borne out by the artist's own discussion of the source for the planar motifs of this period—the topographical maps that indicate altitude by the superpositioning of flat planes. In Villon's paintings, as in these maps, a sense of volume emerges from flatness; the object exists as a stratified cross-sectioned form.

Both the imagery and the composition of *Spaces* recall the overlapping and multicolored rectangles of *Tu m'*, 1918 (Collection Yale University Art Gallery, New Haven), by Villon's brother Duchamp.

* *Jacques Villon*, ed. D. Robbins, Cambridge, Mass., 1976, p. 161.

L.F.

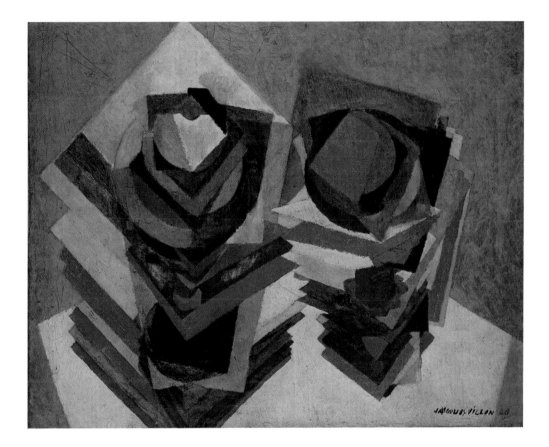

Raymond Duchamp-Villon 1876-1918

Raymond Duchamp-Villon was born Pierre-Maurice-Raymond Duchamp on November 5, 1876, in Damville, near Rouen. His brothers were the artists Marcel Duchamp and Jacques Villon. From 1894 to 1898 he studied medicine at the University of Paris. When illness forced him to abandon his studies, he decided to make a career in sculpture, until then an avocation. During the early years of the century he moved to Paris, where he exhibited for the first time at the Salon de la Société Nationale des Beaux-Arts in 1902. His second show was held at the same Salon in 1903, the year he settled in Neuilly-sur-Seine. In 1905 he had his first exhibition at the Salon d'Automne and a show at the Galerie Legrip in Rouen with Villon, with whom he moved to Puteaux two years later.

His participation in the jury of the sculpture section of the Salon d'Automne began in 1907 and was instrumental in promoting the Cubists in the early teens. About this time he, Villon and Duchamp attended weekly meetings of the Puteaux group of artists and critics. In 1911 he exhibited at the Galerie de l'Art Contemporain in Paris; the following year the Duchamp brothers organized a show at the Salon de la Section d'Or at the Galerie de la Boétie, in which his work was included. Duchamp-Villon's work was exhibited at the Armory Show in New York in 1913 and the Galerie André Groult in Paris, the Galerie S.V.U. Mánes in Prague and the gallery of Der Sturm in Berlin in 1914. During World War I Duchamp-Villon served in the army in a medical capacity, but was able to continue work on his major sculpture *The Horse*. He contracted typhoid fever in late 1916 while stationed at Champagne; the disease ultimately resulted in his death on October 9, 1918, in the military hospital at Cannes.

15 **The Horse.** 1914 (cast ca. 1930)

Bronze, 17³⁄₁₆ x 6⅛″ (43.6 x 41 cm.)
76.2553 PG 24; PG coll. cat. 50

Duchamp-Villon began work on the plaster original of *The Horse,* a composite image of an animal and machine, in 1914, finishing it on leaves from military duty in the fall. It was preceded by numerous sketches and by several other versions initiated in 1913. The original conception did not include the machine and was relatively naturalistic, as is evident in the early states of the small *Horse and Rider* of 1914. Duchamp-Villon then developed an increasingly dynamic, smooth-surfaced and geometric synthesis of horse and machine. The Guggenheim version is highly abstract and parts of the horse's physiognomy are replaced by machine elements. Nonetheless, echoes of the original pose remain. As in the second state of *Horse and Rider* (Collection Judith Riklis, New York), the animal appears to be gathering its hooves, summoning strength to jump. Duchamp-Villon closely observed the dynamics of the movement of horses during his experience in the cavalry; he also studied the subject in the late nineteenth-century photographic experiments of Eadweard Muybridge and Etienne-Jules Marey.

With a handful of other sculptors, such as Archipenko, Brancusi and Boccioni, Duchamp-Villon overturned conventional representation of form to suggest instead its inner forces. He associated these forces with the energy of the machine. The visual movement of the pistons, wheels and shafts of this sculpture turns a creature of nature into a poised mechanical dynamo. The fusion of the horse, traditional symbol of power, and the machine that was replacing it reflects the emerging awareness of the new technological age.

The entire series was cast in bronze after the artist's death.*

* For discussion of the casting of various versions of *The Horse,* see Rudenstine, pp. 271-276.

L.F.

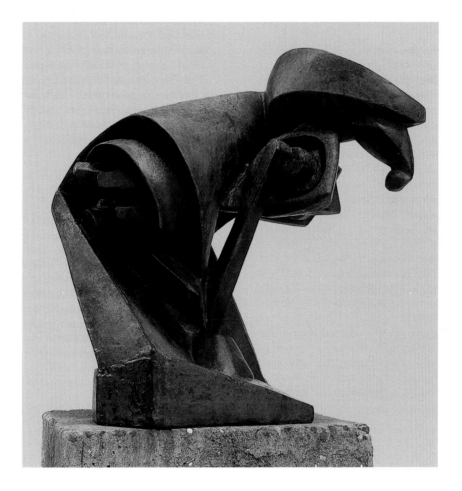

Henri Laurens 1885-1954

Henri Laurens was born on February 18, 1885, in Paris, where he attended drawing classes in 1899. The sculpture he produced during the early years of the twentieth century reflects the influence of Auguste Rodin. In 1911 the sculptor entered into a lifelong friendship with Braque, who introduced him to Cubism. Laurens participated for the first time in the Salon des Indépendants in Paris in 1913, and two years later met Picasso, Gris and Amedeo Modigliani. From 1916 Laurens executed Cubist collages and constructions. He became a friend of Pierre Reverdy in 1915 and illustrated his *Poèmes en prose* that same year.

The artist was given a one-man show at Léonce Rosenberg's Galerie l'Effort Moderne in Paris in 1917, and signed a contract there the following year. During the 1920s he executed designs for various architectural projects and stage decors. From 1932 to 1933 he divided his time between Paris and nearby Etang-la-Ville, where his neighbors were Aristide Maillol and Ker-Xavier Roussel. Laurens contributed substantially to the World's Fair in Paris in 1937. In 1938 he shared an exhibition with Braque and Picasso that traveled from Oslo to Stockholm and Copenhagen. His work was shown in 1945 at the Galerie Louis Carré in Paris and in 1947 at the Buchholz Gallery in New York. About this time Laurens made prints for book illustrations. He was represented at the Venice Biennale in 1948 and 1950. An important exhibition of his work was organized by the Palais des Beaux-Arts in Brussels in 1949, and a major Laurens retrospective took place at the Musée National d'Art Moderne in Paris in 1951. The following year he received a commission for a monumental sculpture for the University of Caracas. He exhibited extensively in Europe and the United States during the early 1950s, and received the Prize of the IV Centenary of São Paulo at the São Paulo Bienal in 1953. Laurens died in Paris on May 5, 1954.

16 Head of a Young Girl. 1920 (cast 1959)

Terra-cotta, 13½ x 6½" (34.2 x 16.5 cm.)
76.2553 PG 27; PG coll. cat. 95

Laurens, who associated closely with the avant-garde painters of his native Paris, worked in a Cubist idiom from 1915. In about 1920 he turned from the production of bas-reliefs and frontalized constructions to the execution of more classically ordered, freestanding sculptures. *Head of a Young Girl* may have appeared originally as a drawing (see, for example, *Head* of 1917, Collection Mr. and Mrs. Irving W. Rabb, Cambridge, Massachusetts). However, in this bust Laurens expresses Cubist painting principles in essentially sculptural terms. The tilted surfaces and geometric volumes of the sculpture interpenetrate to constitute a compact whole. Circling the piece, the viewer perceives dramatically different aspects of the head, which provide a variety of visual experiences unexpected in a form so schematically reduced.

The structuring planes of one side of the head are broad and unadorned; its edges and planar junctures form strong, uninterrupted curves and straight lines. The other side is articulated with detail; its jagged, hewn contour describing hair contrasts rhythmically with the sweeping curve of the opposite cheek. Laurens slices into the polyhedron that determines the facial planes to describe nose, upper lip and chin at one stroke. The subtle modeling, particularly of the almond eye and simplified mouth, produces nuanced relations of light and shadow. Despite the geometric clarity of structure, the delicacy of the young girl's features and her self-contained pose create a gentle, meditative quality.

L.F.

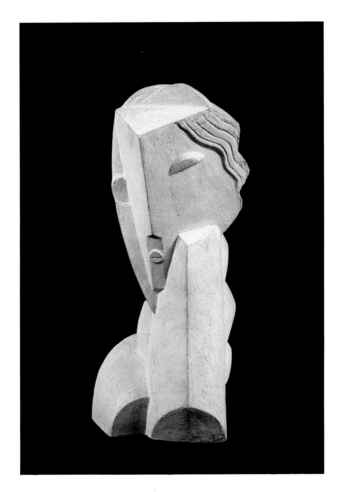

Jacques Lipchitz 1891-1973

Chaim Jacob Lipschitz was born on August 22, 1891, in Druskieniki, Lithuania. At age eighteen he moved to Paris, where he attended the Ecole des Beaux-Arts and the Académie Julian and soon met Picasso, Gris and Braque. In 1912 he began exhibiting at the Salon National des Beaux-Arts and the Salon d'Automne. Lipchitz's first one-man show was held at Léonce Rosenberg's Galerie l'Effort Moderne in Paris in 1920. Two years later he executed five bas-reliefs for The Barnes Foundation in Merion, Pennsylvania. In 1924 the artist became a French citizen and the following year moved to Boulogne-sur-Seine. He received a commission from the Vicomte Charles de Noailles in 1927 for the sculpture *Joy of Life*.

Lipchitz's first important retrospective took place at Jeanne Bucher's Galerie de la Renaissance in Paris in 1930. The Brummer Gallery in New York hosted his first large show in the United States in 1935. In 1941 Lipchitz fled Paris for New York, where he began exhibiting regularly at the Buchholz Gallery (later the Curt Valentin Gallery). He settled in Hastings-on-Hudson, New York, in 1947. In 1954 a Lipchitz retrospective traveled from The Museum of Modern Art in New York to the Walker Art Center in Minneapolis and The Cleveland Museum of Art. In 1958 Lipchitz collaborated with the architect Philip Johnson on the Roofless Church in New Harmony, Indiana. This same year he became a United States citizen. His series of small bronzes *To the Limit of the Possible* was shown at Fine Arts Associates in New York in 1959. He visited Israel for the first time in 1963. From 1964 to 1966 Lipchitz showed annually at the Marlborough-Gerson Gallery in New York. Beginning in 1963 he spent several months of each year casting in Pietrasanta, Italy.

From 1970 until 1973 he worked on large-scale commissions for the Municipal Plaza in Philadelphia, Columbia University in New York and the Hadassah Medical Center near Jerusalem. These projects were completed after Lipchitz's death by his wife Yulla. In 1972 the artist's autobiography was published on the occasion of an exhibition of his sculpture at The Metropolitan Museum of Art in New York. Lipchitz died on May 26, 1973, on Capri, and was buried in Jerusalem.

17 Seated Pierrot. 1922

Lead, including base 13⅛″ (33.5 cm.) high
76.2553 PG 28; PG coll. cat. 98

In 1916 Lipchitz became a close friend of Gris, who inspired him to paint his only completed Cubist oil the following year. Gris, in turn, made a foray into sculpture with his polychromed plaster *Harlequin*, 1917 (Collection Philadelphia Museum of Art), executed with the technical guidance of Lipchitz. *Seated Pierrot* is stylistically close to the Gris sculpture in its squat, massive proportions and the synthesis of angular and curvilinear elements.

By applying an ambiguous formal vocabulary in *Seated Pierrot*, Lipchitz has been able to fuse two recurrent Cubist themes—the commedia dell'arte figure of Pierrot and the still life. The figure's head and neck echo the similarly bifurcated shape of bottle neck and lip in certain of his bas-reliefs. The circular eyes recall the stylized mouth of a bottle; the encircling arms form a recessed oval like that of a compotier; and the configuration of legs and feet resembles the distorted glasses of Cubist painting. These volumes interpenetrate in apparent contradiction to the solidity of the sculptural form. The Cubist exchange of solid for void is wittily effected in the positive-negative handling of the two eyes. Lipchitz's concern with the effects of light is evident in the contrast between broad, deeply shadowed areas and dappled planes animated by surface texture.

L.F.

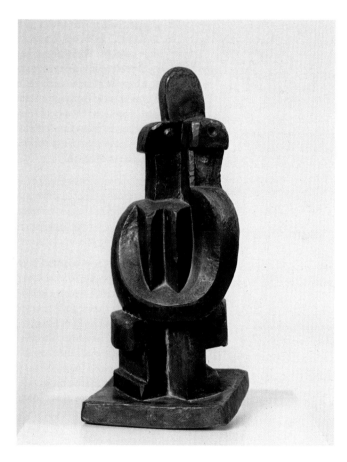

18 Aurelia. 1946

Bronze, 25⅜″ (64.5 cm.) high
76.2553 PG 29; PG coll. cat. 99

A massive bronze rod at the base of *Aurelia* tapers upward, uniting with the elaborate structure above it to
form a bulbous notched mass. This upper structure tilts
slightly, its horizontal protuberances extending from
an axis that is slightly right of center. The appendages
of this central abstract form suggest a zoological or
botanical inspiration. Any such sources, however, have
been transformed by the elaboration of both the front
and back of the sculpture with cascades of flowing,
curved rods. Six of these pierce the uppermost horizontal element of *Aurelia*, their knobby ends fully pene-
trating the frontal surface, and their long curving and
dipping tails dangling over the back. Eight more rods
are supported by a perforated oval which emerges at a
right angle from the central form. These rods surge up,
curve back over their support, and tumble down in
tangled confusion.

Lipchitz mitigates the frontality of his central element
by attaching these curving rods, merging the simple,
symmetrical closed core of the sculpture with the intricate and asymmetrical open network of rods. An
unevenly applied patina offers coloristic variety.

The intricately worked bronze surface replicates the
original model, which was constructed out of small bits
of wax: careful examination reveals the artist's finger-
prints on the bronze surface. Lipchitz may have made
the projecting rods from wax foundry bars, heating and
then bending them into their present shape. As the mold
was baked onto the exterior of the wax, the original
model melted from the mold, and a solid bronze cast
was made. As the unique mold was then destroyed to
retrieve the bronze sculpture, the Peggy Guggenheim
sculpture is the unique cast of *Aurelia* (Rudenstine,
p. 458).

E.C.C.

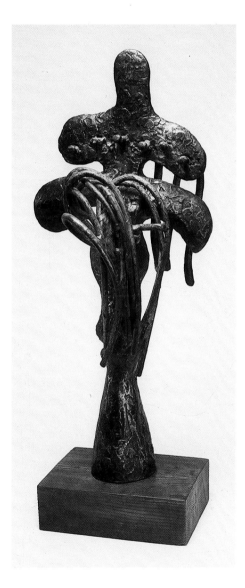

Alexander Archipenko 1887-1964

Alexander Archipenko was born on May 30, 1887, in Kiev, Ukraine, Russia. In 1902 he entered the Kiev Art School where he studied painting and sculpture until 1905. During this time he was impressed by the Byzantine icons, frescoes and mosaics of Kiev. After a sojourn in Moscow Archipenko moved to Paris in 1908. He attended the Ecole des Beaux-Arts for a brief period and then continued to study independently at the Louvre, where he was drawn to Egyptian, Assyrian, archaic Greek and early Gothic sculpture. In 1910 he began exhibiting at the Salon des Indépendants, Paris, and the following year showed for the first time at the Salon d'Automne.

In 1912 Archipenko was given his first one-man show in Germany at the Folkwang Museum in Hagen. That same year in Paris he opened the first of his many art schools, joined the *Section d'Or* group, which included Picasso, Braque, Léger and Duchamp, among others, and produced his first painted reliefs, the *Sculpto-Peintures*. In 1913 Archipenko exhibited at the Armory Show in New York and made his first prints, which were reproduced in the Italian Futurist publication *Lacerba* in 1914. He participated in the Salon des Indépendants in 1914 and the Venice Biennale in 1920. During the war years the artist resided in Cimiez, a suburb of Nice. From 1919 to 1921 he traveled to Geneva, Zürich, Paris, London, Brussels, Athens and other European cities to exhibit his work. Archipenko's first one-man show in the United States was held at the Société Anonyme in New York in 1921.

In 1923 he moved from Berlin to the United States where, over the years, he opened art schools in New York City, Woodstock (New York), Los Angeles and Chicago. In 1924 Archipenko invented his first kinetic work, *Archipentura*. For the next thirty years he taught throughout the United States at art schools and universities, including the New Bauhaus School of Industrial Arts in Chicago. He became a United States citizen in 1928. Most of Archipenko's work in German museums was confiscated by the Nazis in their 1939 purge of *Entartete Kunst* (degenerate art). In 1947 he produced the first of his sculptures that are illuminated from within. He accompanied a one-man exhibition of his work throughout Germany in 1955, and at this time began his book *Archipenko: Fifty Creative Years 1908-1958*, published in 1960. Archipenko died on February 25, 1964, in New York.

19 Boxing. 1935

Terra-cotta, 30⅛″ (76.6 cm.) high
76.2553 PG 26; PG coll. cat. 3

Two plaster versions of this work were made from the same mold in 1913-14 (see Rudenstine, p. 55). One of these, known as *Struggle*, is in the collection of the Solomon R. Guggenheim Museum, New York; the second was given by the artist's widow to the Saarland Museum, Saarbrücken (Rudenstine, p. 56, fn. 6). The Peggy Guggenheim terra-cotta, though very similar to the original plasters, is slightly larger and was executed many years later.

Archipenko disavowed the influence of Cubism on his geometric simplification of form. However, one of his most important contributions to modern sculpture, the breaking up of monolithic form with open spaces, finds its counterpart in the Cubist exchange of solid and void. He also shares with the Cubists an interest in the analysis of space and the interpenetration of planes within it.

The artist explains the choice of subject for this work in a poetic inscription at its base: *«LA BOXE"—C'est la musique monumental* [sic] *des volumes d'éspace* [sic] *et de la matière....* (Boxing—the monumental music of volumes of space and of material.) The thrusting figures of the two contenders are joined inextricably in opposition, forming an aggressively charged sculptural whole. Apart from the work of the Italian Futurists, few sculptures of this period combine radical essentialization of form with virile, assertive dynamism in the manner of *Boxing*. Another is Duchamp-Villon's *The Horse* (cat. no. 15), executed some months after the original version of the Archipenko was completed.

L.F.

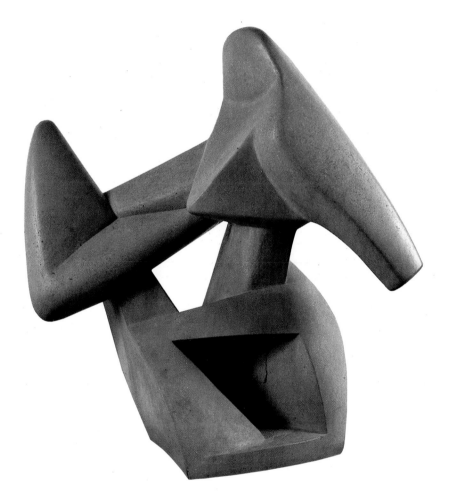

Giacomo Balla 1871-1958

Giacomo Balla was born in Turin on July 18, 1871. In 1891 he studied briefly at the Accademia Albertina di Belle Arti and the Liceo Artistico in Turin and exhibited for the first time under the aegis of the *Società Promotrice di Belle Arti* in that city. He studied at the University of Turin with Cesare Lombroso about 1892. In 1895 Balla moved to Rome, where he worked for several years as an illustrator, caricaturist and portrait painter. In 1899 his work was included in the Venice Biennale and in the *Esposizione Internazionale di Belle Arti* at the galleries of the *Società degli Amatori e Cultori di Belle Arti* in Rome, where he exhibited regularly for the next ten years. In 1900 Balla spent seven months in Paris assisting the illustrator Serafino Macchiati. About 1903 he began to instruct Severini and Boccioni in divisionist painting techniques. In 1903 his work was exhibited at the *Esposizione Internazionale d'Arte della Città di Venezia* and in 1903 and 1904 at the Glaspalast in Munich. In 1904 Balla was represented in the *Internationale Kunstausstellung* in Düsseldorf, and in 1909 exhibited at the Salon d'Automne in Paris.

Balla signed the second Futurist painting manifesto of 1910 with Boccioni, Severini, Carlo Carrà and Luigi Russolo, although he did not exhibit with the group until 1913. In 1912 he traveled to London and to Düsseldorf, where he began painting his abstract light studies. In 1913 Balla participated in the *Erster Deutscher Herbstsalon* at the gallery of Der Sturm in Berlin and in an exhibition at the Rotterdamsche Kunstkring in Rotterdam. In 1914 he experimented with sculpture for the first time and showed it in the *Prima Esposizione Libera Futurista* at the Galleria Sprovieri, Rome. He also designed and painted Futurist furniture and designed Futurist "anti-neutral" clothing. With Fortunato Depero, Balla wrote the manifesto *Ricostruzione futurista dell'universo* in 1915. His first solo exhibitions were held that same year at the *Società italiana lampade elettriche "Z"* and at the Sala d'Arte A. Angelelli in Rome. His work was also shown in 1915 at the *Panama-Pacific International Exposition* in San Francisco. In 1918 he was given a one-man show at the Casa d'Arte Bragaglia in Rome. Balla continued to exhibit in Europe and the United States and in 1935 was made a member of the Accademia di San Luca in Rome. He died on March 1, 1958, in Rome.

20 Abstract Speed + Sound. 1913-14

Oil on board, including artist's painted frame
21½ x 30⅛" (54.5 x 76.5 cm.)
76.2553 PG 31; PG coll. cat. 13

In late 1912 to early 1913 Balla turned from a depiction of the splintering of light to the exploration of movement and, more specifically, the speed of racing automobiles. This led to an important series of studies in 1913-14. The choice of automobile as symbol of abstract speed recalls Filippo Tommaso Marinetti's notorious statement in his first Futurist manifesto, published on February 20, 1909, in *Le Figaro* in Paris, only a decade after the first Italian car was manufactured:

> ...the world's splendor has been enriched by a new beauty: the beauty of speed.... A roaring automobile ...that seems to run on shrapnel, is more beautiful than the Victory of Samothrace.

It has been proposed that *Abstract Speed + Sound* was the central section of a narrative triptych suggesting the alteration of landscape by the passage of a car through the atmosphere.* The related *Abstract Speed* (present whereabouts unknown; formerly Collection Dr. W. Loeffler, Zürich) and *Abstract Speed—The Car Has Passed* (Collection Tate Gallery, London) would have been the flanking panels. Indications of sky and a single landscape are present in the three paintings; the interpretation of fragmented evocations of the car's speed varies from panel to panel. The Peggy Guggenheim work is distinguished by crisscross motifs representing sound and a multiplication of the number of lines and planes.

The original frames of all three panels were painted with continuations of the forms and colors of the compositions, implying the overflow of the paintings' reality into the spectator's own space. Many other studies and variations by Balla on the theme of a moving automobile in the same landscape exist.

* V. Dortch Dorazio, *Giacomo Balla: An Album of His Life and Work,* New York, 1969, figs. 2-4. See also Rudenstine, pp. 92-93, where all three panels are reproduced.

L.F.

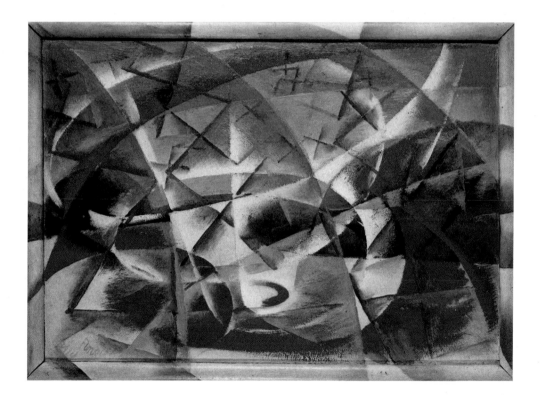

Umberto Boccioni 1882-1916

Umberto Boccioni was born October 19, 1882, in Reggio Calabria, Italy. In 1901 he went to Rome, where he studied design with a sign painter and attended the Scuola Libera del Nudo at the Accademia di Belle Arti. In Rome he and Severini learned the techniques of divisionist painting from Balla. Boccioni traveled in 1902 to Paris, where he studied Impressionist and Post-Impressionist painting. He participated in the *Mostra dei Rifiutati* in 1905 and in the *Esposizione di Belle Arti* in 1906, both in Rome.

After a trip to Russia in 1906, Boccioni visited Padua and then moved to Venice, where he spent the winter of 1906-07 taking life classes at the Accademia di Belle Arti. In 1907 he settled in Milan. In 1909-10 Boccioni began to frequent the *Famiglia Artistica*, a Milanese artists' society that sponsored annual exhibitions. During this period he associated with Carrà and Russolo, and met the poet Filippo Tommaso Marinetti, who had published the first Futurist manifesto in February of 1909. In 1910 Boccioni participated in the formulation of the two Futurist manifestos *Manifesto dei pittori futuristi* and *Manifesto tecnico della pittura futurista*. He, Carrà, Severini and Russolo signed the first, and were joined by Balla in signing the second. That same year Boccioni's first one-man exhibition was held at the Galleria Ca' Pesaro in Venice.

In the fall of 1911 the artist went to Paris, where he met Picasso and Apollinaire through Severini. Boccioni's paintings were shown with those of Carrà, Russolo and Severini in the first Futurist show in Paris, at the Galerie Bernheim-Jeune, in 1912. The exhibition then traveled to London, Berlin and Brussels. In 1912 Boccioni began concentrating on sculpture, and his *Manifesto tecnico della scultura futurista* was published. From 1912 to 1914 he contributed articles to the Futurist publication *Lacerba*. In 1913 the artist showed sculpture and paintings in a one-man show at the Galerie de la Boétie in Paris, and his sculpture was included in the inaugural exhibition of the Galleria Futurista Permanente in Rome. His book *Pittura e scultura futuriste (dinamismo plastico)* appeared in 1914. In July of 1915 Boccioni enlisted in the army with Marinetti, Russolo and Antonio Sant'Elia. He suffered an accident during cavalry exercises in Sorte near Verona, and died on August 17, 1916.

21 Dynamism of a Speeding Horse + Houses. 1914-15

Gouache, oil, wood, cardboard, copper and coated iron, 44½ x 45¼" (112.9 x 115 cm.)
76.2553 PG 30; PG coll. cat. 16

Boccioni turned to sculpture in 1912 after publishing his manifesto on the subject on April 11 of that year. The Futurist aesthetic platform as articulated in this document advocates the use of various materials in a single work, the rejection of closed form and the suggestion of the interpenetration of form and the environment through the device of intersecting planes. In *Dynamism of a Speeding Horse + Houses* Boccioni assembled wood, cardboard and metal, with painted areas showing a Futurist handling of planes influenced by the Cubism of Picasso and Braque. Ironically, his intention of preserving "unique forms" caught in space and time is mocked by the perishability of his materials—the work has been considerably restored and continues to present conservation problems (see Rudenstine, pp. 99-106).

Boccioni, like Duchamp-Villon (see cat. no. 15), made studies of horses from nature before developing the motif into a nonspecific symbol of the modern age. This fully evolved symbol appears in Boccioni's painting *The City Rises* of 1910 (Collection The Museum of Modern Art, New York). In *Dynamism of a Speeding Horse + Houses* he used the horse to demonstrate his observation that the nature of vision produces the illusion of a fusing of forms. When the distance between a galloping horse and a stationary house is visually imperceptible, horse and house appear to merge into a single changing form. Sculptures such as the present example are concerned with the apparent compression of space as an object traverses it and with the nature of the object's redefinition by that space.

In 1913 and 1914 Boccioni made many drawings and watercolors related to the present work that explore the relationship between a galloping horse and a group of houses in close proximity; these are now in the Civica Raccolta Bertarelli in Milan. In some of these studies the speed of the horse's motion serves to dissolve the legs below the muscles of the shanks. Boccioni's original conception of the sculpture gave forceful expression to this concept.

L.F.

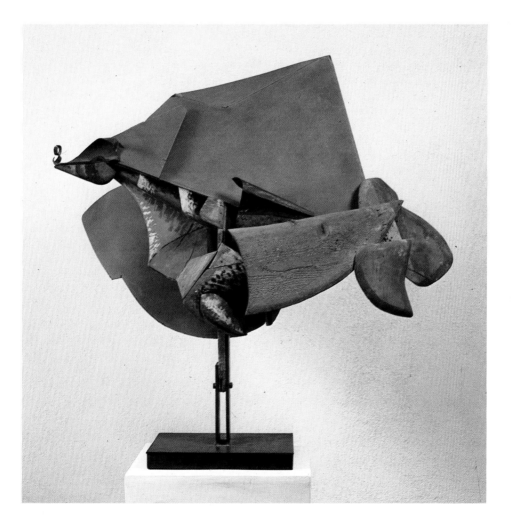

Gino Severini 1883-1966

Gino Severini was born April 7, 1883, in Cortona, Italy. He studied at the Scuola Tecnica in Cortona before moving to Rome in 1899. There he attended art classes at the Villa Medici and by 1901 met Boccioni. Together Severini and Boccioni visited the studio of Balla where they were introduced to painting with "divided" rather than mixed color. After settling in Paris in November 1906, Severini studied Impressionist painting and met the Neo-Impressionist Paul Signac.

Severini soon came to know most of the Parisian avant-garde including Modigliani, Gris, Braque and Picasso, Lugné-Poe and his theatrical circle, the poets Max Jacob, Guillaume Apollinaire and Paul Fort and author Jules Romains. After joining the Futurist movement at the invitation of Marinetti and Boccioni, Severini signed the *Manifesto tecnico della pittura futurista* of April 1910 with Balla, Boccioni, Carrà and Russolo. Severini was less attracted to the subject of the machine than his fellow Futurists and frequently chose the form of the dancer to express Futurist theories of dynamism in art.

Severini helped organize the first Futurist exhibition at Bernheim-Jeune, Paris, in February 1912, and participated in subsequent Futurist shows in Europe and the United States. In 1913 he had one-man exhibitions at the Marlborough Gallery, London, and Der Sturm, Berlin. During the Futurist period Severini acted as an important link between artists in France and Italy. After his last truly Futurist work—a series of paintings on war themes—Severini painted in a Synthetic Cubist mode. By 1920 he was applying theories of Classical balance based on the Golden Section to figurative subjects from the traditional commedia dell'arte. The artist divided his time between Paris and Rome after 1920. He explored fresco and mosaic techniques and executed murals in various media in Switzerland, France and Italy during the 1920s. In the 1950s he returned to the subjects of his Futurist years: dancers, light and movement. Throughout his career Severini published important theoretical essays and books on art. Severini died in Paris on February 26, 1966.

22 Sea = Dancer. January 1914

Oil on canvas, including artist's painted frame
41½ x 33¹³⁄₁₆″ (105.3 x 85.9 cm.)
76.2553 PG 32; PG coll. cat. 162

Toward the end of 1913, after he left Paris for Pienza and Rome, Severini traveled to coastal Anzio for reasons of health. It was after arriving there that he executed *Sea=Dancer*. This painting, in which the sea and a figure are equated, illustrates his notions of "plastic analogies" as outlined in a manifesto he prepared for his one-man exhibition at the Marlborough Gallery in London in 1913. According to Severini, the environment is optically determined and hence fluid, and the human figure is merely a part, albeit an inseparable part, of that metamorphic reality. In this canvas and others the cadences of the swirling motion of the dance and the dancer's costume are compared with those of the sea's movement. The large curling planes are stippled with brilliant staccato dabs of paint that cause all surfaces to vibrate as if with light. As in many other Futurist paintings (see cat. no. 20), the image spills over onto the frame. The divisionist brushstroke derives from Balla and ultimately from the Neo-Impressionists, particularly Georges Pierre Seurat. Works such as *Sea=Dancer* may have a specific source in Seurat's *Le Chahut* of 1889-90 (Collection Rijksmuseum Kröller-Müller, Otterlo).*

The play of cylindrical and flat planes in this painting brings to mind the contemporaneous Cubism of Léger, though the color is closer to the prismatic hues of Robert Delaunay. However, the absence of outline and the dissolution of volume distinguish Severini's work. During this period Severini's analogies of forms divest objects of their usual identities; later in 1914 he would produce entirely nonobjective compositions.

* A. Barr, *Cubism and Abstract Art*, exh. cat., New York, 1936, p. 58.

L.F.

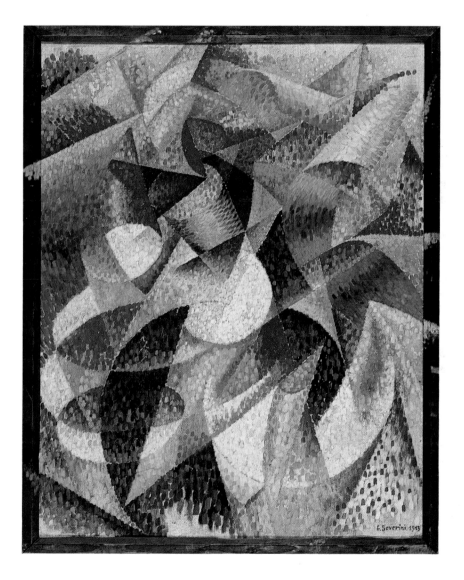

Robert Delaunay 1885-1941

Robert-Victor-Félix Delaunay was born in Paris on April 12, 1885. In 1902, after secondary education, he apprenticed in a studio for theater sets in Belleville. In 1903 he started painting and by 1904 was exhibiting: that year and in 1906 at the Salon d'Automne and from 1904 until World War I at the Salon des Indépendants. Between 1905 and 1907 Delaunay became friendly with Henri Rousseau and Metzinger and studied the color theories of M.-E. Chevreul; he was then painting in a Neo-Impressionist manner. Cézanne's work also influenced Delaunay about this time. From 1907–08 he served in the military in Laon and upon returning to Paris he had contact with the artists who were to develop Cubism, who in turn influenced his work. 1909-10 saw the emergence of Delaunay's personal style: he painted his first *Eiffel Tower* in 1909. In 1910 Delaunay married the painter Sonia Terk, who became his collaborator on many projects.

Delaunay's participation in exhibitions in Germany and association with advanced artists working there began in 1911: that year Kandinsky invited him to participate in the first *Blaue Reiter (Blue Rider)* exhibition in Munich. At this time he became friendly with Apollinaire, Le Fauconnier and Gleizes. In 1912 Delaunay's work was exhibited with that of Laurencin at the Galerie Barbazanges, Paris, and he began his *Window* pictures. Inspired by the lyricism of color of the *Windows*, Apollinaire invented the term "Orphism" or "Orphic Cubism" to describe Delaunay's work. In 1913 Delaunay was given a one-man show at the gallery of Der Sturm in Berlin and became a friend of Blaise Cendrars; this year he also painted his *Circular Form* or *Disc* pictures.

From 1914 to 1920 Delaunay lived in Spain and Portugal and became a friend of Sergei Diaghilev, Igor Stravinsky, Diego Rivera and Leonide Massine. He did the decor for the *Ballets Russes* in 1918. By 1920 he had returned to Paris. Here, in 1922, a major exhibition of his work was held at Galerie Paul Guillaume, and he began his second *Eiffel Tower* series. In 1924 he undertook his *Runner* paintings and in 1925 executed frescoes for the Palais de l'Ambassade de France at the *Exposition Internationale des Arts Décoratifs* in Paris. In 1937 he completed murals for the Palais des Chemins de Fer and Palais de l'Air at the Paris World's Fair. His last works were decorations for the sculpture hall of the Salon des Tuileries in 1938. In 1939 he helped organize the exhibition *Réalités Nouvelles*. Delaunay died in Montpellier on October 25, 1941.

23 **Windows Open Simultaneously 1st Part, 3rd Motif.** 1912

Oil on oval canvas, 22⅜ x 48⅜" (57 x 123 cm.)
76.2553 PG 36; PG coll. cat. 43

Though Delaunay had virtually discarded representational imagery by the spring of 1912 when he embarked on the *Windows* theme, vestigial objects endure in this series. Here, as in *Simultaneous Windows 2nd Motif, 1st Part* (Collection Solomon R. Guggenheim Museum, New York) of the same moment, the centralized ghost of a green Eiffel Tower alludes to his enthusiasm for modern life.

Analytical Cubism inspired Delaunay's fragmentation of form, oval format and organization of the picture's space as a grid supporting intersecting planes. However, unlike the monochromatic, tactile planes of Cubism, those of Delaunay are not defined by line and modeling, but by the application of diaphanous, prismatic color. Delaunay wrote in 1913: "Line is limitation. Color gives depth—not perspectival, not successive, but simultaneous depth—as well as form and movement."[*] As in visual perception of the real world, perception of Delaunay's painting is initially fragmentary, the eye continually moving from one form to others related by hue, value, tone, shape or direction. As focus shifts, expands, jumps and contracts in unending rhythms, one senses the fixed borders of the canvas and the tight interlocking of its contents. Because identification of representational forms is not necessary while the eye moves restlessly, judgements about the relative importance of parts are not made and all elements can be perceived as equally significant. The harmony of the pictorial reality provides an analogy to the concealed harmony of the world. At the left of the canvas Delaunay suggests glass, which, like his chromatic planes, is at once transparent, reflective, insubstantial and solid. Glass may allude as well to the metaphor of art as a window on reality.

[*] Quoted in D. Cooper, *The Cubist Epoch*, London, 1971, p. 84.

L.F.

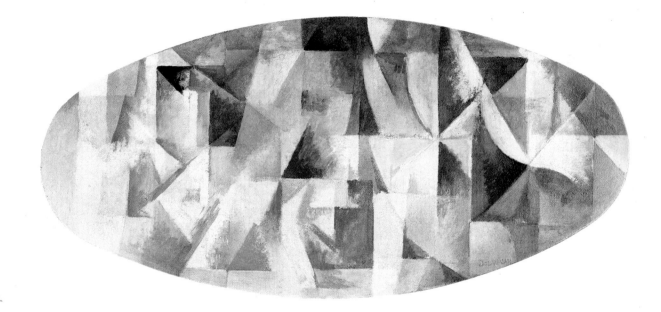

František Kupka 1871-1957

František Kupka was born September 22, 1871, in Opŏcno in eastern Bohemia. From 1889 to 1892 he studied at the Prague Academy. At this time he painted historical and patriotic themes. In 1892 Kupka enrolled at the Akademie der bildenden Künste in Vienna where he concentrated on symbolic and allegorical subjects. He exhibited at the Kunstverein, Vienna, in 1894. His involvement with theosophy and Eastern philosophy dates from this period. By spring 1896 Kupka had settled in Paris; there he attended the Académie Julian briefly and then studied with J. P. Laurens at the Ecole des Beaux-Arts.

Kupka worked as an illustrator of books and posters and, during his early years in Paris, became known for satirical drawings for newspapers and magazines. In 1906 he settled in Puteaux, a suburb of Paris, and that same year exhibited for the first time at the Salon d'Automne. Kupka was impressed by the first Futurist manifesto, published in 1909 in *Le Figaro*. In 1911 he participated in meetings of the Puteaux group, which included his neighbors Villon and Duchamp-Villon as well as Duchamp, Gleizes, Metzinger, Picabia, Léger, Apollinaire and others. In 1912 he exhibited at the Salon des Indépendants in the Cubist room, although he did not wish to be identified with any movement. Later that same year at the Salon d'Automne his paintings caused critical indignation.

La Création dans les arts plastiques (Creation in the Visual Arts), a book Kupka completed in 1913, was published in Prague in 1923. In 1921 his first one-man show in Paris was held at Galerie Povolozky. In 1931 he was a founding member of *Abstraction-Création* with van Doesburg, Auguste Herbin, Vantongerloo, Hélion, Arp and Gleizes; in 1936 his work was included in the exhibition *Cubism and Abstract Art* at The Museum of Modern Art, New York, and in an important two-man show with Alphonse Mucha at the Jeu de Paume, Paris. A major retrospective of his work took place at the Galerie S.V.U. Mánes in Prague in 1946. That same year Kupka participated in the Salon des Réalités Nouvelles, Paris, where he continued to exhibit regularly until his death. During the early 1950s he gained general recognition and had several one-man shows in New York. Kupka died in Puteaux on June 24, 1957.

24 Study for **Amorpha, Warm Chromatics** and for **Fugue in Two Colors**. ca. 1910-11

Pastel on paper, 18¹⁵⁄₁₆ x 19″ (46.8 x 48.3 cm.)
76.2553 PG 13; PG coll. cat. 91

Two of Kupka's earliest purely abstract compositions are *Amorpha, Warm Chromatics* of 1911-12 (Private Collection) and *Amorpha, Fugue in Two Colors* of 1911-12 (Collection Národní Galerie, Prague). The present pastel study reveals an early stage in the formal evolution of both of these paintings (Rudenstine, p. 436). In 1911 Kupka strove to eliminate objective subject matter from his paintings. His development toward abstraction is evident in his work of 1909 to 1911 in his interpretations of motion and of the light and color of Gothic stained-glass windows. The Peggy Guggenheim pastel relates to a series of studies that followed a naturalistic painting of 1908-09 of his stepdaughter Andrée playing naked with a red and blue ball in the garden of their home (Collection Musée National d'Art Moderne, Centre Georges Pompidou, Paris; see Rudenstine, p. 436). More than fifty studies led Kupka from conventional representation of this subject to the abstract formulations of the paintings of 1912. In a note on one of the pencil drawings of *Little Girl with Ball* (Collection The Museum of Modern Art, New York), Kupka details his frustrations: "Here I am only dissecting surfaces. The atmospheric copenetration is yet to be found. As long as there is a distinction in color between ground and flesh, I will fall back into the postcard photograph." (repr. and trans. Rudenstine, p. 436, fig. b)

In the Peggy Guggenheim pastel, Kupka articulated the girl's motion by depicting the continuous penetration of the atmosphere by the ball. A curving brown body shape guides the ball through the blue path of its trajectory. This action occurs on a light green background plane, which suggests the three-dimensional space of the garden. Such residue of naturalistic color is abandoned in culminating versions of the study, such as the *Amorpha, Fugue in Two Colors*, which are conceived in blue, red, black and white. Kupka discerned a musical parallel to these abstract forms in the rhythmic patterns of the fugue, "where the sounds evolve like veritable physical entities, intertwine, come and go."* Kupka's paintings of this period are not simple or formulaic abstractions from ultimate "sources" in nature, but are rather pictorial syntheses of the artist's formal ideas.

* Quoted in M. Rowell, *František Kupka, 1871-1957: A Retrospective*, exh. cat., New York, 1975, p. 184.

E.C.C.

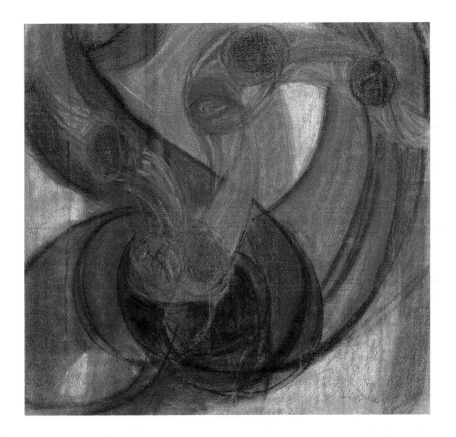

25 Study for **Organization of Graphic Motifs I.** ca. 1911-12

Pastel on paper, 12¹⁵⁄₁₆ x 12⁷⁄₁₆″ (32.9 x 31.6 cm.)
76.2553 PG 15; PG coll. cat. 92

The present work is one of a large group of pastel, ink, pencil and gouache studies executed between 1911 and 1913 for the oils *Organization of Graphic Motifs I* (Collection Thyssen-Bornemisza, Lugano) and *Organization of Graphic Motifs II* (Private Collection), both of 1913 (Rudenstine, p. 440). Kupka articulated the concept of mobile graphics in two manuscripts written between 1910 and 1913. He defines mobile graphics as an outer expression of the artist's inner motivations (or motives), opposing these personal motifs to subject motifs derived from experience in the perceived world. Kukpa describes the process of "organization": "In our inner visions, fragments of images float before our eyes. In order to capture these fragments, we unconsciously trace lines between them and by thus setting up a network of relationships, we arrive at a coherent whole. ... The lines of this network define points in space and directions ... they capture the rhythmic relationships between impressions. And this is the real subject of the painter. ..."*

In the *Organization of Graphic Motifs* studies, Kupka used various approaches to determine spatial relations. In the present example black and brown receding diagonal lines vanish at two different horizon lines. Enigmatic stick-figures may represent human bodies, fence posts or other landscape elements. A blue and green structure on the horizon line on the right suggests the façade of a house. The vibrant orange nexus in the center generates rays of blue, green and gray color which connect these fragmented forms. In the painting *Organization of Graphic Motifs I* Kupka unites a single set of converging diagonals with a constellation of radiating fragments of form and space. Moreover a single large totemic figure dominates the picture field, to which it is fused by gyrating, interconnecting chevrons of color. In *Organization of Graphic Motifs II* the vestiges of receding perspective lines, the landscape framework and the large figure disappear in a dynamic network of interpenetrating spokes of color rotating about a central void. Thus a certain condensation and simplification occurs through which the frenetic action of the Peggy Guggenheim pastel evolves into the more coherently ordered visions of the finished paintings.

* Quoted in M. Rowell, *František Kupka, 1871-1957: A Retrospective*, exh. cat., New York, 1975, pp. 198-200.

E.C.C.

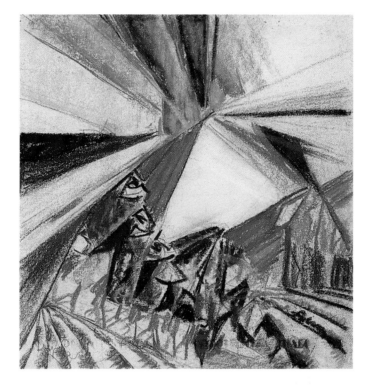

26 Around a Point. ca. 1920-25

Watercolor, gouache and graphite on paper,
7¹⁵⁄₁₆ x 9⅜" (20.1 x 23.8 cm.)
76.2553 PG 16; PG coll. cat. 93

This watercolor belongs to a group of related studies that culminated in the oil painting *Around a Point,* which was begun about 1927 and reworked in 1934 (Collection Musée National d'Art Moderne, Centre Georges Pompidou, Paris; Rudenstine, pp. 443-444). Kupka's first exploratory studies of this theme date from ca. 1911-12 and demonstrate the genesis of the round forms in the lotus-blossom motif in the right foreground of the present study. The exotic water lily, a symbol of life derived from Eastern mystical philosophy, recalls Kupka's interest in theosophy. This involvement is evident in early works such as *The Beginning of Life* of 1900 (Collection Musée National d'Art Moderne, Centre Georges Pompidou, Paris), in which lotus flowers and lily pads appear to generate a human fetus. In the final painting, *Around a Point,* the lotus-flower shape unfolds and evolves to rearticulate another of Kupka's principal early themes, the *Disks of Newton* of 1911-12, in which concentric bands and spheres of brilliant color emanate from a central core of light. Similarly concentric forms unfurl in the studies for *Around a Point,* such as the present work, to suggest the petals of an open flower. Thus Kupka's mystical and biological preoccupations fuse in the formulation of these studies. The development from the abstraction of the *Disks of Newton* to the botanical references in the present work exemplifies Kupka's return after World War I to objective subjects based on biological and botanical themes, such as the 1919-20 series *Tale of Pistils and Stamens* (Rudenstine, p. 443), an example of which is in the collection of the Musée National d'Art Moderne, Centre Georges Pompidou, Paris. Yet the abundant concentric forms in our *Around a Point* defy a literal reading of the image as a mere flower. The duplication and overlapping of the swollen forms, some of which continue beyond the boundaries of the composition, suggest procreation and regeneration on a cosmic order.

Kupka reworked his finished painting *Around a Point* in 1934, covering over many of the original colored motifs with pure white, thus simplifying and opening up the composition. Other works Kupka first painted in the twenties underwent similar transformations.

E.C.C.

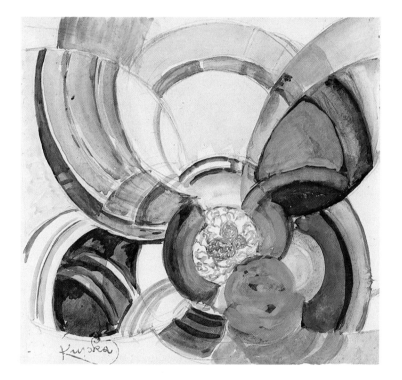

Vasily Kandinsky 1866-1944

Vasily Kandinsky was born on December 4, 1866, in Moscow. From 1886 to 1892 he studied law and economics at the University of Moscow, where he lectured after his graduation. In 1896 he declined a teaching position at the University of Dorpat in order to study art in Munich with Anton Ažbe from 1897 to 1899 and at the Akademie with Franz von Stuck in 1900. From 1901 to 1903 Kandinsky taught at the art school of the *Phalanx,* a group he had co-founded in Munich. One of his students was Gabriele Münter, who remained his companion until 1914. In 1902 Kandinsky exhibited for the first time with the Berlin *Secession* and produced his first woodcuts. In 1903-04 he began his travels in Italy, The Netherlands and North Africa and visits to Russia. He showed frequently at the Salon d'Automne in Paris from 1904.

In 1909 Kandinsky was elected president of the newly founded *Neue Künstlervereinigung München (NKVM).* Their first show took place at the Moderne Galerie (Thannhauser) in Munich in 1909. In 1911 Kandinsky and Marc withdrew from the *NKVM* and began to make plans for the *Blaue Reiter* almanac. The first *Blaue Reiter* exhibition was held in December of that year at the Moderne Galerie. He published *Über das Geistige in der Kunst* in 1911. In 1912 the second *Blaue Reiter* show was held at the Galerie Hans Goltz, Munich, and the *Almanach der Blaue Reiter* appeared. Kandinsky's first one-man show was held at the gallery of Der Sturm in Berlin in 1912. In 1913 one of his works was included in the Armory Show in New York and the *Erster Deutscher Herbstsalon* in Berlin. Except for visits to Scandinavia, Kandinsky lived in Russia from 1914 to 1921, principally in Moscow where he held a position at the People's Commissariat of Education.

Kandinsky began teaching at the Bauhaus in Weimar in 1922. In 1923 he was given his first one-man show in New York by the Société Anonyme, of which he became vice-president. With Klee, Lyonel Feininger and Alexei Jawlensky he was part of the *Blaue Vier (Blue Four)* group, formed in 1924 by Galka Scheyer, who became Kandinsky's representative in the United States. He moved with the Bauhaus to Dessau in 1925 and became a German citizen in 1928. The Nazi government finally closed the Bauhaus in 1933 and later that year Kandinsky settled in Neuilly-sur-Seine near Paris; he acquired French citizenship in 1939. Fifty-seven of his works were confiscated by the Nazis in the 1937 purge of *Entartete Kunst* (degenerate art). Kandinsky died on December 13, 1944, in Neuilly.

27 Landscape with Red Spots, No. 2. 1913

Oil on canvas, 46¼ x 55⅛″ (117.5 x 140 cm.)
76.2553 PG 33; PG coll. cat. 82

From 1908 Kandinsky often stayed in the town of Murnau in upper Bavaria, where his companion Gabriele Münter bought a house in 1909. The landscapes inspired by these Alpine surroundings developed from the flattened, densely colored views of 1908 to the luminous, antimaterial dream visions of 1913, such as this canvas and the closely related *Landscape with Red Spots, No. 1* (Collection Museum Folkwang, Essen).

The motif of the church in a landscape recurs often in Kandinsky's paintings of 1908 to 1913. In examples of 1908 and 1909 the particular design of the Murnau church makes identification possible, though the local topography may not be accurately reflected. By 1911 there is little specifying detail and the tower, which serves to divide the composition, has taken on a generalized, columnar appearance. In *Landscape with Red Spots, No. 2* the tower is replaced by a mysterious elongated vertical form that seems to continue beyond the canvas edge into another realm. Like the nineteenth-century German Romantic painters, Kandinsky presents the landscape as an exalted, spiritualized vision. He achieves the sublimity of the image by freeing color from its descriptive function to reveal its latent expressive content. The chromatic emphasis is on the primary colors, applied thinly over a white ground. The focal point, the red spot that inspires the picture's title, bears out Kandinsky's appraisal of red as an expanding color that pulses forward toward the viewer, in contrast to cooler colors, particularly blue, that recede. Kandinsky indicates the naturalistic content of subject matter with abbreviated signs, emphasizing the purely pictorial aspects of color and form, and thus is able to dematerialize the objective world.

L.F.

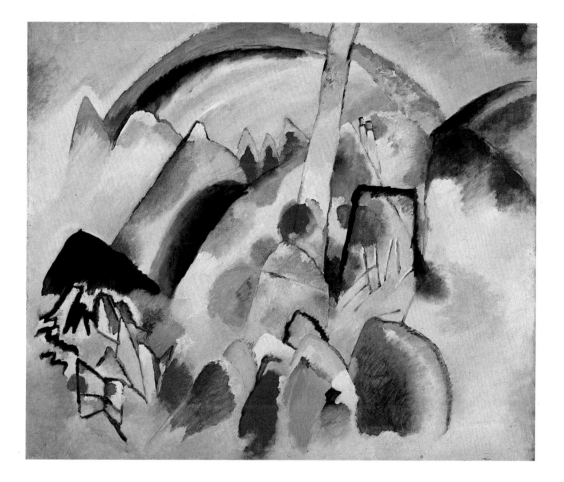

28 White Cross. January–June 1922

Oil on canvas, 39⁹⁄₁₆ x 43⁹⁄₁₆″ (100.5 x 110.6 cm.)
76.2553 PG 34; PG coll. cat. 83

Kandinsky referred to the early 1920s as his "cool period." From this time geometric shapes became increasingly prevalent in his work, often floating in front of or within a broad plane, as in *White Cross*. Here straight lines and circles offset looser, organic forms and irregularly geometric shapes. A corresponding variation of brushstroke produces highly active passages contrasting with less inflected areas. Some shapes may have their distant origins in a naturalistic vocabulary of forms. Thus, the fishlike crescent and the lancing black diagonal that crosses it, which appear also in the related *Red Oval* of 1920 (Collection Solomon R. Guggenheim Museum, New York), may recall the boat with oars in earlier works. However, the motifs are stripped of their representational meaning and do not contribute to an interpretation of the whole in terms of realistic content.

The title isolates a detail of the composition, the white cross at upper right, a formal consequence of the checkerboard pattern (a recurrent motif in works of this period). In this instance negative space is treated as positive form. Once the cross of the title is seen, one begins to perceive throughout the work a proliferation of others, varying in degrees of explicitness. Though Kandinsky, like Malevich, uses it as an abstract element, the cross is an evocative, symbolic form.

The viewer's compulsion to read imagery literally is used to unexpected ends by Kandinsky, who includes two signs resembling the numeral 3 upended and affixed to directional arrows. The variations in direction of the resulting forms suggest the rotation of the entire canvas. The antigravitational feeling of floating forms and the placement of elements on a planar support against an indefinite background in *White Cross* reveal affinities with Malevich's Suprematist works (see cat. no. 30).

L.F.

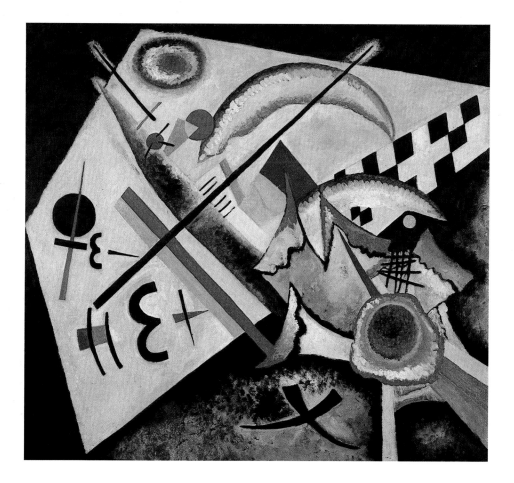

29 Upward. October 1929

Oil on cardboard, 27½ x 19¼" (70 x 49 cm.)
76.2553 PG 35; PG coll. cat. 84

Geometric shapes and sections of circles combine in
Upward in a structure suspended in a field of rich turquoise and green. A partial circle rests delicately on a
pointed base. Another fragment of a circle glides
along its vertical diameter, reaching beyond the circumference of the first form to penetrate the space above it.
Kandinsky achieves an effect of energy rising upward,
while anchoring the forms together by balancing them
on either side of a continuous vertical line. In a closely
related work of the same period, *Depressed* (Collection
Galleria Marescalchi, Bologna), Kandinsky distributes
motifs of partial circles horizontally. Here he represses
the sense of energy found in *Upward* both through his
composition and a subdued palette.

A linear design in the upper right corner of the present
canvas echoes the vertical thrust of the central motif.
This configuration resembles the letter E, as does the
black cutout shape at the base of the central motif.
Another E shape is legible in the upper right corner of a
related drawing (Collection Musée National d'Art
Moderne, Centre Georges Pompidou, Paris; repr.
Rudenstine, p. 421). These forms may at once be independent designs and playful references to the first letter
of *Empor,* the German title of the painting.

The related drawing reveals that the small black circle
and the horizontal bars of the central motif, which have
the physiognomic character of eye and mouth, were not
part of Kandinsky's original design concept and evolved
as he worked on the painting. As he wrote in 1929, the
year he painted *Upward,* "I do not choose form con-
sciously; it chooses itself within me."* The physiognomic character of *Upward* indicates Kandinsky's
association at the Dessau Bauhaus with fellow *Blaue
Vier* artists Klee and Jawlensky. Jawlensky showed
sixteen abstract heads, a motif that appeared in his
work as early as 1918, in an exhibition of the *Blaue
Vier* at the Galerie Ferdinand Möller in Berlin in October 1929. Shown during the month when *Upward*
was completed, these paintings offered Kandinsky the
model of large, abstract faces composed of geometric
planes of non-naturalistic color and accented by bar-
shaped features. However, Kandinsky's working
method more closely resembled that of Klee, who
began with intuitively chosen forms that gradually
suggested counterparts in the natural world, than that
of Jawlensky, who began with the model and moved
toward abstraction. In particular, the whimsy of the
hovering black eye in *Upward* and the incorporation
of a letter as a pictogram with a possible reference to
the title of the painting suggest the reverberations of
Klee's art.

* Quoted in *Kandinsky: Complete Writings on Art,* ed.
  K. C. Lindsay and P. Vergo, Boston, 1982, vol. II, p. 740.

E.C.C.

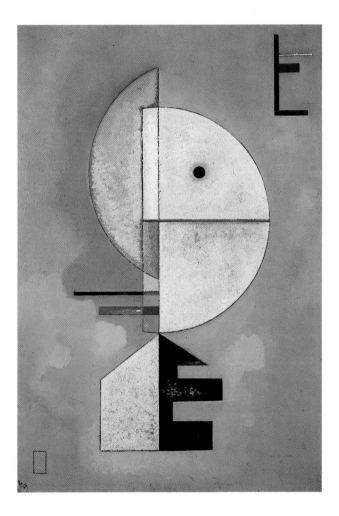

Kazimir Malevich 1878-1935

Kazimir Severinovich Malevich was born on February 26, 1878, near Kiev, Russia. He studied at the Moscow Institute of Painting, Sculpture and Architecture in 1903. During the early years of his career he experimented with various modernist styles and participated in avant-garde exhibitions, such as those of the *Moscow Artists' Association*, which included Kandinsky and Mikhail Larionov, and the *Jack of Diamonds* of 1910 in Moscow. Malevich showed his neo-primitivist paintings of peasants at the exhibition *Donkey's Tail* in 1912. After this exhibition he broke with Larionov's group. In 1913, with composer Mikhail Matiushin and writer Alexei Kruchenykh, he drafted a manifesto for the First Futurist Congress. That same year Malevich designed the sets and costumes for the opera *Victory over the Sun* by Matiushin and Kruchenykh. He showed at the Salon des Indépendants in Paris in 1914.

At the *0.10 Last Futurist Exhibition* in Petrograd in 1915 Malevich introduced his nonobjective, geometric Suprematist paintings. In 1919 he began to explore the three-dimensional applications of Suprematism in architectural models. Following the Bolshevik Revolution in 1917, Malevich and other advanced artists were encouraged by the Soviet government and attained prominent administrative and teaching positions in the arts. At the invitation of Chagall, Malevich began teaching at the Vitebsk Art Institute in 1919; he soon became its director. In 1919-20 he was given a one-man show at the *Sixteenth State Exhibition* in Moscow, which focused on Suprematism and other nonobjective styles. Malevich and his students at Vitebsk formed the Suprematist group *Unovis*. From 1922 to 1927 he taught at the Institute for Artistic Culture in Petrograd and between 1924 and 1926 he worked primarily on architectural models with his students.

In 1927 Malevich traveled with an exhibition of his paintings to Warsaw and also went to Berlin, where his work was shown at the *Grosse Berliner Kunstausstellung*. In Germany he met Arp, Schwitters, Naum Gabo and Le Corbusier and visited the Bauhaus where he met Walter Gropius. The Tretiakov Gallery in Moscow gave Malevich a one-man exhibition in 1929. Because of his connections with German artists, he was arrested in 1930 and many of his manuscripts were destroyed. In his final period he painted in a representational style. Malevich died in Leningrad on May 15, 1935.

30 Untitled. ca. 1916

Oil on canvas, 20⅞ x 20⅞" (53 x 53 cm.)
76.2553 PG 42; PG coll. cat. 104

Malevich proposed the reductive, abstract style of Suprematism as an alternative to earlier art forms, which he considered inappropriate to his own time. He observed that the proportions of forms in art of the past corresponded with those of objects in nature, which are determined by their function. In opposition to this he proposed a self-referential art in which proportion, scale, color and disposition obey intrinsic, nonutilitarian laws. Malevich considered his nonobjective forms to be reproductions of purely affective sensations that bore no relation to external phenomena. He rejected conventions of gravity, clear orientation, horizon line and perspective systems.

Malevich's units are developed from the straight line and its two-dimensional extension, the plane, and are constituted of contrasting areas of unmodeled color, distinguished by various textural effects. The diagonal orientation of geometric forms creates rhythms on the surface of the canvas. The overlapping of elements and their varying scale relationships within a white ground provide a sense of indefinitely extensive space. Though the organization of the pictorial forms does not correspond with that of traditional subjects, there are various internal regulatory principles. In the present work a magnetic attraction and repulsion seem to dictate the slow rotational movement of parts. A preparatory drawing for the painting (Private Collection, U.S.S.R.; see Rudenstine, p. 478, fig. c) diverges slightly from it in the number and placement of the forms.

L.F.

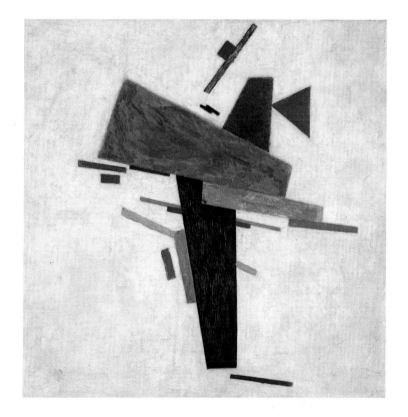

El Lissitzky 1890-1941

El Lissitzky was born Lazar Markovich Lisitskii on November 23, 1890, in Pochinok, in the Russian province of Smolensk, and grew up in Vitebsk. He pursued architectural studies at the Technische Hochschule in Darmstadt from 1909 to 1914, when the outbreak of World War I precipitated his return to Russia. In 1916 he received a diploma in engineering and architecture from the Riga Technological University.

Lissitzky and Malevich were invited by Chagall to join the faculty of the Vitebsk Art Institute in 1919; there Lissitzky taught architecture and graphics. That same year he executed his first *Proun* (acronym in Russian for "project for the affirmation of the new") and formed part of the *Unovis* group. In 1920 he became a member of Inkhuk (Institute for Artistic Culture) in Moscow and designed his book *Pro dva kvadrata (About Two Squares)*. The following year he taught at Vkhutemas (Higher State Art-Technical Studios) with Vladimir Tatlin and joined the Constructivist group. The Constructivists exhibited at the *Erste russische Kunstausstellung* designed by Lissitzky at the Galerie van Diemen in Berlin in 1922. During this period he collaborated with Ilya Ehrenburg on the journal *Veshch/Gegenstand/Objet*.

In 1923 the artist experimented with new typographic design for a book by Vladimir Mayakovsky, *Dlya golosa (For the Voice)*, and visited Hannover where his work was shown under the auspices of the Kestner-Gesellschaft. Also in 1923 Lissitzky created his Proun environment for the *Grosse Berliner Kunstausstellung* and executed his lithographic suites *Proun* and *Victory over the Sun* (illustrating the opera by Alexei Kruchenykh and Mikhail Matiushin), before traveling to Switzerland for medical treatment. In 1924 he worked with Schwitters on the issue of the periodical *Merz* called "Nasci," and with Arp on the book *Die Kunstismen (The Isms of Art)*. The next year he returned to Moscow to teach at Vkhutemas–Vkhutein (Higher State Art-Technical Studios–Higher State Art-Technical Institute), which he continued to do until 1930. During the mid-1920s Lissitzky stopped painting in order to concentrate on the design of typography and exhibitions. He created a room for the *Internationale Kunstausstellung* in Dresden in 1926 (which included works by Mondrian, Léger, Picabia, László Moholy-Nagy and Gabo) and another at the Niedersächsisches Landesmuseum in Hannover in 1927. He also designed the Soviet Pavilion at the exhibition *Pressa* in Cologne in 1928. His essay "Russland: Architektur für eine Weltrevolution" was published in 1930. Lissitzky died on December 30, 1941, in Moscow.

31 Untitled. ca. 1919-20

Oil on canvas, 31⅜ x 19½" (79.6 x 49.6 cm.)
76.2553 PG 43; PG coll. cat. 100

This painting reveals the principles of Suprematism that Lissitzky absorbed under the influence of Malevich in 1919-20. Trained as an engineer and possessing a more pragmatic temperament than that of his mentor, Lissitzky soon became one of the leading exponents of Constructivism. In the 1920s, while living in Germany, he became an important influence on both the Dutch *De Stijl* group and the artists of the German Bauhaus.

Like Malevich, Lissitzky believed in a new art that rejected traditional pictorial structure, centralized compositional organization, mimesis and perspectival consistency. In this work the ladder of vividly colored forms seems to be floating through indeterminate space. Spatial relationships are complicated by the veil of white color that divides these forms from the major gray diagonal. The linkage of elements is not attributable to a mysterious magnetic pull, as in Malevich's painting (see cat. no. 30), but is indicated in a literal way by the device of a connecting threadlike line. The winding line changes color as it passes through the various rectangles that may serve as metaphors for different cosmic planes.

L.F.

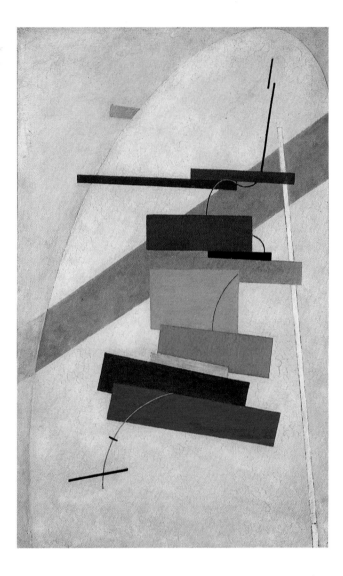

Antoine Pevsner 1884-1962

Antoine Pevsner was born on January 18, 1884, in Orel, Russia. After leaving the Academy of Fine Arts in St. Petersburg in 1911, he traveled to Paris where he saw the work of Robert Delaunay, Gleizes, Metzinger and Léger. On a second visit to Paris in 1913 he met Modigliani and Archipenko, who encouraged his interest in Cubism. Pevsner spent the war years 1915 to 1917 in Oslo with his brother Naum Gabo. On his return to Russia in 1917 Pevsner began teaching at the Moscow Academy of Fine Arts with Kandinsky and Malevich.

In 1920 he and Gabo published the *Realistic Manifesto*. Their work was included in the *Erste russische Kunstausstellung* at the Galerie van Diemen in Berlin in 1922, held under the auspices of the Soviet government. The following year Pevsner visited Berlin, where he met Duchamp and Katherine Dreier. He then traveled on to Paris, where he settled permanently; in 1930 he became a French citizen. His work was included in an exhibition at the Little Review Gallery in New York in 1926. He and Gabo designed sets for the ballet *La Chatte,* produced by Sergei Diaghilev in 1927. In Paris the two brothers were leaders of the Constructivist members of *Abstraction-Création,* an alliance of artists who embraced a variety of abstract styles.

During the 1930s Pevsner's work was shown in Amsterdam, Basel, London, New York and Chicago. In 1946 he, Gleizes, Herbin and others formed the group *Réalités Nouvelles*; their first exhibition was held at the Salon des Réalités Nouvelles in Paris in 1947. That same year Pevsner's first one-man show opened at the Galerie René Drouin in Paris. The Museum of Modern Art in New York presented a *Gabo-Pevsner* exhibition in 1948, and in 1952 Pevsner participated in *Chefs-d'oeuvre du XXᵉ siècle* at the Musée National d'Art Moderne in Paris. The same museum organized a one-man exhibition of his work in 1957. In 1958 he was represented in the French Pavilion at the Venice Biennale. Pevsner died in Paris on April 12, 1962.

32 Anchored Cross. 1933

Glass, marble and brass, 33⁵⁄₁₆″ (84.6 cm.) long (diagonally)
76.2553 PG 60; PG coll. cat. 133

In 1920 Pevsner signed the *Realistic Manifesto* drafted by his brother Naum Gabo, proclaiming the intention of Constructivism as they conceived it. They sought to translate their apprehension of an absolute and essential reality as "the realization of our perceptions of the world in the forms of space and time."[*] They believed that space was given form through implications of depth rather than volume and they rejected mass as the basic sculptural element. Line, rendered dynamic through directionality, established kinetic rhythms. The Constructivists advocated the use of contemporary industrial materials; they did not carve or model these materials according to sculptural conventions, but constructed them according to principles of modern technology. In their words, "The plumb-line in our hand, eyes as precise as a ruler, in a spirit as taut as a compass . . . we construct our work as the universe constructs its own, as the engineer constructs his bridges, as the mathematician his formula of the orbits."[**]

In this work Pevsner complicates the delineation of space by using a transparent substance in conjunction with opaque materials. The glass panes echo both the rounded excised outlines of the construction and its angular metal surfaces. The metal ribs anchor the panes of glass and hinge all planes, real and imagined, resulting in a complex structuring of space. Furthermore, they function visually as an Orthodox cross. The icons of Pevsner's native Russia, which had played a crucial role in the development of his notions of perspective, may have suggested the form.

[*] *Russian Art of the Avant-Garde: Theory and Criticism, 1902-1934*, The Documents of 20th-Century Art, ed. J. E. Bowlt, New York, 1976, p. 213. The entire manifesto, translated by Gabo, appears in this volume.

[**] Ibid.

L.F.

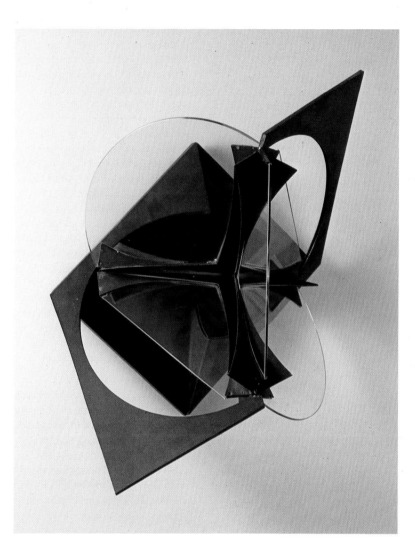

33 Developable Surface. 1941

Bronze and silver plate, 21⅝ x 14¼ x 19⁹⁄₁₆″ (55 x 36.3 x 49.1 cm.)
76.2553 PG 62; PG coll. cat. 135

In *Developable Surface* Pevsner utilizes voids as active structural components, folding, twisting and molding negative space as he does sheets of bronze. The result is a complex three-dimensional statement that demands examination from multiple angles. Viewed from the longer side of their rectangular base, the bronze sheets thrust diagonally upward into opposite directions, liberated from one another at the work's outer dimensions by cone-shaped voids wedged above and beneath the sculpture's center. Viewed from the short side of the base, the upper sheaths of bronze pierce the vertical walls of the structure, folding back into themselves and carrying one's eye along diagonal edges into the surrounding space. The central void, now a single oval, is emphasized by the pattern of the bronze rods that radiate from the twisted contours in the core of the sculpture. An oblique view of the work reveals a deeply cut V-shaped space that penetrates the central torsion, dividing the two sides of the structure which seem to tear apart, alternatively advancing toward and receding from the viewer. Another oblique view reveals the rectangular nature of the construction, the metal sides carving out four distinct corners of a box which are articulated by four dividing spaces. From all points of view, Pevsner balances positive and negative spatial elements to develop form in controlled, symmetrical terms.

The technique employed by Pevsner in the creation of this and other sculptures of the same period (for example, another *Developable Surface,* of 1938, in the Peggy Guggenheim Collection) was painstakingly elaborate (see Rudenstine, pp. 600-601). Pevsner soldered each strand of bronze individually, alternately heating and cooling the material as he worked. The artist created the ridges at the sculpture's edges through the application of a stronger solder, which he then filed down. The sculpture was originally plated in silver, creating a glistening surface which is now largely lost.*

* Repr. in *Mostra di scultura contemporanea,* exh. cat., Venice, 1949, n.p.

E.C.C.

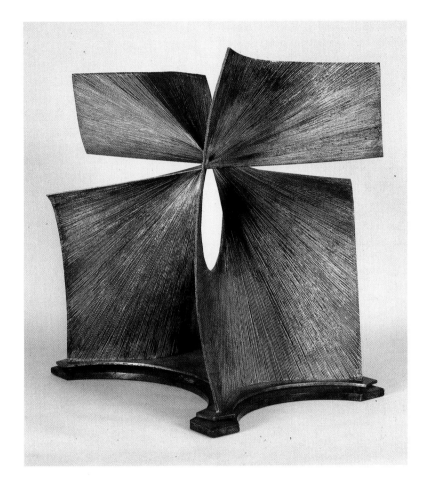

Piet Mondrian 1872-1944

Piet Mondrian was born Pieter Cornelis Mondriaan, Jr., on March 7, 1872, in Amersfoort, The Netherlands. He studied at the Rijksakademie van Beeldende Kunsten, Amsterdam, from 1892 to 1897. Until 1908, when he began to take annual trips to Domburg in Zeeland, Mondrian's work was naturalistic—incorporating successive influences of academic landscape and still-life painting, Dutch Impressionism and Symbolism. In 1909 his work was shown at the Stedelijk Museum, Amsterdam, and that same year he joined the Theosophic Society. In 1909-10 he experimented with Pointillism and by 1911 had begun to work in a Cubist mode. After seeing original Cubist works by Braque and Picasso at the first *Moderne Kunstkring* exhibition in 1911 in Amsterdam, Mondrian decided to move to Paris. In Paris from 1912 to 1914 he began to develop an independent abstract style.

Mondrian was visiting The Netherlands when World War I broke out and prevented his return to Paris. During the war years in Holland he further reduced his colors and geometric shapes and formulated his non-objective Neo-Plastic style. In 1917 Mondrian became one of the founders of *De Stijl*. This group, which included van Doesburg and Vantongerloo, extended its principles of abstraction and simplification beyond painting and sculpture to architecture and graphic and industrial design. Mondrian's essays on abstract art were published in the periodical *De Stijl*. In July 1919 he returned to Paris; there he exhibited with *De Stijl* in 1923 but withdrew from the group after van Doesburg reintroduced diagonal elements into his work about 1924. In 1930 Mondrian showed with *Cercle et Carré (Circle and Square)* and in 1931 joined *Abstraction-Création*.

The growing threat of World War II forced Mondrian to move to London in 1938 and then to New York in October 1940. In New York he joined the *American Abstract Artists* and continued to publish texts on Neo-Plasticism. His late style evolved significantly in response to the city. In 1942 his first one-man show at the Valentine Dudensing Gallery, New York, took place. Mondrian died on February 1, 1944, in New York.

34 The Sea. 1914

Charcoal and gouache on paper mounted on panel, paper 34½ x 47⅜" (87.6 x 120.3 cm.)
76.2553 PG 38; PG coll. cat. 120

Mondrian first treated the theme of the sea in naturalistic works of 1909 to 1911, during lengthy sojourns in the village of Domburg on the coast of Dutch Zeeland. He assimilated and adapted the Cubism of Picasso and Braque in Paris soon after his arrival there in the winter of 1911-12. He returned to The Netherlands in the summer of 1914 and probably in the following war years worked on the studies of the sea that culminated in the *Pier and Ocean* paintings of 1917.*

The oval format and grid structure used in these works are devices derived from Cubism. They serve respectively to resolve the problem of the compositional interference of the corners and to organize and unify the picture's elements. For Mondrian the horizontal-vertical arrangement did not have an exclusively pictorial function, as it did for the Cubists, but carried mystical implications. He viewed the horizontal and vertical as basic oppositional principles that could interact to produce a union symbolizing a state of universal harmony.

Though Mondrian's source exists in the natural world, in the motion of waves and their contact with breakwaters, the signs for this source have been reduced to their most essential pictorial form. The strokes are determined by their structural function rather than their descriptive potential, and there is no sense of perspectival recession despite the atmospheric texture of the gouache highlighting. This highlighting evokes the reflection of light on water and also defines planar surfaces. As Mondrian developed the theories of Neo-Plasticism, these suggestions of natural phenomena disappeared.

* For discussion of the chronology see Rudenstine, pp. 555-557.

L.F.

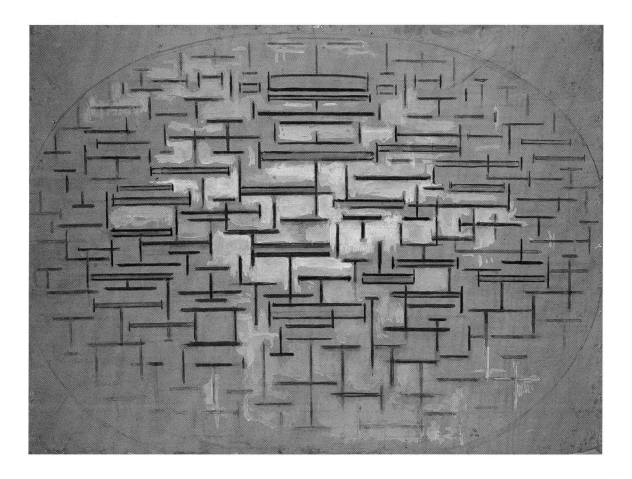

35 Untitled (Oval Composition). 1914

Charcoal on paper mounted on panel, paper 60 x 39⅜″
(152.5 x 100 cm.)
76.2553 PG 37; PG coll. cat. 119

After May 1912 Mondrian regularly employed grid
systems of vertical and horizontal lines in his paintings.
His containment of these linear compositions within
circular or oval perimeters, in examples such as the
present drawing and *The Sea* (cat. no. 34), points to the
influence of oval Analytical Cubist works by Picasso
and Braque. Yet Picasso's shifting Cubist planes coalesce in ambiguous spaces, while Mondrian's shallow
space is united by a network of pure line. Even in this
early Paris period Mondrian's focus on the relationship
between horizontal and vertical elements anticipates
the abstract order of his *De Stijl* compositions later in
the decade.

Mondrian's geometric systems bear witness not to a
calculated formalism, but to a style of construction directed by what he termed "a higher intuition," which
reverberates with a hidden symbolic charge. Mondrian
officially joined the Dutch Theosophic Society in 1909,
testifying to his interest in the mystical philosophies
articulated in the writings of Rudolf Steiner and Mme
H. P. Blavatsky. For Blavatsky, the "philosophical
cross," or the joining of the horizontal and the perpendicular, is a metaphysical form that symbolizes universal principles of human existence.* Mondrian's work
from his Amsterdam period reveals theosophic sympa-
thies in its highly geometricized depiction of trees,

flowers, women and windmills. His Cubist-influenced
works executed in Paris continue to express these
beliefs through emphatic organizations of abstract
vertical and horizontal elements.

Mondrian's search for geometric order in his visual
experience led him to study the rectilinear character of
architecture. In 1913 he began sketching the building
façades of his neighborhood in Paris. He elaborated
some of these sketches into large-scale drawings which
retain some evidence of his initial impression of the
edifice—in the present example, one can still discern
window shapes and suggestions of the relief of the wall.
Thus Mondrian followed a process of abstraction,
ultimately arriving at the rigorously distilled linear
scheme in his painting *Composition in Oval, Tableau
III* (Collection Stedelijk Museum, Amsterdam; repr. and
discussed Rudenstine, pp. 551-552). In the Stedelijk
painting color as well as line assumes a role in main-
taining a harmonious balance among the various parts
of the composition. Hues of rose, tan, pink and gray
give definition to geometric compartments in the painting which, like the Peggy Guggenheim sketch, is more
dense and more fully articulated at its center than at
its periphery.

* See R. P. Welsh, "Mondrian and Theosophy" in
Piet Mondrian 1872-1944: Centennial Exhibition, exh. cat.,
New York, 1971, p. 49.

E.C.C.

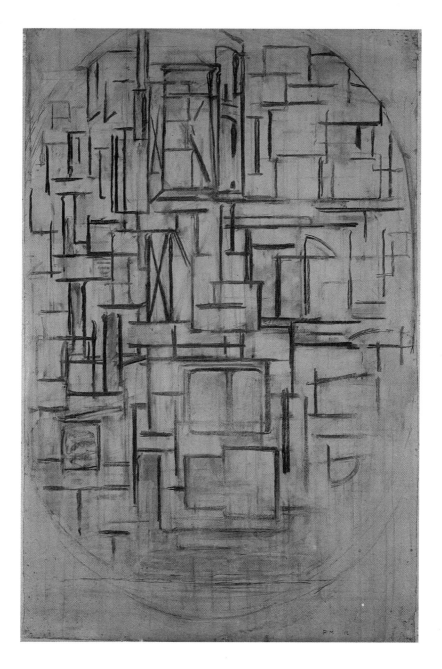

36 Composition. 1938-39

Oil on canvas mounted on wood support, canvas, 41 $\frac{7}{16}$
x 40 $\frac{5}{16}$" (105.2 x 102.3 cm.)
76.2553 PG 39; PG coll. cat. 121

From 1938 to 1940 Mondrian, who had fled wartime
Paris, was established in London near his friends Ben
Nicholson, Barbara Hepworth and Naum Gabo. During this period he continued working in the highly reductivist Neo-Plasticist mode he had developed in
France, in which horizontal and vertical black lines intersect on the canvas in asymmetrically balanced relationships to yield flat white or colored quadrilaterals.
The palette is generally restricted to black, white and
primary colors. The present work is among the more
coloristically austere examples.

By divorcing form completely from its referential meaning, Mondrian hoped to provide a visual equivalent for
the truths that inhabit nature but are concealed in its
random, flawed manifestations. He felt that if he could
communicate these truths by means of a system of re-
solved oppositions, a "real equation of the universal
and the individual,"* the spiritual effect on the viewer
would be one of total repose and animistic harmony.
In order to effect this transmission the artist must sub-
limate his personality so that it does not interfere with
the viewer's perception of the rhythmic equilibrium of
line, dimension and color. These elements, however,
are organized not according to the impersonal dictates
of mathematics but rather to the intuition of the artist.
Likewise, although the artist's gesture is minimized and
the reference to personal experience erased, his presence
can be detected in the stroke of the paintbrush and the
unevenness of the edge of the transcendent line. The
individual consciousness exists in a dialectical relationship with "the absolute," which is realized pictorially
through, in Mondrian's words, the "mutual interaction
of constructive elements and their inherent relations."**
Just as the forms and space of the canvas are abstracted
from life, so the spiritual plane is removed from, though
related to, the work of art. Mondrian sought to unite
art, matter and spirit to discover in all aspects of experience the universal harmony posited in Neo-Plasticism.

* Quoted in *Theories of Modern Art*, ed. H. B. Chipp, Berkeley and Los Angeles, 1968, p. 350.

**Ibid., p. 351.

L.F.

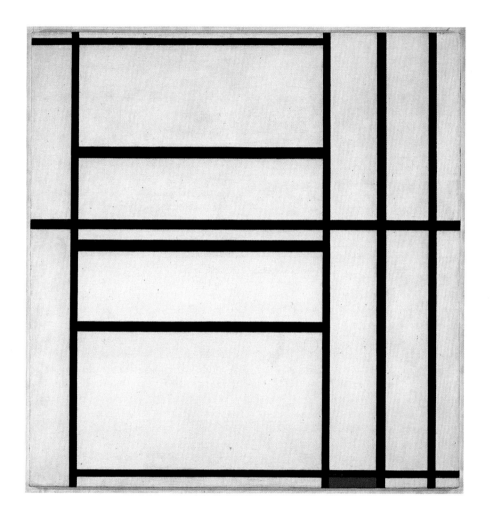

Theo van Doesburg 1883-1931

Christian Emil Marie Küpper, who adopted the pseudonym Theo van Doesburg, was born in Utrecht, The
Netherlands, on August 30, 1883. His first exhibition
of paintings was held in 1908 in The Hague. In the early
teens he wrote poetry and established himself as an art
critic. From 1914 to 1916 van Doesburg served in the
Dutch army, after which time he settled in Leiden and
began his collaboration with the architects J.J.P. Oud
and Jan Wils. In 1917 they founded the group *De Stijl*
and the periodical of the same name; other original
members were Mondrian, Vantongerloo, Bart Van der
Leck and Vilmos Huszár. Van Doesburg executed decorations for Oud's *De Vonk* project in Noordwijker-
hout in 1917.

In 1920 he resumed his writing, using the pen names
I. K. Bonset and later Aldo Camini. Van Doesburg
visited Berlin and Weimar in 1921 and the following
year taught at the Weimar Bauhaus; here he associated
with Mies van der Rohe, Le Corbusier, Raoul Hausmann and Hans Richter. He was interested in Dada at
this time and worked with Schwitters as well as Arp,
Tristan Tzara and others on the review *Mécano* in
1922. Exhibitions of the architectural designs of van
Doesburg, Cor van Eesteren and Gerrit Rietveld were
held in Paris in 1923 at Léonce Rosenberg's Galerie
l'Effort Moderne and in 1924 at the Ecole Spéciale
d'Architecture.

The Landesmuseum of Weimar presented a one-man
show of van Doesburg's work in 1924. That same year
he lectured on modern literature in Prague, Vienna and
Hannover, and the Bauhaus published his *Grundbe-
griffe der neuen gestaltenden Kunst (Principles of Neo-
Plastic Art)*. A new phase of *De Stijl* was declared by
van Doesburg in his manifesto of "Elementarism," published in 1926. During that year he collaborated with
Arp and Sophie Taeuber-Arp on the decoration of the
restaurant-cabaret L'Aubette in Strasbourg. Van Doesburg returned to Paris in 1929 and began working on a
house at Meudon-Val-Fleury with van Eesteren. Also
in that year he published the first issue of *Art Concret,*
the organ of the Paris-based group of the same name.
Van Doesburg was the moving force behind the for-
mation of the group *Abstraction-Création* in Paris. The
artist died on March 7, 1931, in Davos, Switzerland.

37 Composition in Gray (Rag-time). 1919

Oil on canvas, 38 x 23¼″ (96.5 x 59.1 cm.)
76.2553 PG 40; PG coll. cat. 45

In 1917 van Doesburg, Mondrian and other artists and
architects founded the *De Stijl* magazine and group.
The following year they continued elaborating their
theoretical program, which promulgated a new plastic
order of reductivist, nonobjective art. In his painting
van Doesburg followed Mondrian's example by sys-
tematically divesting his imagery of figurative references
and reducing pictorial elements to colors and geometric
forms in oppositional relationships.[*] In so doing, he
hoped to express a universal reality underlying the
capriciously changeable appearances of nature.

This work of 1919 demonstrates van Doesburg's lingering attachment to what he disdainfully referred to as
the "brown" world of Cubism. Reluctant to diffuse the
composition, he structures monochromatic, modulated planes around a central axis and allows the lower
corners to recede, thereby suggesting a Cubist oval.
According to the dogma of the "white" world of Neo-
Plasticism, the focus should be moved from the center
of the canvas to its periphery; the rectangle should not
be construed as a discrete plane but as a shape passively
resulting from the intersection of lines and given substance by color. However, *Composition in Gray (Rag-
time)* incorporates aspects of the Neo-Plastic aesthetic
that distinguish its style from Analytic Cubism. For
example, the edges of its planes have been regularized
and contoured and do not penetrate or overlap one
another. Despite the illusion of bowing in individual
planes, they have been organized with architectural
clarity as a rhythmic composition that is essentially flat
and frontal.

[*] For discussion of the underlying dance and music subject
   of this work, and of its dating, see Rudenstine, pp. 220-
   222, 224-226.

L.F.

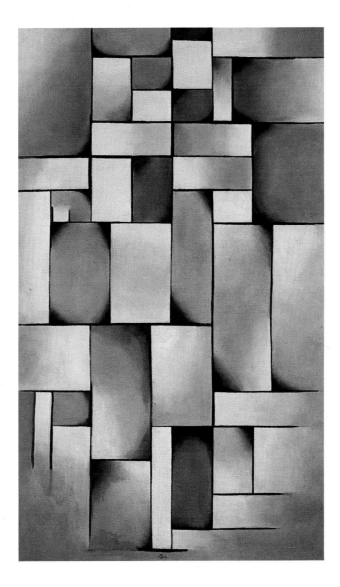

38 Counter-Composition XIII. 1925-26

Oil on canvas, 19⅝ x 19⅝″ (49.9 x 50 cm.)
76.2553 PG 41; PG coll. cat. 46

About 1924 van Doesburg rebelled against Mondrian's programmatic insistence on the restriction of line to vertical and horizontal orientations, and produced his first *Counter-Composition*. The direction consequently taken by Neo-Plasticism was designated "Elementarism" by van Doesburg, who described its method of construction as "based on the neutralisation of positive and negative directions by the diagonal and, as far as color is concerned, by the dissonant. Equilibrated relations are not an ultimate result."* Mondrian considered this redefinition of Neo-Plasticism heretical; he was soon to resign from the *De Stijl* group.

Unlike van Doesburg's *Composition in Gray (Ragtime)* of 1919 (cat. no. 37), this canvas upholds the Neo-Plastic dictum of "peripheric" composition. The focus is decentralized and there are no empty, inactive areas. The geometric planes are emphasized equally, related by contrasts of color, scale and direction. One's eyes follow the trajectories of isosceles triangles and stray beyond the canvas to complete mentally the larger triangles sliced off by its edges. The placement of the vertical axis to the left of center and the barely off-square proportions of the support create a sense of shifting balance.

* Quoted in H. C. L. Jaffé, *De Stijl: 1917-1931: The Dutch Contribution to Modern Art*, Amsterdam, 1956, p. 26.

L.F.

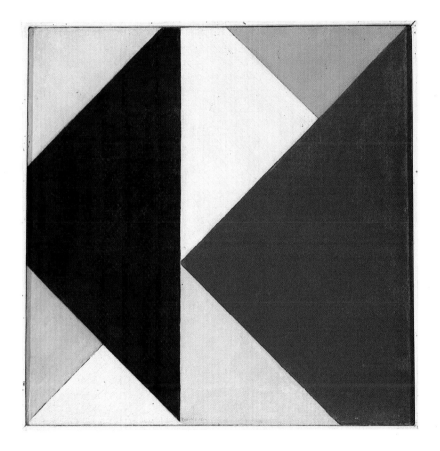

Georges Vantongerloo 1886-1965

Georges Vantongerloo was born on November 24, 1886, in Antwerp. He studied about 1900 at the Académie des Beaux-Arts of Antwerp and of Brussels. He spent the years 1914 to 1918 in The Netherlands, where his work attracted the attention of the Queen. While working on architectural designs there, Vantongerloo met Mondrian, Van der Leck and van Doesburg and collaborated with them on the magazine *De Stijl,* which was founded in 1917. Soon after his return to Brussels in 1918 he moved to Menton, France. In France he developed a close friendship with the artist and architect Max Bill, who was to organize many Vantongerloo exhibitions. In 1924 Vantongerloo published his pamphlet "L'Art et son avenir" in Antwerp.

In 1928 the artist-architect-theorist moved from Menton to Paris; there, in 1931, he became vice-president of the artists' association *Abstraction-Création,* a position he held until 1937. His models of bridges and a proposed airport were exhibited at the Musée des Arts Décoratifs in Paris in 1930. In 1936 he participated in the exhibiton *Cubism and Abstract Art* at The Museum of Modern Art in New York. His first one-man show was held at the Galerie de Berri in Paris in 1943. Vantongerloo shared an exhibition with Bill and Pevsner in 1949 at the Kunsthaus Zürich. His seventy-fifth birthday was observed with a solo exhibition at the Galerie Suzanne Bollag in Zürich in 1961. The following year Bill organized a large Vantongerloo retrospective for the Marlborough New London Gallery in London. Vantongerloo died on October 5, 1965, in Paris.

39 Construction of Volumetric Interrelationships Derived from the Inscribed Square and the Square Circumscribed by a Circle. 1924

Cast cement with paint, $11\frac{13}{16}$ x $10\frac{1}{16}''$ (30 x 25.5 cm.) 76.2553 PG 59; PG coll. cat. 174

Vantongerloo, who accepted the *De Stijl* restriction of line to horizontal and vertical in 1919, based his sculpture on the volumetric translation of this principle. The variation of volume and proportion in his work was determined geometrically, often according to mathematical formulae. Mathematics was for Vantongerloo a convention that established order in the world, a rationalization of nature that could be combined successfully with an aesthetic intention to result in the production of a work of art. In this approach he felt closest to the medieval artist who composed within the constraints of geometric convention, and to the ancient Egyptians, whose solution to the "problem" of the pyramid of Cheops consisted in "the inscribed and circumscribed squares of a circle."[*]

In one of his books Vantongerloo juxtaposed a diagram for the present work with an analytic sketch of the rose window at the cathedral of Amiens.[**] The asymmetry of the *De Stijl* image distinguishes it from the medieval subject. As the diagram shows and the title indicates, the extensions of the sculpture are determined by the lines of the inscribed and circumscribed squares of a circle. The relationships of its volumes result as much from the creative selectivity of the artist as from mathematical regulation. The effects of changing light produce subtle coloristic modulation and a relationship with the environment approaching that of architecture.

[*] G. Vantongerloo, *Paintings, Sculptures, Reflections*, New York, 1948, p. 22.

[**]Ibid., p. 23.

L.F.

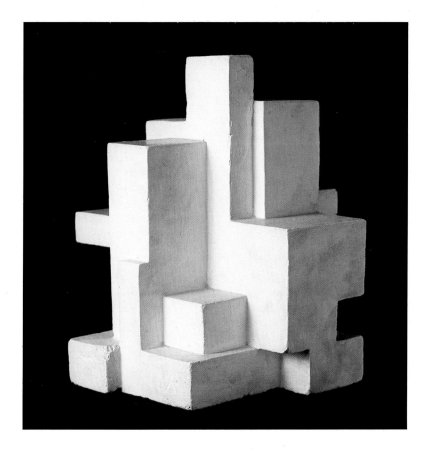

Amédée Ozenfant 1886-1966

Amédée J. Ozenfant was born on April 15, 1886, in Saint-Quentin, Aisne, France. At age fourteen he began painting, and in 1904 he attended the Ecole Municipale de Dessin Quentin-La Tour in Saint-Quentin. The following year Ozenfant moved to Paris, where he entered an architecture studio. At this time he also studied painting with Charles Cottet at the Académie de la Palette, where he became a friend of La Fresnaye and Dunoyer de Segonzac.

Ozenfant's first solo exhibition was held in 1908 at the Salon de la Société Nationale des Beaux-Arts in Paris. In 1910 he contributed works to the Salon d'Automne and in 1911 he participated in the Salon des Indépendants. From about 1909 to 1913 he made trips to Russia, Italy, Belgium and The Netherlands and attended lectures at the Collège de France in Paris. In 1915 Ozenfant founded the magazine *L'Elan,* which he edited until 1917, and began to formulate his theories of Purism. In 1917 the artist met the Swiss architect and painter Charles-Edouard Jeanneret (Le Corbusier); together they articulated the doctrines of Purism in their *Après le Cubisme.* The publication of this book coincided with the first Purist exhibition, held at the Galerie Thomas in Paris in 1917, in which Ozenfant was represented. Ozenfant and Le Corbusier collaborated on the journal *L'Esprit Nouveau,* which appeared from 1920 to 1925.

Ozenfant participated in the second Purist exhibition at the Galerie Druet, Paris, in 1921. In 1924 he and Léger opened a free studio in Paris where they taught with Laurencin and Alexandra Exter. Ozenfant and Le Corbusier wrote *La Peinture moderne* in 1925. During that year Ozenfant exhibited at the controversial Pavillon de l'Esprit Nouveau at the *Exposition des Arts Décoratifs* in Paris. The artist was given a one-man show at Galerie L. C. Hodebert, Paris, in 1928. His book *Art* was published in French in 1928; an English edition appeared as *The Foundations of Modern Art* in London and New York in 1931. In Paris Ozenfant taught at the Académie Moderne in 1929 and founded the Académie Ozenfant in 1932. From 1935 to 1938 he operated the Ozenfant Academy in London and during this time also taught at the French Institute in that city. From 1939 to 1955 he taught at the Ozenfant School of Fine Arts in New York. His one-man show at The Arts Club of Chicago was held in 1940. Ozenfant taught and lectured widely in the United States until 1955, when he returned to France. He remained there the rest of his life, and died in Cannes on May 4, 1966.

40 Guitar and Bottles. 1920

Oil on canvas, 31¹¹⁄₁₆ x 39⁵⁄₁₆″ (80.5 x 99.8 cm.)
76.2553 PG 24; PG coll. cat. 131

Two other versions of this work exist. One of these, *Still Life,* is in the collection of the Solomon R. Guggenheim Museum, New York; the whereabouts of the other is presently unknown. The composition is informed by the Purist aesthetic as developed by Ozenfant and Le Corbusier in 1918. Drawing on pre-1914 Cubism, particularly the coolly rational interpretation of Gris, they dismissed its subsequent evolution as too decorative and unordered. They felt that the chaos of the natural world should be dispelled by the organizing mechanisms of the human mind. This conviction became a moral imperative that Ozenfant and Le Corbusier attempted to uphold in their work.

Ozenfant used the following metaphor to describe the function of rational thought: "A lens concentrates the diffuse rays of the sun and creates fire by converging those rays. To converge is to refine something in nature, so as to render it more concentrated, compact, penetrative, intense: it helps to facilitate the manifestations of that phenomenon and to render it effective and useful for humanity."* Ozenfant's application of this principle to paintings such as *Guitar and Bottles* resulted in compositions that are lucid and geometric but somewhat dry.

* A. Ozenfant, *Foundations of Modern Art,* trans. J. Rodker, New York, 1952, p. 191.

L.F.

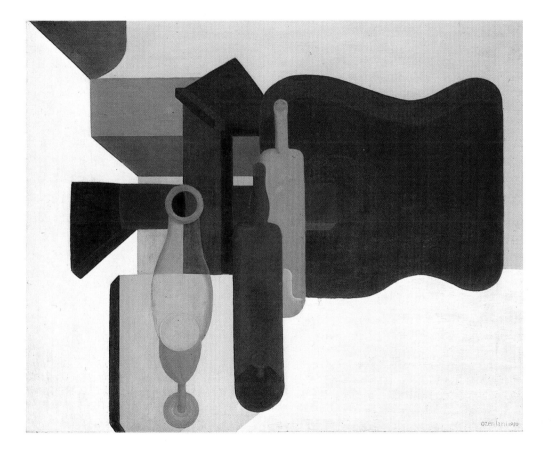

Jean Hélion b. 1904

Jean Hélion was born on April 21, 1904, in Couterne, France. He entered the Institut Industriel du Nord in Lille to study chemistry in 1920 but left the following year to become an architectural apprentice in Paris. He painted while working as an architectural draftsman in the early 1920s. Hélion attracted the attention of the collector Georges Bine in 1925 and was soon able to devote himself entirely to painting. In 1927 he met Joaquín Torres-García, who collaborated on *L'Acte*, a short-lived magazine founded by Hélion and others.

Hélion first exhibited at the Salon des Indépendants in 1928. Shortly thereafter he became acquainted with Arp, Pevsner and Mondrian. By 1929 his work was nonfigurative. With van Doesburg and others in 1930 he formed the artists' association and periodical *Art Concret*. This group was succeeded by *Abstraction-Création* the next year. In 1931, after traveling through Europe and the Soviet Union, Hélion returned to Paris, where he met Ernst, Tristan Tzara and Duchamp. His first one-man show was held at the Galerie Pierre in Paris in 1932. That same year Hélion made his first visit to New York, where he was given a one-man exhibition at the John Becker Gallery at the end of 1933. After returning to Europe from a second trip to the United States in 1934, he met Miró, Lipchitz and Nicholson. In 1936 he settled in the United States, dividing his time between Virginia and New York. That year one-man shows of his work took place at the Galerie Cahiers d'Art in Paris and the Valentine Gallery in New York. The artist traveled to Paris in 1938 on the occasion of his solo exhibition at the Galerie Pierre, and he became a friend of Tanguy, Paul Eluard and Matta.

Shortly after joining the French army in 1940 he was taken prisoner and sent to a camp in Pomerania and then Stettin. Hélion escaped in 1942 and that same year made his way to France and then the United States. In 1943 he began to paint in a figurative style again. His book *They Shall Not Have Me* was published in 1943, a year in which he was given one-man shows at The Arts Club of Chicago and Peggy Guggenheim's Art of This Century, New York. Hélion returned to Paris in 1946. Throughout the 1950s and 1960s his work was shown in Europe and New York. During the 1970s he exhibited primarily in France. Hélion now lives in Paris.

41 Equilibrium. 1933-34

Oil on canvas, 38⅜ x 51⅝″ (97.4 x 131.2 cm.)
76.2553 PG 44; PG coll. cat. 77

Between 1932 and 1935 Hélion created a series of paintings exploring states of visual equilibrium. Among the earliest of these is *Equilibrium* (Collection Mr. and Mrs. Roy Friedman, Chicago), a simple composition of 1932 in which two curved rectangular shapes are held in balance by two slightly curved lines. In his working journal Hélion recorded the following observations about this work: "In searching for the effect of space and movement on the elements, that is to say in constructing a work in movement, rather in creating equilibrium out of movement, my images have become more pliant.... To establish relations between surfaces as complex as those which are defined by curves, it is necessary to arrange nuances." (Quoted in Rudenstine, p. 404. Author's translation)

Following this initial experimentation, Hélion composed several variations on the theme of equilibrium. Generally he worked with drawings and oil studies before reaching the formal solutions of his large canvases. His concern in the present work is to establish a balance between the blocky, simple, essentially rectangular mass on the right with the more complex, more colorful and varied forms on the left. The construction on the left, which is composed of overlapping and interpenetrating curves, bars and lines, is not continuous. Careful inspection reveals that the unit of four elements in the upper left corner (the red, gray and black bars and the green shape) does not touch the forms immediately below it. A similarly strategic use of discontinuous forms occurs in other works in the *Equilibrium* series. In the present painting the subtly disconnected arrangement contributes to the sense of movement and dispersion of the left side of the composition. The multiple hues used at the left also generate visual complexity. The horizontal curves on the left all point to the central white void which is embraced by the more rigidly horizontal dark blue and light green arms of the stable construction on the right. Vibrant red and red orange bars unite the edges of the composition with central forms and bind together right and left halves. A state of visual balance is thus achieved without resorting to the purely rectilinear, often programmatic formulations of the *De Stijl* artists who had influenced Hélion. The *Equilibrium* series, embodying ideas of suspension and tension of two-dimensional forms, inspired Calder who was contemporaneously developing his wind-driven mobiles (see cat. no. 98).*

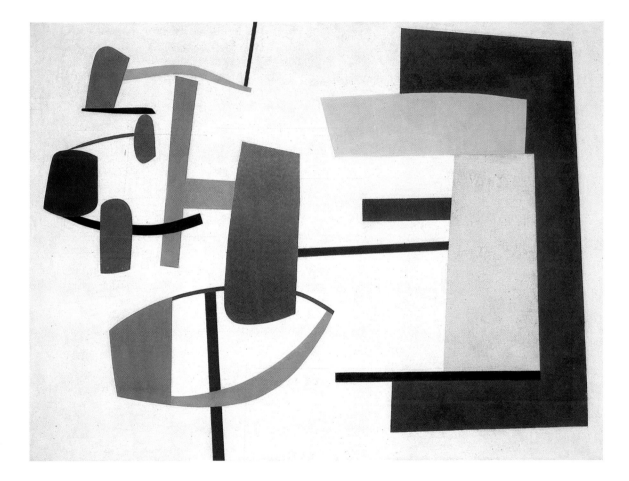

* M. Schipper, "Jean Hélion" in *Abstract Painting and Sculpture in America 1927-1944*, exh. cat., Pittsburgh, 1983, p. 168.

E.C.C.

42 Composition. August-December 1935

Oil on canvas, 57⅛ x 78¹³⁄₁₆″ (145 x 200.2 cm.)
76.2553 PG 45; PG coll. cat. 78

The hard-edged crispness of shapes and the underlying grid structure of this painting are lingering hints of an affinity with Neo-Plasticism, an influence that had dominated Hélion's work until 1931. Here, within a shallow picture space he distributes tubular forms, modeled to provide the illusion of curves, and flat, angular blocks of color. Though he accepts the *De Stijl* practice of basing compositions on the equilibrium of dissimilar parts, Hélion rejects other tenets of the movement. His shapes have an irregular, cutout appearance and float free of the organizing grid, which is sensed rather than fully elaborated. His palette is eccentric, including secondary and tertiary colors: green, auburn, pale yellow, steel blue, gray, orange, pale pinkish whites and black.

The large format (initiated the previous year in *Composition* [Collection Solomon R. Guggenheim Museum, New York]), the treatment of form and the figure-ground relationship invite associations with architectural settings and figures.

L.F.

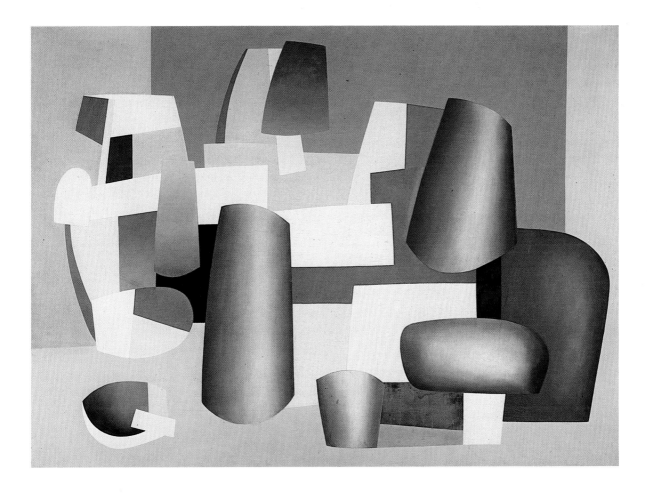

Constantin Brancusi 1876-1957

Constantin Brancusi was born on February 19, 1876, in the village of Hobitza, Rumania. He studied art at the Craiova School of Arts and Crafts from 1894 to 1898 and at the Bucharest School of Fine Arts from 1898 to 1901. Eager to continue his education in Paris, Brancusi arrived there in 1904 and enrolled in the Ecole des Beaux-Arts in 1905. The following year his sculpture was shown at the Salon d'Automne, where he met Rodin.

Soon after 1907 his mature period began. The sculptor had settled in Paris but maintained close contact with Rumania throughout this period, returning frequently and exhibiting in Bucharest almost every year. In Paris his friends included Modigliani, Léger, Matisse, Duchamp and Rousseau. In 1913 five of Brancusi's sculptures were included in the Armory Show in New York. Alfred Stieglitz presented the first one-man show of Brancusi's work at his gallery "291" in New York in 1914. Brancusi was never a member of any organized artistic movement, although he associated with Tristan Tzara, Picabia and many other Dadaists in the early 1920s. In 1921 he was honored with a special issue of *The Little Review*. He traveled to the United States twice in 1926 to attend his one-man shows at Wildenstein and at the Brummer Gallery in New York. The following year a major trial was initiated in U. S. Customs Court to determine whether Brancusi's *Bird in Space* was liable for duty as a manufactured object or was a work of art. The court decided in 1928 that the sculpture was a work of art.

Brancusi traveled extensively in the 1930s, visiting India and Egypt as well as European countries. He was commissioned to create a war memorial for a park in Turgu Jiu, Rumania, in 1935 and designed a complex which included gates, tables, stools and an *Endless Column*. In 1937 Brancusi discussed a proposed Temple of Meditation in India with the Maharajah of Indore (who had purchased several of his sculptures), but the project was never realized. After 1939 Brancusi worked alone in Paris. His last sculpture, a plaster *Grand Coq*, was completed in 1949. In 1952 Brancusi became a French citizen. He died in Paris on March 16, 1957.

43 Maiastra. 1912 (?)

Polished brass, including base 29" (73.1 cm.) high
76.2553 PG 50; PG coll. cat. 17

According to Brancusi's own testimony, his preoccupation with the image of the bird as a plastic form began as early as 1910. With the theme of the *Maiastra* in the early teens he initiated a series of about thirty sculptures of birds.

The word "*maïastra*" means "master" or "chief" in Brancusi's native Rumanian, but the title refers specifically to a magically beneficent, dazzlingly plumed bird in Rumanian folklore. Brancusi's mystical inclinations and his deeply rooted interest in peasant superstition make the motif an apt one. The golden plumage of the *Maiastra* is expressed in the reflective surface of the bronze; the bird's restorative song seems to issue from within the monumental puffed chest, through the arched neck, out of the open beak. The heraldic, geometric aspect of the figure contrasts with details such as the inconsistent size of the eyes, the distortion of the beak aperture and the cocking of the head slightly to one side. The elevation of the bird on a saw-tooth base lends it the illusion of perching. The subtle tapering of form, the relationship of curved to hard-edge surfaces and the changes of axis tune the sculpture so finely that the slightest alteration from version to version reflects a crucial decision in Brancusi's development of the theme.

Seven other versions of *Maiastra* have been identified and located: three are marble and four bronze. The Peggy Guggenheim example apparently was cast from a reworked plaster (now lost but visible in a 1955 photograph of Brancusi's studio.)* This was probably also the source for the almost identical cast in the collection of the Des Moines Art Center.

* Reproduced in A. Spear, *Brancusi's Birds*, New York, 1969, p. 55.

L.F.

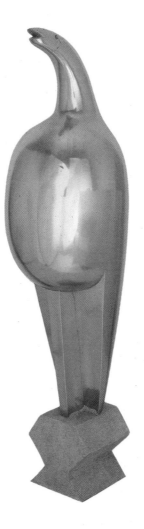

44 Bird in Space. 1932-40

Polished brass, 53″ (134.7 cm.) high
76.2553 PG 51; PG coll. cat. 18

The development of the bird theme in Brancusi's oeuvre can be traced from its appearance in the *Maiastra* sculptures (see cat. no. 43), through the *Golden Bird* group and, finally, to the *Bird in Space* series. Sixteen examples of the *Bird in Space* sequence, dating from 1923 to 1940, have been identified. The streamlined form of the present *Bird in Space,* stripped of individualizing features, communicates the notion of flight itself rather than describing the appearance of a particular bird. A vestige of the open beak of the *Maiastra* is retained in the beveled top of the tapering form, a slanted edge accelerating the upward movement of the whole.

This bronze, closely related to a marble version completed in 1931 (Collection Kunsthaus Zürich), could have been cast as early as 1932 and finished in 1940 (see Rudenstine, pp. 124-125). Though the shaft of the first *Bird in Space* (Private Collection, New York) was mounted on a discrete conical support, the support of the present example is incorporated as an organically irregular stem, providing an earthbound anchor for the sleek, soaring form.

As was customary in Brancusi's work, the bronze is smoothed and polished to the point where the materiality of the sculpture is dissolved in its reflective luminosity. Brancusi's spiritual aspirations, his longing for transcendence of the material world and its constraints, are verbalized in his description of the *Bird in Space* as a "project before being enlarged to fill the vault of the sky."*

* Quoted in S. Geist, *Brancusi: A Study of the Sculpture,* New York, 1968, pp. 113-114.

L.F.

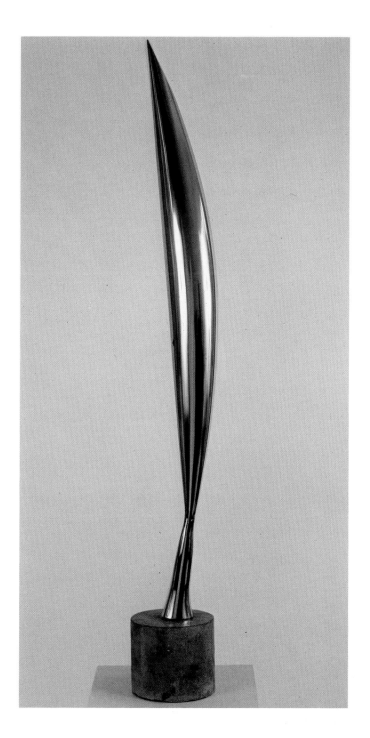

Paul Klee 1879-1940

Paul Klee was born on December 18, 1879, in Münchenbuchsee, Switzerland, into a family of musicians. His childhood love of music was always to remain profoundly important in his life and work. From 1898 to 1901 Klee studied in Munich, first with Heinrich Knirr, then at the Akademie under Franz von Stuck. Upon completing his schooling, he traveled to Italy: this was the first in a series of trips abroad that nourished his visual sensibilities. He settled in Bern in 1902. A series of his satirical etchings was exhibited at the Munich *Secession* in 1906. That same year Klee married and moved to Munich. Here he saw the work of James Ensor, Cézanne, van Gogh and Matisse. Klee's work was shown at the Kunstmuseum Bern in 1910 and at Heinrich Thannhauser's Moderne Galerie in Munich in 1911. In 1911 he began to keep a record of his work in his *Oeuvre Catalogue*, with listings from as early as 1884.

Klee met Kandinsky, August Macke, Franz Marc, Jawlensky and other avant-garde figures in 1911; he participated in important shows of advanced art, including the second *Blaue Reiter (Blue Rider)* exhibition, 1912, and the *Erster Deutscher Herbstsalon*, 1913. In 1912 he visited Paris for the second time, where he saw the work of Picasso and Braque and met Robert Delaunay, whose essay "On Light" he translated. Klee helped found the *Neue Münchner Secession* in 1914. Color became central to his art only after a revelatory trip to North Africa in 1914.

In 1920 a major Klee retrospective was held at the Galerie Hans Goltz, Munich, his *Schöpferische Konfession (Creative Credo)* was published and he was appointed to the faculty of the Bauhaus. Klee taught at the Bauhaus in Weimar from 1921 to 1926 and in Dessau from 1926 to 1931. During his tenure he was in close contact with other Bauhaus masters such as Kandinsky, Feininger and Moholy-Nagy. In 1924 the *Blaue Vier (Blue Four)*, consisting of Klee, Kandinsky, Feininger and Jawlensky, was founded. Among Klee's notable exhibitions of this period were his first in the United States at the Société Anonyme, New York, 1924; his first major show in Paris the following year at the Galerie Vavin-Raspail; and an exhibition at The Museum of Modern Art, New York, 1930. He went to Düsseldorf to teach at the Akademie in 1931. Forced by the Nazis to leave his position in Düsseldorf in 1933, Klee settled in Bern. Major Klee exhibitions took place in Bern and Basel in 1935 and in Zürich in 1940. Klee died on June 29, 1940, in Muralto-Locarno, Switzerland.

45 Portrait of Frau P. in the South. 1924

Watercolor and oil transfer drawing on paper mounted on gouache-painted board, including mount 16¾ x 12¼" (42.5 x 31 cm.)
76.2553 PG 89; PG coll. cat. 86

Klee's vacation in Sicily during the summer of 1924 provided him with the subjects for several watercolors that capture the color, light and mood of a specific geographical location and cast of characters. This portrait and that of *Frau R. on a Journey to the South*, also of 1924 (present whereabouts unknown), are good-natured caricatures of what might be two prim northern ladies whose absurd hats insufficiently shield them from the intensity of the Mediterranean sun.

The registers that break Frau R. into horizontal sections do not so rigidly stratify Frau P.; her hat dips at a jaunty angle. The vivid, warm color that thickens and thins atmospherically over the surface of the page is incised with simplified graphic contours. The black smudges on the surface result from the use of a transfer technique often employed by Klee in this period. In this technique, one side of a sheet of paper was coated with black oil and laid against a blank support. Then a drawing was placed on top of these two layers and its lines traced with a stylus, transferring the outline to the lower sheet.* Finally, watercolor was added.

The heart shape on Frau P.'s chest appears frequently in Klee's work, sometimes as a mouth, nose or torso. The motif bridged the organic and inorganic worlds for the artist by symbolizing life forces while serving as a "mediating form between circle and rectangle."**

* See J. Glaesmer, *Paul Klee Handzeichnungen I*, Bern, 1973, pp. 258-260.

** P. Klee, *Notebooks: Volume 2: The Nature of Nature*, ed. J. Spiller, trans. H. Norden, New York, 1973, p. 106.

L.F.

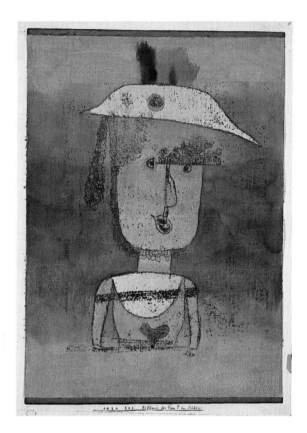

46 Magic Garden. March 1926

Oil on plaster-filled wire mesh, including artist's
frame 20⅞ x 17¾" (52.9 x 44.9 cm.)
76.2553 PG 90; PG coll. cat. 87

Magic Garden was executed in 1926, the year Klee
resumed teaching at the Bauhaus at its new location in
Dessau. During his Bauhaus period he articulated and
taught a complex theoretical program that was supported and clarified by his painting and drawing.
Theory, in turn, served to elucidate his art. Based on
probing investigation and carefully recorded observation, his work in both areas reveals analogies among
the properties of natural, of man-made and of geometric forms.

Studies of plants illustrating growth processes appear
often in Klee's notebooks as well as in his paintings
and drawings. He was also interested in architecture
and combined images of buildings with vegetal forms
in *Magic Garden* and several other works of 1926. Pictorial motifs often arise from geometric exercises: the
goblet shape that dominates the lower center of this
composition appeared also in a nonrepresentational
drawing exploring the development from point to line
to surface to volume.

The surface Klee creates with the medium of *Magic
Garden* resembles that of a primordial substance worn
and textured by its own history. A cosmic eruption
seems to have spewed forth forms that are morphologi-
cally related but differentiated into various genera.
Though excused from the laws of gravity, each of these
forms occupies a designated place in a new universe,
simultaneously as fixed and mobile as the orbits of
planets or the nuclei of organic cells. Klee's cosmic
statements are gleefully irreverent; he writes of his
work: "Ethical gravity rules, along with hobgoblin
laughter at the learned ones."*

* Quoted in W. Grohmann, *Paul Klee*, New York, 1954,
  p. 191.

L.F.

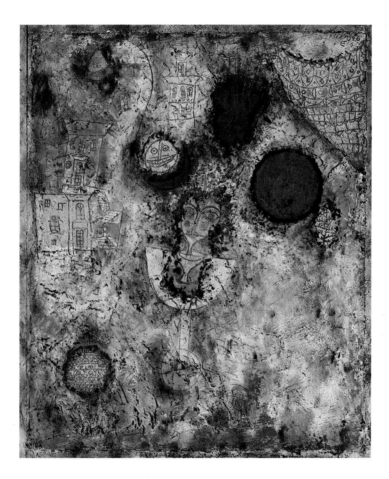

Marc Chagall 1887-1985

Marc Chagall was born on July 7, 1887, in the Russian town of Vitebsk. From 1906 to 1909 he studied in St. Petersburg at the Imperial School for the Protection of the Arts and with Léon Bakst. In 1910 he moved to Paris where he associated with Apollinaire and Robert Delaunay and encountered Fauvism and Cubism. He participated in the Salon des Indépendants and the Salon d'Automne in 1912. His first one-man show was held in 1914 at the gallery of Der Sturm in Berlin.

Chagall returned to Russia during the war, settling in Vitebsk, where he was appointed Commissar for Art. He founded the Vitebsk Academy and directed it until disagreements with the Suprematists resulted in his resignation in 1920. He moved to Moscow and executed his first stage designs for the State Jewish Kamerny Theater there. After a sojourn in Berlin Chagall returned to Paris in 1923 and met Ambroise Vollard. His first retrospective took place in 1924 at the Galerie Barbazanges-Hodebert, Paris. During the thirties he traveled to Palestine, The Netherlands, Spain, Poland and Italy. In 1933 the Kunsthalle Basel held a major retrospective of his work.

During World War II Chagall fled to the United States; The Museum of Modern Art, New York, gave him a retrospective in 1946. He settled permanently in France in 1948 and exhibited in Paris, Amsterdam and London. During 1951 he visited Israel and executed his first sculptures. The following year the artist traveled in Greece and Italy. In 1962 he designed windows for the synagogue of the Hadassah Medical Center near Jerusalem and the cathedral at Metz. He designed a ceiling for the Opéra in Paris in 1964 and murals for the Metropolitan Opera House, New York, in 1965. An exhibition of the artist's work from 1967 to 1977 was held at the Museé National du Louvre, Paris, in 1977-78. Chagall died in St. Paul de Vence, France, on March 28, 1985.

47 Rain. 1911

Oil (and charcoal?) on canvas, 34⅛ x 42½″ (86.7 x 108 cm.)
76.2553 PG 63; PG coll. cat. 29

Chagall's early work is characterized by a neo-primitive style derived primarily from Russian icons and folk art. When he moved from Russia to Paris in the summer of 1910, the artist took with him several of these paintings depicting the life and customs of his native Vitebsk. During the next year he reworked them and also painted new compositions with similar motifs, infused with nostalgia for his homeland, but now adapted according to techniques and concepts he acquired from exposure to current French art.

Nondescriptive, saturated color is used in *Rain* in combination with assertive areas of white and black to produce a highly ornamental and vivid surface. Chagall's use of color was influenced by that of Matisse and Robert Delaunay, whose work he saw almost immediately upon his arrival in Paris. The breaking up of some areas of the composition into shaded planes, for example the roof of the house and the left foreground, has its source in Cubism, though this device is handled somewhat randomly.

L.F.

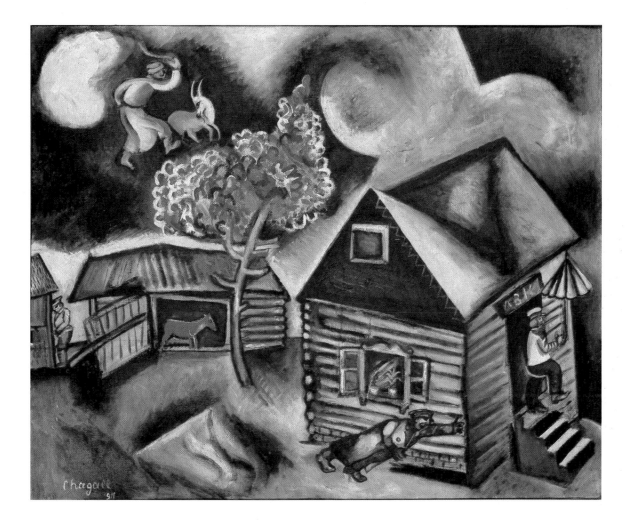

Giorgio de Chirico 1888-1978

Giorgio de Chirico was born to Italian parents in Vólos, Greece, on July 10, 1888. In 1900 he began studies at the Athens Polytechnic Institute and attended evening classes in drawing from the nude. About 1906 he moved to Munich, where he attended the Akademie der bildenden Künste. At this time he became interested in the art of Arnold Böcklin and Max Klinger and the writings of Friedrich Nietzsche and Arthur Schopenhauer. De Chirico moved to Milan in 1909, to Florence in 1910 and to Paris in 1911. In Paris he was included in the Salon d'Automne in 1912 and 1913 and in the Salon des Indépendants in 1913 and 1914. As a frequent visitor to Apollinaire's weekly gatherings, he met Brancusi, André Derain, Max Jacob and others. Because of the war, in 1915 de Chirico returned to Italy, where he met Filippo de Pisis in 1916 and Carrà in 1917; they formed the group that was later called the *Scuola Metafisica*.

The artist moved to Rome in 1918, and was given his first solo exhibition at the Casa d'Arte Bragaglia in that city in the winter of 1918-19. In this period he was one of the leaders of the *Gruppo Valori Plastici*, with whom he showed at the Nationalgalerie in Berlin. From 1920 to 1924 he divided his time between Rome and Florence. A one-man exhibition of de Chirico's work was held at the Galleria Arte in Milan in 1921, and he participated in the Venice Biennale for the first time in 1924. In 1925 the artist returned to Paris, where he exhibited that year at Léonce Rosenberg's Galerie L'Effort Moderne. In Paris his work was shown at Galerie Paul Guillaume in 1926 and 1927 and at the Galerie Jeanne Bucher in 1927. In 1928 he was given one-man shows at the Arthur Tooth Gallery in London and the Valentine Gallery in New York. In 1929 de Chirico designed scenery and costumes for Diaghilev's production of the ballet *Le Bal*, and his book *Hebdomeros* was published. The artist designed for the ballet and opera in subsequent years, and continued to exhibit in Europe, the United States, Canada and Japan. In 1945 the first part of his book *Memorie della mia vita* appeared. De Chirico died on November 20, 1978, in Rome, his residence for over thirty years.

48 The Red Tower. 1913

Oil on canvas, 28¹⁵⁄₁₆ x 39⅝″ (73.5 x 100.5 cm.)
76.2553 PG 64; PG coll. cat. 30

De Chirico's enigmatic works of 1911 to 1917 provided a crucial inspiration for the Surrealist painters. The dreamlike atmosphere of his compositions results from irrational perspective, the lack of a unified light source, the elongation of shadows and a hallucinatory focus on objects. Italian piazzas bounded by arcades or classical façades are transformed into ominously silent and vacant settings for invisible dramas. The absence of event provokes a nostalgic or melancholy mood if one senses the wake of a momentous incident; if one feels the imminence of an act, a feeling of anxiety ensues.

De Chirico remarked that "every object has two appearances: one, the current one, which we nearly always see and which is seen by people in general; the other, a spectral or metaphysical appearance beheld only by some individuals in moments of clairvoyance and metaphysical abstraction, as in the case of certain bodies concealed by substances impenetrable by sunlight yet discernible, for instance, by X-ray or other powerful artificial means."[*] Traces of concealed human presences appear in the fraught expanse of this work. One is the partly concealed equestrian monument often identified as Carlo Marochetti's 1861 statue of King Carlo Alberto in Turin,[**] which also appears in the background of de Chirico's *The Departure of the Poet* of 1914 (Private Collection). In addition, in the left foreground overpainting barely conceals two figures (or statues?), one of which resembles a shrouded mythological hero by the nineteenth-century Swiss painter Böcklin. The true protagonist, however, is the crenellated tower; in its imposing centrality and rotundity it conveys a virile energy that fills the pictorial space.

[*] Quoted in W. Rubin, "De Chirico and Modernism," *De Chirico*, exh. cat., New York, 1982, p. 57.

[**] J. T. Soby, *De Chirico*, exh. cat., New York, 1955, pp. 49-50.

L.F.

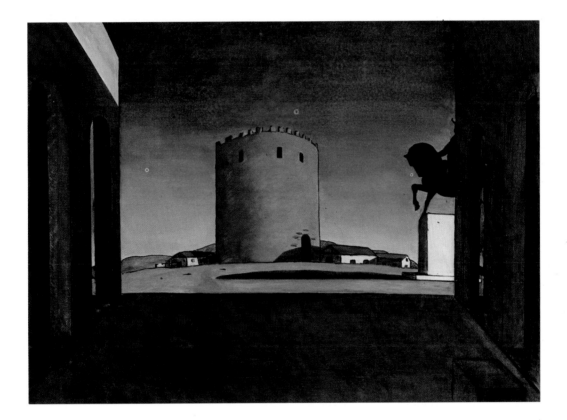

49 The Nostalgia of the Poet. 1914

Oil and charcoal on canvas, 35⁹⁄₁₆ x 16″ (89.7 x 40.7 cm.)
76.2553 PG 65; PG coll. cat. 31

This work belongs to a series of paintings of 1914 on the subject of the poet, the best known of which is the *Portrait of Guillaume Apollinaire* (Collection Musée National d'Art Moderne, Centre Georges Pompidou, Paris; repr. Rudenstine, p. 162). Recurrent motifs in the sequence are the plaster bust with dark glasses, the mannikin and the fish mold on an obelisk. These objects, bearing no evident relationships to one another, are compressed here into a narrow vertical format that creates a claustrophobic and enigmatic space.

As in *The Red Tower* (cat. no. 48), the use of inanimate forms imitating or alluding to human beings has complex ramifications. The sculpture at the lower left is a painted representation of a plaster cast from a stone, marble or metal bust by an imaginary, or at present unidentified, sculptor. The character portrayed could be mythological, historical, symbolical or fictional. The fish is a charcoal drawing of a metal mold that could produce a baked "cast" of a fish made with an actual fish. The fish has additional connotations as a religious symbol, and the hooklike graphic sign toward which its gaping mouth is directed has its own cryptic allusiveness. The mannikin is a simplified cloth cast of a human figure—a mold on which clothing is shaped to conform to the contours of a person. Each object, though treated as solid and static, dissolves in multiple significations and paradoxes. Such amalgams of elusive meaning in de Chirico's strangely intense objects compelled the attention of the Surrealists.

L.F.

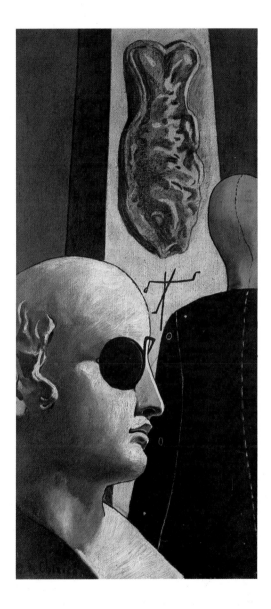

50 The Gentle Afternoon. Before July 1916

Oil on canvas, 25¹¹⁄₁₆ x 22¹⁵⁄₁₆″ (65.3 x 58.3 cm.)
76.2553 PG 66; PG coll. cat. 32

In *The Gentle Afternoon* de Chirico manipulates perspective and scale, the conventional tools of pictorial illusion, to subvert the realism of a meticulously rendered scene. The result is a haunting sense of unreality. Edges of objects in the background form receding orthogonals which lead the eye to multiple vanishing points, revealing the presence of conflicting perspective systems. Diagrams and lines without apparent function suggest some impenetrable or secret system of logic. Radical tilting and foreshortening of other objects further contribute to a visual dilemma of spatial dislocation. Access to the rapidly receding background is blocked by a cluttered, impassable foreground, thus denying the viewer the satisfaction of spatial continuities. This jammed conflation of near and far is enhanced by distortions of scale in the contrasts of small and large. The visual jolt produced by such inexplicable combinations results in a confounding enigma.

The six objects contained in the wooden box in the right foreground pique our curiosity. They appear to be an ordinary candy cane and five biscuits. Yet these banal foods are presented in such self-conscious display as to suggest that they embody extraordinary associa-tions. Pastries appear in numerous paintings by de Chirico dating from 1915 until late 1918, the period of his assignment to an army post in Ferrara (for example *Evangelical Still-Life,* 1917-18, Private Collection). In Ferrara de Chirico was exposed for the first time to Jewish traditions: he later recalled having been inspired in the ghetto by the metaphysical forms of sweets and biscuits. In *The Gentle Afternoon* these pastries testify to his fascination with Jewish culture (see Rudenstine, p. 168). Their arrangement in the foreground of the picture also suggests a parody of war decorations: de Chirico here mocks the seriousness with which such medals are ceremoniously awarded and displayed.

By depicting quotidian objects out of their daily context, de Chirico purges his art of the expected, serving his ambition "to rid art of all that has been its familiar content until now; all subject, all idea, all thought, all symbol must be put aside."* The presentation of these cakes in their wooden box, which stands in front of yet another box, suggests a series of frames within the actual frame of the painting. Through this device, as well as in his distortion of perspective, de Chirico calls our attention to the artifice of picture making.

* Quoted in J. T. Soby, *De Chirico,* exh. cat., New York, 1955, p. 246.

E.C.C.

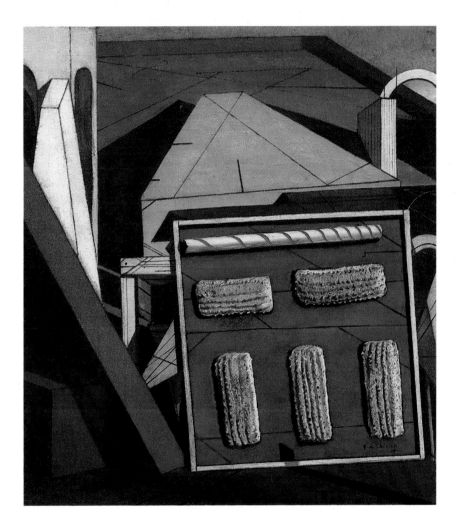

Man Ray 1890-1976

Man Ray (a pseudonym adopted by the artist) was born on August 27, 1890, in Philadelphia, and moved to New York with his family seven years later. In New York he frequented Alfred Stieglitz's gallery "291" in 1911 and attended classes at the Ferrer Center in 1912. In 1915 his first one-man show was held at the Daniel Gallery, New York. About this time he took up photography, the medium for which he was to become best known. He entered into a lifelong friendship with Duchamp, with whom he and Walter Arensberg founded the Society of Independent Artists in 1916. With Duchamp, Katherine Dreier, Henry Hudson and Andrew McLaren, Man Ray established the Société Anonyme, which he named, in 1920. Before the artist moved from New York to Paris in 1921, Man Ray and Duchamp published the single issue of *New York Dada*.

In Paris Man Ray was given a one-man exhibition at the Librairie Six in 1921. His first Rayographs (photographic images produced without a camera) were published in *Les Champs délicieux, rayographies* in 1922, the year the artist participated in the *Salon Dada* at the Galerie Montaigne in Paris. With Arp, de Chirico, Ernst, Masson, Miró and Picasso he was represented in the first Surrealist exhibition at the Galerie Pierre in Paris in 1925. From 1923 to 1929 he made the films *Le Retour à la raison, Emak Bakia, L'Etoile de mer* and *Les Mystères du château de dé*. In 1932 Man Ray's work was included in *Dada, 1916-1932* at the Galerie de l'Institut in Paris and in a Surrealist show at the Julien Levy Gallery in New York. He collaborated with Paul Eluard on the books *Facile* in 1935 and *Les Mains libres* in 1937. In 1936 he went to New York on the occasion of the *Fantastic Art, Dada, Surrealism* exhibition at The Museum of Modern Art, in which his work appeared.

The artist left France in 1940, shortly before the German occupation, making his way to Hollywood and then to New York. In 1951 he returned to Paris, where he was given a one-man show at the Galerie Berggruen. In 1959 a solo exhibition of Man Ray's work was held at the Institute of Contemporary Art in London. His autobiography *Self Portrait* was published in 1963. Ten years later The Metropolitan Museum of Art in New York presented one hundred and twenty-five of his photographic works. Man Ray died on November 18, 1976, in Paris.

51 Silhouette. 1916

India ink and charcoal (and gouache?) on board, 20¹⁵⁄₁₆ x 25¼″ (51.6 x 64.1 cm.)
76.2553 PG 68; PG coll. cat. 105

In 1915 Man Ray abandoned what he called his "Romantic-Expressionist-Cubist" style and adopted a mechanistic, graphic, flattened idiom like that developed by Picabia and Duchamp during the same period. This drawing is preparatory to his most successful painting in this style, *The Rope Dancer Accompanies Herself with Her Shadows* of 1916 (Collection The Museum of Modern Art, New York; repr. Rudenstine, p. 483), the subject of which was inspired by a vaudeville dancer whose movement he wished to suggest in a series of varying poses.* Man Ray's interest in frozen sequential movement may derive from the experiments in photography he initiated about this time.

The particularized features of the figures in this drawing are eliminated to produce two-dimensional patterned forms that are silhouetted against black oval shadows. The dancer is accompanied not only by her shadow but also by music, concisely indicated by the voluted head of an instrument at the lower right of the support, the strings across the bottom and the music stand at left. The position of her feet on the strings, which may double as a stave, may be meant to convey a specific sequence of notes, as if the dancer were indeed accompanying herself musically. It seems likely that this drawing represents the first stage in the conception of the painting. In the canvas the three positions of the dancer are superimposed and appear at the top of the composition, with the greater part of the field occupied by her distorted, enlarged and vividly colored cutout shadows.

* Man Ray discusses the genesis of this work in his autobiography, *Self-Portrait*, Boston and Toronto, 1963, pp. 66-67, 71.

L.F.

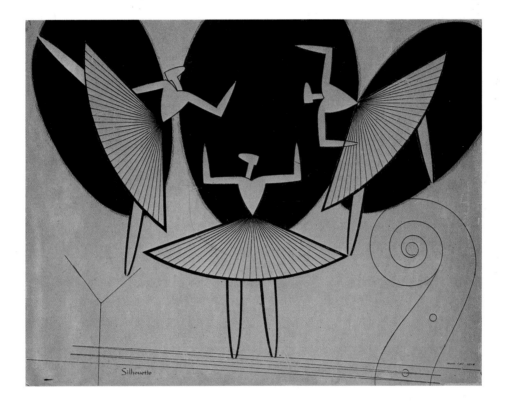

Silhouette

52 Untitled. 1923

Rayograph, gelatin silver print, 11⅜ x 9¼″
(28.8 x 23.5 cm.)
76.2553 PG 69a; PG coll. cat. 106

A Rayograph is not a photograph in the true sense of the word—it is Man Ray's name for a photogram, a unique work of art made without camera or film. The artist first made such images in Paris in 1921, when he accidentally placed objects on an unexposed sheet of photographic paper that had fallen into the developing tray. When he turned on an overhead light, an image began to form, "not quite a simple silhouette of the objects as in a straight photograph, but distorted and refracted by the glass [objects] more or less in contact with the paper and standing out against a black background, the part directly exposed to the light."* In developing his technique, he experimented with various laboratory and household objects, including a key, a glass funnel, pencils, a brush, candles and twine.

It is difficult to identify the objects used to make this Rayograph. Perhaps wire spirals (which Man Ray recalls making in his early days of experimentation with the technique) cast the curling shadows which emanate from the core of this abstract composition. Wire-mesh screens and graters may have created the textured rectangles. The objects' identities remain ambiguous however, more suggestive than explicit in their references. Man Ray's Rayographs received immediate praise in his Parisian Dada circle, and his friend Tzara acclaimed them as "pure Dada creations" and superior to works made in 1918 with a similar process by the Zürich Dadaist Christian Schad. The process itself was, in fact, invented by neither Man Ray nor Schad. In 1833 William Henry Fox Talbot produced "photogenic drawings," images similar to Rayographs in their black backgrounds, silhouetted light forms and subtle middle tonalities. But Talbot's ambitions were scientific rather than artistic, and it remained for the Dadaists to transform this technique into a novel art form.

Schad made his photograms (or "Schadographs") by arranging cutout paper and flat objects on light-sensitive paper. These sharp contours lacked the mysterious shadows and textures created by Man Ray's use of three-dimensional objects. Concurrently with Man Ray's experiments, Moholy-Nagy made photograms from three-dimensional objects at the Bauhaus in Weimar. Some authors claim that Tzara led Man Ray and Moholy-Nagy to their experiments by showing them Schadographs. Man Ray's Rayographs were widely appreciated by the Surrealists, and were published, often anonymously, in their periodicals such as *La Révolution Surréaliste*.

* Man Ray, *Self-Portrait,* Boston and Toronto, 1963, p. 129.

E.C.C.

Man Ray

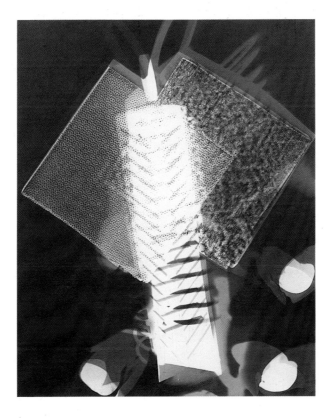

53 Untitled. 1927

Rayograph, gelatin silver print, $11^{15}/_{16}$ x 10″
(30.4 x 25.4 cm.)
76.2553 PG 69b; PG coll. cat. 107

This Rayograph of 1927 offers an intriguing juxtaposition of machine parts and body parts, a combination found in the work of many artists in the 1920s.
Here, long strands of hair and four fingers of a human
hand are identifiable, separated by two white wheel-
shaped forms that suggest an empty film reel. The reel
is an object both ubiquitous in the photographic
laboratory and representative of an important aspect
of Man Ray's artistic career.

Man Ray's involvement with film began as early as
1920, when he collaborated with Duchamp on his
*Anemic Cinema.** In 1923, at Tzara's request, Man Ray
produced a Dada film, *Le Retour à la raison,* in which
he used his Rayograph technique. In 1926, the year
before he created the present Rayograph, he made the
film *Emak Bakia.* This film opposes representational
sequences (involving people and still-life objects, for
example) with abstract images (some of which are film
Rayographs). In his ciné-poem the objective or representational parts visually punctuate the abstract sequences of the movement of light. The present
Rayographs). In his ciné-poem the objective or repre-
unreadable forms with more readily identifiable
objects. The two work together to interest, confuse and
delight the viewer. Tzara's introduction to the album
of twelve Rayographs *Les Champs délicieux* stresses
the powerful beauty of Man Ray's unconventional
images, evoking the poetry of this particular Rayograph:
"He had invented the force of a tender and fresh light-
ning which exceeded in importance all the constellations intended for our visual pleasures. The precise,
unique and exact mechanical deformation was fixed,
filtered like hair through a comb of light."

* C. I. Belz, "The Film Poetry of Man Ray" in *Man Ray,*
  exh. cat., Los Angeles, 1966, pp. 42-52; reprinted from
  Criticism, Spring 1965.

E.C.C.

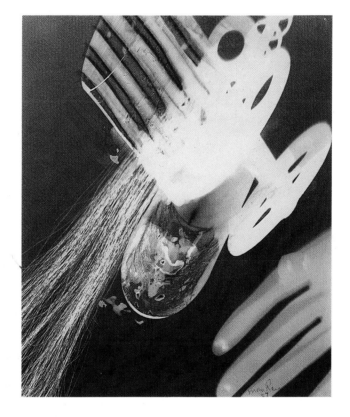

Francis Picabia 1879-1953

François Marie Martinez Picabia was born on or about January 22, 1879, in Paris, of a Spanish father and French mother. He was enrolled at the Ecole des Arts Décoratifs in Paris from 1895 to 1897 and later studied with Albert Charles Wallet, Ferdinand Humbert and Fernand Cormon. He began to paint in an Impressionist manner in the winter of 1902-03 and started to exhibit works in this style at the Salon d'Automne and the Salon des Indépendants of 1903. His first one-man show was held at the Galerie Haussmann, Paris, in 1905. From 1908 elements of Fauvism and Neo-Impressionism as well as Cubism and other forms of abstraction appeared in his painting, and by 1912 he had evolved a personal amalgam of Cubism and Fauvism. Picabia worked in an abstract mode from this period until the early 1920s.

Picabia became a friend of Duchamp and Apollinaire and associated with the Puteaux group in 1911-12. He participated in the 1913 Armory Show, visiting New York on this occasion and frequenting avant-garde circles. Alfred Stieglitz gave him a one-man exhibition at his gallery "291" this same year. In 1915, which marked the beginning of Picabia's machinist or mechanomorphic period, he and Duchamp, among others, instigated and participated in Dada manifestations in New York. Picabia lived in Barcelona in 1916-17; in 1917 he published his first volume of poetry and the first issues of 391, his magazine modeled after Stieglitz's periodical 291. For the next few years Picabia remained involved with the Dadaists in Zürich and Paris, creating scandals at the Salon d'Automne, but finally denounced Dada in 1921 for no longer being "new." He moved to Tremblay-sur-Mauldre, outside Paris, the following year and returned to figurative art. In 1924 he attacked Breton and the Surrealists in 391.

Picabia moved again in 1925, this time to Mougins. During the thirties he became a close friend of Gertrude Stein. By the end of World War II Picabia returned to Paris. He resumed painting in an abstract style and writing poetry, and in March 1949 a retrospective of his work was held at the Galerie René Drouin in Paris. Picabia died in Paris on November 30, 1953.

54 Very Rare Picture on the Earth. 1915

Oil and metallic paint on board, and silver and gold leaf on wood, including artist's painted frame
49½ x 38½" (125.7 x 97.8 cm.)
76.2553 PG 67; PG coll. cat. 136

In 1915 Picabia abandoned his exploration of abstract form and color to adopt a new machinist idiom that he used until about 1923. Unlike Robert Delaunay or Léger, who saw the machine as an emblem of a new age, he was attracted to machine shapes for their intrinsic visual and functional qualities. He often used mecanomorphic images humorously as substitutes for human beings; for example, in *Here, This Is Stieglitz,* 1915 (Collection The Metropolitan Museum of Art, New York), the photographer Alfred Stieglitz is portrayed as a camera. In *Very Rare Picture on the Earth* a self-generating, almost symmetrical machine is presented frontally, clearly silhouetted against a flat, impassive background. Like Picabia's own *Amorous Parade* of 1917 (Collection Mr. and Mrs. Morton G. Neumann, Chicago) or Duchamp's *The Bride Stripped Bare by Her Bachelors, Even* of 1915-23 (Collection Philadelphia Museum of Art), the present work might be read as the evocation of a sexual event in mechanical terms. This dispassionate view of sex is consonant with the anti-sentimental attitudes that were to characterize Dada. The work has also been interpreted as representing an alchemical processor, in part because of the coating of the two upper cylinders with gold and silver leaf respectively.*

Not only is *Very Rare Picture on the Earth* one of Picabia's earliest mecanomorphic works, but it has been identified as his first collage.** Its mounted wooden forms and integral frame draw attention to the work as object—the picture is not really a picture, making it "very rare" indeed. Thus, an ironic note is added to the humorous pomposity of the inscription at upper left.

* U. Linde, *Francis Picabia*, exh. cat., Paris, 1976, p. 24.

** W. A. Camfield, *Francis Picabia: His Art, Life and Times*, Princeton, N.J., 1979, p. 88.

L.F.

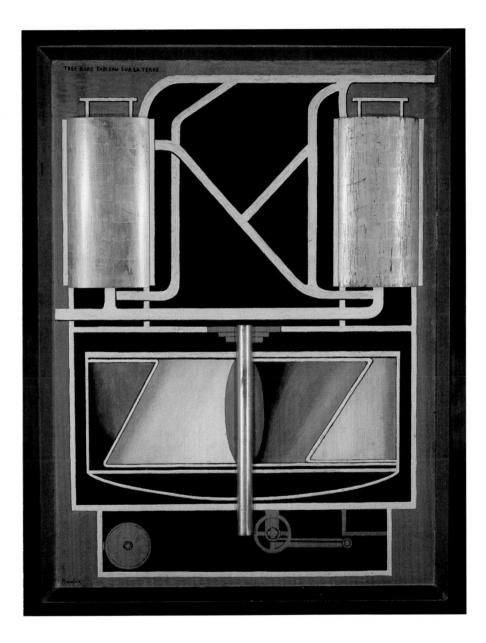

Max Ernst 1891-1976

Max Ernst was born on April 2, 1891, in Brühl, Germany. He enrolled in the University at Bonn in 1909 to study philosophy but soon abandoned this pursuit to concentrate on art. At this time he was interested in psychology and the art of the mentally ill. In 1911 Ernst became a friend of Macke and joined the *Rheinische Expressionisten* group in Bonn. Ernst showed for the first time in 1912 at the Galerie Feldman in Cologne. At the *Sonderbund* exhibition of that year in Cologne he saw the work of van Gogh, Cézanne, Munch and Picasso. In 1913 he met Guillaume Apollinaire and Robert Delaunay and traveled to Paris. Ernst participated that same year in the *Erster Deutscher Herbstsalon*. In 1914 he met Arp, who was to become a lifelong friend.

Despite military service throughout World War I, Ernst was able to continue painting and to exhibit in Berlin at Der Sturm in 1916. He returned to Cologne in 1918. The next year he produced his first collages and founded the short-lived Cologne Dada movement with Johannes Theodor Baargeld; they were joined by Arp and others. In 1921 Ernst exhibited for the first time in Paris, at the Galerie Au Sans Pareil. He was involved in Surrealist activities in the early twenties with Paul Eluard and André Breton. In 1925 Ernst executed his first frottages; a series of frottages was published in his book *Histoire Naturelle* in 1926. He collaborated with Miró on designs for Sergei Diaghilev this same year. The first of his collage-novels, *La Femme 100 têtes*, was published in 1929. The following year the artist collaborated with Dalí and Luis Buñuel on the film *L'Age d'or*.

His first American show was held at the Julien Levy Gallery, New York, in 1932. In 1936 Ernst was represented in *Fantastic Art, Dada, Surrealism* at The Museum of Modern Art in New York. In 1939 he was interned in France as an enemy alien. Two years later Ernst fled to the United States with Peggy Guggenheim, whom he married early in 1942. After their divorce he married Dorothea Tanning and in 1953 resettled in France. Ernst received the Grand Prize for painting at the Venice Biennale in 1954 and in 1975 the Solomon R. Guggenheim Museum, New York, gave him a major retrospective, which traveled in modified form to the Musée National d'Art Moderne, Paris, in 1975. He died on April 1, 1976, in Paris.

55 Little Machine Constructed by Minimax Dadamax in Person. 1919-20

Hand printing(?), pencil and ink frottage, watercolor and gouache on paper, 19½ x 12⅜" (49.4 x 31.5 cm.)
76.2553 PG 70; PG coll. cat. 51

Little Machine . . . was executed in Cologne the year Dada was established there. It belongs to a series of about fifty works dating from 1919-20, based on diagrams of scientific instruments, in which Ernst used printer's plates to reproduce preexisting images. The impressions, once altered by traditional coloristic and modeling effects, occupy a position between found object and artistic product, like his collages.

In both subject and style the series can be compared with Picabia's mecanomorphic drawings and paintings. Ernst shared with Picabia an interest in typography, printed images and language; many of the forms in the present work can be read as letters. They function as well to describe a mechanical structure that can be seen as a symbol of sexual activity, like Picabia's *Very Rare Picture on the Earth* (cat. no. 54) and his *The Child Carburetor*, 1919 (Collection Solomon R. Guggenheim Museum, New York), or Duchamp's *The Bride Stripped Bare by Her Bachelors, Even*, 1915-23 (Collection Philadelphia Museum of Art). Ernst's machine is a fantasized solution to the psychological pressures of sexual performance, as announced in the humorously heroic inscription at the bottom of the sheet: *Little machine constructed by minimax dadamax in person for fearless pollination of female suckers at the beginning of the change of life and for other such fearless functions.* The right side of the machine seems to comprise a miniature laboratory for the production of semen, which is indicated as a red drop that courses through passageways to the left side of the apparatus. The drop finally issues from the yellow faucet, accompanied by a whimsically self-assured and cheerful *"Bonjour."* Alternatively, the machine can be seen as a combination of male and female halves. The female (at the right) is dowdy and angular; the more brilliantly colored male (at the left) "fearlessly" points away from her.

L.F.

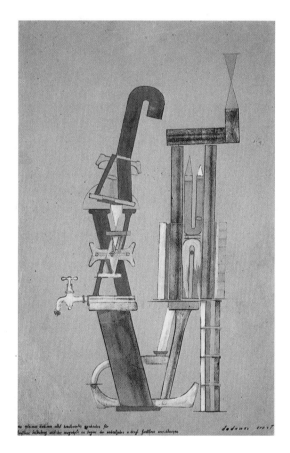

56 The Kiss. 1927

Oil on canvas, 50¾ x 63½″ (129 x 161.2 cm.)
76.2553 PG 71; PG coll. cat. 52

From humorously clinical depictions of erotic events in the Dada period, such as *Little Machine*...(cat. no. 55), Ernst moved on to celebrations of uninhibited sexuality in his Surrealist works. His liaison and marriage with the young Marie-Berthe Aurenche in 1927 may have inspired the erotic subject matter of this painting and others of this year. The major compositional lines of this work may have been determined by the configurations of string that Ernst dropped on a preparatory surface, a procedure according with Surrealist notions of the importance of chance effects. However, Ernst used a coordinate grid system to transfer his string configurations to canvas, thus subjecting these chance effects to conscious manipulation. Visually, the technique produces undulating calligraphic rhythms, like those traced here against the glowing earth and sky colors.

The centralized, pyramidal grouping and the embracing gesture of the upper figure in *The Kiss* have lent themselves to comparison with Renaissance compositions, specifically the *Madonna and Saint Anne* by Leonardo da Vinci (Collection Musée National du Louvre, Paris).* The Leonardo work was the subject of a psychosexual interpretation by Freud, whose writings were important to Ernst and other Surrealists. The adaptation of a religious subject would add an edge of blasphemy to the exuberant lasciviousness of Ernst's picture.

* See N. and E. Calas's interpretation of this work in *The Peggy Guggenheim Collection of Modern Art*, New York, 1966, pp. 112-113.

L.F.

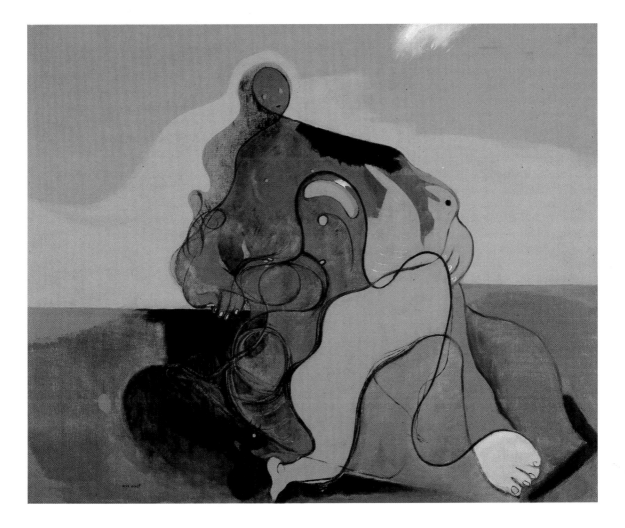

57 The Forest. 1927-28

Oil on canvas, 37⅞ x 51″ (96.3 x 129.5 cm.)
76.2553 PG 72; PG coll. cat. 53

André Breton's *Surrealist Manifesto* of 1924 proclaimed "pure psychic automatism" as an artistic ideal, emphasizing inspiration derived from the chance juxtaposition of forms and the haphazard use of materials. Ernst came under the influence of Breton's ideas in 1924, and soon thereafter developed his frottage or rubbing technique.* In making his first frottages, he dropped pieces of paper at random on floor boards, and rubbed them with pencil or chalk, thus transferring the design of the wood grain to the paper. He next adapted this technique to oil painting, scraping paint from prepared canvases laid over materials such as wire mesh, chair caning, leaves, buttons or twine (see cat. no. 59). His repertory of objects closely parallels that used by Man Ray in his experiments with Rayograms during the same period (see cat. nos. 52, 53). Using his grattage (scraping) technique, Ernst covered his canvases completely with pattern and then interpreted the images that emerged, thus allowing texture to suggest composition in a spontaneous fashion. In *The Forest* the artist probably placed the canvas over a rough surface (perhaps wood), scraped oil paint over the canvas and then rubbed, scraped and overpainted the area of the trees (Rudenstine, pp. 287-289).

The subject of a dense forest appears often in Ernst's work of the late twenties and early thirties. These canvases, of which *The Quiet Forest,* 1927 (Collection Kunstmuseum Basel), is another example, generally contain a wall of trees, a solar disk and an apparition of a bird hovering amid the foliage. Ernst's attitude toward the forest as the sublime embodiment of both enchantment and terror can be traced to his experiences in the German forest as a child.** His essay "Les Mystères de la Forêt," published in *Minotaure* in 1934, vividly conveys his fascination with the various kinds of forests. The Peggy Guggenheim canvas resonates with those qualities he identified with the forests of Oceania: "They are, it seems, savage and impenetrable, black and russet, extravagant, secular, swarming, diametrical, negligent, ferocious, fervent and likeable, without yesterday or tomorrow. . . . Naked, they dress only in their majesty and their mystery." (Author's translation)

* For Ernst's own account of frottage see M. Ernst, "Favorite Poets and Painters of the Past" in *Beyond Painting,* New York, 1948, p. 7.

** M. Ernst, "Some Data on the Youth of M.E. as told by himself" in *Beyond Painting,* New York, 1948, p. 27.

E.C.C.

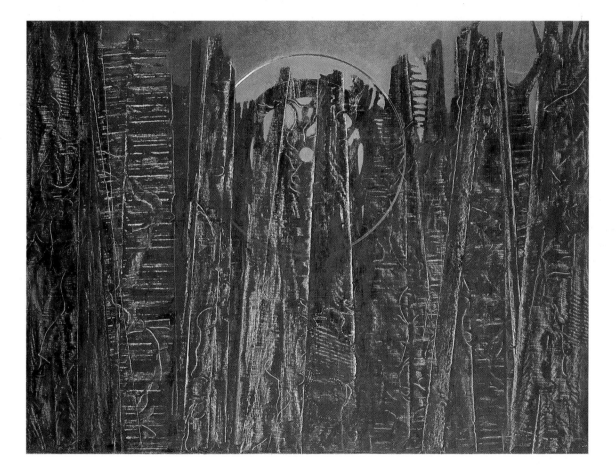

58 The Postman Cheval. 1932

Paper and fabric collage with pencil, ink and gouache
on paper, 25⅜ x 19¼″ (64.3 x 48.9 cm.)
76.2553 PG 74; PG coll. cat. 55

Evidence of Max Ernst's obsession with birds first
emerged in his *Dove* series of the mid-twenties, and
then reappeared in 1929 with his creation of an imaginary alterego, Loplop, Superior of the Birds. Loplop
figures prominently in Ernst's paintings, frottage drawings and collages, both in the naturalistic form of an
attenuated bird and in a schematic, rectangular idiom.
Loplop assumes both these forms in *The Postman
Cheval*, one of a group of some sixty-four works made
between 1929 and 1932 in which the bird persona appears. The more naturalistic Loplop, perched in the blue
black rectangle at the left, is a collage element cut from
one of Ernst's grattage compositions of birds. The second, more abstract guise of Loplop appears on the right
in *The Postman Cheval*: a large, rectangular body, an
abbreviated head (here, as in many other examples,
only a circle) and two stout, blocky feet comprise the
bird's form, and also suggest an artist's easel.
This abstract guise appears in at least forty-three collages and paintings entitled *Loplop Introduces...*.*
In this series, Loplop introduces or presents a wide
variety of motifs, including flowers, grapes, a personi-
fication of the Marseillaise, a young girl or another
depiction of Loplop.

In the present example Loplop's body-easel of blue and
white printed, marbleized paper is pierced by three
voyeuristic holes which reveal details of a young girl's
face and clothing. Yet another rectangular form to the
lower right, a torn envelope, reveals similarly teasing
fragments: the corner of an antique postcard of scantily
clothed women, and through the address window of
the envelope, another card of reclining female torsos.
Loplop first introduced a young girl in a collage of 1930
(Private Collection, Paris) in which three-dimensional
attributes (a lock of hair, bows) substitute for a depiction of the girl in her framed portrait. Provocative
photographs and drawings of female bodies appear,
however, in several collages of 1932 in addition to the
present example. In one of these works, *Du Verre*, 1932
(Private Collection, Stuttgart), Ernst places an erotic
photograph behind the envelope window of a Parisian
electric bill, perhaps implying the sexual "voltage"
of such imagery.

The title of the present collage refers to Ferdinand
Cheval, the postman who constructed the enormous
Ideal Palace of found objects and stones between 1879
and 1912 (Rudenstine, pp. 294-297). His fantastic
structure became an object of inspiration for many
Surrealist artists and writers.

* See W. Spies, *Max Ernst: Oeuvre-Katalog, Werke
  1929-1938,* Cologne, 1979, vol. IV, among nos. 1700-1867.

E.C.C.

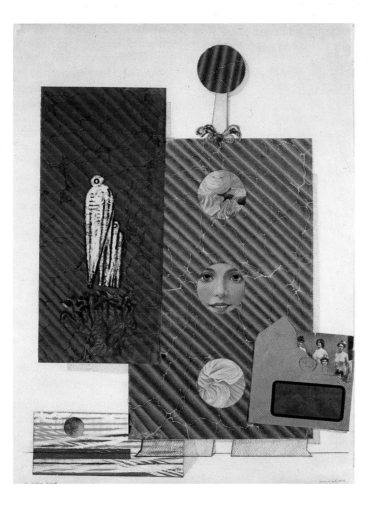

59 Zoomorphic Couple. 1933

Oil on canvas, 36¼ x 28⅞" (91.9 x 73.3 cm.)
76.2553 PG 75; PG coll. cat. 56

By 1925 Ernst had developed his frottage (rubbing) technique, which he associated with a childhood memory of accidental forms materializing within the grooves of wooden floor boards. He also acknowledged the influence of his later discovery of Leonardo's *Treatise on Painting,* in which artists are advised to gaze at the stains on walls until figures and scenes emerge. In the *Hordes* series of 1926 to 1932 Ernst placed twine beneath his canvases and then rubbed pigment over their surfaces. The meanderings of the twine were thus revealed; these chance configurations were then manipulated to elicit imagery. In *Zoomorphic Couple,* the appearance of light, sinuous channels through dark painted areas produces a relief-like effect suggestive of frottage. However, the artist created the effect here by putting paint-laden string or rope on top of the canvas and spraying over it (Rudenstine, p. 299). The image of the bird, which recurs frequently in Ernst's work from 1925, had become an almost obsessive preoccupation by 1930. In the present painting one can discern a vaguely birdlike form and a caressing humanoid arising from the primordial material that gives them their substance. It has been suggested that the atavistic imagery in Ernst's work of this period alludes to the failure of European civilization in the face of the rising National Socialist threat in Germany.* (Ernst was blacklisted by the party in 1933 when Hitler became Chancellor of the Third Reich.) Though a sensitivity to the current political climate may be inferred, it is not confirmed by anecdotal detail. The forms have the effect of dream or poetic apparition.

The sense of genesis and evolutionary stirrings in *Zoomorphic Couple* is complemented by the creative inventiveness of the artist, who combines layers of pastel color under spattered, blown and dripped paint.

* U. M. Schneede, *Max Ernst,* New York and London, 1972, p. 134.

L.F.

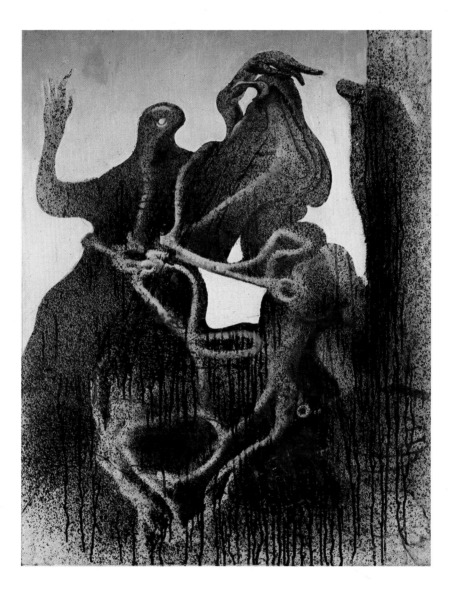

60 The Entire City. 1936-37

Oil on canvas, 38 x 63⅛" (96.5 x 160.4 cm.)
76.2553 PG 77; PG coll. cat. 58

Between 1935 and 1937 Max Ernst painted a group of thirteen architectural fantasies with similar titles, such as *The Petrified City, The Imaginary City* and *The Entire City.** In these works panoramas of tiered and pyramidal structures call forth visions of archeological exploration and discovery. Frequently, an aggressive curtain of exotic foliage engulfs the walls of ruins, overwhelming structures in states of decay and collapse. In others, Atlantean remnants of civilizations appear to wait in timeless limbo for the return of a vanished society. Yet not all of Ernst's cities suggest abandoned ruins—some may be occupied, functioning acropolises of the imagination: often a solar or lunar disc hovers over the scene, invoking the arch convention of nostalgia developed a century earlier by German Romantic artists (for example, *The Entire City,* 1935-36, Collection Kunsthaus Zürich). In the present painting, the thick vegetal foreground and the terra-cotta colored architecture recall the jungle environment of Mesoamerican ruins. No literal connection, however, should be drawn between specific sites and Ernst's architectural and botanical inventions.

Dense vegetation became an independent subject in Ernst's paintings about 1936. In works such as *The Joy of Life,* 1936 (Private Collection, England), man-sized insects and carnivorous plants inhabit jungle scenes that recall the profusion (if not the whimsy) of Rousseau's vegetation. One can discover amid the dense foliage at the left in the Peggy Guggenheim canvas a headless female torso, emerging as an offshoot from the stem of a mammoth plant. Furthermore, an iguanalike form, perhaps a reincarnation of Loplop in reptilian guise, can be perceived in the foliage at the far right. Similarly, close scrutiny of other paintings by Ernst, such as the *The Antipope* (cat. no. 62), reveals frottagelike matrixes composed of numerous hidden creatures. In the present work, this bizarre fruit of the encroaching vines bears a promise of the cyclical regeneration of life, even in the face of civilization's entropic decay.

* W. Spies, *Max Ernst: Oeuvre-Katalog, Werke 1929-1938,* Cologne, 1979, vol. IV, nos. 2208-2220, 2260, 2261.

E.C.C.

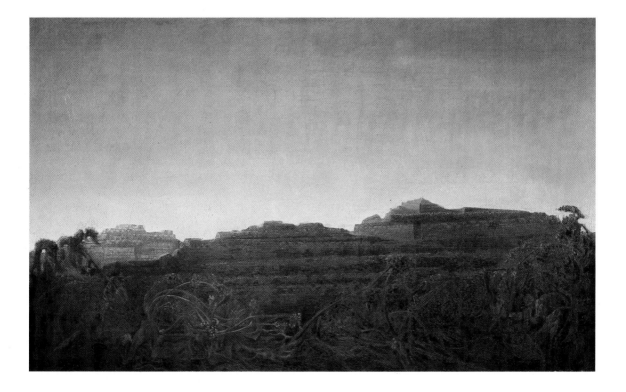

61 Attirement of the Bride. 1940
Oil on canvas, 51 x 37⅞″ (129.6 x 96.3 cm.)
76.2553 PG 78; PG coll. cat. 59

Attirement of the Bride is an example of Ernst's veristic or illusionistic Surrealism, in which a traditional technique is applied to an incongruous or unsettling subject. The theatrical, evocative scene has roots in late nineteenth-century Symbolist painting, especially that of Gustave Moreau. It also echoes the settings and motifs of sixteenth-century German art. The willowy, swollen-bellied figure types recall those of Lucas Cranach the Elder in particular. The architectural backdrop with its strong contrast of light and shadow and its inconsistent perspective shows the additional influence of de Chirico, whose work had overwhelmed Ernst when he first saw it in 1919.

The pageantry and elegance of the image are contrasted with its primitivizing aspects—the garish colors, the animal and monster forms—and the blunt phallic symbolism of the poised spearhead. The central scene is contrasted as well with its counterpart in the picture-within-a-picture at the upper left. In this detail the bride appears in the same pose, striding through a landscape of overgrown classical ruins. Here Ernst has used the technique of decalcomania invented in 1935 by Oscar Domínguez, in which diluted paint is pressed onto a surface with an object that distributes it unevenly, such as a pane of glass. A suggestive textured pattern results.

The title of this work had occurred to Ernst at least as early as 1936, when he italicized it in a text in his book *Beyond Painting*. Ernst had long identified himself with the bird, and had invented an alter ego, Loplop, Superior of the Birds, in 1929. Thus one may perhaps interpret the bird-man at the left as a depiction of the artist; the bride may in some sense represent the young English Surrealist artist Leonora Carrington.

L.F.

Ernst

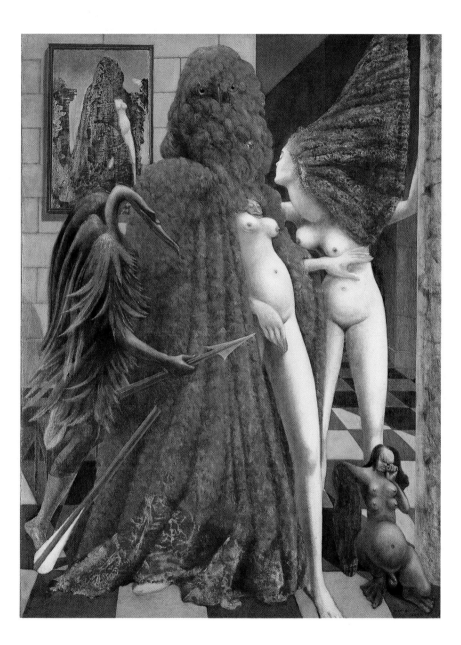

133

62 The Antipope. December 1941-March 1942

Oil on canvas, 63¼ x 50" (160.8 x 127.1 cm.)
76.2553 PG 80; PG coll. cat. 61

Ernst settled in New York in 1941 after escaping from
Europe with the help of Peggy Guggenheim. The same
year he executed a small oil on cardboard (now in the
Peggy Guggenheim Collection) that became the basis
for the large-scale *The Antipope.* When Peggy Guggenheim saw the small version, she interpreted a dainty
horse-human figure on the right as Ernst, who was being
fondled by a woman she identified as herself. She wrote
that Ernst conceded that a third figure, depicted in a
three-quarter rear view, was her daughter Pegeen; she
did not attempt to identify another horse-headed female
to the left.* When Ernst undertook the large version
from December to March he changed the body of the
"Peggy" figure into a greenish column and transferred
her amorous gesture to a new character, who wears a
pink tunic and is depicted in a relatively naturalistic
way. The "Pegeen" figure in the center appears to have
two faces, one of a flayed horse that looks at the horse-
woman at the left. The other, with only its cheek and
jaw visible, gazes in the opposite direction, out over the
grim lagoon, like a pensive subject conceived by Caspar
David Friedrich.

The great upheavals in Ernst's personal life during this
period encourage such a biographical interpretation.
Despite his marriage to Peggy Guggenheim, he was
deeply involved with Leonora Carrington at this time,
and spent hours riding horses with her. As birds were
an obsession for Ernst, so horses were for Carrington.
Her identification with them is suggested throughout
her collection of stories *La Dame Ovale,* published in
1939 with seven illustrations by Ernst, two of which include metamorphosed horse creatures. It seems plausible that the alienated horse-woman of *The Antipope,*
who twists furtively to watch the other horse-figure,
represents a vision of Peggy Guggenheim. (Rudenstine,
pp. 315-317). Like the triumphal bride in *Attirement
of the Bride* (cat. no. 61), she wears an owl headgear.
Her irreconcilable separation from her companion is
expressed graphically by the device of the diagonally
positioned spear that bisects the canvas. The features of
the green totemic figure resemble those of Carrington,
whose relationship with Ernst was to end soon after
the painting was completed, when she moved to
Mexico with her husband.

* See P. Guggenheim, *Out of This Century: Confessions of
an Art Addict,* New York, 1979, pp. 261-262.

L.F.

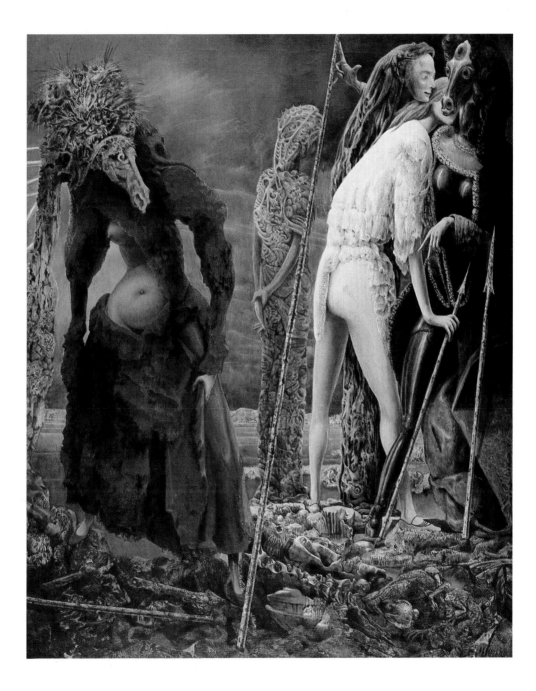

63 In the Streets of Athens. 1960 (cast January 1961)

Bronze, including base 38¾ x 19⁹⁄₁₆ x 7³⁄₁₆″
(98.4 x 49.7 x 18.3 cm.)
76.2553 PG 82; PG coll. cat. 63

Although Ernst produced several Dada assemblages, his serious interest in sculpture developed only in the mid-1930s.* In 1934 he worked briefly with Giacometti in Maloja, Switzerland, where the two artists carved and painted large granite stones to create ovoid abstract sculptures. Fascinated and inspired by the smooth surfaces of Giacometti's Surrealist sculptures, Ernst subsequently modeled numerous works in plaster. Although *In the Streets of Athens* was executed in 1960, it embodies many sculptural formulations Ernst had first explored in the mid-1930s. These include a carefully smoothed surface and a combination of thin, tabular elements into a compressed relief intended to be viewed primarily from the front. Two small secondary figures with flat, tabular faces are attached to the rectangular torso of the main figure, creating accents in high relief. The small winged-creature that hovers over the right shoulder of the central figure may be either bird or man. In the lower left corner, Ernst attaches a reclining female with yet another tabular face. A disembodied head emerges from beneath this female figure.

A large tabular head first appears in Ernst's work about 1934 in *Bird-Head* (De Menil Collection, Houston). Here a curious bird emerges from the forehead of a massive, squarish head which doubles as torso. The combination of bird and man motifs occurs again in Ernst's fantastic cement sculptures executed in 1938 when he renovated a farmhouse at Saint-Martin d'Ardèche in France. *In the Streets of Athens* is neither anthropomorphic nor zoomorphic, but suggests an emblematic union of both the human and the animal. The symbolic character of the sculpture is conveyed by the masklike faces which deny specific association with any one natural source.

A simplified version of the tabular structure of the present sculpture appears in another work of the same year, *A Lost Chinese* (De Menil Collection, Houston). In both examples, small secondary figures are united with the main torsos by a rhyming of mask shapes arranged in parallel planes. It is difficult to determine if Ernst developed any of these mask motifs in response to specific primitive masks (see Rudenstine, pp. 323-324). Ernst's own art collection included Hopi Kachina dolls, which are characterized by simple block forms, and the protuberant carved masks and totems of the Northwest Coast. Indeed many of the formal solutions in his sculptures share the geometric simplicity, planarity and schematic design of some typologies of American Indian Art.

* On Ernst's sculptural development, see W. Spies, *Max Ernst: Inside the Sight,* exh. cat., Houston, 1973, pp. 27-31.

E.C.C.

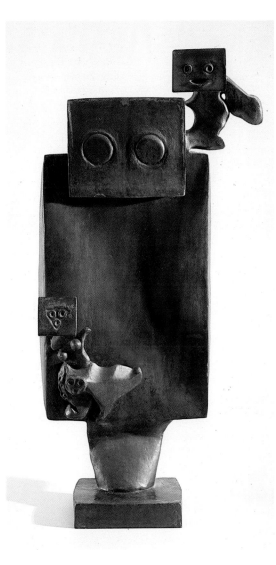

Jean Arp 1886-1966

Jean (Hans) Arp was born on September 16, 1886, in Strasbourg, Alsace. In 1904, after leaving the Ecole des Arts et Métiers in Strasbourg, he visited Paris and published his poetry for the first time. From 1905 to 1907 Arp studied at the Kunstschule of Weimar and in 1908 went to Paris, where he attended the Académie Julian. In 1909 he moved to Switzerland and, in 1911, was a founder of the *Moderner Bund* group there. The following year he met Robert and Sonia Delaunay in Paris and Kandinsky in Munich. Arp participated in the *Erster Deutscher Herbstsalon* in 1913 at the gallery of Der Sturm in Berlin. After returning to Paris in 1914, he became acquainted with Max Jacob, Picasso and Apollinaire. In 1915 he moved to Zürich where he executed collages and tapestries, often in collaboration with his future wife Sophie Taeuber.

In 1916 Hugo Ball opened the Cabaret Voltaire, which was to become the center of Dada activities in Zürich for a group including Arp, Tristan Tzara, Marcel Janco and others. Arp continued his involvement with Dada after moving to Cologne in 1919, contributing to Ernst's periodical *Die Schammade* and creating with him and Baargeld their collaborative collages or *Fatagagas*. In 1922 he participated in the *Kongress der Konstructivisten* in Weimar. Soon thereafter he began contributing to magazines such as *Merz*, *Mécano*, *De Stijl* and, in 1925, *La Révolution Surréaliste*. Arp's work appeared in the first exhibition of the Surrealist group at the Galerie Pierre in Paris in 1925. With Taeuber and van Doesburg he undertook a commission to decorate the cabaret L'Aubette in Strasbourg in 1926. This same year he settled in Meudon, France.

In 1931 Arp associated with the Paris-based group *Abstraction-Création* and the periodical *Transition*. Throughout the 1930s and until the end of his life he continued to write and publish poetry and essays. In 1942 he fled Meudon for Zürich; he was to make Meudon his primary residence again in 1946. The artist visited New York in 1949 on the occasion of his one-man show at Curt Valentin's Buchholz Gallery. In 1950 he was invited to execute a relief for the Harvard Graduate Center in Cambridge, Massachusetts. In 1954 Arp received the International Prize for Sculpture at the Venice Biennale. He was commissioned to design reliefs for the Ciudad Universitaria in Caracas in 1955. In 1960 he traveled to the Middle East. A large retrospective of his work was held at The Museum of Modern Art in New York in 1958, followed by another at the Musée National d'Art Moderne in Paris in 1962. Arp died on June 7, 1966, in Basel.

64 Large Collage. 1955 reconstruction of original of ca. 1918

Paper collage, watercolor, metallic and oil paint on Masonite, 38⅜ x 30⅝" (97.6 x 77.8 cm.)
76.2553 PG 52; PG coll. cat. 4

In 1915, shortly before he joined the Zürich Dada group, Arp produced what he described as his "first 'essential' picture," the simplified geometric elements of which he associated with children's building blocks organized in a spirit of play. By 1918 the artist, influenced by the rectilinear strictness of Taeuber's work, eliminated curves and diagonals from his collages (Rudenstine, pp. 62-64). As the upheaval and anxiety associated with World War I subsided, he concentrated on distilling a world of calm, simplicity and order in his work. His collages literally emphasized the constructive activity of the artist in opposition to or in disregard of the explicitly destructive, iconoclastic attitudes promulgated by the Dadaists.

Arp bases the composition of the present collage on modular rectangles of two sizes distributed along a grid. The proportional ratio of each module is one to one and one-quarter. The only vertically aligned rectangle, at upper center, is inconsistently small and superimposed on another rectangle. The cream-colored areas serve as a ground in which either vertical or horizontal rectangles can be visualized, thereby introducing an element of uncertainty into a composition that at first appears clear and declarative. The way in which collaged elements are integrated with the support results in an ambiguous relationship between figure and ground.

This work, damaged beyond repair, was reconstructed by the artist in 1955 (Rudenstine, p. 60).

L.F.

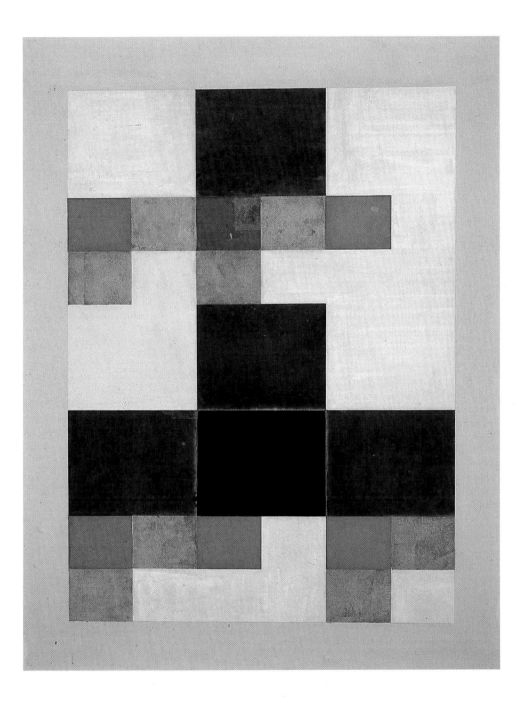

65 Overturned Blue Shoe with Two Heels Under a Black Vault. ca. 1925

Painted wood, 31¼ x 41⅛ x 2″ (79.3 x 104.6 x 5 cm.)
76.2553 PG 53; PG coll. cat. 5

Arp participated in Dada activities in Zürich in the teens; during the mid-twenties he allied himself to a certain extent with Surrealism, which had assimilated many of the tendencies of Dada. Though Arp resisted the program of the Surrealists, he shared their faith in unfettered creativity, their celebration of spontaneity and their antirational stance.

He executed his first monochrome wood reliefs in 1914, adding the element of color two years later. Comprised of discrete wood forms mounted individually on wood supports, these reliefs are assembled like collages rather than carved. Arp continued to make reliefs throughout his life. By combining aspects of painting, collage and sculpture, the reliefs of the teens and twenties served in some sense as a bridge to his sculpture in the round. Arp regarded his simplified forms as emblems of natural growth processes. As he wrote: "I looked for new constellations of form such as nature never stops producing. I tried to make forms grow. I put my trust in the example of seeds, stars, clouds, plants, animals, men, and finally in my innermost being."[*] According to Arp, his works carried their own momentum and arrived at organic solutions subject as much to the laws of chance as to his conscious manipulations. He commented on the "ridiculous" analogies of forms that resulted from this process; his descriptive titles, such as that of the present work or *Shirt Front and Fork* or *Dress with Eye and Navel* were often correspondingly whimsical.

[*] J. Arp, "Looking," *Arp*, exh. cat., New York, 1958, p. 12.

L.F.

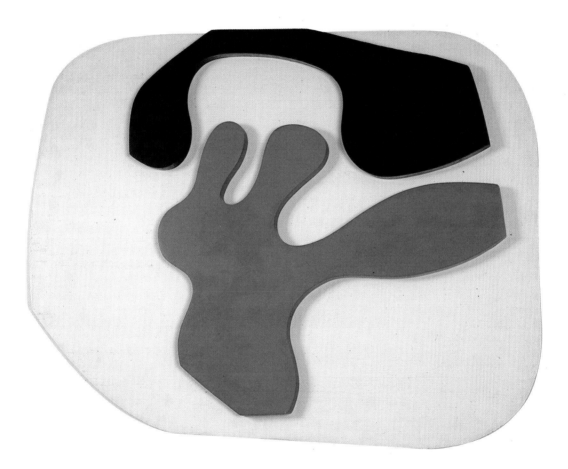

66 Head and Shell. ca. 1933

Polished brass, 2 pieces, total 7¾ x 8⅞″ (19.7 x 22.5 cm.)
76.2553 PG 54; PG coll. cat. 6

Arp's transition from his painted wooden wall reliefs of the 1920s (see cat. no. 65) to his freestanding sculpture of the 1930s (see cat. no. 67) occurred about 1930. At this time he executed some freestanding reliefs, which rested either on carved bases or directly on the ground (for example, *Shell Profiles,* 1930, Private Collection, Switzerland). Biomorphic elements like those attached to the wall reliefs gradually separated into independent forms and assumed positions in fully three-dimensional ensembles, such as *Bell and Navels,* 1931 (Collection The Museum of Modern Art, New York). When, in 1931, Arp began sculpting wood and modeling plaster in the round, he made figurative torsos. He next embarked on a series of abstract forms called *Concretions,* usually carved in plaster and some later cast in bronze. These sculptures, such as *Human Concretion,* 1934 (Collection Musée National d'Art Moderne, Centre Georges Pompidou, Paris), suggest general processes of growth, crystallization and metamorphosis, rather than specific motifs drawn from nature. The present sculpture shares the bulbous, protuberant character of the *Concretions,* its curved and coiled base expressing the spontaneous energy of pullulation.

Head and Shell, however, is not one continuous form but two separable elements. A spike attached to the base section supports the upper portion, which may easily be removed. Both conceptually and physically, this work is a unit composed of discrete parts (Rudenstine, p. 70). The object's small size and its partite nature suggest that Arp intended the original plaster version to be handled. During the 1930s, the artist produced several small works made of multiple elements that the viewer could pick up, separate and rearrange into new configurations. Peggy Guggenheim's fascination with this cast of the plaster original arose from her delight in handling the small sculpture.[*]

Arp's titles, such as *Head and Shell* or *Metamorphosis: Shell-Swan* (Collection Solomon R. Guggenheim Museum, New York), suggest counterparts in nature for his ambiguous organic forms. Such titles should not be considered too literally, however, as they were no doubt inspired by the completed sculptures. As Arp explains his working process, "Each of these bodies has a definite significance, but it is only when I feel there is nothing more to change that I decide what each means, and it is only then that I give it a name."[**]

[*] P. Guggenheim, *Out of This Century: Confessions of an Art Addict,* New York, 1979, p. 162.

[**] J. Arp, "Germe d'une Nouvelle Sculpture," *Jours effeuillés. Poèmes, essais, souvenirs. 1920-1965,* preface by Marcel Jean, Paris, 1966, p. 323. Author's translation.

E.C.C.

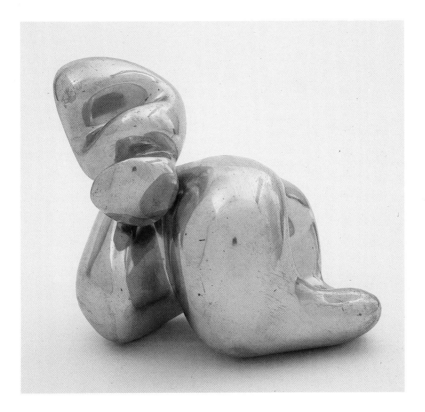

67 Crown of Buds I. 1936

Limestone, 19⅜ x 14¾″ (49.1 x 37.5 cm.)
76.2553 PG 56; PG coll. cat. 7

In 1930 Arp executed his first freestanding sculptures. While the planarity of the early examples links them with his reliefs (see cat. no. 65), by 1931 he was carving and modeling sculpture fully in the round. During the early 1930s he developed works which, though abstract in effect, were intended as "concrete" expressions of natural properties and processes. They emerged from his conviction that all things proliferating in nature could be seen as variations on a few basic forms. He compared his voluptuously rounded biomorphic shapes with fruit and children, endowed with life by the progenitor, but nonetheless thriving independently.

Arp said that "the content of a sculpture should reveal itself on tiptoe, without pretension, like the track of an animal in the snow."* *Crown of Buds I* is presented as an unspecified organic growth, but implicitly invites associations with the human body, particularly with female breasts. The ripening, merging forms of the buds press out centrifugally from the central opening, to point in different directions. Similarly turgid, sensuous forms emerge along a vertical axis in Arp's *Growth* of 1938 (Collection Solomon R. Guggenheim Museum, New York). *Crown of Buds I* in the Peggy Guggenheim Collection is made of porous limestone; versions exist in other media as well (see Rudenstine, p. 74). The slightly larger *Crown of Buds II* (repr. Rudenstine, p. 75, fig. b), was also executed in 1936.

* J. Arp, "Memories and Observations" in *Jean Arp*, exh. cat., New York, 1975, n.p.

L.F.

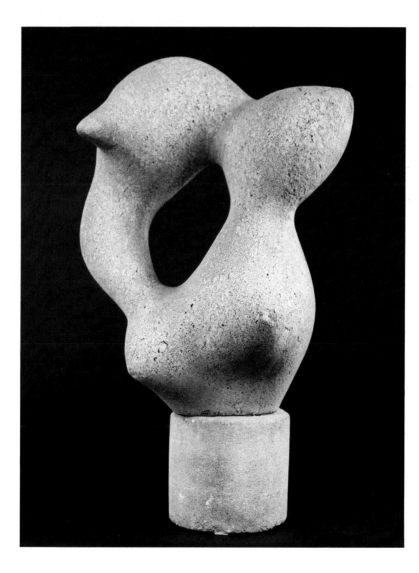

68 Amphora-Fruit. 1946(?) (cast 1951)

Bronze, 29⅜ x 38¹⁵⁄₁₆″ (74.5 x 99 cm.)
76.2553 PG 58; PG coll. cat. 10

By hyphenating the title *Amphora-Fruit*, Arp associates his sculpture simultaneously with man-made shapes and with natural botanical form. An amphora is a particular kind of ancient vessel, most often used for the storage of wine or oil, which has a narrow, cylindrical neck and a bulbous, oval body that tapers to a narrow base. While Arp's abstract form lacks the cavity, the perfect symmetry and the handles of a Greek amphora, its bulging form tapering at either end evokes the general shape of such a vessel. The swelling core of the sculpture, whose lopsided distribution is most easily apprehended from above, embodies ripeness and inner procreative energy. Its two tips extend in opposite directions, stretching away from the center as if sprouting into new life forms. Arp's reference to "fruit" could signify either zoological or botanical issue, and complements the notion of plentitude and abundance present in the concept of amphora as vessel.

A suggestion of surging upward growth in the abstract form and its smooth, luminous surface recall the sculptures of Brancusi, such as *The Seal* of 1924-36 (Collection Solomon R. Guggenheim Museum, New York; repr. Rudenstine, p. 81, fig. b) and *Bird in Space* of 1932-40 (cat. no. 44). Arp's work is less streamlined and fluid in its contours, and less suggestive of rapid movement than *Bird in Space*, however, belonging more to a terrestrial than to an aerial domain. Although by 1929 Arp was well aware of the model of Brancusi's sculpture, he strove to distinguish his work from that of the Rumanian master.[*] The present work probably originated in 1946 in a plaster sculpture entitled simply *Amphora*.[**] Arp subsequently used this basic form in the creation of three distinct bronzes. The plaster first served as the model from which the present sculpture was cast in 1951. In 1957 Arp manipulated the relation of the sculpture to its base by standing the mass on its tip. In 1965 Arp split the original form into sections, which he then reassembled along the new faces to compose yet another three-dimensional statement.

The reflective surface of the sculpture represents a cultivated patina, or layer of corrosion allowed to accumulate on the surface of the bronze. Arp allowed the foundry that cast his sculptures to create the first patina, but he generally applied the second one himself, rubbing oil or wax into his sculpture, and allowing the piece to weather naturally outdoors until it acquired an opaque, dark surface.[***] The present green color of *Amphora-Fruit* results from its prolonged exhibition outside.

[*] S. Poley, *Hans Arp: Die Formensprache im plastischen Werk*, Stuttgart, 1978, p. 143.

[**] Rudenstine, pp. 80-82, where a development of the Amphora theme is proposed and discussed.

[***] Poley, p. 42.

E.C.C.

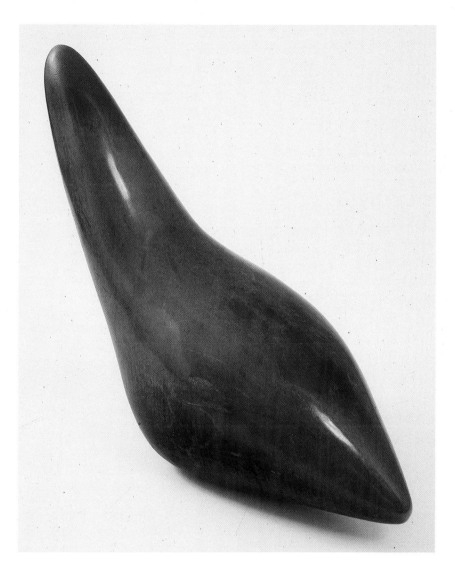

Kurt Schwitters 1887-1948

Herman Edward Karl Julius Schwitters was born in Hannover on June 20, 1887. He attended the Kunstgewerbeschule in Hannover from 1908 to 1909 and from 1909 to 1914 studied at the Kunstakademie Dresden. After serving as a draftsman in the military in 1917, Schwitters experimented with Cubist and Expressionist styles. In 1918 he made his first collages and in 1919 invented the term "*Merz*," which he was to apply to all his creative activities: poetry as well as collage and constructions. This year also marked the beginning of his friendships with Arp and Hausmann. Schwitters's earliest *Merzbilder* date from 1919, the year of his first exhibition at the gallery of Der Sturm, Berlin, and the first publication of his writings in the periodical *Der Sturm*. Schwitters showed at the Société Anonyme in New York in 1920.

With Arp he attended the *Kongress der Konstructivisten* in Weimar in 1922. There Schwitters met van Doesburg, whose *De Stijl* principles influenced his work. Schwitters's Dada activities included his *Merz-Matineen* and *Merz-Abende* at which he presented his poetry. From 1923 to 1932 he published the magazine *Merz*. About 1923 the artist started to make his first *Merzbau*, a fantastic structure he built over a number of years; the *Merzbau* grew to occupy much of his Hannover studio. During this period he also worked in typography. Schwitters was included in the exhibition *Abstrakte und surrealistische Malerei und Plastik* at the Kunsthaus Zürich in 1929. The artist contributed to the Parisian review *Cercle et Carré* in 1930; in 1932 he joined the Paris-based *Abstraction-Création* group and wrote for their organ of the same name. He participated in the *Cubism and Abstract Art* and *Fantastic Art, Dada, Surrealism* exhibitions of 1936 at The Museum of Modern Art, New York.

The Nazi regime banned Schwitters's work as *Entartete Kunst* (degenerate art) in 1937. This year the artist fled to Lysaker, Norway, where he constructed a second *Merzbau*. After the German invasion of Norway in 1940, Schwitters escaped to Great Britain, where he was interned for over a year. He settled in London following his release, but moved to Little Langdale in the Lake District in 1945. There, helped by a stipend from The Museum of Modern Art, he began work on a third *Merzbau* in 1947. The project was left unfinished when Schwitters died on January 8, 1948, in Kendal, England.

69 Merz Drawing 75. 1920

Collage, gouache, ink and graphite on papers and fabric, including artist's mat 5¾ x 3¹⁵⁄₁₆″ (14.6 x 10 cm.)
76.2553 PG 85; PG coll. cat. 159

Schwitters, though closely identified with the iconoclastic Dada movement, was also committed to modernist ideals of pure and self-sufficient art. With a connoisseur's discernment he redeemed objects from the detritus of daily life and incorporated them into his *Merz* works. Even the most raw or worn surfaces are endowed with a poetic grace. The designation *Merz* is derived from the truncation of the word *Kommerz*, which appears in an early collage (present whereabouts unknown). Glued or nailed ticket stubs, cigarette wrappings, bits of fabric, wood, tin and pottery interact in his *Merz* collages to produce compositions of compelling structural authority. These objects lose their conventional associations because of the change of context and the formal manipulations to which they are subjected.

Visually these works are related in some respects to the collages of Picasso and Braque, the paintings of Robert Delaunay and the mixed-media sculptures of Boccioni. Like the Cubists, Schwitters often included printed words or letters, which appealed to him for their intrinsic formal qualities. Here he probably intended a wry comment on his work in the clearly legible words on the cigarette package at the lower right: *made of ... best old*. Below, he added the inscription: *Mz 75/K. Sch.20/Zeichnung blass*. Mz stands for *Merzzeichnung* or *Merz Drawing*; *Zeichnung blass* means "pale drawing." Like his other humorously self-deprecating titles (*Nothing At All* or *It's So Lovely*) "pale drawing" seems to be conceived by Schwitters in an irreverent Dada mood.

L.F.

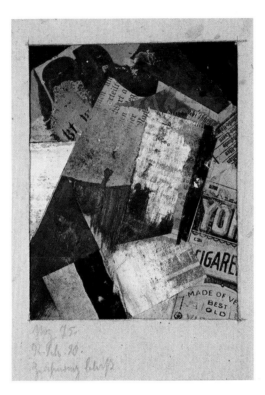

70 Blue in Blue. 1926-29

Collage and lithographic crayon on paper,
14⁷⁄₁₆ x 11¾″ (36.7 x 29.9 cm.)
76.2553 PG 86; PG coll. cat. 160

In *Blue in Blue* Schwitters superimposes six pieces of
paper over a support cut from the same material. The
collage, which now appears almost black, has lost most
of its original blue color (see Rudenstine, p. 696). Edges
of extremely light and extremely dark color emerge in
high contrast to the background. The fragments of
paper, arranged on either side of a slightly off-center
field, balance and stabilize the composition. Their irregular forms, never exactly rectangular, provide variation within the geometric order of the collage, and
the tonal gradations permit a delicate fusion of light
and dark, density and void.

In comparison to Schwitters's *Merz* collages from 1919
to the mid-twenties, which are characterized by diverse
colors, textures and materials, *Blue in Blue* is simple
and restrained. The artist's use here of a single primary
color in a geometric design that stresses horizontal and
vertical relationships points to the impact of the art and
theories of van Doesburg. While the formal relationships of *Blue in Blue* maintain a harmony and balance
characteristic of Neo-Plasticist compositions, the actual
material of the collage recalls Schwitters's Dadaist sensibilities. In the *Merz* pictures old tickets, driftwood,
buttons and rubbish from attics and trash dumps had
been the stuff of his art. To make *Blue in Blue,* Schwitters cut up scraps salvaged from the floors of the
Druckerei Molling in Hannover, where he did typo-
graphical work; the thin cardboard was used to wipe
lithographic stones (Rudenstine, p. 697). Thus he
conserved and transformed a technician's cleaning rags
to create the fabric of collage. As Schwitters stated,
". . . an artist should be permitted to make a painting
merely from two pieces of blotting paper as long as he
is really creating."*

* Quoted in *Kurt Schwitters,* exh. cat., New York, 1963, p. 5.

E.C.C.

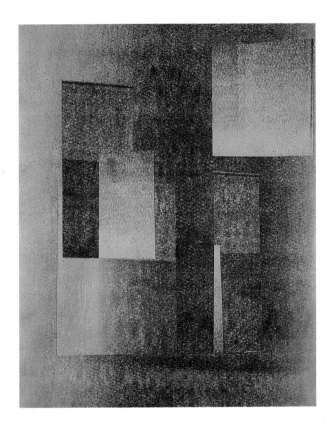

71 Maraak, Variation I. 1930

Oil and assemblage of objects on board, 18⅛ x 14⁹⁄₁₆″
(46 x 37 cm.)
76.2553 PG 87; PG coll. cat. 161

Schwitters abandoned his *Merz* pictures to a large extent during the mid- to late 1920s to concentrate on
paintings, constructions and reliefs in which the influence of Russian Constructivism and the work of his
friend van Doesburg is discernable. He eliminated found
materials from these compositions and thereby reduced
the Dada element of chance they contributed, in order
to achieve a less idiosyncratic and hence more universal
form of expression. This development accorded with his
belief in the ascendancy of formal values, which he felt
should not be jeopardized by references to anything outside the work of art.

When Schwitters returned to the *Merz* idiom in 1930,
he placed more emphasis on the act of painting than he
had in his early collages. Though the planes are shaped
with the impersonality of geometric contour, they are
animated by the variation of rhythmic brushstrokes and
the addition of collaged forms. In the tradition of his
Merz works of the classic period of 1919 to the mid-
1920s, the objects he adopts are disposable articles—the
top of a corroded tin can and a metal butterfly; the picture once included a broken piece of china to the right
of the tin circle and two wooden balls below the butterfly. While the objects function as abstract elements
within the flat confines of the support, their projection
contradicts the two-dimensionality of the picture plane
and implies an extension of the work of art into the observer's world.

L.F.

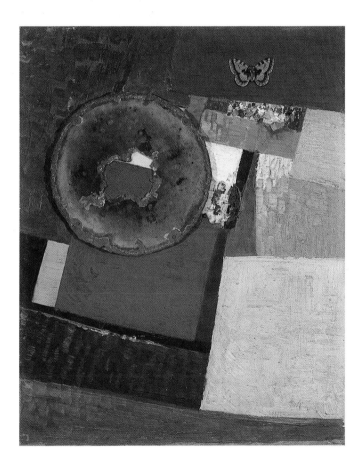

Joan Miró 1893-1983

Joan Miró Ferra was born in Barcelona on April 20, 1893. At the age of fourteen he went to business school in Barcelona and also attended La Lonja, the academy of fine arts in the same city. Upon completing three years of art studies he took a position as a clerk. After suffering a nervous breakdown he abandoned business and resumed his art studies, attending Francesc Galí's Escola d'Art in Barcelona from 1912 to 1915. Miró received early encouragement from the dealer José Dalmau, who gave him his first one-man show at his gallery in Barcelona in 1918. In 1917 he met Picabia.

In 1919 Miró made his first trip to Paris, where he met Picasso. From 1920 Miró divided his time between Paris and Montroig. In Paris he associated with the poets Pierre Reverdy, Tristan Tzara and Max Jacob and participated in Dada activities. Dalmau organized Miró's first one-man show in Paris, at the Galerie La Licorne in 1921. His work was included in the Salon d'Automne of 1923. In 1924 Miró joined the Surrealist group. His one-man show at the Galerie Pierre in Paris in 1925 was a major Surrealist event; Miró was included in the first Surrealist exhibition at the Galerie Pierre that same year. He visited The Netherlands in 1928 and began a series of paintings inspired by Dutch Masters. This year he also executed his first *papiers collés* (pasted papers) and collages. In 1929 he started his experiments in lithography, and his first etchings date from 1933. During the early 1930s he made Surrealist sculpture-objects incorporating painted stones and found objects. In 1936 Miró left Spain because of the Civil War; he returned in 1941.

An important Miró retrospective was held at The Museum of Modern Art in New York in 1941. This year Miró began working in ceramics with Lloréns Artigas and started to concentrate on prints: from 1954 to 1958 he worked almost exclusively in these two media. In 1958 Miró was given a Guggenheim International Award for murals for the UNESCO Building in Paris; the following year he resumed painting, initiating a series of mural-sized canvases. During the sixties he began to work intensively in sculpture. In 1965 he again collaborated with Artigas, on the ceramic tile mural *Alicia* commissioned by Harry F. Guggenheim in memory of his late wife, Alicia Patterson Guggenheim; Miró designed the work for a specific wall of the Solomon R. Guggenheim Museum in New York. A major Miró retrospective took place at the Grand Palais in Paris in 1974. In 1978 the Musée National d'Art Moderne, Centre Georges Pompidou, Paris, exhibited over five hundred works in a major retrospective of his drawings. Miró died on December 25, 1983, in Palma de Mallorca, Spain.

72 Painting. 1925

Oil on canvas, 45⅛ x 57⅜″ (114.5 x 145.7 cm.)
76.2553 PG 91; PG coll. cat. 116

During the mid- to late 1920s Miró developed a private system of imagery in which the implications of motifs have symbolic meanings that vary according to their context. By studying the constellations of these motifs, one is encouraged to infer meanings appropriate to a particular painting.

In *Painting* two "personages" (the designation Miró used for his abstract figures) and a flame have been identified. The personage on the right can perhaps be read as a female because of the curvaceous nature of the eight-shape, and by analogy with forms in other paintings that are specifically identified by the artist as women. The black dot with radiating lines can be interpreted as the figure's eye receiving rays of light, or as a bodily or verbal emission. The same motif appears in *Personage*, also of 1925, in the collection of the Solomon R. Guggenheim Museum, New York. Moons, stars, suns or planets float at the upper left of several canvases of the mid-1920s. In the present work the semicircular orange-red image not only carries a cosmic implication, but also possibly doubles as the head of the second personage, probably a male. This head is presented in a combined full-face and profile view, in the manner of Picasso's Cubist portraits.

The flame, used repeatedly by Miró in this period, may signify sexual excitation in this context. The erotic content that prevails in much of his work in 1925 is particularly explicit in the *Lovers* series, in which two figures approach each other or are united in sexual embrace. The two figures in *Painting* are less clearly conjoined. The submersion of legible subject matter and the ambiguity of its meaning transfer the emphasis to the purely abstract qualities of the work. Line and color articulate a language as complex and poetic as the hieroglyphic signs that constitute the imagery. The generalized ground, rich in texture from the uneven thinning of paint and the use of shadowy black, provides a warm and earthy support for the expressive black lines, the areas of red and yellow and the staccato rhythm of dots.

L.F.

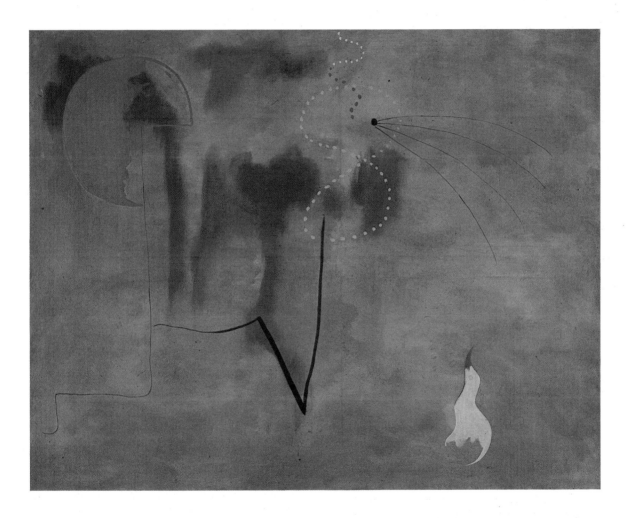

73 Dutch Interior II. Summer 1928

Oil on canvas, 36¼ x 28¾" (92 x 73 cm.)
76.2553 PG 92; PG coll. cat. 117

In 1928 Miró returned to Paris from a trip to The Netherlands with several postcard reproductions of works
by seventeenth-century Dutch artists. At least two of
these have been identified as sources for the *Dutch
Interior* paintings in The Museum of Modern Art, New
York (repr. Rudenstine, p. 544, fig. h), and the Peggy
Guggenheim Collection.* The Guggenheim work is a
transformation of Jan Steen's *The Dancing Lesson*
(Collection Rijksmuseum, Amsterdam; repr. Rudenstine, p. 542, fig. a), and conveys the synthesis of carefully observed, precisely executed detail and imaginative
generalization of form that proceeded from Miró's
encounter with the Dutch Baroque. In this combination
of objective minutiae and abstract vision, *Dutch Interior II* reverts conceptually to works of the early
1920s, such as *The Tilled Field,* 1923-24 (Collection
Solomon R. Guggenheim Museum, New York).

The gradual translation of veristic detail into eccentric,
evocative form can be followed through preliminary
sketches of specific motifs to a meticulously complete
preparatory drawing. A conspicuous modification of
the Dutch original is Miró's enlargement of and focus
on human and animal figures and his concomitant sup-
pression or deemphasis of inanimate objects. Thus a
window at the upper center of the Steen has been greatly
reduced in size, as though it had been sent hurtling
through a vast space. The real subject of the Steen is not
the cat, but the sound, movement and hilarity the dancing lesson provokes. Miró seizes on this anomaly in his
version: although the cat serves as the hub of his cen-
trifugal composition, he emphasizes the cacophony and
animation of the lesson through the swirling motion
of myriad details and the dancing rhythm of points
and counterpoints.

* See W. Erben, *Joan Miró,* New York, 1957, pp. 125-127.

L.F.

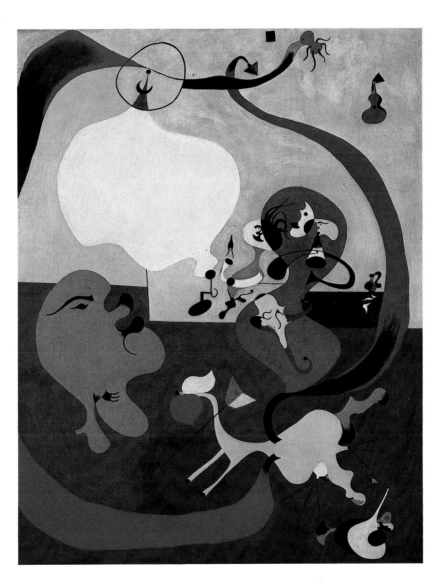

74 Seated Woman II. February 27, 1939

Oil on canvas, 63¾ x 51³⁄₁₆″ (162 x 130 cm.)
76.2553 PG 93; PG coll. cat. 118

The expressionistic *Seated Woman II* can be seen as a
final manifestation of Miró's *peintures sauvages,* works
characterized by violence of execution and imagery. It
was painted at a time when Miró, like Picasso and González (see cat. no. 75), was responding acutely to the
events of the Spanish Civil War.

The human figure has been transmogrified here into a
grotesque and bestial creature. However, the aggressiveness of imagery and formal elements coexists with
fanciful details and cosmic implications. Though the
open, saw-toothed mouth imparts a sense of the woman's voraciousness or anguish, her bottle-breast
implies her generative force. Her expansive torso con-
stitutes an impenetrable ground, its horizon line
described by her squared shoulders, out of which grow
the vegetative stems of arms and neck. The bird and fish
forms floating through the atmosphere become insig-
nias for air and water, while the moon, star and planet
emblems on the woman's collar broaden the associations to encompass the astral plane. The remaining
abstract shapes seem to course slowly in mysterious orbits, passing through and beyond one another, changing
color where they intersect. A cohesive universe is created
despite the dichotomies of light and dark, nurture and
destruction, life and nonexistence. Integration is provided by the repetition of shapes, such as the leaf and
oval, which suggests analogies: the woman's pendant
becomes a moon or vagina, her hair resembles lines of
sight, like those of the fish, or rays of light, her teeth are
equated with the decorative motifs or mountains in the
miniature landscape of her collar.

This work postdates by about two months the more
generalized *Seated Woman I* (Collection The Museum
of Modern Art, New York; repr. Rudenstine, p. 546,
fig. a).

L.F.

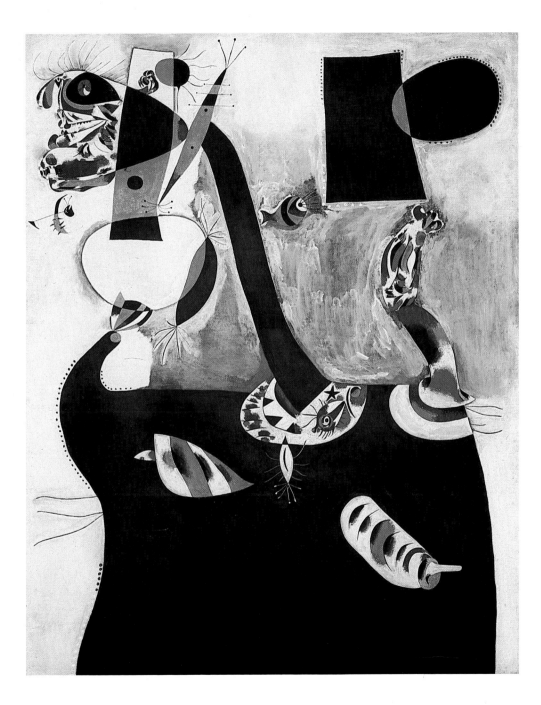

Julio González 1876-1942

Julio González was born in Barcelona on September 21, 1876. With his older brother Joan he worked in his father's metalsmith shop; during the evenings they took classes at the Escuela de Bellas Artes. González exhibited metalwork at the *Exposición de Bellas Artes e Industrias Artísticas* in Barcelona in 1892, 1896 and 1898, and at the *World's Columbian Exposition* in Chicago in 1893. In 1897 he began to frequent Els Quatre Gats, a café in Barcelona, where he met Picasso.

In 1900 González moved to Paris; there he began to associate with Manolo Hugué, Jaime Sabartés, Pablo Gargallo, Max Jacob and Gris. His first embossed metalwork was produced in 1900. He exhibited with the Société Nationale des Beaux-Arts in 1903, 1909 and frequently during the early twenties. González participated in the Salon des Indépendants in 1907 and occasionally thereafter. He first exhibited paintings at the Salon d'Automne in 1909, and showed both sculpture and paintings there regularly during the teens and twenties. In 1918, González worked at the Renault factory at Boulogne-Billancourt, where he learned the techniques of autogenous welding he used later in iron sculptures. In 1920 he became reacquainted with Picasso.

González's first solo exhibition, which included paintings, sculpture, drawings, jewelry and objets d'art, was held in 1922 at the Galerie Povolovsky in Paris. The following year he was given a one-man show of works in similarly varied media at the Galerie Le Caméléon in Paris. In 1923 González participated in the first Salon du Montparnasse, Paris, with Raoul Dufy, Paco Durio, Friesz and others. In 1924 he was included in the exhibition *Les Amis du Montparnasse* at the Salon des Tuileries and the Salon d'Automne in Paris. He made his first iron sculptures in 1927. From 1928 to 1931 González provided technical assistance to Picasso in executing sculptures in iron. In 1930 he was given a one-man sculpture exhibition at the Galerie de France in Paris, and the following year showed at the Salon des Surindépendants for the first time. In 1937 he contributed to the Spanish Pavilion of the World's Fair in Paris and *Cubism and Abstract Art* at The Museum of Modern Art in New York. That same year he moved to Arcueil, near Paris, where he died on March 27, 1942.

75 "Monsieur" Cactus (Cactus Man I). 1939 (cast 1953-54)

Bronze, 25⁵⁄₁₆ x 9³⁄₁₆ x 6¹¹⁄₁₆" (64.3 x 25 x 17 cm.)
76.2553 PG 136; PG coll. cat. 72

During the late 1930s González worked simultaneously in naturalistic and abstract idioms. His abstract mode constituted an important contribution to the development of avant-garde sculpture in both Europe and the United States. This mode is exemplified by *"Monsieur" Cactus* of 1939, in which he returns to the metamorphic theme of several earlier sculptures. As in works by other Spanish artists living abroad during the Civil War, the figure is anguished (see, for example, Miró's *Seated Woman II*, cat. no. 74, or Picasso's *Guernica* of 1937 [Collection Museo Nacional del Prado, Madrid]). Indeed, several of the more literal preparatory drawings for the sculpture, dating from December of 1938, suggest that the figure is shrieking; the prickly nails intensify the aggressive effect of the work, recalling Picasso's use of nails in his *Guitar* of 1926 (Collection Musée Picasso, Paris). Though the distortion and dislocation of anatomical features make positive identification difficult, with the aid of the drawings one can read a raised arm joined to the hip, its five fingers spread like a cluster of cylindrical cactus stems. The analogous five-fingered block to the left of the torso seems to be lowered to a position just above an angular phallus.

The companion to this sculpture, known as *Cactus Man II* or *"Madame" Cactus,* has been interpreted as the image of the Spanish peasant's defiance of Franco's fascist threat.* While the synthesis of human being and cactus may reflect the identification of the Spanish peasant with the land, the metamorphic figure may more generally personify the republican cause. At the end of 1938 Franco launched a major offensive against Catalonia, González's native province, and was to take its capital, Barcelona, in January of 1939, signaling the end of republican hopes. By the time the drawings for the second cactus sculpture appeared in the summer of 1939, Madrid had fallen and Franco's Falange was in full power.

* E. A. Carmean, "Cactus Man Number Two," *The Museum of Fine Arts, Houston: Bulletin,* Fall 1973, p. 41. For discussion of the titles and the meanings of the two works, see M. Rowell, *Julio González: A Retrospective,* exh. cat., New York, 1983, pp. 188, 195, and Rudenstine, p. 364.

L.F.

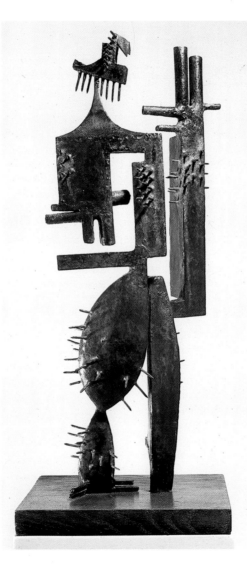

Alberto Giacometti 1901-1966

Alberto Giacometti was born on October 10, 1901, in Borgonovo, Switzerland, and grew up in the nearby town of Stampa. His father Giovanni was a Post-Impressionist painter. From 1919 to 1920 he studied painting at the Ecole des Beaux-Arts and sculpture and drawing at the Ecole des Arts et Métiers in Geneva. In 1920 he traveled to Italy, where he was impressed by the Cézannes and Archipenkos at the Venice Biennale. He was also deeply affected by primitive and Egyptian art and by the masterpieces of Giotto and Tintoretto. In 1922 Giacometti settled in Paris, making frequent visits to Stampa. From time to time over the next several years he attended Bourdelle's sculpture classes at the Académie de la Grande Chaumière.

In 1927 the artist moved into a studio with his brother Diego, his lifelong companion and assistant, and exhibited his sculpture for the first time at the Salon des Tuileries, Paris. His first show in Switzerland, shared with his father, was held at the Galerie Aktuaryus in Zürich in 1927. The following year Giacometti met Masson and by 1930 he was a participant in the Surrealist circle. His first one-man show took place in 1932 at the Galerie Pierre Colle in Paris. In 1934 his first American solo exhibition opened at the Julien Levy Gallery in New York. During the early 1940s he became a friend of Picasso, Jean-Paul Sartre and Simone de Beauvoir. From 1942 Giacometti lived in Geneva, where he associated with the publisher Albert Skira.

He returned to Paris in 1946. In 1948 he had a one-man show at the Pierre Matisse Gallery in New York. The artist's friendship with Samuel Beckett began about 1951. In 1955 he was given major retrospectives at the Arts Council Gallery in London and the Solomon R. Guggenheim Museum in New York. He received the Sculpture Prize at the Carnegie International in Pittsburgh in 1961 and the First Prize for Sculpture at the Venice Biennale of 1962, where he was given his own exhibition area. In 1965 Giacometti exhibitions were organized by the Tate Gallery in London, The Museum of Modern Art in New York, the Louisiana Museum in Humlebaek, Denmark, and the Stedelijk Museum in Amsterdam. That same year he was awarded the Grand National Prize for Art by the French government. Giacometti died on January 11, 1966, in Chur, Switzerland.

76 Woman Walking. 1932

Plaster, including base 59 1/16 x 10 11/16″ (150 x 27.2 cm.)
76.2553 PG 132; PG coll. cat. 67

This sculpture is conceived in the rational and formally serene mode Giacometti pursued concurrently with his dark Surrealist explorations of the subconscious. *Woman Walking* has none of the ferocity of *Woman with Her Throat Cut* (cat. no. 77), though both works were executed during the same period. The graceful, calm plaster seems to have its source in the frontal figures of ancient Egypt, posed with left feet slightly ahead of right in fearless confrontation of death. Despite the pose, the *Woman Walking,* like its Egyptian ancestors, conveys no sense of movement. The plane of the body is only slightly inflected by the projections of breasts, belly and thighs. The long, thin legs are smooth, solid and columnar. In its flatness, the work evokes the traditions of the highly simplified Cycladic figure and the geometric *Kouros* of archaic Greece. Giacometti is known to have copied works of art at the Louvre, during his travels and even from reproductions, showing a preference for models characterized by a high degree of stylization. *Woman Walking* also reflects Giacometti's awareness of twentieth-century sculptors, particularly Brancusi and Archipenko.

Another plaster version of the sculpture, also probably dating from 1932 (formerly Collection Erica Brausen, London), is distinguished by a triangular cavity in the upper abdomen.* The generalization and distortion of form in these works forecast Giacometti's development of the elongated style for which he is best known (see cat. no. 78).

* For discussion of the relationship between the two versions, see Rudenstine, pp. 336-340.

L.F.

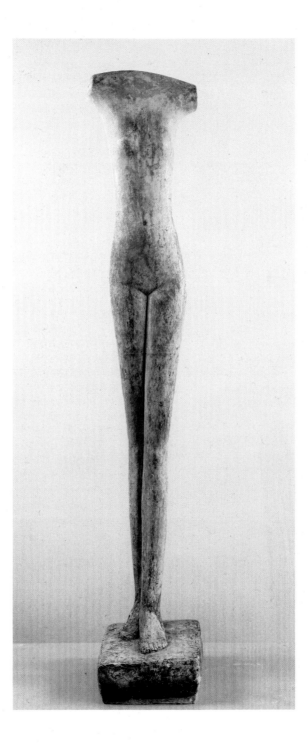

77 Woman with Her Throat Cut. 1932 (cast 1940)

Bronze, 9⅛ x 35 1/16″ (23.2 x 89 cm.)
76.2553 PG 131; PG coll. cat. 68

In a group of works made between 1930 and 1933, Giacometti used the Surrealist techniques of shocking juxtaposition and the distortion and displacement of anatomical parts to express the fears and urges of the subconscious. The aggressiveness with which the human figure is treated in these fantasies of brutal erotic assault graphically conveys their content. The female, seen in horror and longing as both victim and victimizer of male sexuality, is often a crustacean or insectlike form. *Woman with Her Throat Cut* is a particularly vicious image: the body is splayed open, disemboweled, arched in a paroxysm of sex and death. Eros and Thanatos, seen here as a single theme, are distinguished and treated separately in two preparatory sketches (Collection Musée National d'Art Moderne, Centre Georges Pompidou, Paris; repr. Rudenstine, p. 344, fig. b).

Body parts are translated into schematic abstract forms like those in *Cage* of 1930-31 (Collection Moderna Museet, Stockholm), which includes the spoon shape of the female torso, the rib and backbone motif and the pod shape of the phallus. Here a vegetal form resembling the pelvic bone terminates one arm, and a phallus-like spindle, the only movable part, gruesomely anchors the other; the woman's backbone pins one leg by fusing with it; her slit carotid immobilizes her head. The memory of violence is frozen in the rigidity of rigor mortis. The psychological torment and the sadistic misogyny projected by this sculpture are in startling contrast to the serenity of other contemporaneous pieces by Giacometti, such as *Woman Walking* (cat. no. 76).

L.F.

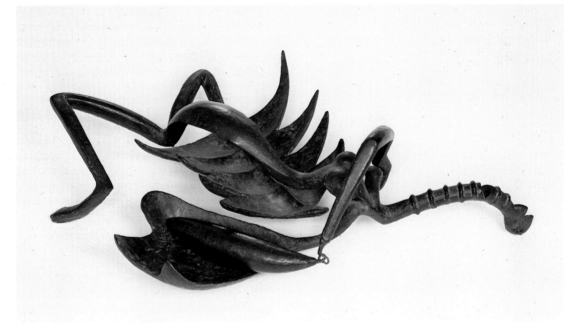

78 Standing Woman ("Leoni"). 1947 (cast November 1957)

Bronze, including base 60¼″ (153 cm.) high
76.2553 PG 134; PG coll. cat. 69

An early example of the mature style with which Giacometti is usually identified, this figure is more elongated and dematerialized than the *Woman Walking* (cat. no. 76), though it retains that sculpture's frontality and immobility. A sense of ghostly fragility detaches the figure from the world around it, despite the crusty materiality of the surfaces, as animated and responsive to light as those of Rodin.

Giacometti exploited the contradictions of perception in the haunting, incorporeal sculptures of this period. His matchstick-sized figures of 1942 to 1946 demonstrate the effect of distance on size and comment on the notion that the essence of an individual persists even as the body appears to vanish, that is, to become nonexistent. Even his large-scale standing women and striding men seem miniaturized and insubstantial. In 1947 the sculptor commented that ". . . lifesize figures irritate me, after all, because a person passing by on the street has no weight; in any case he's much lighter than the same person when he's dead or has fainted. He keeps his balance with his legs. You don't feel your weight. I wanted—without having thought about it—to reproduce this lightness, and that by making the body so thin."* Giacometti sought to convey several notions simultaneously in his attenuated plastic forms: one's consciousness of the nonmaterial presence of another person, the insubstantiality of the physical body housing that presence, and the paradoxical nature of perception. The base from which the woman appears to grow like a tree is tilted, emphasizing the verticality of the figure as well as reiterating the contours of the merged feet.

Giacometti had the present cast made expressly for Peggy Guggenheim.

* Quoted in R. Hohl, *Alberto Giacometti,* New York, 1971, p. 278.

L.F.

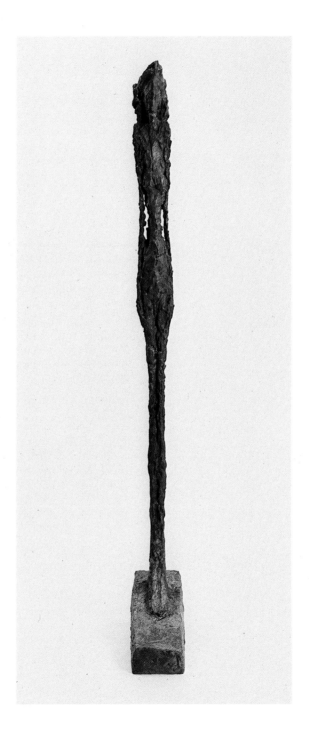

79 Piazza. 1947-48 (cast 1948-49)

Bronze, 8¼ x 24⅝ x 16⅞" (21 x 62.5 x 42.8 cm.)
76.2553 PG 135; PG coll. cat. 70

In the late 1940s Giacometti produced attenuated thin
figures not only of the life-size height of the *Standing
Woman* (cat. no. 78), but also on the miniature scale of
the figures who inhabit his *Piazza* of 1948-49. Four men
stride across a wide plaza, each moving toward center,
yet none apparently directed toward an encounter with
another. A single woman, whose stiff posture recalls the
Standing Woman, stands isolated and motionless near
the center. The featureless figures exist independently
within their haphazardly grouped unity, their multiple,
nonconverging paths suggesting individual ambitions
and absorptions.

The flat bronze slab on which the figures stand serves
both as base and as the plaza setting. Such a tabular
format first appears in *The Palace at 4 a.m.,* 1932-33
(Collection The Museum of Modern Art, New York),
a highly theatrical work of Giacometti's Surrealist
period. Giacometti began placing individual figures on
large bases as early as 1942, but only in 1948, in *Three
Men Walking,* did a group of attenuated figures appear
on a thin square bronze base that also suggests a city
square.

Giacometti's scene derives from modern urban experience. He states:

> *In the street people astound and interest me more
> than any sculpture or painting. Every second the
> people stream together and go apart, then they ap-
> proach each other to get closer to one another. They
> unceasingly form and re-form living compositions in
> unbelievable complexity. . . . It's the totality of this
> life that I want to reproduce in everything I do. . . .*

There are five different casts of this work, and a somewhat larger version with the figures placed in slightly
different positions exists in five casts as well (Rudenstine, p. 354). In all of these sculptures, an eye-level
examination of the work alters the scale of miniaturization first perceived by the viewer. The vastness of the
empty piazza and the anonymity of the figures are
revealed by such closeup scrutiny.

* Quoted in *Alberto Giacometti: A Retrospective Exhibition,*
exh. cat., New York, 1974, p. 31.

E.C.C.

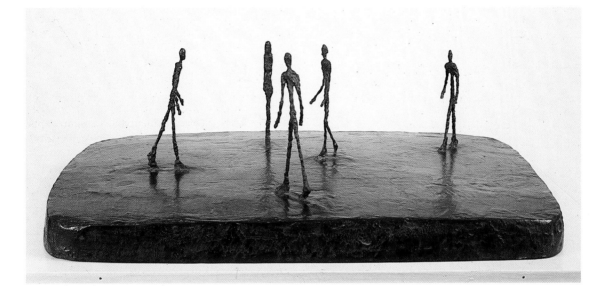

Henry Moore b. 1898

Henry Spencer Moore was born July 30, 1898, in Castleford, Yorkshire, the son of a miner. Despite an early desire to become a sculptor, Moore began his career as a teacher in Castleford. After military service in World War I he attended Leeds School of Art on an ex-serviceman's grant. In 1921 he won a Royal Exhibition Scholarship to study sculpture at the Royal Academy of Art in London. Moore became interested in the Mexican, Egyptian and African sculpture he saw at the British Museum. He was appointed Instructor of Sculpture at the Royal Academy in 1924, a post he held for the next seven years. A Royal Academy traveling scholarship allowed Moore to visit Italy in 1925; there he saw the frescoes of Giotto and Masaccio and the late sculpture of Michelangelo. Moore's first one-man show of sculpture was held at the Warren Gallery, London, in 1928.

In the 1930s Moore was a member of *Unit One,* a group of advanced artists organized by Paul Nash, and was a close friend of Nicholson, Hepworth and the critic Herbert Read. From 1932 to 1939 he taught at the Chelsea School of Art. He was an important force in the English Surrealist movement, although he was not entirely committed to its doctrines; Moore participated in the *International Surrealist Exhibition* at the New Burlington Galleries, London, in 1936. In 1940 Moore was appointed an official war artist and was commissioned by the War Artists Advisory Committee to execute drawings of life in underground bomb shelters. From 1940 to 1943 the artist concentrated almost entirely on drawing. His first retrospective took place at Temple Newsam, Leeds, in 1941. In 1943 he received a commission from the Church of St. Matthew, Northampton, to carve a *Madonna and Child*; this sculpture was the first in an important series of family group sculptures. Moore was given his first major retrospective abroad by The Museum of Modern Art, New York, in 1946. He won the International Prize for Sculpture at the Venice Biennale of 1948.

Moore executed several important public commissions in the 1950s, among them *Reclining Figure,* 1956-58, for the UNESCO Building in Paris. In 1963 the artist was awarded the British Order of Merit. A major retrospective of his work was held at the Forte di Belvedere, Florence, in 1972. A gallery of works Moore donated to the Art Gallery of Ontario in Toronto opened in 1974. The artist's eightieth birthday was celebrated in 1978 with an exhibition of his work at the Serpentine in London organized by the Arts Council of Great Britain; at this time he gave many of his sculptures to the Tate Gallery, London. Moore now lives and works at Perry Green, Much Hadham, Hertfordshire.

80 Three Standing Figures. 1953

Bronze, including base 28¾ x 26¼ x 11⅜"
(73.2 x 68 x 29 cm.)
76.2553 PG 194; PG coll. cat. 127

In its abstraction of the human figure and exaggeration of isolated anatomical features, this work is related to African sculpture and to the Surrealist sculpture of Picasso and Giacometti. Within Moore's own body of work, *Three Standing Figures* can be seen in connection with the "shelter" drawings of the early 1940s, in which the artist explored the psychological interaction of groups, and with the monumental *Three Standing Figures* of 1947-49 erected at Battersea Park in London. Classicizing elements of the latter, however remote, endure in the Guggenheim work. The grouping of three figures, their contrapposto stances, the variety of rhetorical gestures and the echoes of drapery creases and swags provide visual analogies with ancient sources. Typically, Moore conflates the human figure with the forms of inanimate natural materials such as bone and rock. The perforations through the mass of the sculptured bodies suggest a slow process of erosion by water or wind.

At least three preparatory drawings exist for *Three Standing Figures,* which was cast in bronze from a plaster original in an edition of eight, with one artist's proof (discussed and repr. Rudenstine, p. 580). A ten-inch maquette preceding it in 1952 was also cast in bronze. Neither of the original plasters survives. Moore used bronze increasingly from the late 1940s; he has commented on its greater flexibility in comparison with stone, and its relative strength in withstanding the action of the elements.

L.F.

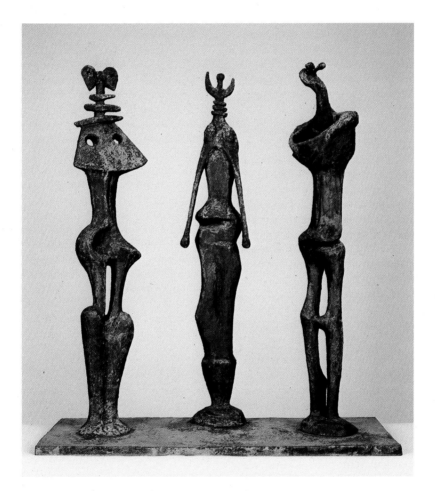

Yves Tanguy 1900-1955

Raymond Georges Yves Tanguy was born on January 5, 1900, in Paris. While attending lycée during the teens, he met Pierre Matisse, his future dealer and lifelong friend. In 1918 he joined the Merchant Marine and traveled to Africa, South America and England. During military service at Lunéville in 1920, Tanguy became a friend of the poet Jacques Prévert. He returned to Paris in 1922 after volunteer service in Tunis and began sketching café scenes that were praised by Maurice de Vlaminck. After Tanguy saw de Chirico's work in 1923, he decided to become a painter. In 1924 he, Prévert and Marcel Duhamel moved into a house that was to become a gathering place for the Surrealists. Tanguy became interested in Surrealism in 1924 when he saw the periodical *La Révolution Surréaliste*. André Breton welcomed him into the Surrealist group the following year.

Despite his lack of formal training, Tanguy's art developed quickly and his mature style emerged by 1927. His first one-man show was held in 1927 at the Galerie Surréaliste in Paris. In 1928 he participated with Arp, Ernst, André Masson, Miró, Picasso and others in the Surrealist exhibition at the Galerie Au Sacre du Printemps, Paris. Tanguy incorporated into his work the images of geological formations he had observed during a trip to Africa in 1930. He exhibited extensively during the 1930s in one-man and Surrealist group shows in New York, Brussels, Paris and London.

In 1939 Tanguy met the painter Kay Sage in Paris and later that year traveled with her to the American Southwest. They married in 1940 and settled in Woodbury, Connecticut. In 1942 Tanguy participated in the *Artists in Exile* show at the Pierre Matisse Gallery in New York, where he exhibited frequently until 1950. In 1947 his work was included in the exhibition *Le Surréalisme en 1947*, organized by Breton and Duchamp at the Galerie Maeght in Paris. He became a United States citizen in 1948. In 1953 he visited Rome, Milan and Paris on the occasion of his one-man shows in those cities. The following year he shared an exhibition with Kay Sage at the Wadsworth Atheneum in Hartford and appeared in Hans Richter's film *8 x 8*. A retrospective of Tanguy's work was held at The Museum of Modern Art in New York eight months after his death on January 15, 1955, in Woodbury.

81 Promontory Palace. 1931

Oil on canvas, 28¾ x 23⅜" (73 x 60 cm.)
76.2553 PG 94; PG coll. cat. 166

Following his trip to Africa in 1930, Tanguy produced a group of landscapes that have been termed *"les coulées"* (or flowing forms) for their molten character. Other paintings in this sequence include *Neither Legends nor Figures*, ca. 1930 (Private Collection, United States), and *The Armoire of Proteus*, 1931 (Private Collection, Paris).* Perhaps the most striking of the series is *Promontory Palace,* in which a rigid multitiered mass dominates a broad, flat plain. This corrugated mesa and other buttes in the center foreground stand firm as the surrounding viscous landscape succumbs to some persistent melting force. The small abstract shapes that inhabit the scene are in various stages of metamorphosis: some appear to melt or ooze, others seem to collapse or deflate and still others secrete or sputter white liquids or gases. Some of these shapes are disturbingly anthropomorphic. A line of globular forms marches down the incline of the promontory to the edge of a cliff, where two forms have already surrendered and begun to melt over the precipice to join the sea of flowing matter below. A five-fingered, bulbous white mass glides over the ground as if on water. Elsewhere steam emerges, both from the pipe-shaped form at the base of the promontory, and from the distant horizon. On the highest peak, or the palace, mysterious sparks emanate from a thornlike tower. To the right a hairlike apparition disappears into the thin atmosphere of an empty sky.

In the natural world such geologic metamorphosis would require intense heat and volcanic activity. Yet Tanguy's restrained grays and muted pinks, accented with cool blue and pale green and yellow, deny the presence of fire and earth. Instead, Tanguy creates a Surrealist terrain where molten and frozen, figurative and abstract, literal and suggestive elements exist in perfect harmony. Tanguy's use of a specific horizon line, his naturalistic modeling of forms and his depiction of landscape evocative of an actual coastline, permit us a conceptual foothold in known experience. Yet our foothold gives way as Tanguy's abstract shapes transform known experience into a familiar but irrational fantasy. The power of Tanguy's imagery derives from the delicate tension he creates between the logic of sensation and the freedom of imagination.

* For further discussion of this sequence, see *Yves Tanguy: Retrospective (1925-1955)*, exh. cat., Paris, 1982, pp. 50-52, 103-105.

E.C.C.

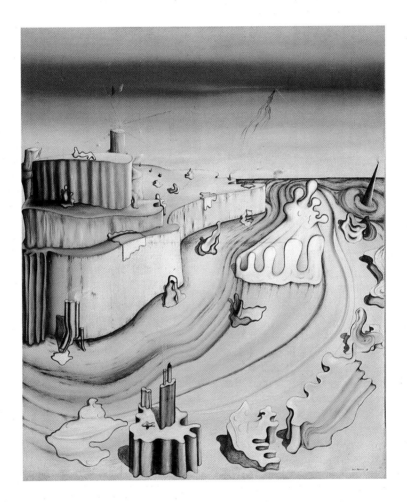

82 The Sun in Its Jewel Case. 1937

Oil on canvas, 45 ⅞₁₆ x 34¹¹⁄₁₆″ (115.4 x 88.1 cm.)
76.2553 PG 95; PG coll. cat. 167

Tanguy arrived at his lunar or submarine morphology
in about 1927, and spent the rest of his artistic career
exploring and elaborating it without changing its essential character. His compositions, arrived at in an unpremeditated manner directly on the canvas, recall the
landscape of Locronan, in the French province of Brittany, where he spent childhood summers at a house
owned by his parents. The repertory of memory was
augmented by his experience of Africa during a trip of
the early 1930s. After this his light becomes clear and
strong and the color schemes more complex. Vegetal
forms are replaced by mineral formations. Dolmens
and menhirs, stone remnants of prehistoric ages, and
fossilized bones are smoothed and tinted in the dream
spaces of his canvases. The assertive shadows cast in
these landscapes recall those of de Chirico, whose example had inspired Tanguy to take up painting in 1923.

The spatial paradox of *The Sun in Its Jewel Case* de-
pends on the merging of sky and earth, achieved
through the continuous gradation of color over the
surface—there is no horizon line—and the device of a
diagonal line of forms shown receding in perspective
from lower right to upper left. Acute angles are suggested throughout, by the placement of objects, by the
relationship of shadows to objects, or by the things
themselves. Geometric precision and a minutely detailed academic technique, in which careful modeling
lends plastic solidity to form, heighten the poetic
strangeness of Tanguy's world.

L.F.

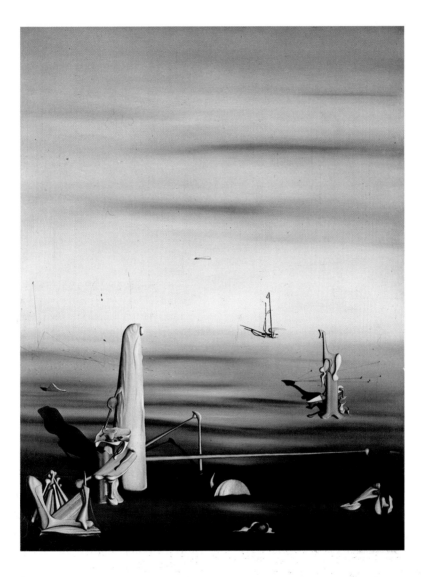

83 Untitled. 1938

Gouache on paper. 3¹¹⁄₁₆ x 9³⁄₁₆″ (9.3 x 23.3 cm.)
76.2553 PG 96; PG coll. cat. 168

In this gouache six abstract forms occupy a space in which the ground merges imperceptibly with the air, the horizon suggested only by a purplish band of atmosphere bisecting the landscape. Converging diagonal lines on the left suggest the orthogonals of a linear perspective system. Yet the receding wavy lines stop short of uniting at a vanishing point, leaving the viewer to complete the ordering of the space in his imagination. A hidden light source casts hard-edged black shadows on the empty ground. The bleached quality of light recalls the intensity and clarity of desert sun which had so impressed Tanguy on his trip to Africa in 1930.

The six forms that inhabit the landscape are arranged in pairs. The two white boxlike forms on the far left sit erect, transmitting some kind of energy or sound from raised antennae. In the middle of the composition, Tanguy paints two horizontal, attenuated configurations in the gray shades of bones or driftwood and in the brown hues of stone. The reclining form with interpenetrating limbs in the right foreground is the most anthropomorphic element. The white strokes that surround its head and disturb the ground at its base may suggest either a slight breeze or a languid movement of the mass toward the left. Two tiny spheres appear in the background, their position unclear in this ambiguous space. Although this picture is extremely small, Tanguy's emphasis on its horizontal dimension results in a sense of vast space.

Tanguy executed several small gouaches with similar imagery as independent works in the late 1930s. Fond of working on an almost miniature scale, he also painted a pair of tiny landscapes on oval earrings for Peggy Guggenheim in 1938.* These earrings and our gouache share an arrangement of bonelike forms in a horizonless landscape, and the presence of tiny spheres in the background. In the earrings as well as the present work, Tanguy required only a minimal surface to project his visions of measureless space.

* Reproduced in P. Guggenheim, *Out of This Century: Confessions of an Art Addict,* New York, 1979, p. 194.

E.C.C.

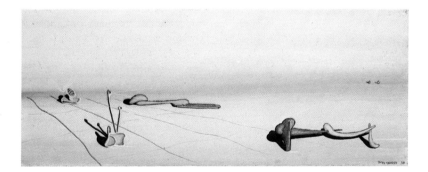

84 In an Indeterminate Place. March 1941

Oil on canvas, 16¹⁵⁄₁₆ x 28⅛″ (43 x 71.4 cm.)
76.2553 PG 98; PG coll. cat. 169

After Tanguy settled in the United States in 1940, his
palette intensified, his abstract forms became more complex and interdependent, and he occasionally worked
on larger canvases than he had previously used. The
first two of these stylistic developments are evident in
the present painting. Fully saturated hues of blue, green,
red and pink appear in addition to the restricted grays,
whites and blacks familiar from his earlier works such
as *Promontory Palace* of 1931 and our untitled gouache
of 1938 (cat. nos. 81, 83). More sweeping brushwork
animates the sky in the present picture and a more
varied terrain characterizes the foreground. The four
distinct configurations that people the landscape show
a new ambition in their wide variety and intricacy of
interlocking shapes.

Breton's poetic description of Tanguy's art as filled
with the "desert's dazzling furniture" is particularly apt
here. The shapes in the foreground simultaneously
suggest animate figures and their places of repose: biomorphic and architectonic features intermingle in odd
society. A thin white line and small secondary forms
scattered on the ground unite the major groups. Similar
connecting devices appear in contemporaneous landscapes by Tanguy such as *Earth and Air,* 1941 (Collection The Baltimore Museum of Art). In these paintings,
as in the present work, Tanguy also distinguishes air
from ground by contrasting blue sky with pervasive
black regions of earth and shadow.

The French title of this picture, *En Lieu oblique,* is
difficult to translate. *In an Indeterminate Place* suggests that the landscape evokes some undefined locale
but describes no particular site. Another translation,
On Slanting Ground, conveys the sense of a tilted foreground that merges with distant background. But neither
translation offers a literal explanation of the imagery.
Tanguy was reluctant to attach specific labels or interpretations to his works, lest he risk enclosing himself in
a definition that could soon become a "prison" for him.*

* See letter from Tanguy to E. Genauer, dated June 20, 1947,
quoted in Rudenstine, p. 715.

E.C.C.

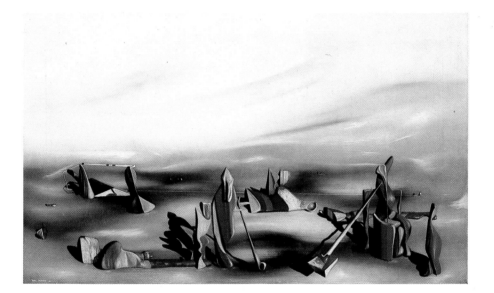

René Magritte 1898-1967

René François Ghislain Magritte was born on November 21, 1898, in Lessines, Belgium. He studied intermittently between 1916 and 1918 at the Académie Royale des Beaux-Arts in Brussels. Magritte first exhibited at the Centre d'Art in Brussels in 1920. After completing military service in 1921, he worked briefly as a designer in a wallpaper factory. In 1923 he participated with Lissitzky, Moholy-Nagy, Feininger and the Belgian Paul Joostens in an exhibition at the Cercle Royal Artistique in Antwerp. In 1924 he collaborated with E.L.T. Mesens on the review *Oesophage*.

In 1927 Magritte was given his first solo exhibition at the Galerie Le Centaure in Brussels. Later that year the artist left Brussels to establish himself in Le Perreux-sur-Marne, near Paris, where he frequented the Surrealist circle, which included Paul Eluard, André Breton, Arp, Miró and Dalí. In 1928 Magritte took part in the *Exposition Surréaliste* at the Galerie Goemans in Paris. He returned to Belgium in 1930, and three years later was given a one-man show at the Palais des Beaux-Arts in Brussels. Magritte's first solo exhibition in the United States took place at the Julien Levy Gallery in New York in 1936, and the first in England at the London Gallery in London in 1938; he was represented as well in the 1936 *Fantastic Art, Dada, Surrealism* exhibition at The Museum of Modern Art in New York.

Throughout the 1940s Magritte showed frequently at the Galerie Dietrich in Brussels. During the following two decades he executed various mural commissions in Belgium. From 1953 he exhibited frequently at the galleries of Alexander Iolas in New York, Paris and Geneva. Magritte retrospectives were held in 1954 at the Palais des Beaux-Arts in Brussels and in 1960 at the Museum for Contemporary Arts, Dallas, and The Museum of Fine Arts in Houston. On the occasion of his retrospective at The Museum of Modern Art in New York in 1965, Magritte traveled to the United States for the first time, and the following year he visited Israel. Magritte died on August 15, 1967, in Brussels, shortly after the opening of a major exhibition of his work at the Museum Boymans-van Beuningen in Rotterdam.

85 Voice of Space. 1931

Oil on canvas, 28⅝ x 21⅜" (72.7 x 54.2 cm.)
76.2553 PG 101; PG coll. cat. 102

Influenced by de Chirico, Magritte sought to strip objects of their usual functions and meanings in order to convey an irrationally compelling image. In *Voice of Space* (of which three other oil versions exist), the bells float in the air; elsewhere they occupy human bodies or replace blossoms on bushes. By distorting the scale, weight and use of an ordinary object and inserting it into a variety of unaccustomed contexts, Magritte confers on that object a fetishistic intensity. He has written of the jingle bell, a motif that recurs often in his work: "I caused the iron bells hanging from the necks of our admirable horses to sprout like dangerous plants at the edge of an abyss."[*]

The disturbing impact of the bells presented in an unfamiliar setting is intensified by the cool academic precision with which they and their environment are painted. The dainty slice of landscape could be the backdrop of an early Renaissance painting, while the bells themselves, in their rotund and glowing monumentality, impart a mysterious resonance.

[*] Quoted in S. Gablik, *Magritte*, Greenwich, Conn., 1970, p. 183.

L.F.

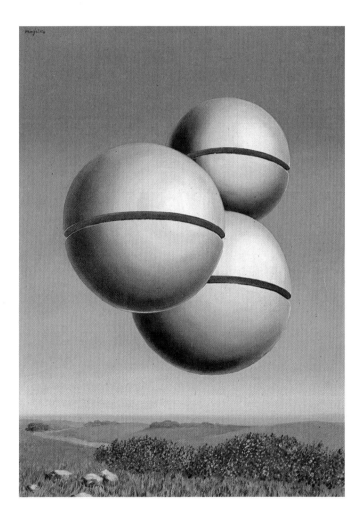

86 Empire of Light. 1953-54

Oil on canvas, 76¹⁵⁄₁₆ x 51⅝″ (195.4 x 131.2 cm.)
76.2553 PG 102; PG coll. cat. 103

In *Empire of Light,* numerous versions of which exist
(see, for example, those at The Museum of Modern Art,
New York, and the Musées Royaux des Beaux-Arts de
Belgique, Brussels), a dark, nocturnal street scene is
set against a pastel blue, light-drenched sky spotted
with fluffy cumulus clouds. With no fantastic element
other than the single paradoxical combination of day
and night, Magritte upsets a fundamental organizing
premise of life. Sunlight, ordinarily the source of clarity,
here causes the confusion and unease traditionally associated with darkness. The luminosity of the sky becomes unsettling, making the empty darkness below
even more impenetrable than it would seem in a normal
context. The bizarre subject is treated in an impersonal,
precise style, typical of veristic Surrealist painting and
preferred by Magritte since the mid-1920s.

L.F.

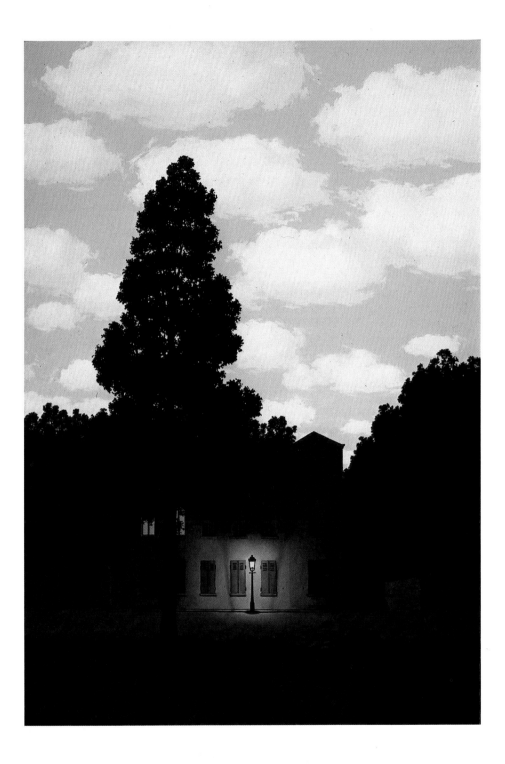

Salvador Dalí b. 1904

Dalí was born Salvador Felipe Jacinto Dalí y Domenech in the Catalonian town of Figueras, Spain, on May 11, 1904. In·1921 he enrolled in the Real Academia de Bellas Artes de San Fernando in Madrid, where he became a friend of the poet Federico García Lorca and Luis Buñuel. His first one-man show was held in 1925 at the Galeries Dalmau in Barcelona. In 1926 Dalí was expelled from the Academia and the following year he visited Paris and met Picasso. He collaborated with Buñuel on the film *Un Chien Andalou* in 1928. At the end of the year he returned to Paris and met Tristan Tzara and Paul Eluard. About this time Dalí produced his first Surrealist paintings and met André Breton and Louis Aragon. He worked with Buñuel and Ernst on the film *L'Age d'or* in 1930. During the 1930s the artist contributed to various Surrealist publications and illustrated the works of Surrealist writers and poets. His first one-man show in the United States took place at the Julien Levy Gallery in New York in 1933.

Dalí was censured by the Surrealists in 1934. Toward the end of the decade he made several trips to Italy to study the art of the sixteenth and seventeenth centuries. In 1940 Dalí fled to the United States, where he worked on theatrical productions, wrote, illustrated books and painted. A major retrospective of his work opened in 1941 at The Museum of Modern Art in New York and traveled through the United States. In 1942 Dalí published his autobiography and began exhibiting at M. Knoedler and Co. in New York. He returned to Europe in 1948, settling in Port Lligat, Spain. His first paintings with religious subjects date from 1948-49. In 1954 a Dalí retrospective was held at the Palazzo Pallavicini in Rome and in 1964 an important retrospective of his work was shown in Tokyo, Nagoya and Kyoto. He continued painting, writing and illustrating during the late 1960s. The Salvador Dali Museum in Cleveland was inaugurated in 1971, and the Dalinian Holographic Room opened at M. Knoedler and Co., New York, in 1973. In 1980 a major Dalí retrospective was held at the Musée National d'Art Moderne, Centre Georges Pompidou, in Paris, and his work was exhibited at the Tate Gallery, London. The artist now lives in Port Lligat.

87 Untitled. 1931

Oil on canvas, 10¹¹⁄₁₆ x 13¾″ (27.2 x 35 cm.)
76.2553 PG 99; PG coll. cat. 40

Dalí's Surrealist landscape combines meticulous optical realism with an elaboration of irrational detail in enigmatic contexts, a style he justified as follows: "My whole ambition . . . is to materialize the images of concrete irrationality with the most imperialist fury of precision.—In order that the world of the imagination and of concrete irrationality may be as objectively evident, of the same consistency, of the same durability, of the same persuasive cognoscitive and communicable thickness as that of the exterior world of phenomenal reality."*

This landscape relates to a series of paintings from 1930-31 of nude or draped figures, whose bodies are often partially composed of shells and pebbles. These figures appear on rocky, desolate beaches which may be inspired by Dalí's native Cadaqués. The high horizon lines, broad expanses of empty space, precisely rendered detail and palettes of restricted tonalities of these pictures all reveal the influence of Tanguy's style on Dalí. Unlike Tanguy's abstract biomorphic forms, however, Dalí's imagery is identifiable. In the present example the woman, whose body is cropped at the hips, cryptically turns away from the viewer, offering only a view of her back and of her head, which is hollowed into a concavity that overflows with sea shells and rocks. Her rib cage serves as a platform for a collection of small pebbles, and the remnants of her hair have congealed into a solid, undulating mass. Dalí charges the scene with erotic implications: the nude's wrist is tied to a feeble branch by a thin dangling rope; on the horizon a faceless white figure peeps tentatively from a hiding place among the rocks.

Dalí's substitution of shells for the woman's head and hair may relate to personal experience. When his father banished him from the family, Dalí shaved his head, buried the hair with empty sea-urchin shells and climbed into the nearby hills of Cadaqués to meditate on the landscape of his youth.** The distant figure's contemplation of the beach from a rocky viewpoint may resonate with Dalí's memories of emotional trauma. But such imagery is, at most, only partly autobiographical, and carries the broader themes of isolation, unfulfillment, sexual longing and metamorphosis through imagination found in Dalí's landscapes of this period (see Rudenstine, pp. 195-196).

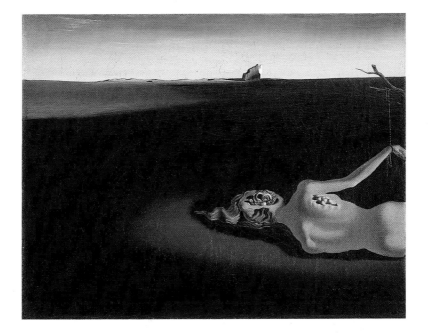

 * Quoted in W. Rubin, *Dada, Surrealism, and Their Heritage*, exh. cat., New York, 1968, p. 111.

** S. Dalí, *La Vie secrète de Salvador Dalí*, Paris, 1952, pp. 196-197.

E.C.C.

88 Birth of Liquid Desires. 1931-32

Oil and collage on canvas, 37⅞ x 44¼″ (96.1 x 112.3 cm.)
76.2553 PG 100; PG coll. cat. 41

By the time Dalí joined the Surrealist group in 1929, he had formulated his "paranoid-critical" approach to art, which consisted in conveying his deepest psychological conflicts to the viewer in the hopes of eliciting an empathetic response. He embodied this theoretical approach in a fastidiously detailed painting style. One of his hallucinatory obsessions was the legend of William Tell, which represented for him the archetypal theme of paternal assault.* The subject occurs frequently in his paintings from 1929, when he entered into a liaison with Gala Eluard, his future wife, against his father's wishes. Dalí felt an acute sense of rejection during the early 1930s because of his father's attitude toward him.

Here father, son and perhaps mother seem to be fused in the grotesque dream-image of the hermaphroditic creature at center. William Tell's apple is replaced by a loaf of bread, with attendant castration symbolism. (Elsewhere Dalí uses a lamb chop to suggest his father's cannibalistic impulses.) Out of the bread arises a lugubrious cloud vision inspired by the imagery of Böcklin. In one of the recesses of this cloud is an enigmatic inscription in French: *Consigne: gâcher l'ardoise totale?*

Reference to the remote past seems to be made in the two forlorn figures shown in the distant left background, which may convey Dalí's memory of the fond communion of father and child. The infinite expanse of landscape recalls Tanguy's work of the 1920s. The biomorphic structure dominating the composition suggests at once a violin, the weathered rock formations of Port Lligat on the eastern coast of Spain, the architecture of the Catalan visionary Antoni Gaudí, the sculpture of Arp, a prehistoric monster and an artist's palette. The form has an antecedent in Dalí's own work in the gigantic vision of his mother in *The Enigma of Desire* of 1929 (Collection Staatsgalerie moderner Kunst, Munich). The repressed, guilty desire of the central figure is indicated by its attitude of both protestation and arousal toward the forbidden flower-headed woman (presumably Gala). The shadow darkening the scene is cast by an object outside the picture and may represent the father's threatening presence, or a more general prescience of doom, the advance of age or the extinction of life.

* S. Dalí interviewed by P. Hultén, "L'Enigme de Salvador Dali," *XXe Siècle*, no. 74, Dec. 1974, p. 92.

L.F.

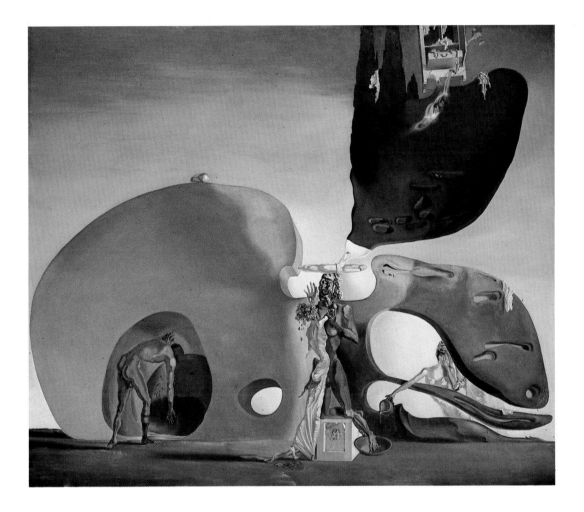

Paul Delvaux b. 1897

Paul Delvaux was born on September 23, 1897, in Antheit, Belgium. At the Académie Royale des Beaux-Arts in Brussels he studied architecture from 1916 to 1917 and decorative painting from 1918 to 1919. During the early 1920s he was influenced by Ensor and Gustave De Smet. In 1936 Delvaux shared an exhibition at the Palais des Beaux-Arts in Brussels with Magritte, a fellow member of the Belgian group *Les Compagnons de l'Art.*

Delvaux was given one-man exhibitions in 1938 at the Palais des Beaux-Arts, Brussels, and the London Gallery in London, the latter organized by E.L.T. Mesens and Roland Penrose. That same year he participated in the *Exposition International du Surréalisme* at the Galerie des Beaux-Arts in Paris, organized by Breton and Eluard, and an exhibition of the same title at the Galerie Robert in Amsterdam. The artist visited Italy in 1938 and 1939. His first retrospective was held at the Palais des Beaux-Arts in Brussels in 1944-45. Delvaux executed stage designs for Jean Genet's *Adame Miroire* in 1947 and collaborated with Eluard on the book *Poèmes, peintures et dessins,* published in Geneva and Paris the next year. After a brief sojourn in France in 1949, the following year he was appointed professor at the Ecole Supérieure d'Art et d'Architecture in Brussels, a position he retained until 1962. From the early 1950s he executed a number of mural commissions in Belgium. About the middle of the decade Delvaux settled in Boitsfort, and in 1956 he traveled to Greece.

From 1965 to 1966 Delvaux served as President and Director of the Académie Royale des Beaux-Arts of Belgium, and about this time he produced his first lithographs. Retrospectives of his work were held at the Palais des Beaux-Arts in Lille in 1965, at the Musée des Arts Décoratifs in Paris in 1969 and at the Museum Boymans-van Beuningen in Rotterdam in 1973. Also in 1973 he was awarded the Rembrandt Prize of the Johann Wolfgang Stiftung. A Delvaux retrospective was shown at The National Museum of Modern Art in Tokyo and The National Museum of Modern Art of Kyoto in 1975. In 1977 he became an associate member of the Académie des Beaux-Arts of France. Delvaux lives and works in Brussels.

89 The Break of Day. July 1937

Oil on canvas, 47¼ x 59¼" (120 x 150.5 cm.)
76.2553 PG 103; PG coll. cat. 44

Like his compatriot Magritte, Delvaux applied a fastidious, detailed technique to scenes deriving their impact from unsettling incongruities of subject. Influenced by de Chirico, he frequently included classicizing details and used perspectival distortion to create rapid, plunging movement from foreground to deep background. Unique to Delvaux is the silent, introspective cast of figures he developed during the mid-1930s. His formidable, buxom nude or seminude women pose immobile with unfocused gazes, their arms frozen in rhetorical gestures, dominating a world through which men, preoccupied and timid, unobstrusively make their way.

Although the fusion of woman and tree in the present picture invites comparison with Greek mythological subjects, the artist has insisted that no such references were intended (Rudenstine, p. 216). The motif of the mirror appears in 1936 in works such as *Woman in a Grotto* (Collection Thyssen-Bornemisza, Lugano) and *The Mirror* (formerly Collection Roland Penrose, London; destroyed during World War II). In *The Break of Day* a new element is introduced; the reflected figure is not present within the scene, but exists outside the canvas field. She is, therefore, in some sense, the viewer, even if that viewer should happen to be male. The irony of the circumstance in which a clothed male viewer could see himself reflected as a nude female torso would have particularly appealed to Duchamp, who appropriated the detail of the mirror in his collage of 1942, *In the Manner of Delvaux* (Collection Vera and Arturo Schwarz, Milan; repr. Rudenstine, p. 217).

L.F.

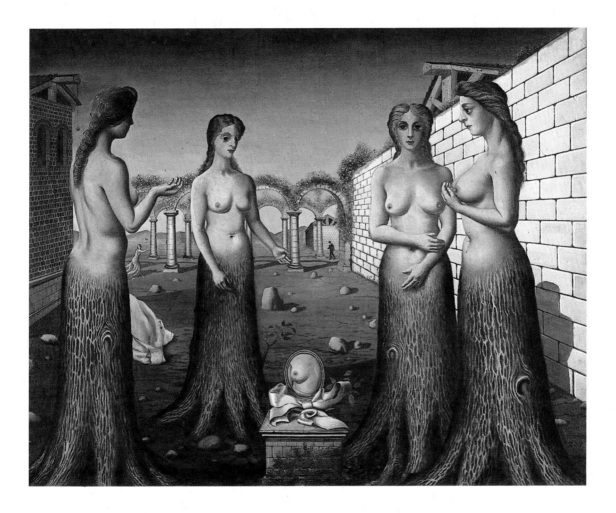

Victor Brauner 1903-1966

Victor Brauner was born on June 15, 1903, in Piatra-Neamt, Rumania. His father was involved in spiritualism and sent Brauner to evangelical school in Braïla from 1916 to 1918. In 1921 he briefly attended the School of Fine Arts in Bucharest, where he painted Cézannesque landscapes. He exhibited paintings in his subsequent expressionist style at his first one-man show at the Galerie Mozart in Bucharest in 1924. Brauner helped found the Dadaist review *75 HP* in Bucharest. He went to Paris in 1925 but returned to Bucharest approximately a year later. In Bucharest in 1929 Brauner was associated with the Dadaist and Surrealist review *UNU*.

Brauner settled in Paris in 1930 and became a friend of his compatriot Brancusi. Then he met Tanguy who introduced him to the Surrealists by 1933. Breton wrote an enthusiastic introduction to the catalogue for Brauner's first Parisian one-man show at the Galerie Pierre in 1934. The exhibition was not well-received, and in 1935 Brauner returned to Bucharest where he remained until 1938. That year he moved to Paris, lived briefly with Tanguy and painted a number of works featuring distorted human figures with mutilated eyes. Some of these paintings, dated as early as 1931, proved gruesomely prophetic when he lost his own eye in a scuffle in 1938. At the outset of World War II Brauner fled to the south of France, where he maintained contact with other Surrealists in Marseille. Later he sought refuge in Switzerland; unable to obtain suitable materials there, he improvised an encaustic from candle wax and developed a graffito technique.

Brauner returned to Paris in 1945. He was included in the *Exposition Internationale du Surréalisme* at the Galerie Maeght in Paris in 1947. His postwar painting incorporated forms and symbols based on Tarot cards, Egyptian hieroglyphics and antique Mexican codices. In the fifties Brauner traveled to Normandy and Italy, and his work was shown at the Venice Biennale in 1954 and in 1966. He died in Paris on March 12, 1966.

90 The Surrealist. January 1947

Oil on canvas, 23⅝ x 17¾″ (60 x 45 cm.)
76.2553 PG 111; PG coll. cat. 21

In *The Surrealist* Brauner borrows motifs from the tarot to create a portrait of himself as a young man. The tarot, a set of seventy-eight illustrated cards used in fortune telling, was a subject of widespread interest to Brauner and other Surrealists. Four of these cards, for example, appeared on Derain's cover for the December 1933 issue of *Minotaure*. A group including Brauner even produced a deck of cards in 1940-41 which was probably a tarot. One tarot card, the Juggler (the first card in the Marseille tarot deck; repr. Rudenstine, p. 135), provided Brauner with a key prototype for his self-portrait: the Surrealist's large hat, medieval costume and the position of his arms all derive from this figure who, like Brauner's subject, stands behind a table displaying a knife, a goblet and coins.* The tarot Juggler appropriately symbolizes the creativity of the Surrealist poet, for it refers to the capacity of each individual to create his own personality through intelligence, wit and initiative, and thus to play with his own future, as the juggler manipulates his baton.

In another tarot deck known as the Waite tarot, the first card of the Major Arcana is the Magician rather than the Juggler, although both share many attributes. A sign of infinity, ∞ (the symbol of life), that appears above the Magician's head is also depicted on the hat of Brauner's Surrealist. Drawing on the Juggler-Magician prototype, Brauner illustrates the traditional signs of the four suits in the tarot deck: wands, cups, swords and coins (symbols of the elements of natural life—fire, water, air and earth, respectively). These objects and all natural life are controlled by the Juggler, just as all creative life is at the disposal of the Surrealist poet, who wields his pen as the Juggler brandishes his wand.

Brauner depicted the Juggler and a Popess (a figure from the Marseille Tarot) in another painting of 1947, *The Lovers* (Private Collection, Paris). The inscriptions at either side of that canvas, *Past—Present—Future* and *Fate/Necessity—Will/Magic—Surreality/Liberty,* are written in Brauner's hand on the back of the Peggy Guggenheim canvas. These inscriptions convey the artist's belief that Surrealism could be a path to artistic freedom.

* See N. and E. Calas, *The Peggy Guggenheim Collection of Modern Art*, New York, 1966, pp. 123-124 and Rudenstine,

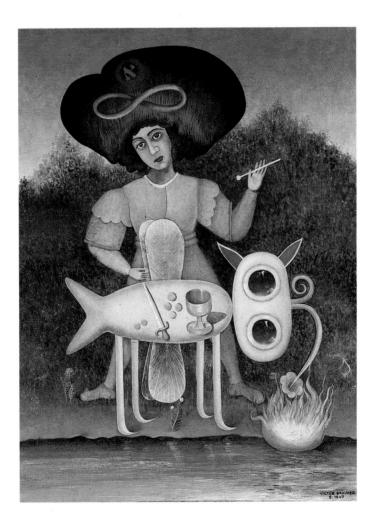

pp. 135-136. Cynthia Goodman's unpublished notes on
The Surrealist offer the most complete discussion of this
tarot iconography.

E.C.C.

91 Téléventré. 1948

Encaustic on board, 28½ x 23⅝" (72.5 x 60 cm.)
76.2553 PG 112; PG coll. cat. 22

Brauner, who was influenced by Surrealism during the
mid-1930s, sought to penetrate his unconscious to discover its fundamental imagery and governing impulses.
His works are a plastic manifestation of this exploration, expressed in primitivizing, iconic forms. In *Téléventré* Brauner uses the primary image of the mother
as devourer and generator, the source of all conflict and
resolution. The erect phallus labeled *Maman* may refer
to the paradoxical identity of male and female in the
moment of conception, the suppressed but urgent inces-
tual longing of son for mother, or the influence of the
mother on the child's sexual development. The metamorphic nature of gestation and growth is translated
into a Surrealist language—the male child enters the
womb as if swallowed by a long-necked animal and
appears to emerge from it through the mouth of another
as a female; the female is seized by the hybrid form of
a bird doubling as the mother's head.* Formally, the
work is characterized by compositional simplicity,
frontality and the rough, layered surface of Brauner's
paintings on wax, several others of which are in the
Peggy Guggenheim Collection.

* For discussion of the relationship of the imagery to Alfred
  Jarry's 'Pataphysics, see Rudenstine, pp. 139-140.

L.F.

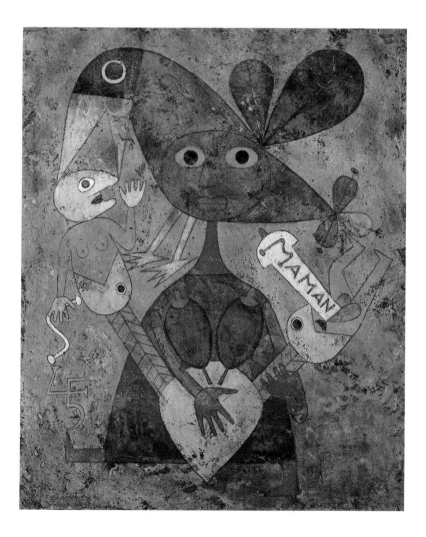

92 Consciousness of Shock. April 1951

Encaustic on board, 25¼ x 31½″ (64 x 80 cm.)
76.2553 PG 113; PG coll. cat. 23

A symbolic struggle is expressed between the human
and bird halves of the hybrid form in *Consciousness of
Shock*, in which Brauner portrays a complex boat-
shaped figure in the course of battling for control of
itself. Drawn in the schematic profile style of Egyptian
hieroglyphs, a large androgynous head unites with the
raised prow of a boat elaborated with breasts. The
body of the vessel, directed by rudderlike legs and feet,
merges at the stern with the upright body of a bird.
Two powerful hands, at the ends of crossed arms, sup-
press the internal battle by restraining the limbs of the
bird, while a third hand doggedly forges progress along
the river by paddling. Thus, in keeping with the nature
of much psychic conflict, a difficult internal struggle
is self-contained, while the vessel-self continues along
a predetermined route.

Nicolas Calas has suggested that Brauner was inspired
by two Egyptian themes, the "Sun Barge" and the
"Heavenly Vault," in the creation of this image.* While
a generalized Egyptian style undoubtedly influenced
Brauner's imagery, it seems more likely that the artist
derived this fantastic visual vocabulary from his own
imagination, rather from specific art-historical sources
(see Rudenstine, p. 142).

* N. and E. Calas, *The Peggy Guggenheim Collection of
Modern Art,* New York, 1966, pp. 124-125.

E.C.C.

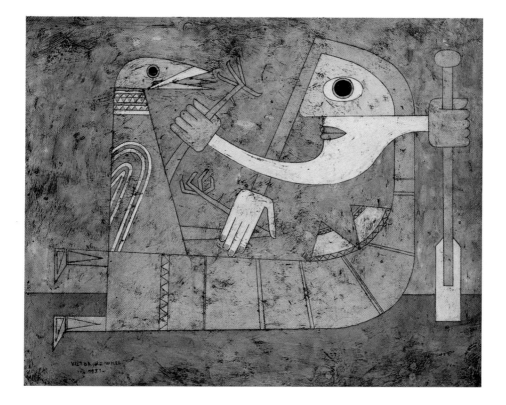

André Masson b. 1896

André Masson was born on January 4, 1896, in Balagny-sur-Oise, France. He studied at the Académie Royale des Beaux-Arts in Brussels and the Ecole Nationale Supérieure des Beaux-Arts in Paris. Masson settled in Paris in 1920. Two years later he met D.-H. Kahnweiler, who served as his principal dealer until 1931. His first one-man show was held at Kahnweiler's Galerie Simon in Paris in 1924. That same year Masson met André Breton and joined the Surrealist group, with which he was initially affiliated until 1928. During his first Surrealist period, Masson made automatic drawings and paintings and experimented with sand paintings. At this time he began to explore violent and erotic themes and was influenced by Analytical Cubism. He illustrated books and his works were reproduced regularly in the magazine *La Révolution Surréaliste*. In 1925 he participated in the first Surrealist exhibition, at the Galerie Pierre in Paris. Two years later he met Giacometti and executed his first sculpture.

After breaking with the Surrealists, Masson worked in various idioms: progressing from violent and erotic themes interpreted with increasingly abstract forms to more figurative landscapes to massacre subjects and finally, when he lived in Spain from 1934 to 1936, Spanish subjects. In 1933 the artist designed sets and costumes for the *Ballets Russes*. Thereafter he frequently designed for the theater, the opera and the ballet. Masson returned to Paris in 1936, and the following year reconciled with the Surrealists. In 1941 he fled German-occupied France for America, where he settled in New Preston, Connecticut. His first major museum exhibition took place at The Baltimore Museum of Art in 1941. During his sojourn in America, Masson showed frequently with artists in exile, for example at the opening exhibition of Peggy Guggenheim's Art of This Century in New York, and delivered lectures on modern art. In 1943 he made his final break with Breton and with official Surrealism.

The artist returned to France in 1945. In the succeeding years he painted landscapes as well as abstract works and continued to explore the violent and erotic imagery of his early years. *Plaisir de peindre*, a volume of Masson's collected writings, was published in 1950. In 1965, at the request of André Malraux and Jean-Louis Barrault, he decorated the ceiling of the Odéon, Théâtre de France, in Paris. In 1976 The Museum of Modern Art in New York held a major Masson retrospective. Masson now lives and works in Paris and Aix-en-Provence.

93 The Armor. January-April 1925

Oil on canvas, 31¾ x 21¼″ (80.6 x 54 cm.)
76.2553 PG 106; PG coll. cat. 110

In *The Armor* Masson has appropriated the visual syntax of Analytical Cubism in his restricted palette, spatial ambiguities and stippled brushwork. He charges his nude subject, however, with an explicit eroticism that is decidedly Surrealist. Masson concentrates on the female torso, not only eliminating limbs, but brutally severing the head from the body. The title suggests that this female form is impregnable, an object of frustrated desire. Perhaps an ironic pun is implied by the French title, *L'Armure*, a word closely resembling *l'amour* which means passion and is the French name of the mythological deity Eros. Masson painted *The Armor* during his initial association with the Surrealist circle, when he first strove to bring philosophical ideas into painting. He described its imagery: "This feminine armor has a crystalline appearance. The head is replaced by a flame. The neck cut. The sexual area with an open pomegranate: the only fruit that bleeds. A bird approaches the armpit (the nest). The armed body is encircled by streamers of paper that imitate the curves of the female body. . . ."*

Many of these elements occur repeatedly in Masson's paintings of 1924-25, including *Man in a Tower*, 1924 (Collection Solomon R. Guggenheim Museum, New York). Because a single motif may evoke multiple associations, a specific reading of their symbolism is problematic. The eroticism of the composition is closely tied to the presence of death. The open pomegranate in classical mythology bears double connotations of death and rebirth. From the fruit's core emerge sinuous blood-colored threads which wrap themselves around symbols of fertility: the seeds of the fruit, and the woman's thighs and abdomen, swelling with the potential of procreation. Yet elsewhere a red filament traces the wound of decapitation, and another assumes the place of a candle's flame, a motif Masson links with destruction.** The necrophilic flame licks the torso and the scroll of paper, threatening to burn and consume even as it embraces.

The connection between eroticism and death is a central motif in the writings of Georges Bataille, whom Masson met in 1924 through Michel Leiris. During 1925 the subconscious power of eroticism became a subject of general interest to Masson's circle when Bataille and Leiris recorded dreams of prostitutes for a review they intended to publish. In the same year Bataille purchased *The Armor*, and he later championed Masson's art in his periodicals, *Documents* (1929-31) and *Acéphale* (1936-37).

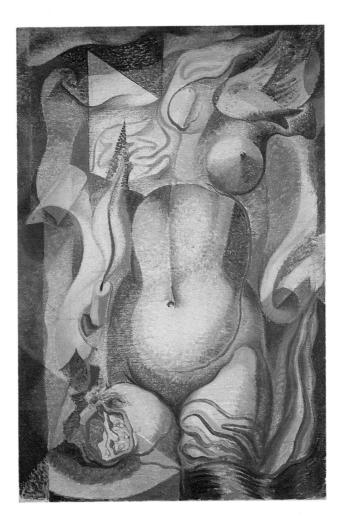

* J.-P. Clébert, *Mythologie d'André Masson*, Geneva, 1971,
  p. 32. Author's translation.

** Ibid., p. 26. For a complete discussion of these motifs in
  the context of Surrealist thought, see Rudenstine,
  pp. 521-525.

E.C.C.

94 Bird Fascinated by a Snake. 1942

Tempera on paper, 22¼ x 29¾" (56.5 x 75.5 cm.)
76.2553 PG 108; PG coll. cat. 112

Masson here depicts a charged confrontation between
a bird and a serpent. A menacing snake with enormous
teeth and spikelike horns emerges from what may be
the open mouth of another creature at the lower center
of the composition. A small red bird with wasplike
wings flutters about the head of the serpent. The two
encounter one another on a green field whose figure-
eight shape suggests the pattern of the bird's flight. The
dotted line enscribes the motion of the snake's head as it
angrily follows the darting and flitting bird. The
sketchily outlined protagonists interact on the flat plane
of the picture surface. Color and line weave behind
them to suggest the symbolic space of their motion.

Bird Fascinated by a Snake dates from Masson's stay
in America, 1941 through 1945, and belongs to the
Telluric series he began at this time. Referring to this
period, Masson stated: "My idea of America was . . .
rooted in Châteaubriand. . . . the might of Nature. . . .
What characterizes my American work is its manner of
expressing this feeling for nature."* The present work
shares the bright palette on dark ground and the zoomorphic motifs of many *Telluric* temperas. The subject is also typical of the series, which explores themes
of germination, gestation and metamorphosis in nature. The serpent's mysterious emergence from the
orifice of another creature may be inspired by Native
American mythology, a subject of great interest to
Masson's friend, André Breton, the magus of Surrealism. Masson himself frequented the American Museum
of Natural History and the Museum of the American
Indian in New York in 1941. Such visits reflected his
growing interest in what he has called the cthonic or
subterranean forces of nature—the mysteries of creation
and the metamorphosis of one natural form into another. Perhaps a metamorphosis of the snake fascinates
the bird in the present work.

Serpent and Butterfly (Collection Mr. and Mrs. Dan R.
Johnson, New York) is a similar composition in oil on
panel, which Masson probably executed a short time
after *Bird Fascinated by a Snake* (see Rudenstine,
p. 528). Here the enlarged, pugnacious head of the
serpent and the whimsical characterization of the bird
in the Peggy Guggenheim work give way to a simpler,
more abstract depiction of animals.

* Quoted in C. Lanchner, "André Masson: Origins and Development" in *André Masson*, exh. cat., New York, 1976,
p. 163.

E.C.C.

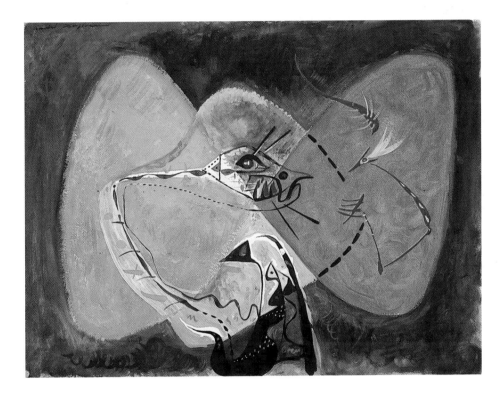

Matta b. 1911

Roberto Sebastian Antonio Matta Echaurren was born on November 11, 1911, in Santiago, Chile. After studying architecture at the Universidad Católica in Santiago, Matta went to Paris in 1934 to work as an apprentice to the architect Le Corbusier. By the mid-thirties he knew the poet Federico García Lorca, Dalí and André Breton; in 1937 he left Le Corbusier's atelier and joined the Surrealist movement. This same year Matta's drawings were included in the Surrealist exhibition at Galerie Wildenstein in Paris. In 1938 he began painting with oils, executing a series of fantastic landscapes which he called "inscapes" or "psychic morphologies."

Matta fled Europe for New York in 1939, where he associated with other Surrealist emigrés including Ernst, Tanguy, Masson and Breton. The Julien Levy Gallery in New York presented his first one-man show of paintings in 1940, and he was included in the *Artists in Exile* exhibition at the Pierre Matisse Gallery in New York in 1942. During the forties Matta's painting anticipated many innovations of the Abstract Expressionists and influenced artists such as Gorky and Motherwell. Towards the end of the war he evolved increasingly monstrous imagery; the appearance of mechanical forms and cinematic effects in Matta's work reflects the influence of Duchamp, whom he met in 1944. He broke with the Surrealists in 1948 and returned to Europe, settling in Rome in 1953. A mural for the UNESCO Building in Paris was executed by the artist in 1956.

In 1957 The Museum of Modern Art in New York gave him a major retrospective, which traveled to the Institute of Contemporary Art in Boston and the Walker Art Center in Minneapolis. His work was exhibited at the São Paulo Bienal in 1962, in Berlin in 1970 and Hannover in 1974. The artist now lives in Tarquinia, Italy, and in Paris.

95 The Dryads. 1941

Pencil and crayon on paper, 22¹⁵⁄₁₆ x 28¹⁵⁄₁₆"
(58.2 x 73.4 cm.)
76.2553 PG 109; PG coll. cat. 113

This early drawing by Matta is one of several that reflect his interest in film, particularly the process of animation. Scenes are divided by a grid that invites a sequential reading from left to right and top to bottom. The pseudomythological content is treated with Surrealist violence and distortion in quick, spontaneous pencil strokes.

In describing his notion of "psychic morphology" and how it applied to his work of this period, Matta has said, "I had all sorts of propositions, for example, I had the propositions of—morphology of meeting—the man meeting with another man in which the effect of the meeting changed the form of the one met, etc."* Such a proposition is made in this narrative, in which three dryads (wood nymphs of classical mythology) are espied by three centaurs who cavort, couple and eventually fuse with them to create new winged-creatures. One couple is isolated in the central frame, and their history is followed. Theirs is a less than harmonious transmutation, and though the creature they become struggles to fly away as the others have, its wings are abruptly amputated. In the final compartment it pulls a fire-issuing tank. The frothy color lends the work a lyrical tone at odds with the drama of the content.

* M. Kozloff, "An Interview with Matta," *Artforum*, vol. IV, Sept. 1965, p. 25.

L.F.

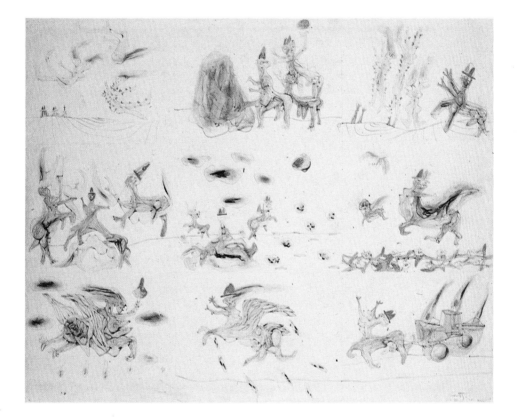

96 The Un-Nominator Renominated. 1952-53

Oil on canvas, 47⅜ x 68⅞″ (120.4 x 175 cm.)
76.2553 PG 110; PG coll. cat. 114

When Matta arrived in New York in 1939, he brought
with him a Surrealist repertory of fantastic imagery,
including a menagerie of anthropomorphic creatures
found only in drawings of his Parisian period. In America, these beasts emerged in his paintings, beginning in
1944 with a portrait of André Breton as a horned
demon. Matta's large canvases of the mid-1940s, whose
scale inspired early Abstract Expressionists, contained
numerous imaginary anthropoids with grotesque insectile heads and stiff limbs set in mechanical postures.
In paintings from the mid-1940s to the mid-1950s such
as this Peggy Guggenheim picture, these organisms, fre-
created in terms of Matta's personal cybernetics, frequently convene around transparent rectangular planes
as if engaged in futuristic board games or in directing
the control panels of arcane machines. Matta may have
been stimulated initially by Julien Levy's exhibition in
1945 on the theme of chess, which included Duchamp,
Max Ernst and Man Ray as well as Matta, who contributed a drawing. In the *Un-Nominator Renominated*
the salmon-colored figure extends its arms to a monolithic companion whose arms rest on the right edge of
the table. The game played by these beings is less important than the relationship implied between them—
the table is a device used to unite the unconnected. As
Matta said in 1955, "I use sheets of glass, transparent
planes in my paintings too. This is because I am more
interested in what exists between objects than in the
object itself, what goes on between things. . . . We must
paint man and his daily galaxy."*

The present canvas reinterprets a subject that emerged
in at least two works of 1952 entitled *The Un-
Nominator (I and II)*.** The dominant insectile beings
in these canvases share stiff extended arms and the
suggestion of an open visceral or genital cavity. The
meaning of the figure's renomination or renaming referred to by the title of the present work is unclear—
it may simply imply that the earlier theme of the
un-nominator has been restated.

* "Matta on his paintings," in *Sebastian Matta*, exh. cat.,
  Stockholm, 1959, p. 32; reprinted from interview with
  I. Gustafson in *Salamander*, no. 2, 1955.

** A. Jouffroy, "Le réalisme ouvert de Matta," *Cahiers d'Art*,
  vol. XXVIII, June 1953, repr. pp. 113, 115.

E.C.C.

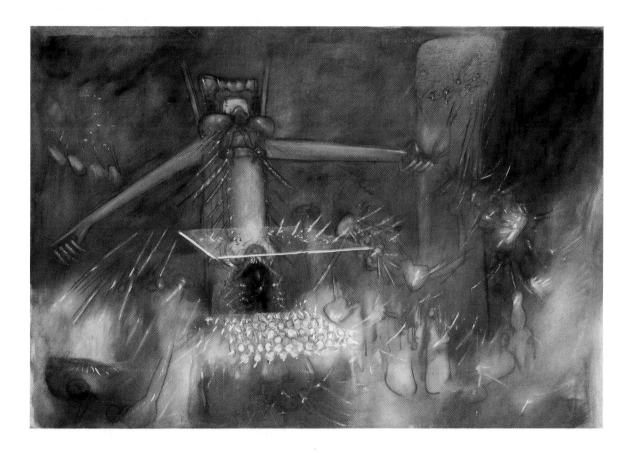

John Tunnard 1900-1971

John Tunnard was born on May 7, 1900, in Bedford-shire, England. He graduated with a diploma in design from the Royal College of Art in London in 1923 and for the next four years worked as a textile designer in Manchester. In 1929 he gave up commercial work to become a painter, supporting himself as a part-time teacher of design at the Central School of Arts and Crafts in London. Tunnard showed for the first time in 1931, at the Royal Academy of Arts and with the *London Group*. He did not show again at the Royal Academy until 1960, but continued to exhibit annually with the *London Group* until 1950, becoming a member in 1934.

Tunnard's first one-man show was held at the Redfern Gallery in London in 1933. Most of the works presented depicted the landscape of Cornwall, where the artist and his wife had settled and established a hand-blocked printed silk business. Tunnard began at this time to revive his early interest in natural science, collecting entomological specimens on the moors for the British Museum of Natural History and observing the minutiae of nature that provided a source of imagery for his art. Although he never formally joined the Surrealist movement, Tunnard participated in several of the group's exhibitions in the 1930s, including *Surrealism*, held in 1939 at Gordon Fraser Gallery in Cambridge, which featured works by Max Ernst, Klee, Magritte, Miró and others. That same year Peggy Guggenheim gave Tunnard a show at her gallery Guggenheim Jeune in London.

Tunnard enlisted as an auxiliary coast guard in 1940 and served for the duration of the war. During this period he participated in group shows in London at the Redfern Gallery, the Zwemmer Gallery and Alex Reid and Lefevre. The British Council included his work in three survey exhibitions in Australia and South America between 1940 and 1949, and in 1944 the artist was given a one-man show at the Nierendorf Gallery in New York. Tunnard resumed teaching design in 1946 at Wellington College, Berkshire, and two years later at Penzance School of Art, Cornwall. Also in 1946 he was featured in *Contemporary British Art*, which traveled to the Toledo Museum of Art, Ohio, the Albright Art Gallery, Buffalo, and the City Art Museum, St. Louis. In 1949 his work was shown at the Salon des Réalités Nouvelles in Paris. The artist designed a mural for the Festival of Britain in 1951 and the following year he showed at Durlacher Brothers in New York, where he would have a solo exhibition in 1960. Tunnard was elected an Associate of the Royal Academy in 1967. In 1971 he was represented in *The British Contribution to Surrealism* at Hamet Gallery in London. The artist died that year on December 18.

97 Psi. 1938

Oil, gesso, gouache, pastel (?) and wax crayon on board, 31 7/16 x 47 3/16" (79.9 cm. x 119.8 cm.)
76.2553 PG 47; PG coll. cat. 171

Tunnard's paintings of the late 1930s and early 1940s present intricate constructions in states of taut equilibrium. The core of his imagery is usually constituted of dominant hard-edged forms through which are threaded a network of connecting lines, overlapping bars, geometric shapes and Greek characters. In *Psi* of 1938 Tunnard's apparatus is suspended in a textured atmosphere of blue, gray and white. This aerated space of what has been termed "plein-air abstraction" permits Tunnard to create abstract form in fully three-dimensional terms.[*] Here a dark gray and black armature whose limbs project in four directions recalls the work of Tunnard's friend Henry Moore, who in 1937 began incorporating tightly-drawn string into open spaces in his sculpture. Tunnard's affinity with Moore extends beyond the realm of form to that of their fidelity to media: Tunnard compares his sensitivity to the physical potential of paint to that of a sculptor who allows the stone to suggest the direction of creation.[**]

Tunnard's machinery is generally descended from irrational Surrealist designs drafted from fantasy by Max Ernst, Miró and Klee, but his imagery more often refers to real machines or engineering equipment. Regular curves and Greek characters derived from calculus and algebra, the vocabulary of the engineer, appears in *Psi* as well. A tiny white theta (Φ) appears at upper left, and elsewhere are three psi (Ψ): atop the white plane at upper right; inscribed on the black sphere at the left; and in elongated form at lower right. Draped between these last two psi figures is a wavy, transparent musical score, composed of six lines rather than the conventional five. Notes assume their positions on the score in syncopated fashion, suggesting the rhythms of jazz, which Tunnard played in semiprofessional bands. Perhaps an allusion to a stringed instrument can be found in the seven lines, the fret-shaped yellow orange bar and stylized black and white sound hole suspended together under the right arm of the central structure. While Tunnard's enterprise should not be misread as some fantastic aeolian harp, aural sensations are clearly invoked. Both in the development of such musical allusion and in his subtly textured surfaces, Tunnard was inspired by the art of Klee.

[*] J. A. Thwaites, "The Technological Eye," in *John Tunnard*, exh. cat., London, 1977, p. 50, reprinted from *The Art Quarterly*, Detroit Institute of Arts, Spring 1946.

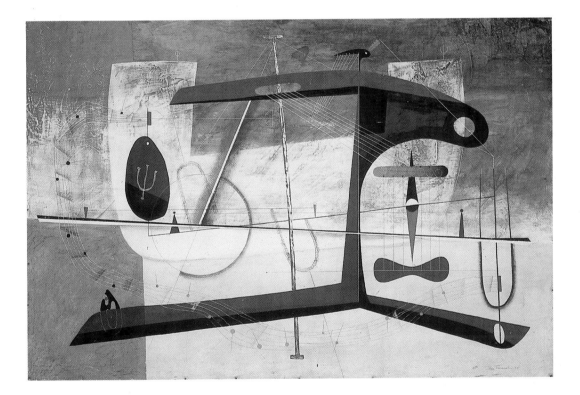

** R. Myerscough-Walker, "Modern Art Explained by
   Modern Artists, Part II," *The Artist*, vol. 27, Apr. 1944,
   p. 44.

E.C.C.

Alexander Calder 1898-1976

Alexander Calder was born on July 22, 1898, in Lawnton, Pennsylvania, into a family of artists. In 1919 he received an engineering degree from Stevens Institute of Technology in Hoboken, New Jersey. Calder attended the Art Students League in New York from 1923 to 1926, studying briefly with Thomas Hart Benton and John Sloan, among others. As a free-lance artist for the *National Police Gazette* in 1925 he spent two weeks sketching at the circus; his fascination with the subject dates from this time. He also made his first sculpture in 1925; the following year he made several constructions of animals and figures with wire and wood.

Calder's first exhibition of paintings took place in 1926 at The Artist's Gallery in New York. Later this year he went to Paris and attended the Académie de la Grande Chaumière. In Paris he met Stanley William Hayter, exhibited at the 1926 Salon des Indépendants and in 1927 began giving performances of his miniature circus. The first show of his wire animals and caricature portraits was held at the Weyhe Gallery, New York, in 1928. That same year he met Miró, who became his lifelong friend. Subsequently Calder divided his time between France and the United States. In 1929 the Galerie Billiet gave him his first one-man show in Paris. He met Léger, Frederick Kiesler and van Doesburg and visited Mondrian's studio in 1930. Calder began to experiment with abstract sculpture at this time and in 1931-32 introduced moving parts into his work. These moving sculptures were called mobiles; the stationary constructions were to be named stabiles. He exhibited with the *Abstraction-Création* group in Paris in 1933. In 1943 The Museum of Modern Art in New York gave him a major one-man exhibition.

During the 1950s Calder traveled widely and executed *Towers* (wall mobiles) and *Gongs* (sound mobiles). He won First Prize for Sculpture at the 1952 Venice Biennale. Late in the decade the artist worked extensively with gouache; from this period he executed numerous major public commissions. In 1964-65 the Solomon R. Guggenheim Museum, New York, presented a major Calder retrospective. He began the *Totems* and the *Animobiles,* variations on the standing mobile, in 1966 and 1971, respectively. An important Calder exhibition was held at the Whitney Museum of American Art in New York in 1976. Calder died in New York on November 11, 1976.

98 Mobile. ca. 1934

Glass, china, iron wire and thread, ca. 65¾ x 46¹⁄₁₆″ (ca. 167 x 117 cm.)
76.2553 PG 139; PG coll. cat. 24

When Calder visited Mondrian's studio in 1930, he was intrigued by rectangles of colored paper the painter had tacked to a white wall. Calder aspired to infuse motion into this abstract order of color, by discovering a way to make the rectangles oscillate. Subsequently he experimented with abstract painting and then with abstract stationary sculpture, encouraged in these directions by Miró, Arp and Duchamp. Calder's fascination with movement led him to incorporate motion into his abstract constructions in 1931, which he powered with small electric motors or hand cranks. In such mobiles of geometric forms, many of which recall didactic scientific models, Calder sought to express the underlying form systems of the universe.

In 1932 Calder made his first wind mobiles, abandoning mechanisms that controlled the set patterns of movement. His mobiles subsequently lost their resemblance to astrological models, as he moved away from spherical structures to configurations suspended from a network of horizontal bars. The spontaneous movement of the elements continued to express for Calder the rhythms and principles of cosmic motion. The thread used in wind mobiles, such as the present one, allows them to move more freely than did the wire used in earlier constructions. Calder often incorporated found objects into his mobiles of 1934-35, suspending various fragments of broken glass, china, buttons and kitchen utensils from wire frameworks. Such objects were chosen for their texture and color, and lack, for the most part, the poetic evocativeness of the found objects in Surrealist constructions by Miró, Man Ray and others. The viewer experiences the mobile in constant flux, as occasional breezes propel the disparate elements through space. The unfinished, rough quality of the glass and pottery shards adds further variety and unpredictability to the configurations as the mobile hovers overhead in ever changing patterns of color and motion.

E.C.C.

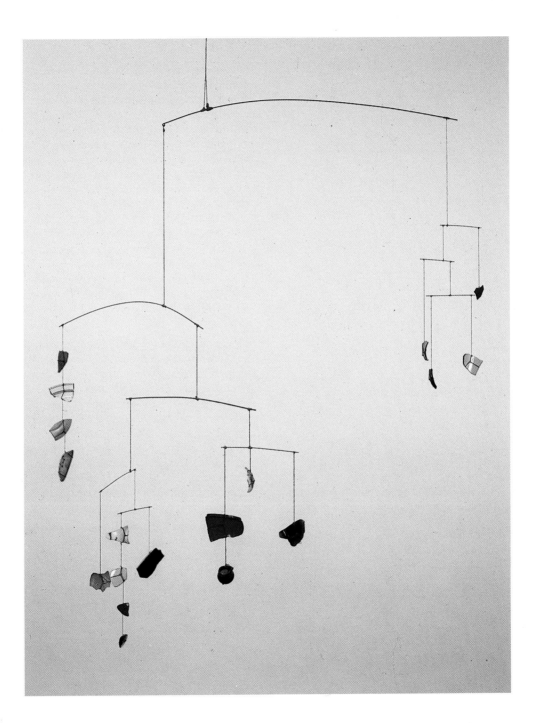

99 Mobile. 1941

Painted and unpainted aluminum and iron wire,
ca. 84¼″ (214 cm.) high
76.2553 PG 137; PG coll. cat. 25

During the early 1930s Calder, a pioneering figure in
the development of kinetic art, created sculptures in
which balanced components move, some driven by
motor, and others impelled by the action of air currents.
Duchamp first applied the descriptive designation
"mobiles" to those reliant on air alone. Either suspended or freestanding, these constructions generally
consist of flat pieces of painted metal connected by wire
veins and stems. Their biomorphic shapes recall the
organic motifs of the Surrealist painting and sculpture
of his friends Miró and Arp. Calder, a fastidious craftsman, cut, bent, punctured and twisted his materials
entirely by hand, the manual emphasis contributing to
the sculptures' evocation of natural form. Shape, size,
color, space and movement combine and recombine in
shifting, balanced relationships that provide a visual
equivalent to the harmonious but unpredictable activity
of nature.

The present mobile is organized as an antigravitational
cascade in which large, heavy, mature shapes sway
serenely at the top, while small, undifferentiated, agitated new growth dips and rocks below. Calder left one
of the upper leaves as well as the lowest group unpainted, revealing the aluminum surface and under-
scoring the sense of variety he considered vital to the
success of a work of art. As he wrote, "Disparity in
form, color, size, weight, motion, is what makes a
composition. . . . It is the apparent accident to regularity which the artist actually controls by which he
makes or mars a work."*

* Quoted in J. Lipman, *Calder's Universe*, exh. cat., New
    York, 1976, p. 33.

L.F.

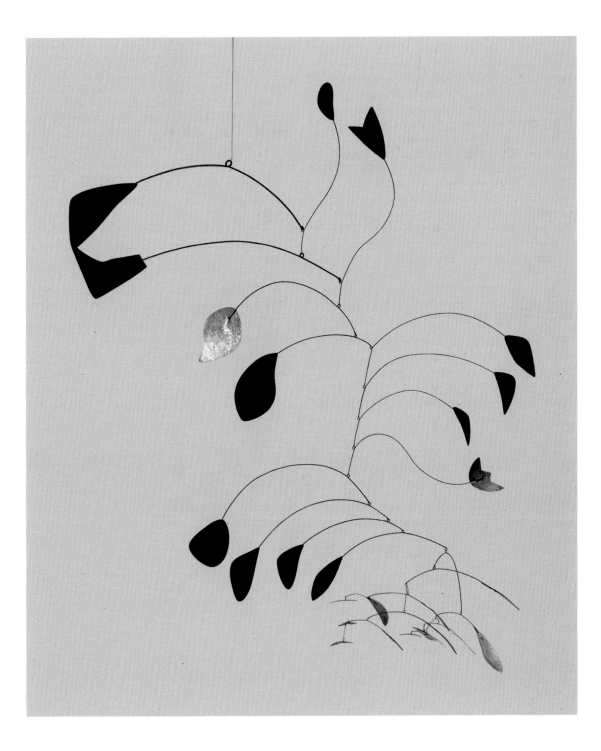

100 Silver Bedhead. Winter 1945-46

Silver, 63 x 51⅞₆″ (160 x 131 cm.)
76.2553 PG 138; PG coll. cat. 26

In New York in the winter of 1945-46, Peggy Guggenheim commissioned Calder to make a silver bedhead.* His design combines fish, insect and plant motifs in an exuberant conflation of the worlds of sea and garden. The two fish at the lower left are free-hanging elements. Calder also suspends an insect, probably a bee or dragonfly, from a silver link chain which may be dangled from various locations on the sculpture. Since the insect may fly in any of several possible positions, realms of sea and sky are not separated into distinct areas—rather, the bedhead is a whimsical fantasy in which flora and fauna from both regions coexist. The outer curve of a large spiral comprises the basic circular structure of the bedhead, which is elaborated with decorations of hammered and cut silver. Although these botanical forms are fixed permanently in position, their curving, twisting contours nonetheless convey a sense of perpetual natural motion.

Calder first twisted wire into three-dimensional forms in his wire sculptures of the mid-1920s. Subsequently, he twisted, cut and hammered wire and gold, silver and brass into jewelry for his friends and patrons. It has been suggested that the delicate and slender forms of some of Calder's metal constructions of the early 1940s are indebted to his jewelry of the 1930s, which includes both simple animal motifs and curvilinear or spiraling abstract forms.** Calder's book illustrations also contributed to the development of a graphic lyricism in his sculpture. Many of the vegetal forms in the bedhead share the spontaneity and inventiveness of Calder's line-etching illustrations. In particular, the soaring zigzag fern motif on the left and the numerous spiral shaped blossoms anticipate the illustrations executed in 1946 for Eunice Clark's *Fables of La Fontaine* (for example, the "Stag and the Vine").

The compressed, shallow relief of this piece answers neatly the practical demands of Peggy Guggenheim's commission for a bedhead. This project allowed Calder to exercise his calligraphic skills not only in the more conventional realm of book illustration but also in drawing on a blank wall with a line of silver metal. The worked surface of the hammered silver, which reflects light in countless directions, adds variety and a three-dimensional presence to each of Calder's lines.

* P. Guggenheim, *Out of This Century: Confessions of an Art Addict*, New York, 1979, p. 318.

** J. Lipman, *Calder's Universe*, New York, 1976, p. 209.

E.C.C.

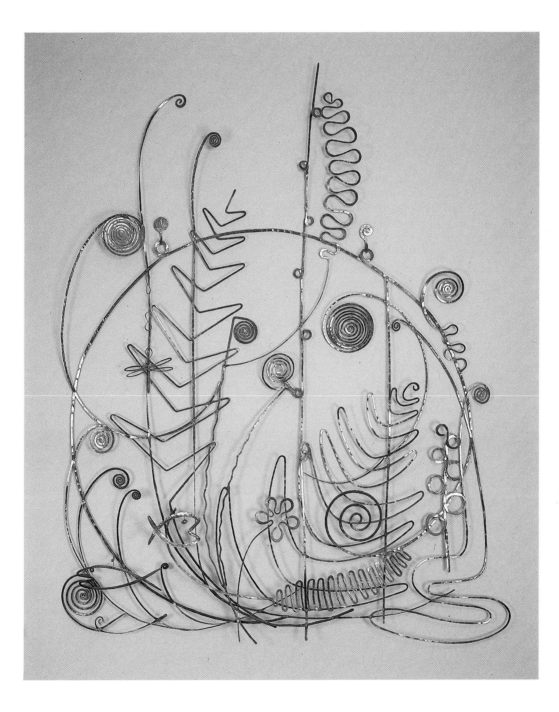

Joseph Cornell 1903-1972

Joseph Cornell was born on December 24, 1903, in Nyack, New York. From 1917 to 1921 he attended Phillips Academy in Andover, Massachusetts. He was an avid collector of memorabilia and, while working as a woolen-goods salesman in New York for the next ten years, developed his interest in ballet, literature and the opera.

In the early thirties Cornell met Surrealist writers and artists at the Julien Levy Gallery in New York and saw Ernst's collage-novel *La Femme 100 têtes.* Cornell's early constructions of found objects were first exhibited in *Surrealism,* presented at the Wadsworth Atheneum in Hartford and subsequently at Julien Levy's in 1932. From 1934 to 1940 Cornell supported himself by working at the Traphagen studio in New York. During these years he became familiar with Duchamp's *Readymades* and Schwitters's box constructions. Cornell was included in the 1936 exhibition *Fantastic Art, Dada, Surrealism* at The Museum of Modern Art, New York. Always interested in film and cinematic techniques, he made a number of movies, including *Rose Hobart* of 1931, and wrote two film scenarios. One of these, *Monsieur Phot* of 1933, was published in 1936 in Levy's book *Surrealism.*

Cornell's first one-man exhibition took place at the Julien Levy Gallery in 1939 and included an array of objects, a number of them in shadow boxes. During the forties and fifties he made *Medici* boxes, boxes devoted to stage and screen personalities, *Aviary* constructions, *Observatories, Night Skies, Winter Night Skies* and *Hotel* boxes. In the early 1960s Cornell stopped making new boxes and began to reconstruct old ones and to work intensively in collage. Major Cornell retrospectives were held in 1967 at the Pasadena Art Museum and the Solomon R. Guggenheim Museum, New York. In 1971 The Metropolitan Museum of Art in New York mounted an exhibition of his collages. Cornell died on December 29, 1972, at his home in Flushing, New York.

101 Fortune Telling Parrot. ca. 1937-38

Box construction, 16¹⁄₁₆ x 8¼ x 6¹¹⁄₁₆″ (40.8 x 22.2 x 17 cm.)
76.2253 PG 126; PG coll. cat. 35

Cornell lived an isolated life with his mother at their home in Flushing, New York, from which he made frequent excursions into Manhattan to gather objects for his constructions. His diaries record his alternating feelings of being trapped at home, and then of release when he escaped to Manhattan. Working on his boxes at home in his cellar became a substitute for traveling, the arrangement of imaginary souvenirs inducing the excitement of voyages.

Fortune Telling Parrot offers many associations with exotic travels. First, the box construction itself resembles the apparatus of a hurdy-gurdy, invoking the bohemian world of the traveling gypsy musician. The crank on the right exterior of the construction turns a broken music box, hidden in the lower right corner of the sculpture. The music box in turn is attached by a thin rod to the cylinder above it, which is intended to revolve while music plays.

The cylinder is covered with decorations, some of which suggest the paraphernalia and practices of the fortune-teller: playing cards such as the King of Hearts and the Jack of Clubs; the numbers one through nine; a picture of two hands playing cat's cradle, recalling the entertainments of the gypsy; and the picture of a gypsy woman in elaborate costume. Small stars on the cylinder and a map of the constellation of Ursa Minor, "Little Bear" in the lower left corner of the box, also allude to astrology and divination. The parrot itself is a common attribute of the itinerant fortune teller. Facing the revolving cannister, this bird assumes the role of a soothsayer's assistant. Exotic birds, including parrots, parakeets and cockatoos, appear in some eighteen boxes by Cornell, the present example being the earliest and the others dating from the forties and fifties (Rudenstine, p. 178). In other boxes, birds are caged and chained on their perches, captured as exotic pets. Cornell recalls in his diary some of the experiences that contributed to his obsession with parrots: "magic windows of yesterday . . . pet shop windows splashed with white tropical plumage / the kind of revelation symptomatic of city wanderings in another era. . . . scintillating songs of Rossini and Bellini and the whole golden age of the bel canto . . . indelible childhood memory of an old German woman a neighbor's pet parrot may have added to the obsession of these . . . feathered friends."*

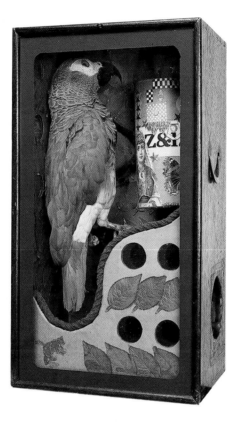

* Quoted in D. Ades, "The Transcendental Surrealism of
  Joseph Cornell," *Joseph Cornell*, exh. cat., New York,
  1980, p. 37.

E.C.C.

102 Swiss Shoot-the-Chutes. 1941

Box construction, 21¹⁄₁₆ x 13¹³⁄₁₆ x 4⅛″
(53.8 x 35.2 x 10.5 cm.)
76.2553 PG 127; PG coll. cat. 36

More prosaic in its connotations than many of Cornell's boxes, *Swiss Shoot-the-Chutes* playfully combines real objects with reproductions to identify a locale—the Swiss Alps. Like other works of the period by Cornell, the box has been devised as a sophisticated toy that requires the viewer's imaginative participation. In order for this ingeniously constructed work to be activated, the wooden ball resting inside the box must be extracted, inserted through the hatch at the top of the right side of the frame and released. The ball then rolls along the ramps within the box, hitting bells of various sizes, appearing and disappearing behind the punctured façade of the map in an energetic crisscross downhill route, ultimately emerging through the hatch at the lower right.

Not only does the ball enact the Shoot-the-Chutes amusement park ride, but, as it plows through a topsy-turvy map of Switzerland and surroundings, it also mimics the course of the skier who appears in a vignette at the center. Cornell wittily seizes on the mapmaker's miniaturization of scale to suggest a family of mammoth balls tunneling through Alpine Europe, processing the land into a surface with the aerated texture of Swiss cheese. In striking the bells, the ball evokes Switzerland's dairyland by producing the cacophony of a herd of cows, such as those shown stolidly grazing over the upper half of the composition. In his investigation of potential, interrupted and completed movement Cornell makes reference in this construction to photography in general and to cinematic technique in particular.

L.F.

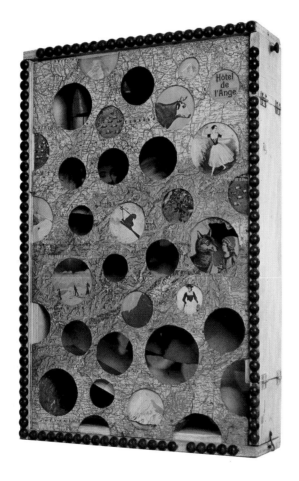

103 Untitled (Pharmacy). ca. 1942

Box construction, 14 x 12¹/₁₆ x 4³/₈"
(35.5 x 30.6 x 11.1 cm.)
76.2553 PG 128; PG coll. cat. 38

Cornell's obsession with the collection, isolation, combination and preservation of found objects is revealed in a fastidiously compartmentalized form in the *Pharmacy* boxes of the 1940s and 1950s. Like Duchamp's *Box in a Valise* of 1941 (an example of which is in the Peggy Guggenheim Collection), this work is a miniature museum dedicated to the protection and presentation of its contents. The care with which the collection has been selected and displayed invests it with a potency the individual objects do not ordinarily convey.*

Each apothecary jar presents a diorama of poetically allusive natural or man-made forms. The natural world is present in sand, stones, shells, plant and insect parts, feathers and wood; the constructed world appears in mechanisms, toys, maps and prints. The environments invoked range from the seashore, where man's importance is negligible, to the Renaissance palace, one of the most sophisticated expressions of his material and intellectual achievement. Like the alchemist, Cornell transforms ordinary objects into precious things; in one jar he even seems to have fulfilled the ultimate alchemical aspiration of transmuting base metal into gold. By presenting these inviolable jars in a pharmaceutical context, he may also allude to the universal restorative powers that alchemists hoped to discover. The mirroring of the back wall of the box, typical of apothecaries' cabinets, multiplies the contents and reflects the viewer, whom it affords the unexpected opportunity to study the reverse of objects without moving around them.

* For discussion of the state of incompletion of this example, see Rudenstine, pp. 187-188.

L.F.

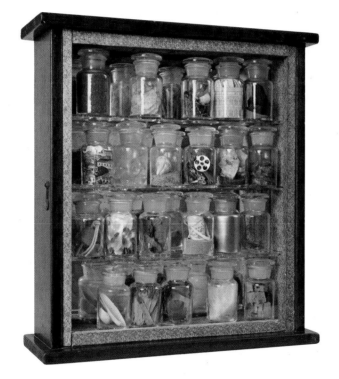

104 Setting for a Fairy Tale. 1942

Box construction, 11⁹⁄₁₆ x 14⅜ x 3⅞″ (29.4 x 36.6 x 9.9 cm.)
76.2553 PG 125; PG coll. cat. 37

In contrast to the cluttered assemblage of juxtaposed objects of varying scales in other boxes, Cornell here creates a coherent miniaturized world. A black painted border on the surface of the glass frames a white palace and serves as a proscenium that invokes the world of theater and spectacle. The title *Setting for a Fairy Tale* enhances the stage-model associations of the construction. Cornell's setting is a reproduction of Jacques Androuet du Cerceau's engraving, first published in 1576, of the Château de Madrid in Paris. Reproductions of this same engraving appear in at least nine of his palace constructions, for example, *Untitled (Pink Palace)*, ca. 1946-48 (Collection San Francisco Museum of Modern Art). The Peggy Guggenheim work is the first of these boxes, which were created between 1942 and the mid-1950s (see Rudenstine, p. 184).

For Cornell, fairy tales had specific associations with the romantic ballet. His favorite ballets included classics such as *Swan Lake, The Nutcracker, Ondine* and, of special relevance to the present discussion, *Sleeping Beauty*. Cornell's friend Tamara Toumanova, whom he met in 1940, often performed the role of Princess Aurora in Diaghilev's revival of the ballet *Sleeping Beauty* by Petipa, with music by Tchaikovsky.* About 1941 the artist made several objects resembling glass Christmas ornaments that contained cutout pictures of Toumanova dancing Aurora. Certain details of *Setting for a Fairy Tale*, such as the bramble of twigs suggesting a dense forest around the palace, may derive from the *Sleeping Beauty* story. Both the balletic rendition of the fairy tale and Cornell's shadow box conjure up fantasies of romantic love and historic pageantry.

In other constructions (cat. nos. 101 and 102) Cornell invites the viewer's imaginative participation in the work through means such as a hatch that may be opened or a tempting crank of a hurdy-gurdy that may be turned. In the present construction, the imagined participation is not physical, but psychological and creative. The viewer may be playwright, choreographer, director and performer in the spectacle of his choice. In a careful scrutiny of the work, the mirrored surfaces not only offer the illusion of shimmering glass windows, but also engage the viewer in a multifaceted reflection and discovery of himself.

* On Cornell and Toumanova, see *Joseph Cornell and the Ballet,* exh. cat., New York, 1983, pp. 36-40, 59-70.

E.C.C.

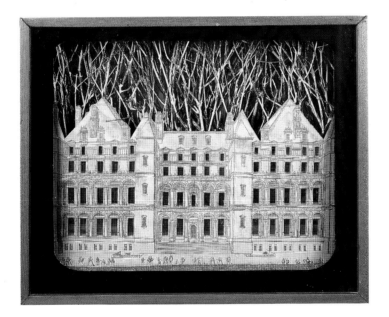

Morris Hirshfield 1872-1945

Morris Hirshfield was born on April 10, 1872, near the German border of Russian Poland. Although as a youth in Poland he carved wooden sculptures of religious subjects, he became a serious artist only during the last decade of his life. At the age of eighteen Hirshfield immigrated to the United States, where he pursued a business career in the clothing industry first as a dress and suit manufacturer and subsequently as a successful slipper manufacturer in Brooklyn. Forced into retirement by ill health in 1935, he began to paint in 1937. Entirely self-taught, Hirshfield painted women, children, animals and architecture. He eschewed the use of live models, working from memory, from imagination and occasionally from postcards or other printed images. His artistic goal was the literal representation of his motifs, and he aspired to the factual precision of photography. His paintings have generally been appreciated, however, more for their decorative qualities of pattern, for their symmetrical designs and for their naive illusionism than for any qualities of mimetic realism.

In 1939 Sidney Janis introduced Hirshfield's work by including two of his paintings in the exhibition *Unknown Americans* at The Museum of Modern Art, New York. In 1941 The Museum of Modern Art first purchased works by Hirshfield, and his paintings were exhibited at the San Francisco Museum of Art and at the Stendhal Galleries in Los Angeles. In 1943 The Museum of Modern Art held a retrospective of his paintings. In the catalogue, Janis championed the work in the context of a Surrealist aesthetic. The show, which was a subject of widespread controversy among critics, was attended by such figures as Breton, Duchamp and Mondrian.

Additional exhibitions of Hirshfield's work were held at the Julien Levy Gallery in New York and at the Vigeveno Gallery in Los Angeles in 1945. Hirshfield died in New York on July 28, 1945. A memorial exhibition of his work was held at Peggy Guggenheim's Art of This Century Gallery in New York in 1947.

105 **Two Women in Front of a Mirror.** 1943
Oil on canvas, 52⅜ x 59⅞″ (133 x 152 cm.)
76.2553 PG 122; PG coll. cat. 79

Here, as in many of his compositions, the women's bodies contain several anatomical distortions. The legs of the black-haired woman on the left are painted in profile, but her buttocks are depicted from another angle. On the right, Hirshfield shows the blonde woman's body in profile, the hourglass outline of her torso recalling the dressmaker forms familiar to the artist throughout his life in the garment industry. Yet imposed on the front of the profile form is the woman's left breast, which suggests that her chest faces the viewer, as does the position of her head. Her long blonde hair spreads evenly over her chest, masking details and thus mitigating the anatomical confusion. The mirror does not reflect, as expected, the front of either body. Instead, it shows their backs, restating the spectator's view of the women, but in reverse. Such doubling also substitutes for true reflection in Hirshfield's *Girl in a Mirror*, 1940, and *Inseparable Friends*, 1941 (both Collection The Museum of Modern Art, New York).

Hirshfield did not paint these women from live models but drew preliminary full-scale sketches or patterns which he transferred to his canvases. His distinct outlining of figures, his flat, patterned detail, minimal modeling and the symmetrical positioning of his figures attest to his linear sensibility, one probably reinforced by years of arranging tailors' patterns on material. His restricted palette of gray, black and yellow harmonizes the multiple patterns and figures in the present composition.

Although the subjects in *Two Women in Front of a Mirror* are depicted in intimate moments of grooming, the setting is not domestic. A framing curtain or proscenium of black and yellow stripes transforms the private scene into a more public event. A similar curtain, decorated with teasing putti, frames and presents a woman in Hirshfield's *Nude with Cupids* (Collection Sidney Janis Gallery, New York), painted in 1944. Hirshfield's paintings of women are concerned with themes of inspection and display: on the one hand, the nudes' examination and presentation of themselves; and on the other, the artist's own consideration of their bodies both as pleasing subjects and as linear shapes to be arranged in an overall pattern.

E.C.C.

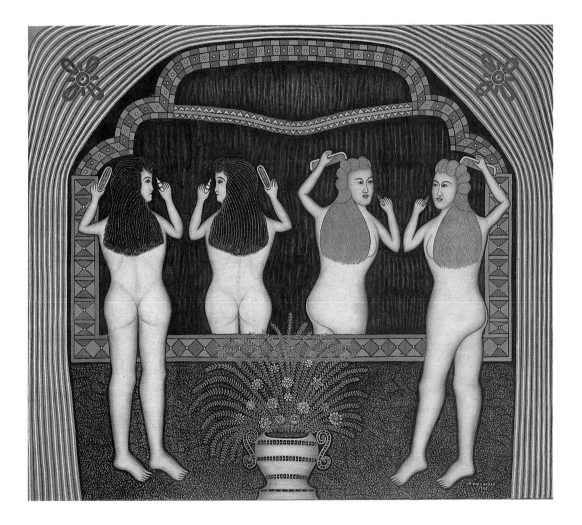

John Ferren 1905-1970

John Ferren was born in Pendleton, Oregon, on October 17, 1905. He grew up in California and worked briefly as an engineer before turning his attention to art. He apprenticed to an Italian stonecutter, carving tombstones and ornamental building-block. In 1926 he began to sculpt portrait busts. Ferren visited Europe for the first time in 1929. With Hans Hofmann he attended a Matisse exhibition in Munich that so excited his interest in color that he abandoned sculpture for painting. The following year Ferren's first one-man exhibition was held at the Art Center in San Francisco.

Ferren returned in 1931 to Paris, where, except for a year spent in Mallorca, he remained until 1938. He soon achieved recognition as an abstract artist and befriended many of the artists working in that city, including Picasso, Miró, Mondrian and Hélion. Ferren frequented the Parisian art academies and studied at the Sorbonne and other European universities. His first group show in Paris was held in 1932 at the Galerie Zak. He showed regularly with the *Abstraction-Création* group and *Le Groupe d'artistes anglo-américains*. Ferren studied printmaking with Hayter at his Atelier 17. In 1936 Pierre Loeb gave Ferren his first solo exhibition in Paris, and in 1936, 1937 and 1938 the artist had one-man shows at the Pierre Matisse Gallery in New York.

In 1938 he returned to the United States. Two years later The Corcoran Gallery, Washington, D.C., held a solo exhibition of his work. Ferren's painting career was interrupted by four years of service in the Office of War Information, which took him to North Africa and Europe. Upon his release from the army in 1946, he took a teaching position at the Brooklyn Museum Art School. The following year he also began teaching at Cooper Union and in 1952 at Queens College, Ferren was a member of The Club, an informal group that constituted the social and intellectual center of the New York School of Abstract Expressionists. He became president of The Club in 1955. The Stable Gallery in New York held a one-man show of his work each year from 1954 to 1958. The artist participated in the Carnegie International, Pittsburgh, in 1955. That year and again in 1958 he served as artistic consultant to Alfred Hitchcock on the films *The Trouble with Harry* and *Vertigo*. In 1961 Ferren was included in the Guggenheim Museum's *Abstract Expressionists and Imagists*. He was the first recipient of an American Specialists Abroad Grant awarded by the United States State Department; this allowed him to spend 1963-64 lecturing on contemporary American art in Beirut and elsewhere in the Middle East, Pakistan and India. Ferren died on July 24, 1970, in East Hampton, New York.

106 Tempora. 1937

Plaster print, ink and tempera, image 11¹³⁄₁₆ x 9⁷⁄₁₆″ (30 x 24 cm.); plaster 15 x 12⅝″ (38.1 x 32.1 cm.) 76.2553 PG 49; PG coll. cat. 64

In 1935 Ferren studied printmaking in Hayter's Atelier 17 in Paris, where he was introduced to the abstract styles of Miró, Max Ernst, Hayter himself and others. He experimented there with a nineteenth-century technique of plaster relief-printing which had been revived by Hayter. (An example of Hayter's plaster prints, *Defeat* of 1938-39, is in the Peggy Guggenheim Collection.) Between 1935 and 1938 Ferren made fifty-five plaster reliefs (Rudenstine, p. 326). To make a plaster print, an engraved or etched plate is inked and placed faceup on a glass surface.* A deep wooden frame is then placed around the plate and is filled with plaster of Paris. When the plate is removed, a printed image appears on the smooth plaster.

Ferren contributed a variety of additional steps to this basic process. He usually carved several areas defined by the printed line while the plaster was still slightly damp. In some works he used layers of colored plaster, and here this sculpting process exposed colored strata. In other works, such as *Tempora*, Ferren allowed the carved relief to dry and then painted selected planes in bright colors. He also elaborated the flat plaster surfaces with scored or hatched white lines or tiny pinholes, or he imbedded small glass mosaics in hollowed areas to provide textural variety.

These plaster reliefs are three-dimensional studies that treat the same concerns Ferren explored in his abstract oils. In his paintings of the mid-thirties he created complex textures by using thick mixtures of sand and paint, or by incising deep outlines around individual shapes. Often Ferren graded his palette from light to dark values or from cool to warm hues within each rolling abstract form, as in *Untitled (J F 7)*, 1937 (Collection Solomon R. Guggenheim Museum, New York). The artist achieved an optical illusion of similar color modulations in many of the plaster reliefs, including the present example. Here, Ferren carved parallel diagonal lines across the background. Although most of the sculpted facets between the printed lines are left white, Ferren painted three of them in blue, red and orange. Other colors appear on the sides of sculpted curved surfaces as well. When viewed frontally, a white surface reflects the color next to it, producing the visual effect of graded monochrome. When viewed obliquely, from either side, the colors shift, thereby revealing the relief to be simultaneously print, painting and sculpture.

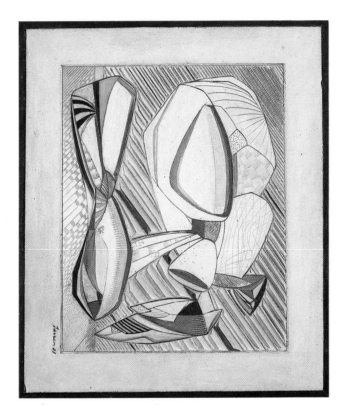

* On the plaster print technique, see G. Peterdi, *Printmaking:*
  Methods Old and New, rev. ed., New York, 1971,
  pp. 183-189.

E.C.C.

Arshile Gorky 1904-1948

Arshile Gorky was born Vosdanik Adoian in the village of Khorkom, province of Van, Armenia, on April 15, 1904. The Adoians became refugees from the Turkish invasion; Gorky himself left Van in 1915 and arrived in the United States about March 1, 1920. He stayed with relatives in Watertown, Massachusetts, and with his father who had settled in Providence, Rhode Island. By 1922 he lived in Watertown and taught at the New School of Design in Boston. In 1925 he moved to New York and changed his name to Arshile Gorky. He entered the Grand Central School of Art in New York as a student but soon became an instructor of drawing; from 1926 to 1931 he was a member of the faculty. Throughout the 1920s Gorky's painting was influenced by Cézanne, Braque and, above all, Picasso.

In 1930 Gorky's work was included in a group show at The Museum of Modern Art in New York. During the thirties he associated closely with Stuart Davis, John Graham and de Kooning; he shared a studio with de Kooning late in the decade. Gorky's first one-man show took place at the Mellon Galleries in Philadelphia in 1931. From 1935 to 1937 he worked under the WPA Federal Art Project on murals for the Newark Airport. His involvement with the WPA continued into 1941. Gorky's first one-man show in New York was held at the Boyer Galleries in 1938. The San Francisco Museum of Art exhibited his work in 1941.

In the 1940s he was profoundly affected by the work of European Surrealists, particularly Miró, Masson and Matta. By 1944 he met Breton and became a friend of other Surrealist emigrés in this country. Gorky's first exhibition at the Julien Levy Gallery in New York took place in 1945. From 1942 to 1948 he worked for part of each year in the countryside of Connecticut or Virginia. A succession of personal tragedies, including a fire in his studio that destroyed much of his work, a serious operation and an automobile accident, preceded Gorky's death by suicide on July 21, 1948, in Sherman, Connecticut.

107 Untitled. Summer 1944

Oil on canvas, 65¾ x 70³⁄₁₆″ (167 x 178.2 cm.)
76.2553 PG 152; PG coll. cat. 73

Gorky spent the greater part of 1944 at Crooked Run Farm in Hamilton, Virginia, where he produced a large number of drawings, many of which were conceived as preliminary studies for paintings. This work is preceded by such a study, a closely related untitled drawing of 1944 (Private Collection; repr. Rudenstine, p. 669, fig. a) that sets out its motifs, their ordering within the composition and the arrangement of color. Apart from the transformation of an empty contour at the upper center into a solid, anchored black form, only insignificant compositional and coloristic changes appear in the finished painting.

Gorky's enthusiastic response to the natural surroundings of rural Virginia infused his work with expressive freedom. Landscape references appear in *Untitled*; though the white ground is uniform, it is empty at the very top of the canvas, suggesting a slice of sky, while the "earth" below is replete with vegetal shapes and floral colors. A clear gravitational sense is produced by the dripping of paint thinned with turpentine, a technique suggested by Matta. As in *They Will Take My Island* of the same year (Collection Art Gallery of Ontario, Toronto), an aggressive diagonal accent cuts through the upper center of the canvas.

The techniques and content of Surrealism influenced the development of Gorky's language of free, organic, vitally curvilinear forms. Miró's example is particularly evident here, in the disposition of floating abstract units on an indeterminate background, and in details such as flamelike shapes, dotted ovals and suggestions of genitals. Unlike Miró, however, Gorky enmeshes his forms with one another to create the overall structure. Textured, insubstantial clouds of color occasionally pertain to the graphic form they accompany, but more often are independent elements, as in the work of Kandinsky. The curves, inflections and directionality of Gorky's line likewise free it from descriptive function. In his emphasis on the autonomous expressive potential of line, form and color, Gorky anticipated the concerns of Abstract Expressionism.

L.F.

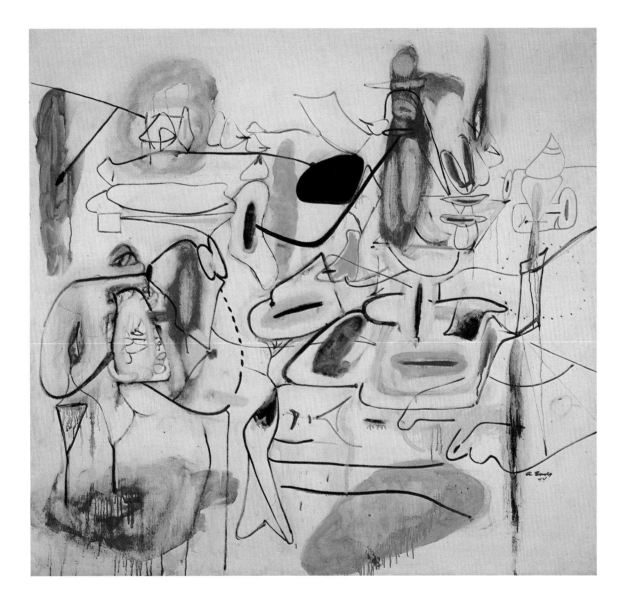

Willem de Kooning b. 1904

Willem de Kooning was born April 24, 1904, in Rotterdam. From 1916 to 1925 he studied at night at the Academie voor Beeldende Kunsten en Technische Wetenschappen, Rotterdam, while apprenticed to a commercial art and decorating firm and later working for an art director. In 1924 he visited museums in Belgium and studied further in Brussels and Antwerp. De Kooning came to the United States in 1926 and settled briefly in Hoboken, New Jersey. He worked as a house painter before moving to New York in 1927, where he met John Graham, Stuart Davis and Gorky. He took various commercial art and odd jobs until 1935-36, when he was employed in the mural and easel divisions of the WPA Federal Art Project. Thereafter he painted full-time. In the late 1930s his abstract as well as figurative work was primarily influenced by the Cubism and Surrealism of Picasso and also by Gorky, with whom he shared a studio.

In 1938 de Kooning started his first series of *Women,* which would become a major recurrent theme. During the 1940s he participated in group shows with other artists who would form the New York School of Abstract Expressionism. De Kooning's first one-man show, which took place at the Egan Gallery in New York in 1948, established his reputation as a major artist; it included a number of the allover black-and-white abstractions he had initiated in 1946. The *Women* of the early 1950s were followed by abstract urban landscapes, *Parkways,* rural landscapes and, in the 1960s, a new group of *Women.*

In 1968 de Kooning visited The Netherlands for the first time since 1926 for the opening of his major retrospective at the Stedelijk Museum in Amsterdam. In Rome in 1969 he executed his first sculptures—figures modeled in clay and later cast in bronze—and in 1970-71 he began a series of life-size figures. In 1974 the Walker Art Center in Minneapolis organized a show of de Kooning's drawings and sculpture that traveled throughout the United States, and in 1978 the Solomon R. Guggenheim Museum, New York, mounted an important exhibition of his recent work. In 1979 de Kooning and Eduardo Chillida received the Andrew W. Mellon Prize, which was accompanied by an exhibition at the Museum of Art, Carnegie Institute, in Pittsburgh. De Kooning lives in The Springs, East Hampton, Long Island, where he settled in 1963.

108 Untitled. 1958

Oil on paper mounted on Masonite mounted on wood, 23 x 29⅛″ (58.5 x 74 cm.)
76.2553 PG 158; PG coll. cat. 89

De Kooning, like Pollock and Motherwell, was a leader in the development of Abstract Expressionism, an American movement strongly influenced by European Surrealist notions of automatism and free expression. De Kooning does not use preliminary studies but paints directly on the support, manipulating pigment in vigorous, uninhibited gestures, expressing his subjective apprehensions of the material world in both figurative and abstract compositions. During the late fifties he temporarily abandoned the depiction of the human figure, which had preoccupied him since the beginning of his career, to evoke parkway and urban landscapes in abstract terms. As he wrote: "The pictures done since the *Women,* they're emotions, most of them. Most of them are landscapes and highways and sensations of that, outside the city, or coming from it."[*] The quality of light and the freshness of color in the present painting communicate a sense of landscape. Nevertheless, the subject relates, however indirectly, to the artist's obsession with the image of woman, whose contours he has sublimated in abstract natural forms; it is present here in the flesh tones and the lithe curves playing against an implied grid.

In the late fifties de Kooning reduced the frenzied proliferation of stroke, form and plane that had characterized his preceding work to effect compositions of relative restraint and clarity. Each area of color, contoured only by the physical edges of the paint, is applied expansively. The broad simplification makes conspicuous the manner of paint application and the resultant textural complexities of the medium. Movement, conflict and resolution take place on the flat surface of the canvas, while shifting penetrations into an illusory depth are made by color areas that advance and recede according to value, overlap or shading.

[*] Quoted in *Willem de Kooning,* exh. cat., Pittsburgh, 1979, p. 28.

L.F.

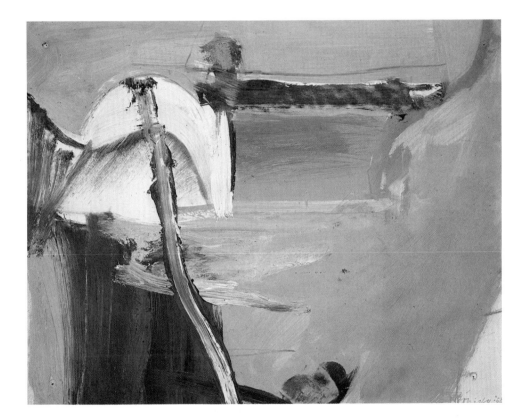

109 Untitled. 1958

Pastel and charcoal on paper, 22⁷⁄₁₆ x 30½″
(57 x 77.5 cm.)
76.2553 PG 159; PG coll. cat. 88

In the late 1950s de Kooning executed a number of abstract drawings in pastel and charcoal in which he renounced the emphatic references to female figures and features prevalent in his works of the preceding years. His broad strokes of charcoal suggest the human form in lines that are independent of any underlying color area, and which may be read simultaneously as the physical evidence of gesture and the descriptive line of representation. In the present work traces of a female form may be discerned in the flowing contours that sweep from the upper left to the lower center of the composition. Perhaps outlines of arms, a head, a torso and two bent legs of a reclining nude may be discerned. But their presence in no way detracts from the inherent beauty of these marks as compelling abstract elements. Clement Greenberg's description, in a 1953 critique, of the formal ambiguity of de Kooning's work may be applied to the Peggy Guggenheim drawing:

*The supple line that does most of the work in de Kooning's pictures . . . is never a completely abstract element but harks back to the contour, particularly that of the human form. . . . it is a disembodied contour. . . . he wants in the end to recover a distinct image of the human figure, yet without sacrificing anything of abstract painting's decorative and physical force.**

In the present work the artist first laid down thin layers of pastel crayon on the paper, scraping the pastel particularly lightly across the surface at the periphery of the composition. Small portions of the paper were left blank, most notably in a triangular area at the lower right corner. Next, colors were laid one on top of the other: fuchsia over orange, tan and orange over blue, and green over orange. In some areas, such as the top center and right, thick applications of the crayon were left untouched. In other areas, such as the center of the paper, hues have been gently rubbed so that they merge delicately to produce a luminous, multicolored membrane which appears to palpitate on the surface of the paper. Contrasting hues of orange and blue or yellow and purple vibrate in relation to one another, animating the surface and urging the eye to move from one richly colored area to the next.

De Kooning applied strokes of charcoal in varying widths and densities over this fabric of color, subtly fusing the lines into gray areas, as in the left center, and elsewhere, as in the lower right, allowing powerful, hard-edged strokes to stand independently: the varying densities of the blacks and the colors create an illusion of depth. Finally, de Kooning touched a pale gray or white crayon to the surface to mediate between areas of dark gray and high-keyed hues, such as the oranges in the center. The overall result is a composition at once poignant in its delicacy and powerfully expressive in its contrasts of color and line.

* Quoted in T. B. Hess, *Willem de Kooning*, exh. cat., New York, 1968, pp. 138-139, fn. 11.

E.C.C.

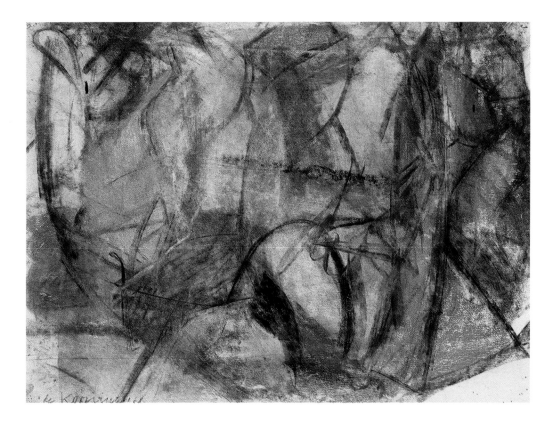

Jackson Pollock 1912-1956

Paul Jackson Pollock was born January 28, 1912, in Cody, Wyoming. He grew up in Arizona and California and in 1928 began to study painting at the Manual Arts High School in Los Angeles. In the autumn of 1930 Pollock came to New York and studied under Thomas Hart Benton at the Art Students League. Benton encouraged him throughout the succeeding decade. By the early 1930s Pollock knew and admired the murals of José Clemente Orozco and Diego Rivera. Although he traveled widely throughout the United States during the 1930s, much of Pollock's time was spent in New York, where he settled permanently in 1935 and worked on the WPA Federal Art Project from 1935 to 1942. In 1936 he worked in David Alfaro Siqueiros's experimental workshop in New York.

Pollock's first one-man show was held at Peggy Guggenheim's Art of This Century gallery in New York in 1943. Peggy Guggenheim gave him a contract that lasted through 1947, permitting him to devote all his time to painting. Prior to 1947 Pollock's work reflected the influence of Picasso and Surrealism. During the early 1940s he contributed paintings to several exhibitions of Surrealist and abstract art, including *Natural, Insane, Surrealist Art* at Art of This Century in 1943, and *Abstract and Surrealist Art in America*, organized by Sidney Janis at the Mortimer Brandt Gallery in New York in 1944.

From the autumn of 1945, when Lee Krasner and Pollock were married, they lived in The Springs, East Hampton. In 1952 Pollock's first one-man show in Paris opened at the Studio Paul Facchetti and his first retrospective was organized by Clement Greenberg at Bennington College in Vermont. He was included in many group exhibitions, including the annuals at the Whitney Museum of American Art, New York, from 1946 and the Venice Biennale in 1950. Although his work was widely known and exhibited internationally, the artist never traveled outside the United States. He was killed in an automobile accident August 11, 1956, in The Springs.

110 **The Moon Woman.** 1942

Oil on canvas, 69 x 43¹⁄₁₆" (175.2 x 109.3 cm.)
76.2553 PG 141; PG coll. cat. 142

Like other members of the New York School, Pollock was influenced in his early work by Miró and Picasso, and seized on the Surrealists' concept of the unconscious as the source of art. In the late 1930s Pollock introduced imagery based on totemic or mythic figures, ideographic signs and ritualistic events that have been interpreted as pertaining to the buried experiences and cultural memories of the psyche.

The Moon Woman suggests the example of Picasso, particularly his *Girl Before a Mirror* of 1932 (Collection The Museum of Modern Art, New York). The palettes are similar, and both artists describe a solitary standing female as if she had been X-rayed, her backbone a broad black line from which her curving contours originate. Frontal and profile views of the face are combined to contrast two aspects of the self, one serene, and public, the other dark and interior.

The subject of the moon woman, which Pollock treated in several drawings and paintings of the early 1940s, could have been available to him from various sources. At this time many artists, among them Pollock's friends Baziotes and Motherwell, were influenced by the fugitive, hallucinatory imagery of Charles Baudelaire and the French Symbolists. In his prose poem "Favors of the Moon" Baudelaire addresses the "image of the fearful goddess, the fateful godmother, the poisonous nurse of all the moonstruck of the world." The poem, which is known to have inspired Baziotes's *Mirror at Midnight*, completed in 1942 (Collection Rudi Blesh, New York), alludes to "ominous flowers that are like the censers of an unknown rite," a phrase uncannily applicable to Pollock's bouquet at the upper right. Though it is possible that Pollock knew the poem, it is likelier that he was affected in a more general way by the interest in Baudelaire and the Symbolists that was pervasive during the period.

L.F.

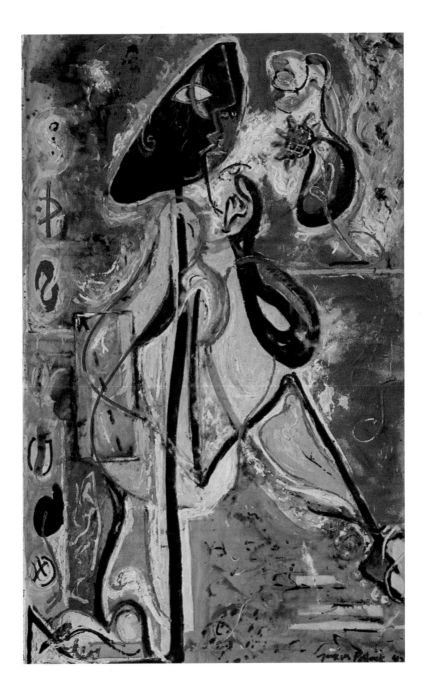

111 Two. 1943-45

Oil on canvas, 76 x 43¼″ (193 x 110 cm.)
76.2553 PG 143; PG coll. cat. 144

As in *The Moon Woman* (cat. no. 110), Pollock depicts in *Two* a figurative subject in emblematic, abstract terms. Rapidly applied strokes of thick black paint harshly delimit the two totemic figures. A columnar figure on the left, probably male, faces the center. Black contours only partially delineate the white and flesh colored areas that signify his body, as Pollock separates and liberates line from a descriptive function. The figure on the right, possibly female, bends and thrusts in approaching the static figure on the left—a sexual union between the two is implied at the juncture of their bodies in the center of the canvas.

Careful examination of the paint surface reveals that the gray "ground" is actually extensive overpainting which covers and redefines broad areas of flesh color, white and a lighter gray. Many of the harshest contours, such as the inner sides of the figures' upper torsos, are defined by this intrusive field of gray. Broad black strokes were applied on top of the overpainted ground in several areas: Pollock's imagery emerges with the painting process. A statement made by Pollock in 1947 about his mature art holds true for this earlier work as well: "The source of my painting is the unconscious. I approach painting the same way I approach drawing. That is direct—with no preliminary studies."*

At about the same time he executed the present work, Pollock painted another encounter between two totemic beings, *Male and Female* (Collection Mrs. H. Gates Lloyd, Haverford, Pennsylvania). Ciphers and mathematical signs appear in both canvases. In *Two* several numerals, including 2, 3 and 6 (and possibly others between 1 and 8), may be discerned at the far right. In both works numerals serve at once as calligraphic marks and as signs: they reinforce the generally symbolic character of the painting without being invoked as specific references. Also, in both paintings two figures are brought together in agitated union, perhaps signifying the primacy of the male and the female in the genesis of human life. To be intrigued by such basic concepts, Pollock need not have relied, as is sometimes suggested, on Jungian psychology or American Indian mythology. Rather, he was interested in such phenomena because he sought to explore universal principles through his work.

* Quoted in F.V. O'Connor, *Jackson Pollock,* exh. cat., New York, 1967, p. 40.

E.C.C.

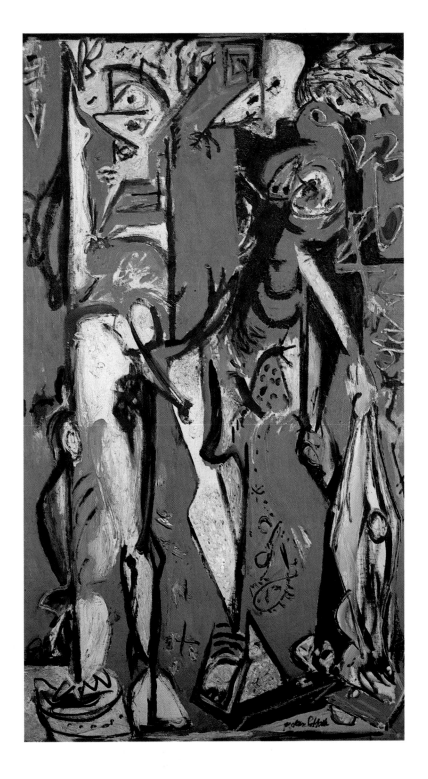

112 Direction. October 1945

Oil on canvas, 31¾ x 21¹⁵⁄₁₆″ (80.6 x 55.7 cm.)
76.2553 PG 144; PG coll. cat. 145

In *Direction* Pollock emphasizes a palette of bold primary hues, white and black. He squeezes much of his dark blue and white pigment directly from the tube into rapidly drawn thick lines and dollops of paint that are intentionally crude. Varied peaks and crusts of the surface bear witness to the artist's aggressive treatment of his materials. Visible beneath the turquoise ground are traces of a deep maroon pigment, suggesting that the final color is a hard-won solution in the evolution of the painting.

The vertical orientation of the composition permits one to discern a highly schematic stick figure on the right side of the canvas. Perhaps as many as three rudimentary blue arms merge with the blue torso at the base of the yellow head. It has been suggested that the imagery of *Direction* was specifically inspired by the stick figures in paintings by Miró, such as *Dancer* of 1935 (Collection Pierre Matisse Gallery, New York) and other works seen by Pollock in the Miró exhibition at The Museum of Modern Art in New York in 1941.* These paintings share with the Pollock a reduction of form to the simplified language of bold line. Miró's works, however, are executed with a greater degree of poetic whimsy, while *Direction* is characterized by a more restless, even volatile linear energy.

The existence of figurative or numerical pictorial elements in Pollock's early work has invited a wide range of speculation. The white motifs in the lower right corner of the present canvas, for example, have been interpreted by some critics as the inverted numbers 4 and 6. It is unclear whether these marks have any symbolic significance in Jungian terms, as has been suggested by some authors. It is likely, however, that they retain a specific autobiographical meaning in that they comprise the numbers in one of Pollock's former street addresses.** In using motifs that are simultaneously abstract marks and personal symbols, Pollock sought to express his unconscious associations. Pollock's invoking of the unconscious in his development of a highly personalized imagery testifies to the importance of the model of European Surrealism in his emerging style.

* G. Levin, "Miró, Kandinsky and the Genesis of Abstract Expressionism," in *Abstract Expressionism: The Formative Years*, Ithaca, New York, 1978, p. 31.

** W. Rubin, "Pollock as Jungian Illustrator: The Limits of Psychological Criticism," *Art in America*, vol. 67, Dec. 1979, p. 83.

E.C.C.

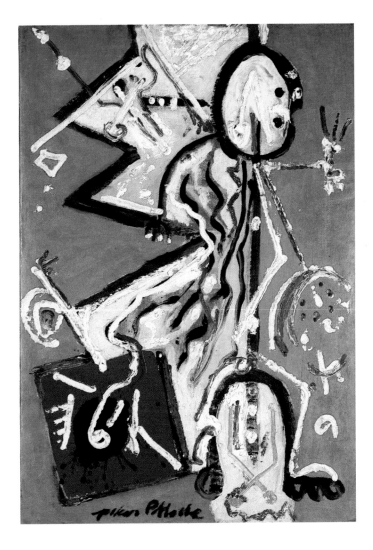

113 Circumcision. January 1946

Oil on canvas, 56⅟₁₆ x 66⅛" (142.3 x 168 cm.)
76.2553 PG 145; PG coll. cat. 146

In this transitional work of 1946 the subtle persistence
of the Cubist grid system is felt in the panels that organize the composition and orient major pictorial details in vertical or horizontal positions. However,
Pollock's dependence on Picasso has virtually dissolved,
giving way to a more automatic, fluidly expressive style.
Line loses its descriptive function and begins to assume
a self-sufficient role, the rhythm, duration and direction
of each brushstroke responding to the artist's instinc-
tual gesture. The compositional focus is multiplied and
decentralized and areas of intense activity fill the entire
surface. Fragmented figural elements are increasingly
integrated into the shallow pictorial space, as background, foreground and object merge and the texture
of the paint gains in importance. By 1945 the vigor and
originality of Pollock's work had prompted the critic
Clement Greenberg, one of his earliest champions, to
write in *The Nation* of April 7: "Jackson Pollock's
second one-man show at Art of This Century . . . estab-
lishes him, in my opinion, as the strongest painter of
his generation and perhaps the greatest one to appear
since Miró."

Primitive art-forms are alluded to in the crudely drawn
arrows, cult and stick figures and ornamental markings
discernable in *Circumcision*. Totemic figures (the rotund being standing at the left and the owllike creature
at upper center) are posed stiffly, observing what seems
to be a scene of violence in the center of the canvas. The
enactment of a rite of passage is suggested, but the
visual evidence does not encourage a specific reading.
Pollock's concern with archetypal imagery and pan-
cultural rituals and mythologies is evoked with varying
degrees of specificity in his work.

Lee Krasner suggested the title to Pollock after the
painting was completed (see Rudenstine, pp. 634-635).

L.F.

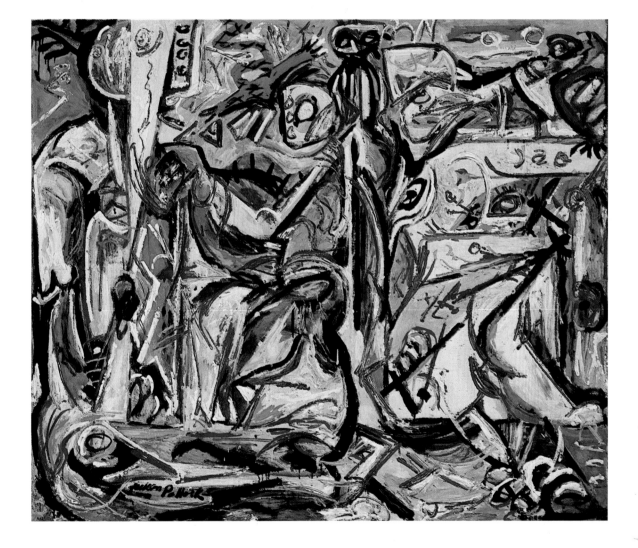

114 Eyes in the Heat. 1946

Oil (and enamel?) on canvas, 54 x 43″
(137.2 x 109.2 cm.)
76.2553 PG 149; PG coll. cat. 150

Eyes in the Heat heralds the poured paintings Pollock
initiated in the winter of 1946-47. It is part of *Sounds
in the Grass,* a series of seven canvases that also includes
Croaking Movement in the Peggy Guggenheim Collection (cat. no. 115). Pollock had moved to a house on
Long Island in 1945, and early the next summer began
using one of the bedrooms as a studio. Later in 1946
he arranged with Peggy Guggenheim to have a show
at her Art of This Century gallery, to open in January
of 1947; in preparation for this exhibition he worked
with great intensity on *Sounds in the Grass* and the
series *Accabonac Creek.*

Visible effects of the move from New York City to the
more rural environment of East Hampton were a light-
ening of palette and the introduction of themes alluding
to nature. Though the light and flora and fauna of Long
Island are evoked in a general sense in *Eyes in the Heat,*
particularized figurative references are almost entirely
submerged in the layers of impasto that build up the
surface. Pollock no longer applies paint with a brush,
but squeezes pigment onto the canvas directly from the
tube, pushing and smearing it with blunt instruments to
create a thick, textured crust. One's gaze is carried
along broad swathes of color that swoop, careen,
double back, rise and fall rhythmically over the entire
canvas. The watchful eyes of creatures concealed in the
paint appear here and there, in their proliferation
mimicking the restless movement of the viewer's eyes.

L.F.

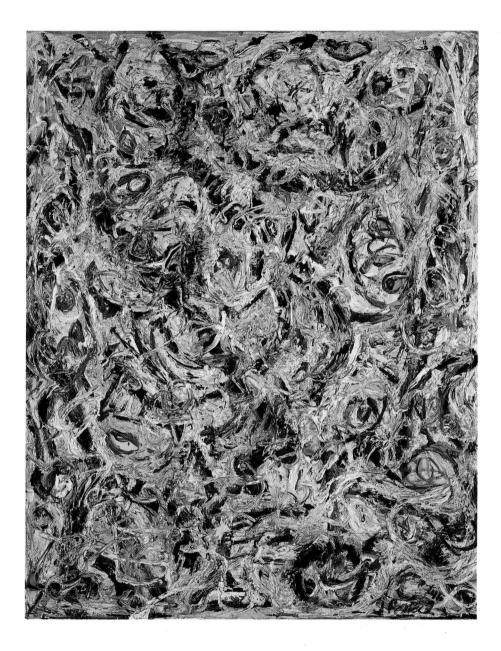

115 Croaking Movement. 1946

Oil on canvas, 54 x 44⅛″ (137 x 112 cm.)
76.2553 PG 148; PG coll. cat. 149

Croaking Movement, like *Eyes in the Heat* (cat. no. 114), belongs to Pollock's *Sounds in the Grass* series of paintings. Here, as in *Eyes in the Heat*, Pollock applied layers of moist pigment, often squeezing the paint directly from a tube, and swirling it about using the blunt end of a paintbrush, a palette knife, or the metal tip of the paint tube. These pigments mix freely in variegated crusts of impasto in *Eyes in the Heat*. In the present canvas, however, the artist established distinct color zones of pure yellow, dark green, red, blue, orange and purple at early stages of the composition. He maintained the integrity of this patchwork effect in the subsequent process of repeated scratching and dredging of the paint surface. In the final stages of the composition a firm, confident movement of the white paint across the canvas created an elaborate structure of segments and splinters of bold white line. Shorter, more staccato movements produced circles, crescents and coils of white. This network of pulsating line on the surface suggests the hidden limbs and features of beings that move amidst the camouflage of vibrant hue. A cacophony reverberating in nature is evoked by the exuberant profusion of color. The idea of sound, conveyed by both the title of the series and of this individual painting, is thus transformed from an aural to a visual sensation.

E.C.C.

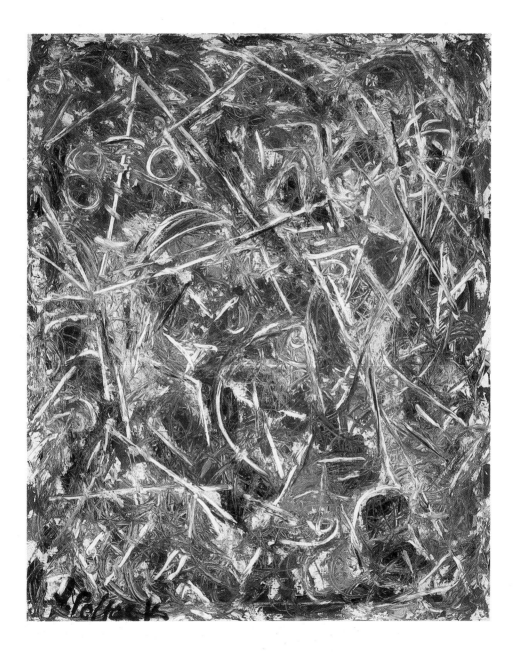

116 Alchemy. 1947

Oil, aluminum (and enamel?) paint and string on
canvas, 45⅛ x 87⅛″ (114.6 x 221.3 cm.)
76. 2553 PG 150; PG coll. cat. 152

Alchemy is one of Pollock's earliest poured paintings,
executed in the revolutionary technique that constituted
his most significant contribution to twentieth-century
art. After long deliberation before the empty canvas, he
used his entire body in a picture-making process that
can be described as drawing in paint. By pouring
streams of commercial paint onto the canvas from a can
with the aid of a stick, Pollock made obsolete the conventions and tools of traditional easel painting. He often
tacked the unstretched canvas onto the floor in an approach he likened to that of the Navajo Indian sand-
painters, explaining that "on the floor I am more at ease.
I feel nearer, more a part of the painting, since this way
I can walk around it, work from the four sides and literally be *in* the painting."* Surrealist notions of chance
and automatism are given full expression in Pollock's
classic poured paintings, in which line no longer serves
to describe shape or enclose form, but exists as an autonomous event, charting the movements of the artist's
body. As the line thins and thickens it speeds and slows,
its appearance modified by chance behavior of the
medium such as bleeding, pooling or blistering.

When *Alchemy* is viewed from a distance, its large scale
and even emphasis encourage the viewer to experience
the painting as an environment. The layering and interpenetration of the labyrinthine skeins give the whole a
dense and generalized appearance. The textured surface
is like a wall on which primitive signs are inscribed with
white pigment squeezed directly from the tube. Interpretations of these markings have frequently relied on
the title *Alchemy*; however, this was assigned not by
Pollock, but by Ralph Manheim and his wife, neighbors of the Pollocks in East Hampton.

* J. Pollock, "My Painting," *Possibilities*, no. 1, New York,
  Winter 1947-48, p. 79.

L.F.

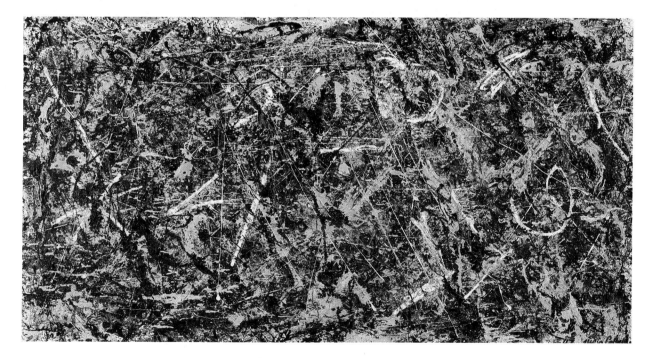

117 Enchanted Forest. 1947

Oil on canvas, 45⅛ x 87⅛″ (114.6 x 221.3 cm.)
76.2553 PG 151; PG coll. cat. 151

Like *Alchemy* (cat. no. 116), *Enchanted Forest* exemplifies Pollock's mature abstract compositions created by
the pouring, dripping and splattering of paint on large,
unstretched canvases. In *Enchanted Forest* Pollock
opens up the more dense construction of layered color
found in works such as *Alchemy,* by allowing large
areas of white to breathe amidst the network of moving,
expanding line. He also reduces his palette to a restrained selection of gold, black, red and white.
Pollock creates a delicate balance of form and color
through orchestrating syncopated rhythms of lines that
surge, swell, retreat and pause only briefly before
plunging anew into continuous, lyrical motion. One's
eye follows eagerly, pursuing first one dipping rope of
color and then another, without being arrested by any
dominant focus. Rather than describing a form,
Pollock's line thus becomes continuous form itself.

Michael Fried has described Pollock's achievement:
"[his] all-over line does not give rise to positive and
negative areas. . . . There is no inside or outside to
Pollock's line or to the space through which it moves.
And this is tantamount to claiming that line, in Pollock's all-over drip paintings of 1947-50, has been freed
at last from the job of describing contours and bounding shapes."[*] It is this redefinition of the traditional
capacity of the artist's formal means that distinguishes
Pollock's art in the history of modernism.

[*] M. Fried, *Three American Painters*, exh. cat., Cambridge,
   Mass., 1965, p. 14.

E.C.C.

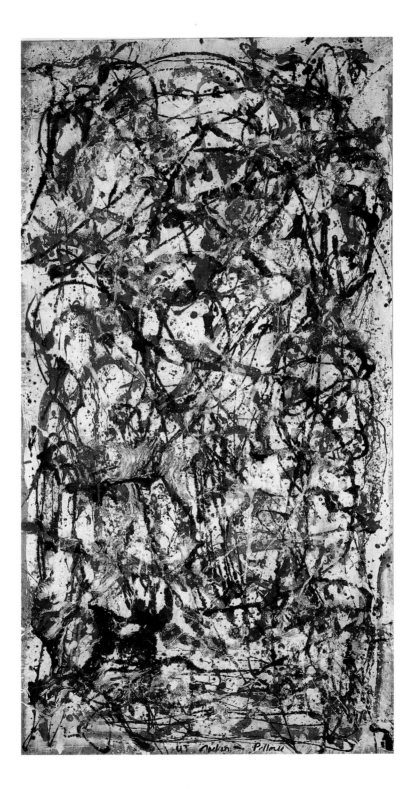

William Baziotes 1912-1963

William Baziotes was born to parents of Greek origin on June 11, 1912, in Pittsburgh. He grew up in Reading, Pennsylvania, where he worked at the Case Glass company from 1931 to 1933, antiquing glass and running errands. At this time he took evening sketch classes and met the poet Byron Vazakas, who became his life-long friend. Vazakas introduced Baziotes to the work of Baudelaire and the Symbolist poets. In 1931 Baziotes saw the Matisse exhibition at The Museum of Modern Art in New York and in 1933 he moved to that city to study painting. From 1933 to 1936 Baziotes attended the National Academy of Design.

In 1936 he exhibited for the first time in a group show at the Municipal Art Gallery, New York, and was employed by the WPA Federal Art Project as an art teacher at the Queens Museum. Baziotes worked in the easel division of the WPA from 1938 to 1941. He met the Surrealist emigrés in New York in the late thirties and early forties, and by 1940 knew Matta, Jimmy Ernst and Gordon Onslow-Ford. He began to experiment with Surrealist automatism at this time. In 1941 Matta introduced Baziotes to Motherwell, with whom he formed a close friendship. Masson invited Baziotes to participate with Motherwell, Hare and others in the 1942 exhibition *First Papers of Surrealism* at the Whitelaw Reid Mansion in New York. In 1943 he took part in two group shows at Peggy Guggenheim's Art of This Century, New York, where his first one-man exhibition was held the following year. With Motherwell, Rothko and Hare, Baziotes founded The Subjects of the Artist school in New York in 1948. Over the next decade Baziotes held a number of teaching positions in New York: at the Brooklyn Museum Art School and at New York University from 1949 to 1952; at the People's Art Center, The Museum of Modern Art, from 1950 to 1952; and at Hunter College from 1952 to 1962. Baziotes died in New York on June 6, 1963. A memorial exhibition of his work was presented at the Solomon R. Guggenheim Museum, New York, in 1965.

118 Untitled. 1943

Gouache on paper mounted on cardboard, 9 1/16 x 12" (23 x 30.5 cm.)
76.2553 PG 157; PG coll. cat. 14

In this untitled gouache Baziotes weaves a dense fabric of intersecting strands of vibrant color, laying down a complex web of undulating, exploratory line. The black color of the paper support lends a luminous quality to the layers of gouache. Blocks of scumbled color, composed of white subtly modulated with grays, blues or pinks, create a rich sense of textured depth. Red, blue, orange and yellow threads meander freely, bounding irregular blocks that appear momentarily frozen in states of expansion or contraction. One's eye is drawn repeatedly to a haunting motif in the center, where a mysterious pale turquoise oval hovers suspended on a radiating sphere of yellow. This oval, reminiscent of Miró's shapes, invites association with a wide variety of terrestrial and oceanic life-forms, particularly protozoa, amoebae and arachnids.

Such imagery combines elements of the grotesque with the elusive attraction of the unknown—a potent amalgam that links Baziotes's aesthetic to that of French Symbolist poets, whose works he knew extremely well.* Like these poets, Baziotes sought to express subjective, personal truths rather than empirical reality. And like them, Baziotes created his intimate language of expression out of intuition and gradual revelation, rather than out of preconceived ideas or theories. He stated about his art:

> There is no particular system I follow when I begin a painting. Each painting has its own way of evolving. . . . Each beginning suggests something. Once I sense the suggestion, I begin to paint intuitively. The suggestion then becomes a phantom that must be caught and made real. . . . I work on many canvases at once. . . . They are my mirrors. They tell me what I am like at the moment.**

* See B. Cavaliere, "An Introduction to the Method of William Baziotes," *Arts*, vol. 51, Apr. 1977, pp. 124-131.

** W. Baziotes, "I Cannot Evolve Any Concrete Theory," *Possibilities*, no. 2, Winter 1947-48, p. 2.

E.C.C.

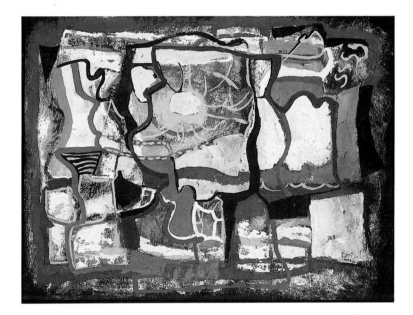

119 The Room. 1945

Gouache on board, 17¹⁵⁄₁₆ x 24″ (45.6 x 61 cm.)
76.2553 PG 156; PG coll. cat. 15

Baziotes and other members of the New York School
were influenced by the European Surrealists who had
fled to the United States during World War II. Like the
Surrealists, Baziotes used objects in his environment as
triggers for the memory of early sensations or as con-
duits to the unconscious. This procedure produced in
him an acutely sensitized state of mind that he attempted
to formulate visually in his paintings. Baziotes saw this
visual manifestation of states of mind as parallel to the
literary achievement of the Symbolist poets and of
Marcel Proust, whose work he much admired.

Baziotes makes allusions in his paintings to the external
world of objects, but these remain elusive and changeable. He usually added his titles after the compositions
had emerged through intuitive decisions. Though the
titles do not identify subject matter, they nevertheless
guide interpretation. Thus, the title of the present work
may encourage one to experience the mood of an interior space illuminated by diffused twilight. An atmosphere of nostalgic reverie is evoked by scumbled,
weathered layers of gouache in which pastel colors predominate. Unlike Baziotes's most characteristic works,
in which biomorphic shapes float free on an indefinite
background, *The Room* is constructed architectonically. The gridded structure derives from Mondrian
and the Cubists, models for Baziotes before his encounter with the Surrealists.

L.F.

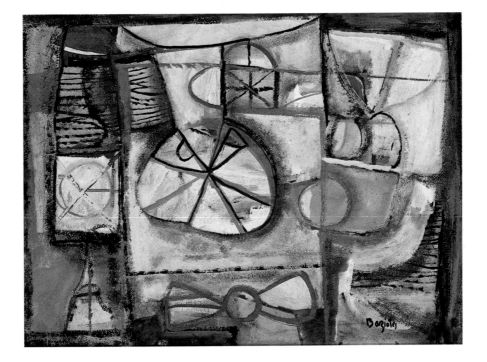

Robert Motherwell b. 1915

Robert Motherwell was born January 4, 1915, in Aberdeen, Washington. He was awarded a fellowship to the Otis Art Institute in Los Angeles at age eleven, and in 1932 studied painting briefly at the California School of Fine Arts in San Francisco. Motherwell received a B.A. from Stanford University in 1937 and enrolled for graduate work later that year in the Department of Philosophy at Harvard University, Cambridge, Massachusetts. He traveled to Europe in 1938 for a year of study abroad. His first one-man show was presented at the Raymond Duncan Gallery in Paris in 1939.

In September of 1940 Motherwell settled in New York City, where he entered Columbia University to study art history with Meyer Schapiro, who encouraged him to become a painter. In June 1941 Motherwell traveled to Mexico with Matta, and remained there until December. After returning to New York, his circle came to include Baziotes, Pollock, de Kooning and Hans Hofmann. In 1942 Motherwell was included in the exhibition *First Papers of Surrealism* at the Whitelaw Reid Mansion, New York. In 1944 Motherwell became editor of The Documents of Modern Art series of books, and he has contributed frequently to the literature on modern art since that time.

A one-man exhibition of Motherwell's work was held at Art of This Century in 1944. In 1946 he began to associate with Rothko, Barnett Newman and Herbert Ferber, and spent his first summer in East Hampton, Long Island. This year Motherwell was given one-man exhibitions at The Arts Club of Chicago and the San Francisco Museum of Art, and he participated in *Fourteen Americans* at The Museum of Modern Art in New York. The artist has subsequently taught and lectured throughout the United States, and has continued to exhibit extensively in the United States and abroad. In 1956 Motherwell began spending summers in Provincetown, Massachusetts. A Motherwell exhibition took place at the Städtische Kunsthalle, Düsseldorf, the Museum des 20. Jahrhunderts, Vienna, and the Musée d'Art Moderne de la Ville de Paris in 1976-77. He was given important one-man exhibitions at the Royal Academy, London, and the National Gallery, Washington, D.C., in 1978. A retrospective of his works organized by the Albright-Knox Art Gallery, Buffalo, traveled in the United States from 1983 to 1985. Since 1971 the artist has lived and worked in Greenwich, Connecticut.

120 Personage (Autoportrait). December 9, 1943

Paper collage, gouache and ink on board,
40⅞ x 25¹⁵⁄₁₆″ (103.8 x 65.9 cm.)
76.2553 PG 155; PG coll. cat. 128

In 1943 Motherwell and Pollock experimented with collage in response to Peggy Guggenheim's initial preparations for a show of works in the medium at Art of This Century. The exhibition was to include examples by the foremost European practitioners, such as Picasso, Schwitters and Matisse. Though Pollock's interest in the technique soon waned, Motherwell's concern with it endured. *Personage (Autoportrait)* (which has previously been known as *Surprise and Inspiration,* a title assigned by Peggy Guggenheim or someone in her circle*) was one of several important examples Motherwell produced in 1943-44.

Motherwell has acknowledged that the work might, in a sense, evoke an embodiment of self-image (Rudenstine, pp. 585-586). Although a blocky, somewhat mournful figure can be imagined, *Personage (Autoportrait)* is more readily perceived as a nonreferential coloristic and spatial construction. A jagged horizontal-vertical mesh organizes the composition. The alignment of the edges of the cut, torn and glued paper provides the grid, which has a physical, planar dimension. Not only does the paper structure the work architectonically, but it serves as a support for vigorously applied paint. The energy of handling and the uneven oval shapes separated by a black line in this early collage foreshadow the powerful facture and recurrent motifs of Motherwell's later work.

* See H. H. Arnason, *Robert Motherwell*, rev. ed., New York, 1982, n.p.

L.F.

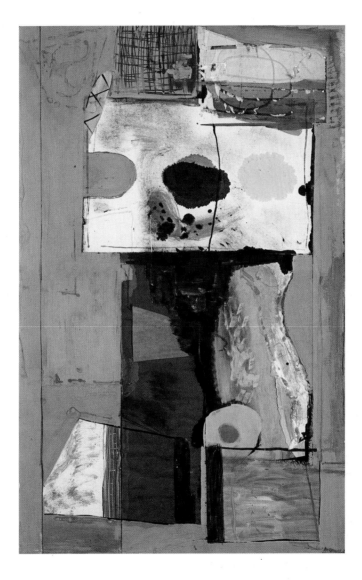

Mark Rothko 1903-1970

Marcus Rothkowitz was born in Dvinsk, Russia, on September 25, 1903. In 1913 he left Russia and settled with the rest of his family in Portland, Oregon. Rothko attended Yale University in New Haven on a scholarship from 1921 to 1923. That year he left Yale without receiving a degree and moved to New York. In 1925 he studied under Max Weber at the Art Students League. He participated in his first group exhibition at the Opportunity Galleries in New York in 1928. During the early 1930s Rothko became a close friend of Milton Avery and Adolph Gottlieb. His first one-man show took place at the Portland Art Museum in 1933.

Rothko's first one-man exhibition in New York was held at the Contemporary Arts Gallery in 1933. In 1935 he was a founding member of *The Ten,* a group of artists sympathetic to abstraction and expressionism. He executed easel paintings for the WPA Federal Art Project from 1936 to 1937. By 1936 Rothko knew Newman. In the early forties he worked closely with Gottlieb, developing a painting style with mythological content, simple flat shapes and imagery inspired by primitive art. By mid-decade his work incorporated Surrealist techniques and images. Peggy Guggenheim gave Rothko a one-man show at Art of This Century in New York in 1945.

In 1947 and 1949 Rothko taught at the California School of Fine Arts, San Francisco, where Still was a fellow instructor. With Baziotes, Hare and Motherwell, Rothko founded the short-lived The Subjects of the Artist school in New York in 1948. The late forties and early fifties saw the emergence of Rothko's mature style in which frontal, luminous rectangles seem to hover on the canvas surface. In 1958 the artist began his first commission, monumental paintings for the Four Seasons Restaurant in New York. The Museum of Modern Art, New York, gave Rothko an important one-man exhibition in 1961. He completed murals for Harvard University in 1962 and in 1964 accepted a mural commission for an interdenominational chapel in Houston. Rothko took his own life in his New York studio on February 25, 1970. A year later the Rothko Chapel in Houston was dedicated.

121 Sacrifice. April 1946

Watercolor, gouache and India ink on paper,
39⅞6 x 25⅞″ (100.2 x 65.8 cm.)
76.2553 PG 154; PG coll. cat. 157

During the late 1930s and early 1940s Rothko, like Baziotes, Gottlieb and Theodoros Stamos, combined mythical themes with primordial imagery in order to express universal experiences. In his work of this period evanescent biomorphic shapes float within an atmospheric haze. Resembling rudimentary life forms or primitive subaquatic plants and creatures, these shapes are intended to provide a visible equivalent of images lodged in the subconscious. Though he drew primarily on his innermost sensations, Rothko also looked toward earlier art. The example of Miró is evoked in *Sacrifice* in the dotted line, the flame, the amorphic personage at the lower left and in the meandering threadlike tendrils.

Figurative and literary allusions, albeit disguised, persist here. Architectural elements contrast with the aquatic forms and nebulous milieu: the horizontal registers are articulated like moldings, as in an untitled oil painting of 1939-40 by Rothko (Collection Mr. and Mrs. Richard E. Lang, Medina, Washington), in which a frieze of faces appears between an undulating cornice and two ornamental tiers. The title may be inspired by Rothko's interest in Greek tragedy and Nietzsche's examination of its origins. Despite the persistence of these references, overtly representational images have disappeared, signaling a move toward the complete abstraction of Rothko's mature style. In its horizontal zoning, cloudlike texture and blurred contours, *Sacrifice* anticipates his characteristic, fully evolved colorfield paintings.

L.F.

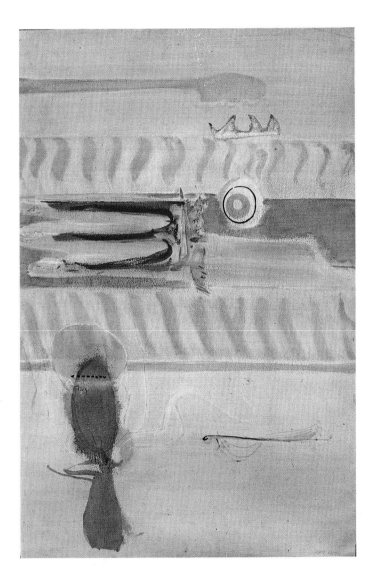

Clyfford Still 1904-1980

Clyfford Still was born in Grandin, North Dakota, on November 30, 1904. He attended Spokane University in Washington for a year in 1926, and again from 1931 to 1933. After graduation he taught at Washington State College in Pullman until 1941. Still spent the summers of 1934 and 1935 at the Trask Foundation (now Yaddo) in Saratoga Springs, New York. From 1941 to 1943 he worked in defense factories in California. In 1943 his first one-man show took place at the San Francisco Museum of Art, and he met Rothko in Berkeley. That same year Still moved to Richmond, Virginia, where he taught at the Richmond Professional Institute.

When Still was in New York in 1945, Rothko introduced him to Peggy Guggenheim who gave him a one-man exhibition at her Art of This Century gallery in early 1946. Later that year the artist returned to San Francisco, where he taught for the next four years at the California School of Fine Arts. Solo exhibitions of his work were held at the Betty Parsons Gallery in New York in 1947, 1950 and 1951 and at the California Palace of the Legion of Honor in San Francisco in 1947. In New York in 1948 Still worked with Rothko and others on developing the concept of the school which became known as The Subjects of the Artist. He re-settled in San Francisco for two years before returning again to New York. A major Still retrospective took place at the Albright Art Gallery, Buffalo, in 1959. In 1961 he settled on his farm near Westminster, Maryland.

Solo exhibitions of Still's paintings were presented by the Institute of Contemporary Art of the University of Pennsylvania in Philadelphia in 1963 and at the Marlborough-Gerson Gallery in New York in 1969-70. He received the Award of Merit for Painting in 1972 from the American Academy of Arts and Letters, of which he became a member in 1978, and the Skowhegan Medal for Painting from the Skowhegan School of Painting and Sculpture in Maine in 1975. Also in 1975 a permanent installation of a group of his works opened at the San Francisco Museum of Modern Art. The Metropolitan Museum of Art in New York gave him a major exhibition in 1980; Still died on June 23 of that same year in Baltimore.

122 Jamais. May 1944

Oil on canvas, 65$\frac{1}{16}$ x 32$\frac{1}{4}$″ (165.2 x 82 cm.)
76.2553 PG 153; PG coll. cat. 163

Like the examples by Baziotes, Motherwell and Rothko in the Peggy Guggenheim Collection (cat. nos. 119-121), *Jamais* dates from the formative, exploratory period of Abstract Expressionism. Though the influence of Surrealism pervaded the work of these artists in the early forties, they were moving toward distinctive independent styles.

Until 1946-47 the single upright figure dominated Still's painting. In its elongation and expressionistic distortion, this element is reminiscent of figures painted by Miró and Picasso in the 1930s. Here the figure is barely particularized, appearing as a black flame or cleft in the blazing environment that surrounds it. Later it was to disappear entirely within the craggy, tenebrous abstractions for which Still is best known. The sphere, which interrupts the thrusting verticality of his tense lines in several of these early works, was also to vanish. Concern with the contrast of light and dark was to become increasingly important, and was emphasized by jarring color juxtapositions. The canvas, already large in this example, was to reach monumental proportions and create an impact rivaling that of the viewer's own environment.

The present painting is one of the few by Still bearing its original title. He disdained titles, and discarded those he had given to early works because he considered that they too strongly influenced the observer's experience of the painting. Indeed, *Jamais* (French for "never") lends an air of finality and melancholy to this scene, and encourages one to read the figure as howling in protest or despair above a setting sun.

L.F.

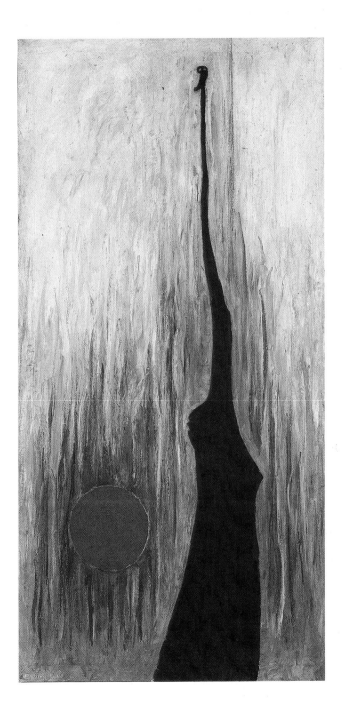

Mark Tobey 1890-1976

Mark Tobey was born on December 11, 1890, in Centerville, Wisconsin. From 1906 to 1908 he attended Saturday classes at The Art Institute of Chicago. In 1911 Tobey moved to New York, where he worked as a fashion illustrator for *McCall's* magazine. His first one-man show was held at M. Knoedler & Co., New York, in 1917.

In 1918 Tobey converted to the Bahā'ī World Faith, which led him to explore the representation of the spiritual in art. Four years later he moved to Seattle and began teaching at the Cornish School of Allied Arts. Also that year he began to explore Chinese calligraphy. The artist went to Paris in 1925, beginning his lifelong travels. While in the Middle East in 1926, he became interested in Persian and Arabic script. Upon returning to Seattle in 1928, Tobey cofounded the Free and Creative Art School. From 1931 to 1938 he was resident artist at Dartington Hall, a progressive school in Devonshire, England. His tenure there was punctuated with frequent absences for travel to Mexico, the United States and the Orient. Tobey spent a month in a Zen monastery outside Kyoto in 1934; the following year he began his "white writing" paintings, which were shown for the first time at the Willard Gallery, New York, in 1944. Tobey exhibited regularly at the Willard Gallery thereafter.

Tobey returned in 1938 to Seattle where, in addition to painting and teaching, he studied the piano and music theory. During this period he executed several paintings inspired by Seattle's open-air market. The Arts Club of Chicago held one-man shows of Tobey's work in 1940 and 1946. He was given a solo exhibition in 1945 at the Portland Museum of Art, Oregon. In 1951, at the invitation of Albers, Tobey spent three months as guest critic of graduate art-students' work at Yale University. Also that year the artist's first retrospective was held, at the Palace of the Legion of Honor in San Francisco. A one-man show of Tobey's work took place in 1955 at the Galerie Jeanne Bucher in Paris. The next year he was elected to the National Institute of Arts and Letters, and he received a Guggenheim International Award. In 1957 he began his Sumi ink paintings. Tobey was awarded the City of Venice painting prize at the Venice Biennale the following year. The artist settled in Basel in 1960, and in 1961 he became the first American painter to be honored with a one-man exhibition at the Musée des Arts Décoratifs in Paris. Solo presentations of Tobey's work were held at The Museum of Modern Art, New York, in 1962, and at the Stedelijk Museum in Amsterdam in 1966. A major retrospective of the artist's work took place at the National Collection of Fine Arts in Washington, D.C., in 1974. Tobey died in Basel on April 24, 1976.

123 Advance of History. 1964

Gouache and watercolor on paper, 25⅝ x 19¹¹⁄₁₆″ (65.2 x 50.1 cm.)
76.2553 PG 140; PG coll. cat. 170

Mark Tobey's animated matrices of brushed line, like the mature works of Pollock, are allover compositions. That is, unlike conventional representational paintings, they have no discernable center of focus, no single emphasized portion. Even Cubist works maintain vestiges of pictorial illusionism through an increased density of form at their centers (see cat. no. 1). Yet in viewing a work such as *Advance of History*, the eye moves easily from edge to edge without halting at any particular configuration, dipping, plunging, swirling and doubling back to pursue the network of dynamic strokes that expand and breathe on the white surface of the paper. The support thus becomes but a portion of a composition that seems to extend beyond the physical limitations of edges or frames. As Tobey wrote, "I have sought to make my painting 'whole' but to attain this I have used a whirling mass. I take up no definite position."*

Although the development of allover compositions in abstract painting is often associated with Pollock (cat. nos. 110-117), Tobey in fact exhibited works without compositional focus or orientation as early as 1944, two years before Pollock made his first allover painting. In 1935 Tobey introduced his white writing, the characteristic network of white line that covers the surfaces of his works. This innovation followed Tobey's discovery of Oriental traditions of ink brushwork in China and Japan, where he found himself "freed from form by the influence of the calligraphic."** The spontaneity and energy conveyed in his first white writing compositions is still evident in the Peggy Guggenheim work, executed nearly thirty years later. But the frenetic impulses of line in early examples, such as *Broadway Norm*, 1935 (Collection Carol Ely Harper, Seattle), have subsided into the more intricate and delicate fabric of lines of varying widths, densities and color of *Advance of History*.

* Quoted in *Mark Tobey*, exh. cat., Amsterdam, 1966, n.p.

** Ibid., n.p. On the development of white writing, see W. Seitz, *Mark Tobey*, exh. cat., New York, 1962, pp. 50-51.

E.C.C.

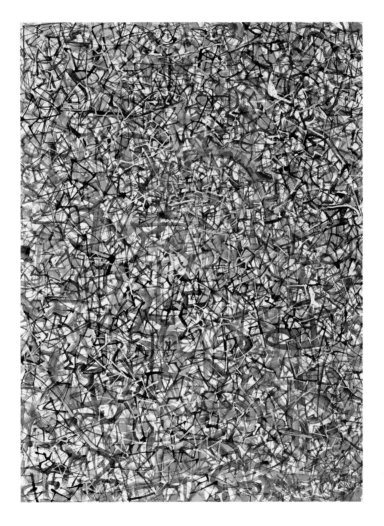

Ibram Lassaw b. 1913

Ibram Lassaw was born of Russian parents in Alexandria, Egypt, on May 4, 1913. He lived for short periods in Naples, Tunis, Malta, the Crimea and Constantinople before emigrating to the United States and settling in Brooklyn, New York, with his family. He learned traditional modeling, casting and carving as a young sculpture student at the Brooklyn Children's Museum in 1926, the Clay Club (now the Sculpture Center), Brooklyn, from 1927 to 1932, and when he took evening classes at the Beaux-Arts Institute of Design, New York, in 1931-32, while attending City College, New York. Lassaw's encounter with avant-garde art in the *International Exhibition of Modern Art* organized by the Société Anonyme at the Brooklyn Museum in 1926 made a powerful impression on him.

In the early 1930s he explored new materials and notions of open-space sculpture. The ideas of Moholy-Nagy and Buckminster Fuller were important to him and he knew the work of González, Picasso, the Russian Constructivists and other abstract sculptors through magazines during this early period. A pioneer of abstract sculpture in the United States, in 1936 Lassaw was a founding member of the *American Abstract Artists*. He participated in this group's annual exhibitions from 1937 to 1951 and served as its president from 1946 to 1949. Between 1933 and 1942 Lassaw worked for various federal arts projects: the Public Works of Art Project, the Civil Works Authority and the WPA Federal Art Project. In 1938 he produced his first welded work. From 1942 to 1944 Lassaw served with the United States army, where he learned direct welding techniques. During the forties he experimented with cage constructions and with acrylic plastics, adding color to his sculptures by applying dye directly to their surfaces. In 1949 Lassaw was a founder of The Club: the first meeting of this informal discussion group of New York School artists took place in his studio.

Lassaw used oxyacetylene welding techniques in evolving his mature improvisational manner in the 1950s. His first solo show was held at the Kootz Gallery in New York in 1951 and since that time he has exhibited widely. Deeply interested in biology, cosmology and religion, the artist studied Zen Buddhism with D. T. Suzuki at Columbia University in New York from 1953 to 1955, thereby extending the range of intellectual sources that constitute the theoretical basis of his work. Lassaw executed the first of numerous public commissions in 1953, for Temple Beth-El in Springfield, Massachusetts. His recent shows include a retrospective at the Heckscher Museum in Huntington, New York, in 1973 and a solo exhibition at the Zabriskie Gallery, New York, in 1977. Ibram Lassaw lives and works in The Springs, East Hampton, New York.

124 Corax. December 1953

Chromium bronze and other metals, 19½ x 23 x 10″
(49.5 x 58.8 x 25.5 cm.)
76.2553 PG 202; PG coll. cat. 94

Lassaw executed his first successful welded work, *Sculpture in Steel,* in 1939 (Collection of the artist); reproductions in French periodicals of the early 1930s of constructions by González and Picasso led him to the welding technique. In 1951, using new welding techniques learned in the army during World War II, Lassaw developed his mature sculpture style in which a wide variety of metals are welded and melted onto open armatures of iron wire. He eschews preliminary drawings on paper, and instead designs each work in three dimensions—heating, bending and stretching wire into an open framework intended to be viewed from all sides.

Using an oxyacetylene torch, the artist then builds up the surface of the armature with molten metal. Often, as in the present sculpture, the form is further elaborated by melting and applying a metal rod like a stick of sealing wax, to create small lumps and clusters over the wire structure. He has compared this process to that of a medieval alchemist-philosopher who, in laboring to make gold, entered "the most profound levels of being, philosophizing over the melting and mixing of his ingredients."*

The titles of Lassaw's sculptures such as *Corax* are often selected after the pieces are finished. They are derived from a wide variety of sources and bear no literal relationship to the form of his work.

* L. Campbell, "Lassaw makes a sculpture," *Art News,* vol. 53, Mar. 1954, p. 66.

E.C.C.

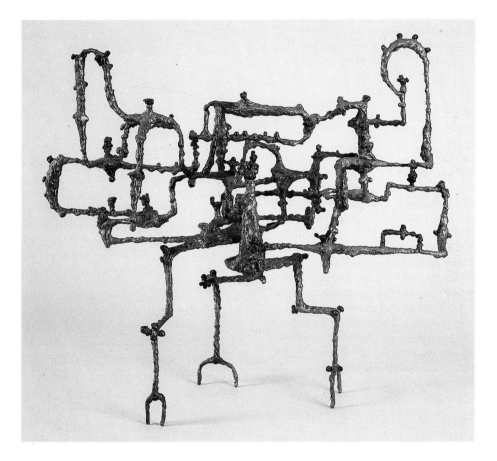

David Hare b. 1917

David Hare was born on March 10, 1917, in New York. From 1936 to 1937 he studied biology and chemistry at Bard College in Annandale-on-Hudson, New York. In the late thirties he began to experiment with color photography, which the Walker Galleries in New York exhibited in 1939. Hare opened a commercial photography studio in New York in 1940, and in the same year the Julien Levy Gallery, New York, gave him a solo exhibition. During the early forties Hare came into contact with a number of the Surrealist emigrés in New York and in 1942 he started to make sculpture. From 1942 to 1944 Hare founded and edited the Surrealist magazine VVV with André Breton, Duchamp and Max Ernst. Peggy Guggenheim presented one-man shows of Hare's work in her Art of This Century gallery from 1944 to 1947. In 1948 he was a founding member, together with Motherwell, Baziotes and Rothko, of The Subjects of the Artist school in New York and he became friendly with Jean-Paul Sartre. This same year he moved to Paris where he met Balthus, Brauner, Giacometti and Picasso. He returned to New York in 1953 but spent the next two summers in Paris.

Hare was included in the São Paulo Bienal of 1951 and 1957, and in 1958 he received a sculpture commission for the Uris building at 750 Third Avenue, New York. Hare began to concentrate on painting in the sixties. From the mid-sixties into the seventies Hare held teaching positions at the Philadelphia College of Art, the University of Oregon, Eugene, and the Tamarind Institute at the University of New Mexico, Albuquerque. He was included in the *Dada, Surrealism and Their Heritage* exhibition of 1968 at The Museum of Modern Art, New York. The following year he received an honorary doctorate from the Maryland Institute of Art, Baltimore. In the late sixties the artist began his *Cronus* series of drawings, collages, paintings and sculpture, which was the subject of a one-man exhibition at the Solomon R. Guggenheim Museum in 1977. In the same year he was included in *Dada and Surrealism Revisited* at the Hayward Gallery, London, and in 1978 he showed in *American Painting of the 1970's* at the Albright-Knox Art Gallery, Buffalo. Hare lives and works in New York.

125 Moon Cage. 1955

Welded steel, 30⅛″ (76.5 cm.) high
76.2553 PG 201; PG coll. cat. 75

Moon Cage is, according to the artist, neither abstract nor representational. Hare has stated that this sculpture "is not figurative literally. A combination of images is more interesting to me. Ambiguity is important; a confusion of images makes you more conscious of the image you are interested in." (Quoted in Rudenstine, p. 380) In approaching the work from any side, one encounters the ambiguity described by the artist in the powerful suggestions of a window, a moon and a human figure.

The central configuration, which is literally drawn in space, is created by the union of four steel rods welded about a central rod. This form both supports and is pierced by two framing rectangles which intersect at right angles at its core. These frames are at once windows that open into space, and the bars of a cage that enclose. The artist says of this spatial dualism, "you are in a house and would like to get out, or you are out and would like to be in." (Quoted in Rudenstine, p. 380) The piece is contained within a square space defined by the welded pedestal, establishing a dialogue between the closed plane of the base and the open space of the construction above it. The configuration is held aloft by the stem of a crescent-shaped abstract form, which may be the moon referred to by the title. This form rhymes with a smaller crescent at the top of the sculpture, from which an arabesque line falls gracefully and dips into the space below the frame of the cage. This continuous arabesque unites the piece by mediating between the empty space at the base of the work and the complex, elongated structure over it.

Hare was an American heir to the Surrealist tradition brought to New York in the early 1940s by European emigré artists. During his stay in Paris between 1948 and 1953, Hare became friends with Giacometti. In its evocation of a female figure caged within an architectural setting, the present work recalls enigmatic sculptures by Giacometti such as *Invisible Object (Hands Holding the Void)* of 1934-35 (Collection Yale University Art Gallery, New Haven). But the elaborate, varied surfaces in *Moon Cage* link Hare not to the heritage of Surrealism but rather to a generation of American sculptors—among them Lassaw (see cat. no. 124), Seymour Lipton and Theodore Roszak—who experimented with complicated molded, pitted and encrusted surfaces of welded metal.

E.C.C.

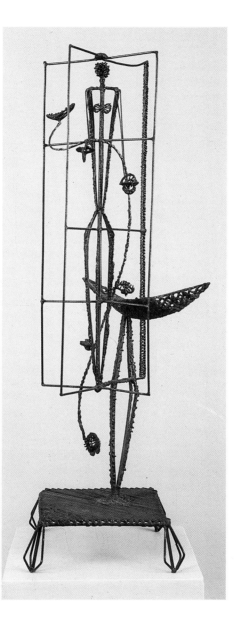

Massimo Campigli 1895-1971

Massimo Campigli was born in Florence on July 4, 1895. In 1909 he moved with his family to Milan, where he came into contact with the Futurist painters. His aspirations, however, were then primarily literary. After military service during World War I, Campigli moved to Paris in 1919. In Paris he worked for nine years as a journalist for *Corriere della Sera*, during which time he began to paint. His first one-man show took place in 1923 at the Galleria Bragaglia in Rome. Self-taught as a painter, he was initially drawn to Purism, Léger, the neoclassicizing works of Picasso and Metaphysical painting. Campigli also admired the preclassical works in the Louvre, but it was only in 1928, when he saw the Etruscan collection at the Villa Giulia in Rome, that he was profoundly affected by ancient art. His love of archaism and of hieratic and abstract form led him to find sources in Cretan, Pompeian and Coptic as well as Etruscan art and to turn to Seurat among the moderns. Campigli's interest in ancient art may have been encouraged by his affiliation with *Sette italiani di Parigi*, the group he formed with de Chirico, Severini and others in 1929. This same year his mature, characteristic works were exhibited, to considerable acclaim, in his first solo show in Paris, at the Galerie Jeanne Bucher.

During the thirties Campigli settled once more in Milan. The artist visited Paris and continued to exhibit there during this time. He showed in 1931, 1935 and 1939 at the Julien Levy Gallery in New York, a city he traveled to in 1935 and 1939. In 1933, with de Chirico, Achille Funi and Mario Sironi he executed murals, now destroyed, at the Palazzo dell'Arte in Milan: this was the first of his several mural projects. After a period of renewed residence in Paris, Campigli returned again to Italy, spending the war years in Venice and Milan.

After 1949 Campigli divided his time among Paris, Milan, Rome and St. Tropez. His first one-man exhibition in a museum was held at the Stedelijk Museum in Amsterdam in 1946 and he participated in the Venice Biennale in 1948, 1958, 1960 and 1962. Among his many one-man shows were presentations at the Stedelijk Museum, Amsterdam, the Gemeentemuseum, The Hague, and the Kunsthalle, Bern, in 1955, and the Palazzo Reale, Milan, in 1967. Campigli illustrated numerous books, including Marco Polo's *Il Milione*, 1942, and André Gide's *Theseus*, 1948, and wrote several texts of an autobiographical-critical nature. The artist died in St. Tropez on May 31, 1971.

126 The Ball Game. 1946

Tempera with gesso on canvas, 26¼ x 23⁷⁄₁₆"
(66.5 x 59.5 cm.)
76.2553 PG 160; PG coll. cat. 27

Here, as in a number of his other paintings of the 1940s, Campigli depicts two women playing a ball game in an empty space undefined by a system of perspective or an architectural setting. Gray brushstrokes partially outline the women's figures, silhouetting them in this ambiguous space. The body of the woman on the left disappears below her waist and to the right of her arm. Her rigid arms cannot throw the balls gracefully; rather they awkwardly present the spheres as emblems of the game. Campigli attaches her arms to sloping shoulders, preserving the angularity introduced by the diamond-shaped upper torso. Her partner is locked into a similarly rigid position, and balances a fifth ball on her head, a detail which removes the scene from the realm of conventional experience. The two women gaze in different directions—they are united not by action or space, but by the balls of their game. As in many of Campigli's works, the viewer is left to speculate whether the figures actually play together, or merely juggle their balls in self-absorbed isolation.

The women's angular torsos, long necks and tiered necklaces recall Cretan and Etruscan figurines. In addition, the use of profile and the suggestion of recession in space through the placement of smaller figures in midair reveal the influence of Egyptian mural painting. Many of these traditions of archaic forms reached Campigli through the filter of Picasso's art, which he had admired and emulated beginning in the 1920s.* Furthermore, Campigli's figures were also influenced by the hourglass-shaped contours of women, many depicted in profile, in Seurat's *A Sunday Afternoon on the Island of La Grande Jatte*, 1884-86 (Collection The Art Institute of Chicago, Helen Birch Bartlett Memorial Collection). Eclectic in origin, these various models merge in Campigli's simple yet sophisticated interpretations of ball games.

* "Intervista con Campigli," *Domus*, no. 223-225. Oct.-Dec. 1947, p. 35.

E.C.C.

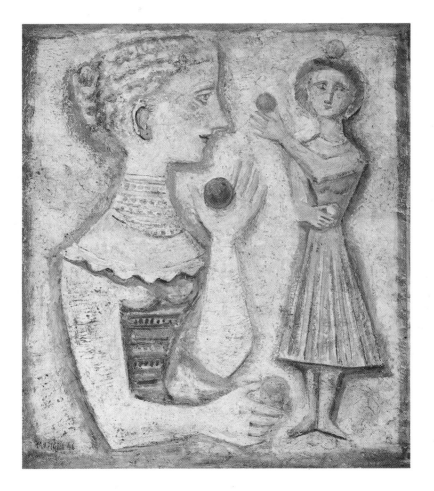

Ben Nicholson 1894-1982

Ben Nicholson was born on April 10, 1894, in Denham, Buckinghamshire, England. Both his parents were painters. Nicholson attended the Slade School of Fine Art in London in 1910-11; between 1911 and 1914 he traveled in France, Italy and Spain. He lived briefly in Pasadena, California, in 1917-18. His first one-man show was held at the Adelphi Gallery in London in 1922. Shortly thereafter he began abstract paintings influenced by Synthetic Cubism. By 1927 he had initiated a primitive style inspired by Rousseau and early English folk art.

From 1931 Nicholson lived in London; his association with Moore and Barbara Hepworth dates from this period. In 1932 he and Hepworth visited Brancusi, Arp, Braque and Picasso in France. Herbin and Hélion encouraged them to join *Abstraction-Création* in 1933. Nicholson made his first wood relief in 1933; the following year, he met Mondrian and married Hepworth. In 1937 Nicholson edited *Circle: International Survey of Constructivist Art*, which he had conceived in 1935.

After moving to Cornwall in 1939, the artist resumed painting landscapes and added color to his abstract reliefs. In 1945-46 he turned from reliefs to linear, abstract paintings. Nicholson was commissioned to paint a mural for the Time-Life Building in London in 1952. He was given retrospectives at the Venice Biennale in 1954, and at the Tate Gallery, London, and the Stedelijk Museum, Amsterdam, in 1955. Nicholson moved to Castagnola, Canton Ticino, Switzerland, in 1958 and began to concentrate once more on painted reliefs. In 1964 he made a concrete wall relief for the *Documenta III* exhibition in Kassel, Germany, and in 1968 was awarded the Order of Merit by Queen Elizabeth. The Albright-Knox Art Gallery, Buffalo, organized a retrospective of his work in 1978. Ben Nicholson died on February 6, 1982, in London.

127 February 1956 (menhir). 1956

Oil and ink(?) on board, 39⅛ x 11¹³⁄₁₆″
(99.4 x 30 cm.)
76.2553 PG 46; PG coll. cat. 129

In the early thirties Nicholson began carving reliefs. By 1934 these were composed of circular and rectilinear elements that he painted white. The first series was completed in 1939. When Nicholson focused again on the medium in the mid-1950s, the reliefs became subtly varied in coloration and texture. The present example is particularly severe, the absence of curved or diagonal lines recalling the work of Mondrian, whom Nicholson knew and admired. The muted, chalky color evokes early Italian Renaissance frescoes and shards of classical pottery.

The parenthetical *menhir* (Breton for "long stone") in the title refers to the simple prehistoric stone slabs found throughout western Europe, especially in Brittany. The association is reinforced by the vertical format and the hewn monochromatic surface of the board. The balance of shape, proportion and placement, apparently so simple, is achieved adroitly. The thickness of the central rectangle decreases gradually from top to bottom, so that the form projects where it meets the upper rectangle, while lying flush above the lower rectangle. This manipulation produces a tapering shadow that softens the strictly perpendicular alignment of the relief to produce a work of austere harmony.

L.F.

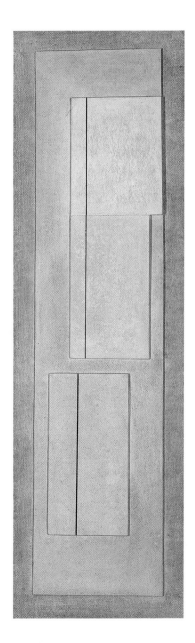

Germaine Richier 1902-1959

Germaine Richier was born in Grans, Bouches-du-Rhône, France, on September 16, 1902. After six years at the Ecole des Beaux-Arts in Montpellier, she moved to Paris in 1926 where she studied privately with Antoine Bourdelle from 1927 to 1929. Her first one-woman exhibition was held at the Galerie Max Kaganovitch in Paris in 1934. Richier was granted a sculpture prize in 1936 by the Blumenthal Foundation in New York, and in 1937 took part in the Paris World's Fair, where she received an award. Also in 1937 she participated in an exhibition of European women artists at the Musée du Jeu de Paume in Paris. Richier showed with Braque, Chagall, Robert Delaunay, Derain, Pierre Bonnard, Lipchitz and others in the French Pavilion at the 1939 World's Fair in New York.

Richier lived primarily in Switzerland and Provence during World War II. In Switzerland she exhibited at the Kunstmuseum Winterthur in 1942 and shared an exhibition with Marini, Fritz Wotruba and Arnold d'Altri at the Kunstmuseum Basel in 1944. After her return to Paris in 1946 she developed her metamorphic imagery. She became increasingly well-known after the war and during the late 1940s and the 1950s exhibited widely in the United States and Europe. Her work was represented at the Venice Biennale in 1948, 1952 and 1954. In 1948 she exhibited with Arp and Laurens at the Galerie d'Art Moderne in Basel and was given an important one-woman show at the Galerie Maeght in Paris. She executed a Crucifixion for the church of Assy in 1950. Richier was awarded a sculpture prize in 1951 at the São Paulo Bienal. Following an important retrospective at the Musée National d'Art Moderne in Paris in 1956, she settled again in Provence. The next year her first solo show in New York took place at the Martha Jackson Gallery. In 1958 Richier participated in group exhibitions at the Kunsthalle Bern and the Musée Rodin, Paris, and was given her first one-woman presentation in an American museum at the Walker Art Center in Minneapolis. She returned to Paris in 1959, visiting Antibes that summer on the occasion of her solo exhibition at the Musée Grimaldi, Château d'Antibes. Richier died in Montpellier on July 31, 1959.

128 Tauromachy. 1953

Bronze, figure 43⅞″ (111.5 cm.) high; base 37¹¹⁄₁₆ x 20⅝″ (95.7 x 52.5 cm.)
76.2553 PG 205; PG coll. cat. 155

Richier's investigation of the composition and decomposition of organic materials situates her work in the vitalist current of twentieth-century sculpture, which concerns itself with natural processes. In an assault on closed form, she breaks through her heavily-worked surfaces to expose the structural armature and hollow spaces within the bodies they describe.

In subject matter and style this sculpture recalls both Picasso's Surrealist bullfight imagery of the 1930s and his sculptures of the early 1950s. Richier, who was herself familiar with the bullfight, shared with Picasso an interest in its mythic, archaic implications.[*] In addition, the robust three-dimensionality, raw surfaces and incorporation of found objects in *Tauromachy* may constitute a response to works such as Picasso's *She-Goat* of 1950 and *Goat Skull and Bottle* of 1951-52. Like Moore during the same year (see cat. no. 80), Richier places her forms in situational relationships. As she wrote: "Finally, the sculpture is a *place*, an entity, a synthesis of movements. I don't know if the *Tauromachy* evokes the sand, but no form, it seems to me, can be separated from the universe, the elements. It is therefore something more than an image."[**]

This bronze was produced in an edition of ten.

[*] For discussion of Richier's references to her native Provence, see Rudenstine, pp. 686-687.

[**] Quoted in *Art du XXᵉ siècle: Fondation Peggy Guggenheim, Venise,* exh. cat., Paris, 1974, p. 106. Author's translation.

L.F.

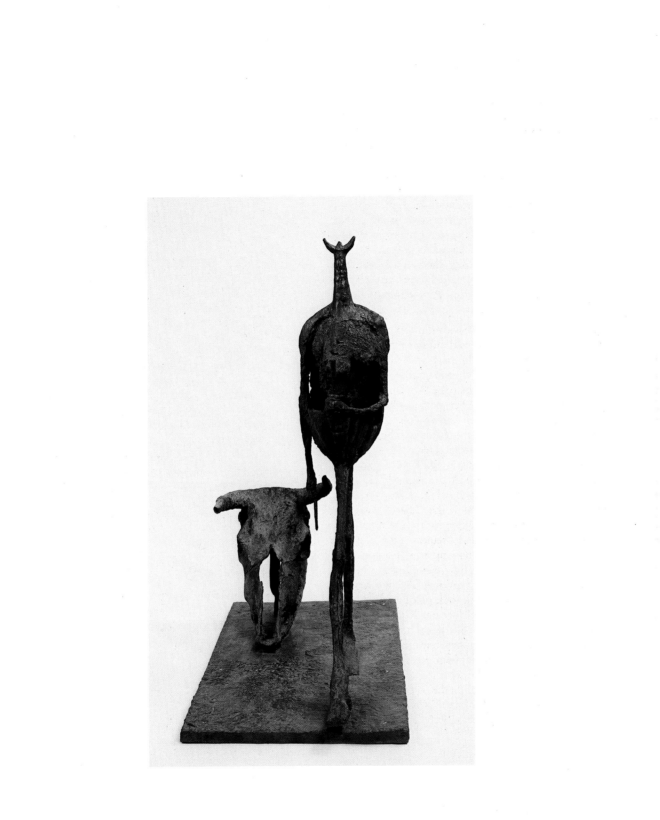

Eduardo Paolozzi b. 1924

Eduardo Paolozzi was born to Italian parents in Leith, near Edinburgh, Scotland, on March 7, 1924. He took evening classes at the Edinburgh College of Art in 1943 and studied at the Slade School of Fine Art, London, from 1947 to 1949. His first one-man exhibition took place at the Mayor Gallery, London, in 1947. From 1947 to 1949 Paolozzi lived in Paris, where he knew Brancusi, Tzara, Giacometti and Dubuffet. Deeply interested in Dada, Surrealism and *Art Brut* in this period, he was especially drawn to the chance effects and incongruous juxtapositions of Surrealist collage. Returning to London in 1949, he associated with Bacon, with whom he shared an enthusiasm for pulp imagery and brutal surfaces. From 1949 to 1955 Paolozzi taught textile design at the Central School of Art and Design, London; this position, which led him to experiment with silkscreen, was the first of many teaching jobs he has held throughout his career.

A leader in the development of British Pop Art, in 1953 Paolozzi was a member of the *Independent Group* of artists and critics in London, influencing its position in favor of popular imagery. He was an organizer of the important *Independent Group* exhibitions *Parallel of Life and Art,* Institute of Contemporary Arts, London, 1953, and *This Is Tomorrow,* Whitechapel Art Gallery, London, 1956. In the 1950s Paolozzi extended the idea of collage into sculpture, and he incorporated found objects into his hulking, rough-surfaced anthropomorphic or animal figures of cast metal. These figures were succeeded in the 1960s by austere polished metal sculptures of simpler monumental components that often included or referred to machine parts, and by dense, elaborate machine constructions. Among the major group shows in which the artist participated during this period were the Venice Biennale, 1952, 1960, and the São Paulo Bienal, 1963. Active as a printmaker since 1950, Paolozzi produced his first unified series of graphics, *All Is When*, a suite of prints on the life and writings of Wittgenstein, in 1964.

During the 1970s he produced compartmentalized boxlike reliefs in wood or bronze as well as freestanding cast metal sculptures with machine references. Doors for the Hunterian Art Gallery, Glasgow University, 1976, and mosaics for the Tottenham Court Road tube station, London, 1980, are recent examples of the numerous public commissions Paolozzi has executed. His major one-man exhibitions include retrospectives at the Tate Gallery, London, 1971, and the Nationalgalerie, Berlin, 1975, and a print retrospective at the Victoria and Albert Museum, London, 1977. The artist, who was elected to the Royal Academy in 1978, lives in London.

129 Chinese Dog 2. May 1958

Bronze, 36⅜ x 25³⁄₁₆″ (92.3 x 64 cm.)
76.2553 PG 200; PG coll. cat. 132

Paolozzi's *Chinese Dog* is an exotic quadruped whose boxlike body and jointless tubular limbs bear little resemblance to any conventional canine. Its overlarge, stocky head, pierced by gaping holes, is joined directly to the body without a neck, and is simultaneously comical and grotesque. It occurred to Paolozzi to identify the creature as a Chinese dog only after the sculpture was completed. The title "is meant to convey the idea that the dog came from another culture, is foreign."[*] Yet that foreign homeland is not truly a geographical region, as the title suggests, but rather a realm of technological detritus which provided the components of the dog's body. In his sculpture of the late 1950s, Paolozzi frequently pressed fragments of scrap metal, wheels, toy numbers, bottle tops and other salvaged junk into tablets of rolled clay, which he sometimes scored and decorated further by hand. For Paolozzi, these separate pieces constitute "sheets of an alphabet of elements awaiting assembly . . . grammar of forms . . . dictionary of design elements."[**] The artist poured wax over the imprinted clay to obtain a wax sheet which he then pressed around other wax sheets, thereby creating the sculpture's core. He then cast the piece, using the lost wax technique. Other grotesque creatures Paolozzi constructed from the impression of machine parts on clay include *Large Frog* of 1958 (Private Collection) or *Chinese Dog 1* (present whereabouts unknown).

Paolozzi's incorporation of such items into these sculptures is a practice rooted in the Surrealist tradition of utilizing the found object. He merged his salvage technique with bronze casting, remaking low materials into art, to produce sculptures that are at once rugged and refined. The discarded materials and crude surfaces of Paolozzi's work recall the *Art Brut* style of Dubuffet's paintings (see cat. no. 134), which he had admired in Paris between 1947 and 1949. Yet unlike Dubuffet, who appeals to primitive art styles and raw, natural materials, Paolozzi debunks a technological aesthetic through the celebration of the machine in a broken and whimsically reordered state.

[*] Letter from the artist to A. Z. Rudenstine, dated Aug. 5, 1983.

[**] Quoted in U. M. Schneede, *Paolozzi*, New York, 1970, p. 12.

E.C.C.

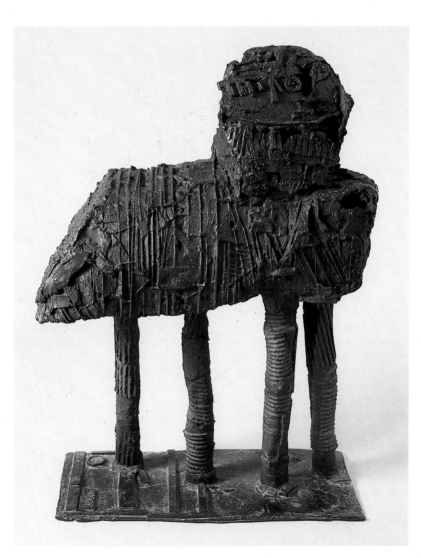

Zoltan Kemeny 1907-1965

Zoltan Kemeny was born on March 21, 1907, in the hamlet of Banica, Transylvania, then part of Hungary. As an adolescent he learned to paint under the tutelage of a naive sign painter. Apprenticed to a cabinet maker in 1921, he began to study technical drawing for furniture making in 1923. From 1924 to 1927 Kemeny took courses in architecture and interior decoration at the School of Decorative Arts in Budapest. Thereafter he enrolled in the School of Fine Arts in Budapest, where he studied painting from 1927 to 1930.

In 1930 Kemeny settled in Paris; he abandoned painting and for the next decade worked as a designer of forged metal objects, a fashion designer and at other trades. After spending the years 1940 to 1942 in Marseille, Kemeny moved to Zürich. There he resumed painting and supported himself as a fashion designer and, from 1952, as an editor for a fashion magazine. His first solo exhibition took place at the Galerie des Eaux-Vives in Zürich in 1945. The following year the artist's first one-man show in Paris was held at the Galerie Kléber, and he met Dubuffet. Subsequent to this encounter with Dubuffet, Kemeny began to introduce commonplace found objects such as pebbles, beads and dried grass into his works, to produce collages and reliefs with crude, rough surfaces.

The character of Kemeny's work changed markedly in 1951 when he made his first translucent, colored reliefs, in which objects are attached to glass sheets. He sometimes enhanced the luminosity of these reliefs by placing an electric light behind the glass. By 1954 the artist began to renounce crude materials in favor of metal, the medium he continued to use throughout his life. Kemeny obtained Swiss citizenship in 1957. In 1959 he was honored with a retrospective at the Kunsthaus Zürich. He gave up his work as a fashion designer to devote himself exclusively to sculpture in 1960, the year of his first one-man exhibition in New York, at the Sidney Janis Gallery. He executed several major commissions in his last years, including a brass sculpture for the municipal theater in Frankfurt. Zoltan Kemeny died on June 14, 1965, in Zürich.

130 Divided Movement. 1957

Copper, copper and iron filings and wood,
31⅛ x 20⅛ x 1″ (79 x 51 x 2.5 cm.)
76.2553 PG 208; PG coll. cat. 85

Kemeny's transition from painting on canvas to sculpting metal reliefs during the period 1946 to 1953 can in part be attributed to the influence of Dubuffet's art. After 1945 Kemeny emulated his friend's *Art Brut* style, by incorporating string, pebbles, rags and buttons into thick collages or low reliefs on plaster, which he often painted.* In 1954 Kemeny's preference for complex, three-dimensional surfaces led him to create low reliefs in metal, a new medium for him. The artist welded or bolted onto wooden and metal supports scrap and ready-made industrial elements in iron, copper, zinc, brass and aluminum. He carefully considered the color of each piece, exploiting the coloristic effects of soldering and using acids to change hues chemically.

In the present example, he organized prefabricated copper elements—most of which are tripartite—into a large oval pattern whose configuration he established in small preparatory sketches. Kemeny then scattered a thin layer of copper and iron filings around the periphery of the oval, leaving a framing ring of smooth copper. A central path, weaving through the oval just below center, divides the configuration in two, so that the sections seem to pull apart as if in the process of fission. The placement of the prefabricated copper units next to each other at irregular intervals and along uneven diagonal axes, contributes to a sense of energy and movement. Other reliefs made by Kemeny in 1957-58, such as *Shadow of a Miracle* (Collection The Museum of Modern Art, New York), convey movement through the relationship of the welded components to empty spaces left on the smooth metal support. These sculptures make no reference to either personal or historical experience: the artist asserts that many of his sources are derived from science and technology.** Although he may seek inspiration from scientific forms and structures (perhaps in the present example a cell in fission), his major concerns are aesthetic and involve the choice of the appropriate industrial materials and techniques to execute his abstract ideas.

* See *Zoltan Kemeny*, exh. cat., Bern, 1982, pp. 45-60.

** Interview in *Zoltan Kemeny: 1907-1965*, exh. cat., London, 1967, n.p.; reprinted from *Le Jardin des Arts*, vol. 77, Apr. 1961.

E.C.C.

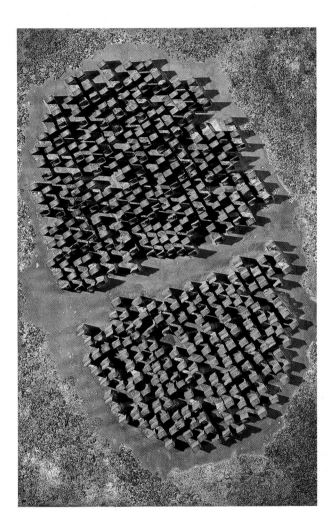

Rufino Tamayo b. 1899

Rufino Tamayo was born August 26, 1899, in Oaxaca, Mexico. Orphaned by 1911, he moved to Mexico City to live with an aunt who sent him to commercial school. Tamayo began taking drawing lessons in 1915 and by 1917 had left commercial school to devote himself entirely to the study of art. In 1921 he was appointed head of the Department of Ethnographic Drawing at the Museo Nacional de Arqueología, Mexico City, where his duties included drawing pre-Columbian objects in the museum's collection. Tamayo integrated the forms and slatey tones of pre-Columbian ceramics into his early still lifes and portraits of Mexican men and women.

The first exhibition of Tamayo's work in the United States was held at the Weyhe Gallery, New York, in 1926. The first of his many mural commissions was given to him by the Escuela Nacional de Música in Mexico City in 1932. In 1936 the artist moved to New York, and throughout the late thirties and early forties the Valentine Gallery, New York, gave him shows. He taught for nine years, beginning in 1938, at the Dalton School in New York. In 1948 Tamayo's first retrospective took place at the Instituto de Bellas Artes, Mexico City. Tamayo was influenced by European modernism during his stay in New York and when he traveled in Europe in 1957. In that year he settled in Paris, where he executed a mural for the UNESCO Building in 1958. Tamayo returned to Mexico City in 1964, making it his permanent home. The French government named him Chevalier and Officier de la Légion d'Honneur in 1956 and 1969, respectively, and he has been the recipient of numerous other honors and awards. His work has been exhibited internationally in group and one-man shows. Important Tamayo retrospectives took place at the São Paulo Bienal in 1977 and the Solomon R. Guggenheim Museum, New York, in 1979. The artist lives and works in Mexico City.

131 **Heavenly Bodies.** 1946

Oil with sand on canvas, 34⅛ x 66¹⁵⁄₁₆″ (86.6 x 170 cm.) 76.2553 PG 119; PG coll. cat. 165

Tamayo filters his pre-Columbian heritage through the pictorial tradition of European modernism in images of man's confrontation with the forces of nature and the universe. In several paintings of 1946-47 he shows primitivized figures gesticulating in terror, awe or longing at the patterns of astral and planetary orbits.

The lines traversing the sky in *Heavenly Bodies* may represent light emanating from stars or the tails of meteors, and may also indicate the mental constructs that join stars in constellations. These lines dissect the rich blue sky into flat planes and simultaneously provide the illusion of movement through a vast space. The purity of the sky's geometry is contrasted with the unevenly curving contours of the human figure, associated formally with the earth. A setting sun is evoked by the red strip on the hill and is reflected on the man's face. While bearing some relation to Mexican folk art, the treatment of the figure derives more directly from the work of Picasso. The combination of frontal and profile view, the gaping mouth and conical eye, the shorthand outlining of the face and outstretched childlike hand have analogies in works such as Picasso's *Guernica* of 1937 (Collection Museo Nacional del Prado, Madrid), which Tamayo had occasion to see in New York.

L.F.

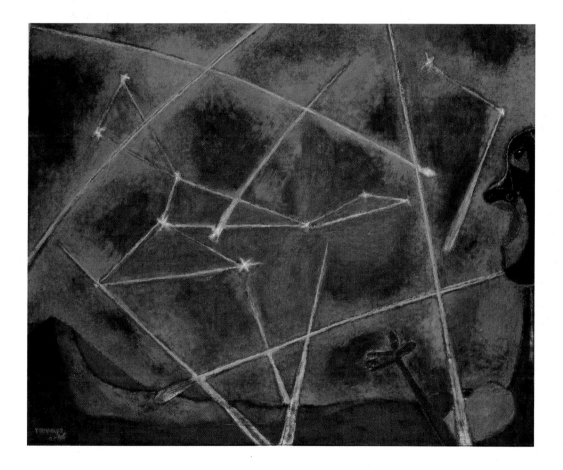

Graham Sutherland 1903-1980

Graham Vivian Sutherland was born on August 24, 1903, in London. From 1921 to 1926 he attended The Goldsmiths' College of Art, London, where he concentrated on engraving. His work was shown for the first time in 1923 at the Royal Academy, London, where he exhibited frequently until 1929. His first solo exhibition took place in London at the Twenty-One Gallery in 1925. Sutherland was an associate of the Royal Society of Painter-Etchers and Engravers from 1925 until 1933. He taught at the Chelsea School of Art in London from 1928 to 1939, and abandoned engraving for painting in the early 1930s. From the mid-1930s Sutherland made frequent trips to Wales.

His paintings were first exhibited at the Rosenberg and Helft Gallery in London in 1938. At the outbreak of World War II he fled to the relative safety of Tetbury in Gloucestershire on the invitation of his friend and patron Kenneth Clark. In the capacity of War Artist from 1940 to 1945, Sutherland executed numerous official commissions. His first New York exhibition took place at Curt Valentin's Buchholz Gallery in 1946. The following year Sutherland met Picasso and Matisse during a visit to southern France. One-man shows of his work opened in 1948 at the Hanover Gallery in London and the Buchholz Gallery in New York.

Sutherland visited Italy on the occasion of his one-man show at the Venice Biennale of 1952; the exhibition was expanded to constitute a retrospective presented at the Musée National d'Art Moderne in Paris that same year. Another Sutherland retrospective, organized by the Arts Council of Great Britain in 1953, was shown at the Stedelijk Museum in Amsterdam, the Kunsthaus Zürich and the Tate Gallery in London. The artist began a portrait commission of Sir Winston Churchill in 1954. From 1955 he divided his time between Venice and Menton. Paul Rosenberg and Co. in New York organized a one-man show of his work in 1959. Other Sutherland exhibitions were held in 1966 at Marlborough Fine Art in London and in 1967 at the Wallraf-Richartz-Museum in Cologne and the Gemeentemuseum in The Hague. He was elected to the American Academy of Arts and Letters in New York in 1972. Sutherland died in London on February 17, 1980.

132 Organic Form. 1962-68

Oil on canvas, 51¼ x 38⅜″ (130.2 x 97.4 cm.)
76.2553 PG 120; PG coll. cat. 164

Sutherland, a Roman Catholic convert, frequently depicted religious imagery, most notably in his tapestry commission for the Cathedral of Coventry, completed in 1961. An echo of the Coventry commission is to be found even in a work as abstract as *Organic Form*. The small crucifixion and flanking sun and moon that appear in the lower part of the tapestry find abstract counterparts here in the monstrance-like shape on the gray platform. Superpositioned on the cross is a humanoid form, rising out of a pod shape that is similar to the fruit form in Sutherland's gouache *Fruit Villefrance* of 1950 (present whereabouts unknown; formerly Collection Galleria Galatea, Turin). The motif resembling a grinning face at the left is composed of elements like those in his *Landscape with Pointed Rocks* series of drawings of 1944. The artist's most literal reference to his own earlier work, however, is the large planetlike globe to the right, which was taken from his 1940 gouache *Design for "The Wanderer" II* (Collection The Hon. Colette Clark, London), a design for a ballet performed by the Vic Wells Company at the New Theatre in London in January of 1941.

L.F.

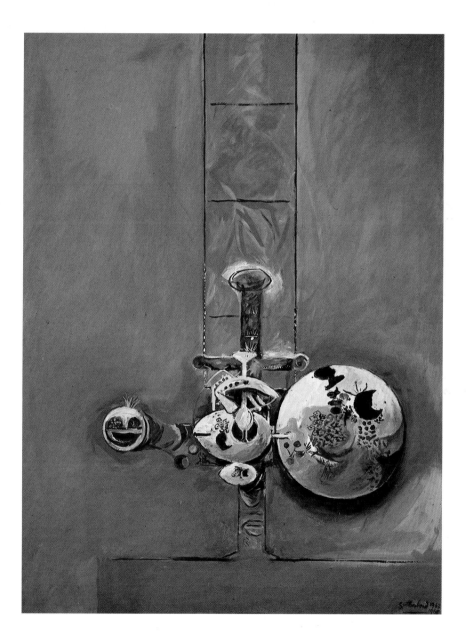

Francis Bacon b. 1909

Francis Bacon was born in Dublin on October 28, 1909. At the age of sixteen he moved to London and subsequently lived for about two years in Berlin and Paris. Although Bacon never attended art school he began to draw and work in watercolor about 1926-27. Picasso's work decisively influenced his painting until the mid-1940s. Upon his return to London in 1929 he established himself as a furniture designer and interior designer. He began to use oils in the autumn of that year and exhibited furniture and rugs as well as a few paintings in his studio. His work was included in a group exhibition in London at the Mayor Gallery in 1933. In 1934 the artist organized his own first one-man show at Sunderland House, London, which he called Transition Gallery for the occasion. He participated in a group show at Thos. Agnew and Sons in London in 1937.

Bacon painted relatively little after his one-man show and in the 1930s and early 1940s destroyed many of his works. He began to paint intensively again in 1944. His first major one-man show took place at the Hanover Gallery in London in 1949. From the mid-1940s to the 1950s Bacon's work reflected the influence of Surrealism. In the 1950s Bacon drew on such sources as Velázquez's *Portrait of Pope Innocent X,* van Gogh's *The Painter on the Road to Tarascon* and Muybridge's photographs. His first one-man exhibition outside England was held in 1953 at the Durlacher Brothers, New York. In 1950-51 and 1952 the artist traveled to South Africa. He visited Italy in 1954 when his work was featured in the British Pavilion at the Venice Biennale. His first retrospective was held at the Institute of Contemporary Art, London, in 1955. Bacon was given a one-man show at the São Paulo Bienal in 1959. In 1962 the Tate Gallery, London, organized a major Bacon retrospective, a modified version of which traveled to Mannheim, Turin, Zürich and Amsterdam. Other important exhibitions of his work were held at the Solomon R. Guggenheim Museum, New York, in 1963 and the Grand Palais in Paris in 1971; paintings from 1968 to 1974 were exhibited at The Metropolitan Museum of Art, New York, in 1975. The artist lives in London.

133 Study for Chimpanzee. March 1957

Oil and pastel on canvas, 60 x 46¹⁄₁₆″ (152.4 x 117 cm.)
76.2553 PG 172; PG coll. cat. 12

Though Bacon is best known for his alienated and often hideously distorted human figures, animals are the subject of at least a dozen of his canvases. He rarely works from nature, preferring photographs, and for images of animals has often consulted Eadweard Muybridge's *Animals in Motion,* Marius Maxwell's *Stalking Big Game with a Camera in Equatorial Africa* and pictures from zoological parks. Intrigued by the disconcerting affinities between simians and human beings, he first compared them in 1949 in *Head IV (Man with a Monkey)* (formerly Collection Geoffrey Gates, New York), in which a man's averted face is concealed by that of the monkey he holds.

Like his human subjects, Bacon's animals are shown in formal portraits or candid snapshots in which they are passive, shrieking or twisted in physical contortions. The chimpanzee in the Peggy Guggenheim work is depicted with relative benevolence, though the blurring of the image, reflecting Bacon's interest in frozen motion and the effects of photography and film, makes it difficult to interpret the pose or expression. In composition and treatment it is close to paintings of simians executed in the fifties by Sutherland, with whom Bacon became friendly in 1946. The faint, schematic framing enables Bacon to "see" the subject better, while the monochrome background provides a starkly contrasting field that helps to define form.

L.F.

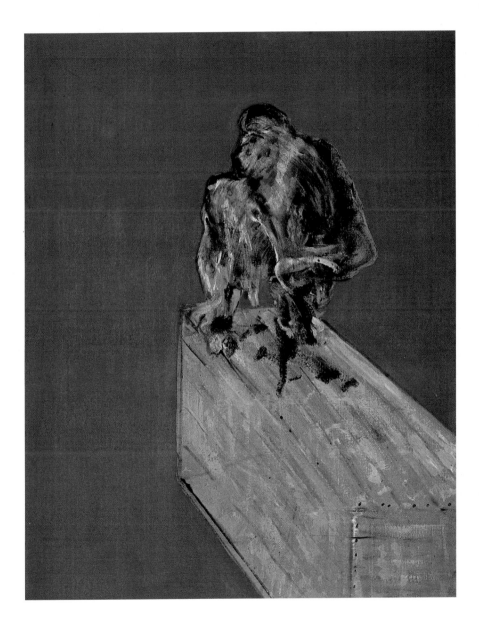

Jean Dubuffet 1901-1985

Jean Dubuffet was born in Le Havre on July 31, 1901. He attended art classes in his youth and in 1918 moved to Paris to study at the Académie Julien, which he left after six months. During this time Dubuffet met Suzanne Valadon, Dufy, Léger and Max Jacob and became fascinated with Hans Prinzhorn's book on psychopathic art. He traveled to Italy in 1923 and South America in 1924. Then Dubuffet gave up painting for about ten years, working as an industrial draftsman and later in the family wine business. He committed himself to becoming an artist in 1942.

Dubuffet's first one-man exhibition was held at the Galerie René Drouin in Paris in 1944. During the forties the artist associated with Charles Ratton, Jean Paulhan, Georges Limbour and André Breton. His style and subject matter in this period owed a debt to Klee. From 1945 he collected *Art Brut,* spontaneous, direct works by untutored individuals, such as mental patients. The Pierre Matisse Gallery gave him his first one-man show in New York in 1947.

From 1951 to 1952 Dubuffet lived in New York; he then returned to Paris, where a retrospective of his work took place at the Cercle Volney in 1954. His first museum retrospective occurred in 1957 at the Schloss Morsbroich, Leverkusen, Germany. Major Dubuffet exhibitions have since been held at the Musée des Arts Décoratifs, Paris, The Museum of Modern Art, New York, The Art Institute of Chicago, the Stedelijk Museum, Amsterdam, the Tate Gallery, London, and the Solomon R. Guggenheim Museum, New York. His paintings of *L'Hourloupe,* a series begun in 1962, were exhibited at the Palazzo Grassi in Venice in 1964. A collection of Dubuffet's writings, *Prospectus et tous écrits suivants,* was published in 1967, the same year he started his architectural structures. Soon thereafter he began numerous commissions for monumental outdoor sculptures. In 1971 he produced his first theater props, the *"practicables."* A major Dubuffet retrospective was presented at the Akademie der Künste, Berlin, the Museum Moderner Kunst, Vienna, and the Joseph-Haubrichkunsthalle, Cologne, in 1980-81. In 1981 the Solomon R. Guggenheim Museum, New York, observed the artist's eightieth birthday with an exhibition. Dubuffet died in Paris on May 12, 1985.

134 Fleshy Face with Chestnut Hair. August 1951

Oil-based mixed media on board, 25 9/16 x 21 1/4″
(64.9 x 54 cm.)
76.2553 PG 121; PG coll. cat. 48

Dubuffet was attracted to the surfaces of dilapidated walls, pitted roads and the natural crusts of earth and rock, and during the 1940s and 1950s sought to create an equivalent texture in his art. He experimented with a variety of materials to produce thick, ruggedly tactile surfaces that constitute deliberately awkward, vulgar and abbreviated imagery, often of grotesque faces or female nudes. Dubuffet made the present work with an oil-based "mortar," applying it with a palette knife, allowing areas to dry partially, then scraping, gouging, raking, slicing or wiping them before applying more medium. The resulting surface is so thick that incisions providing the contours and delineating features seem to model form in relief. He wrote that this mortar enabled him to "provoke systems of relief in objects where reliefs are least expected, and lent itself, at the same time, to very realistic effects of rugged and stony terrains. I enjoyed the idea that a single medium should have this double (ambiguous) power: to accentuate the actual and familiar character of certain elements (notably in figurations of ground and soils), and yet to precipitate other elements into a world of fantasmagoric irreality. . . ."*

Dubuffet's aggressively anticultural, antiaesthetic attitude and spontaneity of expression provided an example for members of the COBRA group in Europe (see cat. nos. 135-137) and New York artists such as Claes Oldenburg and Jim Dine.

* P. Selz and J. Dubuffet, *The Work of Jean Dubuffet*, exh. cat., New York, 1962, p. 66.

L.F.

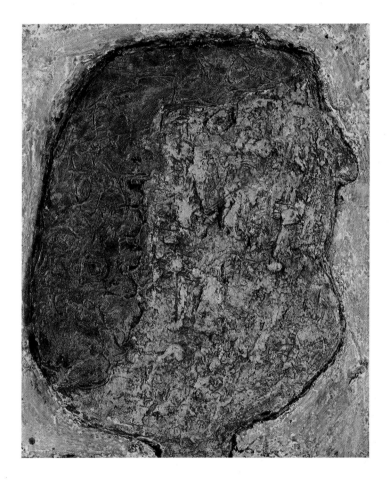

Asger Jorn 1914-1973

Asger Jorn was born Asger Oluf Jørgensen in Vejrum, Jutland, Denmark, on March 3, 1914. He visited Paris in the autumn of 1936, where he studied at Léger's Académie Contemporaine. During the war Jorn remained in Denmark, painting canvases that reflect the influence of Ensor, Kandinsky, Klee and Miró and contributing to the magazine *Helhesten.*

Jorn traveled to Swedish Lapland in the summer of 1946, met Constant in Paris that autumn and spent six months in Djerba, Tunisia, in 1947-48. His first one-man exhibition in Paris took place in 1948 at the Galerie Breteau. At about the same time the COBRA (an acronym for Copenhagen, Brussels, Amsterdam) movement was founded by Appel, Constant, Corneille, Christian Dotremont, Jorn and Joseph Noiret. The group's unifying doctrine was complete freedom of expression with emphasis on color and brushwork. Jorn edited monographs of the Bibliothèque Cobra before disassociating himself from the movement.

In 1951 Jorn returned, poor and ill, to Silkeborg, his hometown in Denmark. He began his intensive work in ceramics in 1953. The following year he settled in Albisola, Italy, and participated in a continuation of COBRA called *Mouvement International pour un Bauhaus Imaginiste.* Jorn's activities included painting, collage, book illustration, prints, drawings, ceramics, tapestries, commissions for murals and, in his last years, sculpture. He participated in the *Situationist International* movement from 1957 to 1961 and worked on a study of early Scandinavian art between 1961 and 1965. After the mid-1950s Jorn divided his time between Paris and Albisola. His first one-man show in New York took place in 1962 at the Lefebre Gallery. From 1966 Jorn concentrated on oil painting and traveled frequently, visiting Cuba, England and Scotland, the United States and the Orient. Jorn died on May 1, 1973, in Aarhus, Denmark.

35 **Untitled.** 1956-57

Oil on canvas, 55½ x 43⅜" (141 x 110.1 cm.)
76.2553 PG 175; PG coll. cat. 81

From about 1948 Jorn filled his canvases with swarming faces and figures, vaporous equivalents of the eccentric visages in crowd scenes by the Belgian artist Ensor. Their scrawled half-innocent, half-demonic features also have antecedents in the creatures of Dubuffet and Klee. These presences hovering on the surface of the canvas are integrated with their surroundings, scarcely distinguishable as representational forms. In the present canvas blobs of paint and linear contours coalesce into a standing, grinning human figure at the right and a bird in the center; a multitude of faces, less acutely defined, emerge, vanish and reappear in the seething environment. Wherever two dots can be interpreted as eyes, a face can be imagined.

The sense of fantasy here is complemented by the candied color applied in thicknesses ranging from thin veneer to heavy ridges. Line incises its way through the fluffy space of this layered pigment to determine boundaries and suggest form. The dots of color sprinkled throughout anticipate the pointillism of the artist's *Luxury Paintings* of the early 1960s, in which paint is dripped onto the canvas from a perforated tin can. The accidental revelation of form and the importance of chance in Jorn's work suggest Surrealist concerns.

L.F.

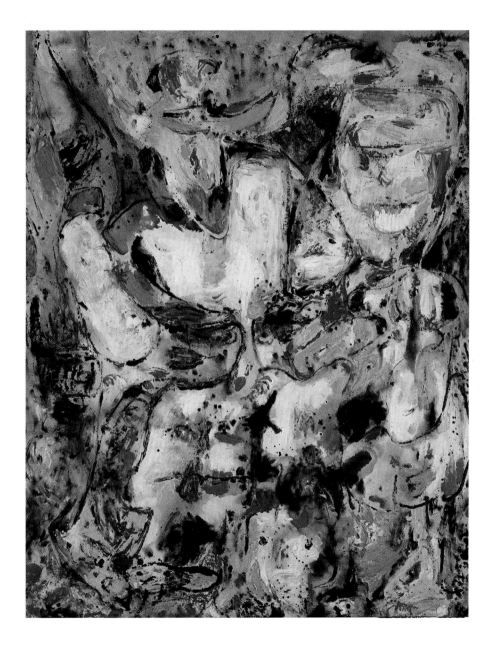

Karel Appel b. 1921

Karel Appel was born on April 25, 1921, in Amsterdam. From 1940 to 1943 he studied at the Rijksakademie van Beeldende Kunsten in Amsterdam. In 1946 his first one-man show was held at Het Beerenhuis in Groningen, The Netherlands, and he participated in the *Jonge Schilders* exhibition at the Stedelijk Museum of Amsterdam. About this time Appel was influenced first by Picasso and Matisse, then by Dubuffet. He was a member of the *Nederlandse Experimentele Groep* and established the COBRA movement in 1948 with Constant, Corneille and others. In 1949 Appel completed a fresco for the cafeteria of the city hall in Amsterdam, which created such controversy that it was covered for ten years.

In 1950 the artist moved to Paris; there the writer Hugo Claus introduced him to Michel Tapié, who organized various exhibitions of his work. Appel was given a one-man show at the Palais des Beaux-Arts in Brussels in 1953. He received the UNESCO Prize at the Venice Biennale of 1954, and was commissioned to execute a mural for the restaurant of the Stedelijk Museum in 1956. The following year Appel traveled to Mexico and the United States and won a graphics prize at the Ljubljana Biennial in Yugoslavia. He was awarded an International Prize for Painting at the São Paulo Bienal in 1959. The first major monograph on Appel, written by Claus, was published in 1962. In the late 1960s the artist moved to the Château de Molesmes, near Auxerre, southeast of Paris. Solo exhibitions of his work were held at the Centre National d'Art Contemporain in Paris and the Stedelijk Museum in Amsterdam in 1968 and at the Kunsthalle Basel and the Palais des Beaux-Arts in Brussels in 1969. During the 1950s and 1960s he executed numerous murals for public buildings. A major Appel show opened at the Centraal Museum in Utrecht in 1970, and a retrospective of his work toured Canada and the United States in 1972. Appel lives in Paris and New York.

136 The Crying Crocodile Tries to Catch the Sun. 1956

Oil on canvas, 57¼ x 44½" (145.5 x 113.1 cm.)
76.2553 PG 174; PG coll. cat. 2

Appel, like Jorn, was a member of the COBRA group, which emphasized material and its spontaneous application. Though the group was short-lived, its concerns have endured in his work. The single standing figures of humans or animals he developed during the 1950s are rendered in a deliberately awkward, naive way, with no attempt at modeling or perspectival illusionism. Thus, the crocodile in this painting is presented as a flat and immobile form, contoured with heavy black lines in the manner of a child's drawing.

Appel's paint handling activates a frenzy of rhythmic movement in *The Crying Crocodile . . .* despite the static monumentality of the subject. Drips and smears are interspersed with veritable stalactites of brilliant, unmodulated color that buckle, ooze, slash, wither and thread their way over the surface. The physicality of the impasto and its topographic variety allow it to reflect light and cast shadows dramatically, increasing the emotional intensity of violent color contrasts. In 1956 Appel summarized the genesis of his work: "I never try to make a painting; it is a howl, it is naked, it is like a child, it is a caged tiger. . . . My tube is like a rocket writing its own space."*

* Quoted in A. Frankenstein, *Karel Appel*, New York, 1980, p. 52.

L.F.

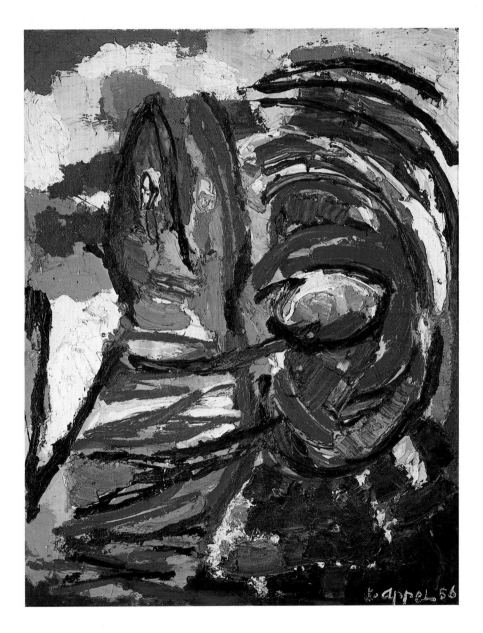

Pierre Alechinsky b. 1927

Pierre Alechinsky was born on October 19, 1927, in Brussels. From an early age Alechinsky was interested in graphic arts and in 1944 he entered the Ecole Nationale Supérieure d'Architecture et des Arts Décoratifs in Brussels, where he studied book illustration and typography. He also painted in a post-Cubist style and later in a manner reminiscent of Ensor. His paintings of monstrous women were shown in his first one-man exhibition at the Galerie Lou Cosyn in Brussels in 1947. That same year he became a member of the group *Jeune Peinture Belge.*

In 1948 expressionist artists including Appel, Jorn, Constant, Carl-Henning Pedersen and Corneille formed the COBRA group. Alechinsky joined COBRA in 1949 and participated in the first *Internationale tentoonstelling experimentele Kunst—COBRA* that year at the Stedelijk Museum in Amsterdam. He became a central figure in the group and organized its second international exhibition in Liège, Belgium, in 1951. Shortly thereafter COBRA disbanded.

Alechinsky moved to Paris in 1951 to study printmaking under a grant from the French government. He studied engraving with Hayter at Atelier 17 in 1952. At about the same time he became fascinated by Japanese calligraphy and in 1955 he went to Tokyo and Kyoto. There he visited masters of the art and produced the award-winning film *Calligraphie japonaise.* In the 1960s Alechinsky traveled extensively in Europe, the United States and Mexico and participated in numerous international exhibitions. An Alechinsky retrospective organized by The Arts Club of Chicago toured the United States in 1965. In 1976 Alechinsky became the first recipient of the prestigious Andrew W. Mellon Prize for artists. The prize was accompanied by a major retrospective of his work in all media at the Museum of Art, Carnegie Institute, Pittsburgh, in 1977. The artist continues to paint and to make prints and book illustrations at his home in Bougival, France.

137 Dressing Gown. 1972

Acrylic on paper mounted on canvas, 38³⁄₁₆ x 60⁷⁄₁₆″ (99.5 x 153.5 cm.)
76.2553 PG 176a; PG coll. cat. 1

Alechinsky's work exhibits a commitment to both spontaneous expression and figuration. Here he combines agitated calligraphic line with vivid washes of thinned paint, out of which simplified figures emerge. The opposition of graphic and painterly effects parallels the tension between representational and abstract forms.

Amid Alechinsky's familiar vocabulary of nonreferential signs, such as the triangle or clusters of loops inscribed in a circle, one can detect the confrontation of two figures, a coiling serpentine form to the left and an anxious childlike presence to the right. Reminiscent of the theme of St. Michael and the dragon, to which he alludes in other works, this scene suggests the conflicts of fundamental impulses. The presence of the blue dressing gown* may suggest a nocturnal setting. Alechinsky has written that "when I paint, I liberate monsters, my own monsters—and for these I am responsible. They are the manifestations of all the doubts, searches and groping for meaning and expression which all artists experience, and at the same time they represent my doubts, my searches and my most profound and diffuse difficulties."**

* Confirmed by the artist in conversation, Apr. 1983, Rudenstine, p. 51.

** Interview by J. Putnam, trans. S. W. Taylor, in *Alechinsky,* exh. cat., New York, 1965, n.p.

L.F.

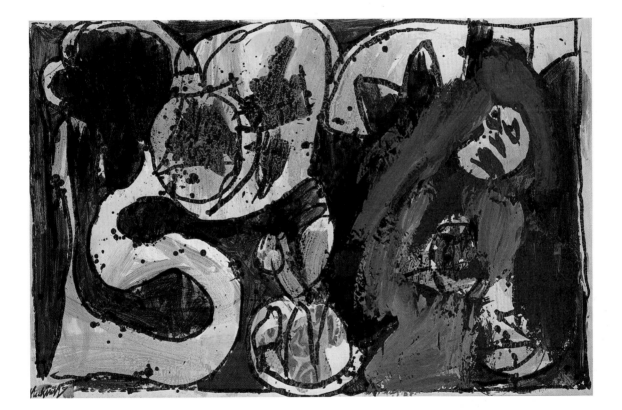

Alan Davie b. 1920

James Alan Davie was born in Grangemouth, Scotland, on September 28, 1920. From 1937 to 1940 he attended the Edinburgh College of Art, where he was awarded Andrew Grant Scholarships in 1938 and 1941. While serving in the Royal Artillery from 1941 to 1946, Davie spent a leave in 1945 in London, where he saw the work of Klee and Picasso. His first one-man show was held in Edinburgh in 1946 at Grant's Bookshop. He used the second Andrew Grant Scholarship in 1948 to visit Paris and traveled to Switzerland, Italy, southern France and Spain. Davie was given a one-man exhibition at Gimpel Fils in 1950 in London, where he has since shown frequently; at this time he met Herbert Read and Roland Penrose.

On the occasion of his solo exhibition at the Catherine Viviano Gallery in New York in 1956 Davie visited the United States for the first time, meeting Motherwell, Pollock, Kline, Rothko and de Kooning. In England later that year he received a Gregory Fellowship in Painting and started to teach at the University of Leeds. A retrospective of his work was held at the Whitechapel Art Gallery in London in 1958. The following year he began to divide his time between Hertfordshire and Cornwall and participated in *II. Documenta* in Kassel.

A major Davie exhibition opened at the Stedelijk Museum in Amsterdam in 1962 and circulated in Europe thereafter. The artist made his first trip to Norway in 1962. Davie was given a one-man show in the British section of the 1963 São Paulo Bienal and he took part in the Salon de Mai in Paris in 1964. Solo exhibitions of his work were organized in 1967 at the Galerie de France, Paris, the Kestner-Gesellschaft Hannover, The Arts Club of Chicago and the University of Minnesota Gallery in Minneapolis. During the 1970s Davie exhibited extensively internationally. An accomplished jazz musician, he gave his first public recital in 1971. He lives and works in Rush Green, Hertfordshire, England, and St. Lucia, West Indies.

138 Peggy's Guessing Box. 1950

Collage and oil on Masonite, 47^{15}/$_{16}$ x 59^{15}/$_{16}$″
(121.7 x 152.2 cm.)
76.2553 PG 169; PG coll. cat. 42

During a visit to Peggy Guggenheim's collection in Venice in 1948, Davie was impressed by Pollock's work, particularly that of his ritualistic, symbolic period of the early 1940s. Davie's large and somber paintings of the 1950s integrate the mythic elements and formal freedom he had discovered in Pollock with the structural rigor of French Cubism.

This early work contains a proliferation of pictographic signs that are open to multiple interpretations. Two stick figures at the lower left represent the fundamental human units of male and female and provide a sense of scale. Measured against this human scale, the other compositional elements become monumental, forming a vast urban environment dimly lit by artificial means. Fragments of words and numbers take on billboard proportions, and, as in Cubist collage, also function as self-representing signs equivalent to invented abstract signs. Bits of collaged newsprint show through here and there, the actual layering of paper on board complementing the illusory layering of forms in paint.

An accomplished jazz musician, Davie has compared his compositional technique in painting to that of jazz improvisation, in which the artist departs from the original structure in an unpremeditated way.

L.F.

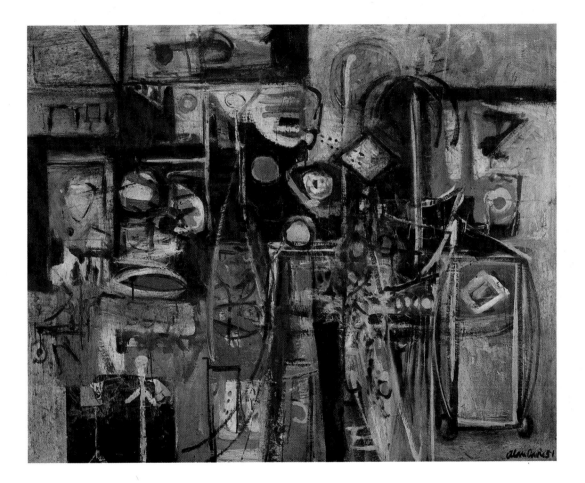

Corneille b. 1922

Corneille was born Corneille Guillaume Beverloo on July 3, 1922, in Liège, Belgium, of Dutch parents. From 1940 to 1943 he studied drawing at the Rijksakademie van Beeldende Kunsten in Amsterdam. His first one-man show was held in 1946 at Het Beerenhuis in Groningen, The Netherlands. Corneille visited Hungary the following year, returning to The Netherlands in 1948 to co-found the *Nederlandse Experimentele Groep* (N.E.G.), which published the periodical *Reflex*, and the COBRA movement, which included Jorn, Appel, Constant, Dotrement and Noiret. Corneille traveled to Tunisia in 1948, and on his return from a summer in Algeria and Tunisia in 1949 participated in the N.E.G. and COBRA exhibitions at the Galerie Colette Allendy in Paris and the Stedelijk Museum in Amsterdam of that year.

In 1950 the artist settled permanently in Paris and began exhibiting at the Salon de Mai. He studied etching with Hayter in 1953 in Paris, and ceramics with Tullio Mazzotti in Albisola, Italy, during the summers of 1954 and 1955. Corneille received the Guggenheim International Award for The Netherlands in 1956, the year of his first one-man exhibition at the Stedelijk Museum, Amsterdam. In 1957 he participated in the Salon des Réalités Nouvelles in Paris. He traveled extensively during this period, visiting Africa, South America, The Netherlands Antilles and the United States.

In 1962 Corneille was given his first solo exhibition in New York at the Lefebre Gallery, where he has since shown frequently. During five successive summers from 1962 through 1966, Corneille worked in the Spanish coastal town of Cadaqués. A Corneille retrospective was held at the Musée d'Antibes, France, in 1963. In 1968 he executed mosaics in Vela-Luka, Yugoslavia, and in 1970 and 1971 he traveled in Mexico. Among his many one-man shows during the 1970s were those presented at Milan's Galleria d'Arte and the Museu de Arte of São Paulo in 1975, at Galerie Espace in Amsterdam in 1977 and at the Galleria C.M. in Rome and the Galerie Kände Malåra, Jönköping, Sweden, in 1978. Corneille now lives and works in Paris.

139 The Great Solar Symphony. 1964

Oil on canvas, 51 1/16 x 63 13/16" (129.6 x 162 cm.)
76.2553 PG 176; PG coll. cat. 34

Brilliant light and intense color characterize Corneille's abstract landscape compositions of the 1950s, painted following his trips to the Sahara Desert. Corneille discovered a new source of inspiration in nature when he spent the summers of 1962 through 1966 painting in the small town of Cadaqués on the coast of Spain. The paintings produced during this period are characterized by a daring, loose application of thin layers of pigment and by dense compositions of large, irregular mosaic-like forms executed in vibrant, primary hues. The shapes in these works often resemble protozoa in cross section and evoke microbiological associations. The potential for germination is implied by the conjunction of ovarian and seedlike forms. Others invite comparison with vegetal and entomological life. Corneille's works of this period, such as the present canvas and *Spell of the Island* of 1965 (Collection Solomon R. Guggenheim Museum, New York), remain abstract, yet his bright palette and organic shapes celebrate the vitality and fecundity of the Cadaqués area.

The Great Solar Symphony has been described by the artist as "an extremely rhythmic work, and also very strong in color" and as very representative of his art.* Bright primary hues of red, blue and yellow and lighter primary values of pink and pale blue dominate a composition accented by pure black, white and secondary tones of green and orange. A vibrant vermillion wheel-shaped disc emerges from the lower edge of the painting, anchoring the dozens of pulsating cellular shapes above it. Several of the elements, such as the green circle in the lower right, are elaborated with seedlike forms which suggest ovarian or vegetal sources. A group of chartreuse spots, like a magnified specimen of multiplying spores, covers a white space at the center of the field. Elsewhere undulating lines surge, creep or drip, independent of any underlying form. Bold outlines in red, black or white encircle and contain many of the amoeba shaped motifs. Corneille has said that "if lines are to be pure, they must reveal the great elemental lines of elemental forces."** The severing of forms at the limits of the canvas implies the continuation of the composition in an infinite field. The presence of universal or cosmic process is indicated by the painting's title, *The Great Solar Symphony*. Corneille depicts in abstract form the energy of the sun and the generative power of its nurturing rays in his orchestration of this joyous cacophony.

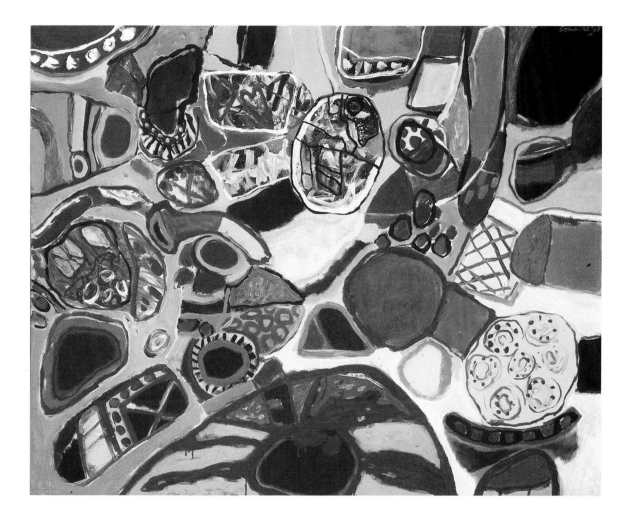

* Letter from the artist to P. Guggenheim, dated July 1964,
  quoted in Rudenstine, p. 175. Author's translation.

** Quoted in F. T. Gribling, "Corneille and luxuriant
   monotony" in *Art and Architecture in the Netherlands*,
   trans. L. Scott, Amsterdam, 1972, p. 8.

E.C.C.

Heinz Mack b. 1931

Heinz Mack was born on March 8, 1931, in Lollar, Germany. In 1949 he moved to Düsseldorf, where he studied painting at the Kunstakademie from 1950 to 1953. He received a degree in philosophy from the University of Cologne in 1956, the year he began to explore problems of movement and of light and its vibration. From 1956 to 1958 Mack developed his light reliefs and light dynamos, works made of polished metal which vibrate and reflect the colors of the surroundings. The Galerie Schmela in Düsseldorf mounted his first one-man exhibition in 1957. In 1957-58, together with Otto Piene, Mack established the *Group Zero*, a loose and continually changing association of artists which included Günther Uecker, Yves Klein, Jean Tinguely and others. Mack renounced color in his painting in 1958, and thereafter produced black or white canvases. In 1958 he also began to formulate his Sahara Project, an environmental work involving proposals for constructions in the desert and the Arctic; this project has continued to preoccupy him. Mack's first one-man show in Paris took place in 1959 at the Galerie Iris Clert.

Since 1960 he has executed numerous architectural-scale works, usually combining industrial materials such as glass, aluminum and stainless steel with light, water, wind, prisms or mirrors. Among these public projects are two water walls for a hospital in Diourbel, Senegal, a light carrousel for the Stedelijk Museum in Amsterdam and a piece for *Expo 70,* Osaka. He made the film *O x O = Kunst* in 1962.

Mack lived in New York during 1965-66 and his first solo exhibition in the United States was held at the Howard Wise Gallery, New York, in 1966. The following year saw the publication of the artist's journal-catalogue *Mackazin.* Major international shows in which Mack has participated include *Documenta III,* Kassel, 1964, and the Venice Biennale, 1970. He designed sets for a 1970 production of *Titus Andronicus* in Düsseldorf as well as other theater decor. In 1976, with the photographer Thomas Hopker, Mack built sculpture gardens in the Sahara and in Greenland: photographs taken of these ephemeral works before the elements destroyed them were published in *Sculpture Safari* in 1977. Mack, who has traveled widely in Europe, Asia and Africa, lives in Mönchengladbach, West Germany.

140 **Cardiogram of an Angel.** 1964

Aluminum mounted on Masonite, 68⅛ x 39⁹⁄₁₆″ (173 x 100.5 cm.)
76.2553 PG 228; PG coll. cat. 101

Mack and the sculptors Piene and Uecker were united by their explorations of the potential of light as subject matter in both sculpture and monochromatic painting when they formed the *Group Zero.* The group appealed for a new beginning for art, akin to the "zone of silence and pure possibility"* embodied by zero, as in the countdown of a rocket launching, a powerful symbol in the late 1950s of new frontiers and infinite potential. Yet in an age of technological advancement, one of the group's most important aims was the reharmonization of "the relations between man and nature—nature offering enormous impulse from the elements...the sky, the sea, the arctic and the desert, air, light, fire, water as means of expression, and not to put the artist in the position of fugitive from the 'modern world.' "** Mack shared with the *Group Zero* artists an interest in the kinetic aspects of light, a concern emerging as early as 1957 in his light reliefs—sculpture constructed of large sheets of polished metal.

In 1961 Mack described light reliefs as "free surfaces in the sky.... it is not the metal that forms the apparition, it is the light relief itself, which outshines and overpowers the materiality of the metal. These light reliefs ...show the ability to change their structure as the light falling on them changes its angle of incidence or its intensity.... Thus the structure is suspended from any fixed identity."*** Mack either folded, pounded or cut polished metal sheets into low reliefs, creating ridges, wedges and fringes that reflect the motion and pattern of incident light. Often he elaborated these basic reflections by placing the relief beneath a sheet of engraved glass or behind a field of electronically charged air which acts as a refracting filter of light. Occasionally he set pieces of metal in motion electronically to control the motion of light. In the Peggy Guggenheim example, however, it is the viewer's own movement in approaching the work that enlivens the polished surface with fluctuating reflections of the gallery environment.

* O. Piene, quoted in C. Barrett, "Group Zero," *Art and Artists,* vol. 1, Dec. 1966, p. 54.

** Ibid., p. 56.

*** H. Mack, "The Sahara Project, Station 10: The Light Reliefs," in *Zero,* trans. and ed. H. Beckmann, Cambridge, Mass., 1973, p. 183.

E.C.C.

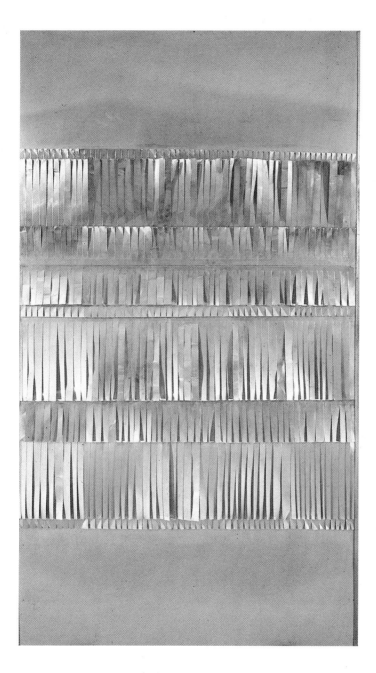

Kenzo Okada 1902-1982

Kenzo Okada was born on September 28, 1902, in Yokohama, Japan. In 1922 he enrolled at the Tokyo Fine Arts University and in 1924 moved to Paris, where he studied with Tsuguji Fujita and was influenced by French painting. Okada exhibited at the Salon d'Automne of 1927 and later that year returned to Japan. His first one-man show took place at the Mitsukoshi Department Store in Tokyo in 1928. The Nichido Gallery, Tokyo, held solo presentations of Okada's work regularly from 1929 to 1935. Also in 1929 two of Okada's paintings were accepted at the sixteenth exhibition of the *Nikakai*, an association of contemporary Japanese artists. Okada was awarded a prize by the *Nikakai* in 1936 and he became a member of the group the following year. During the 1930s, in addition to painting, the artist made illustrations for books and magazines. He taught in Tokyo at the School of Fine Arts, Nippon University, from 1940 to 1942, at the Musashino Art Institute from 1947 to 1950 and at the Tama Fine Arts College in 1949-50. Okada was given solo exhibitions at the Hokuso Gallery, Tokyo, in 1947, 1948 and 1950.

In 1950 the artist moved to New York where, three years later, his first American one-man show was held at the Betty Parsons Gallery. He continued to exhibit there for the rest of his life. In 1954 Okada was awarded the Annual Prize of The Art Institute of Chicago. The following year he represented the United States at the São Paolo Bienal and received the International Prize at the Carnegie International, Pittsburgh. Also in 1955 a one-man show of Okada's work took place at The Corcoran Gallery of Art in Washington, D.C. Okada was the recipient of the Astorre Meyer Prize at the 1958 Venice Biennale, where he represented Japan.

Okada became a United States citizen in 1960. That same year he was awarded a Ford Foundation Grant. In 1965 the Albright-Knox Art Gallery in Buffalo held a retrospective of Okada's work, and The Phillips Collection, Washington, D.C., included him in its exhibition *Three Pioneers of Abstract Painting in 20th-Century Japan* in 1979. Another Okada retrospective took place at the Seibu Museum of Art, Tokyo, in 1982. That year on July 25 the artist died in Tokyo.

141 **Above the White.** 1960

Oil on canvas, 50⅛ x 38¹/₁₆" (127.3 x 96.7 cm.)
76.2553 PG 184; PG coll. cat. 130

Although Okada often derived imagery from nature in his paintings of the late 1950s and early 1960s, *Above the White* is among his more abstract works of this period. Luminous earth tones are layered subtly in large, broad shapes on a field of finely nuanced whites. A blocky rose-colored form penetrates this space, descending from the top edge of the canvas to break the central horizontal tan band and push the left section downward. Lyrical accents of white, blue and red punctuate and lighten the dominant hovering block. Okada animates the white field at the bottom of his canvas with vibrantly colored shapes: the larger forms in the primary hues yellow, blue and red complemented by smaller ones in the secondaries green, orange and purple. Yet the values of all of these hues are restricted and subdued, suggesting a Japanese aesthetic of balance and understatement. This restraint is effected as well through Okada's smooth, chalky surface and the indistinct, blurred edges of his forms. Among the American Abstract Expressionists who inspired Okada, Rothko is clearly important for his large dominant shapes, deep and luminous color and smooth surfaces. Yet Okada merges any American influences with traditional Japanese solutions, such as the asymmetrical placement of the prominent shapes in *Above the White*. In his work the monumental and the delicate fuse, bringing Western and Eastern traditions together in sublime and personal harmony.

E.C.C.

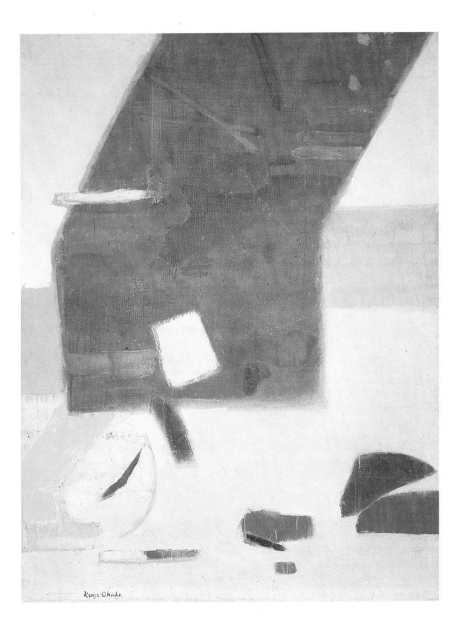

Jean-Paul Riopelle b. 1923

Jean-Paul Riopelle was born in Montreal on October 7, 1923. At an early age he studied painting with Henri Bisson and in 1943 he enrolled at the Ecole du Meuble in Montreal. In 1945 Riopelle began a close association with his instructor Paul-Emile Borduas, Fernand Leduc, Jean-Paul Mousseau and other Canadian avant-garde artists who formed the *Automatiste* group. That year he also traveled to Paris on a Canadian Government Fellowship. In 1946 the artist visited New York, where his work was included in the *International Surrealist Exhibition* and where he met Hayter, Miró and Lipchitz. That same year he participated in *Automatistes* in Montreal.

Riopelle settled in Paris in 1947. He soon met Pierre Loeb and André Breton and befriended writer and aesthetician Georges Duthuit. He also made the acquaintance of many of the artists involved with *art informel*, including Georges Mathieu, Wols and Hans Hartung. In 1948 the *Automatiste* manifesto *Refus global*, which Riopelle signed, was published. Beginning in that year he participated regularly in the Salon de Mai. In 1949 he was represented in the *Salon des Surindépendants* and was given his first one-man exhibition, at the Galerie Nina Dausset. Additional Riopelle shows followed in Paris at the Studio Paul Facchetti and Galerie Pierre and, with Leduc, at Galerie Creuze. He participated in the São Paolo Bienal in 1951 and 1955, receiving an Honorable Mention at the latter. In 1954 and again in 1962 Riopelle was included in the Venice Biennale: he alone represented Canada in 1962 and for his exhibition was awarded the UNESCO Prize. Also in 1954 the first of many Riopelle shows was held at the Pierre Matisse Gallery in New York.

In 1958 Riopelle received an Honorable Mention at the Guggenheim Museum's *Guggenheim International Award* exhibition and a major retrospective of his work was held at the Kölnischer Kunstverein, Cologne. Also that year the artist began to make bronze sculpture using the lost-wax process. His first sculpture exhibition took place at Galerie Jacques Dubourg, Paris, in 1962. Four years later Galerie Maeght, Paris, gave Riopelle the first of several solo shows. Retrospectives of Riopelle's work held in the early 1970s include those at the Fondation Maeght, Saint Paul-de-Vence, France, in 1971, and at the Musée d'Art Moderne de la Ville de Paris the following year. In 1977 the artist began his black and white *Iceberg* series of paintings. Two years later he commenced work on a ceramic wall for the Fondation Maeght, which he completed in 1981. The artist lives and works in Saint Cyr-en-Arthie, France.

142 Painting. 1955

Oil on canvas, 45⅜ x 28⁹⁄₁₆″ (115.2 x 72.5 cm.)
76.2553 PG 187; PG coll. cat. 156

Between 1953 and 1959 Riopelle executed a series of abstract paintings, primarily using a palette knife. The artist laid considerable amounts of paint directly onto the canvas from a tube and then spread the paint with a scraper and knife, creating layers of overlapping thick, multicolored strips. In the present work, most of these strips are bounded by distinct raised edges—evidence of the painter's gesture in scraping the palette knife over the moist paint surface and then lifting it abruptly to leave a hard edge, or implanting the spatula firmly in the bed of wet paint and raising it to leave an exact impression of the contours of the instrument. Some edges drip and fall back into the contiguous strips; others stand firm in sharp raised relief. Between the layers of strips Riopelle used thread to drag blue, black and white paint over the surface, adding spontaneous line to the regularity of the hard-edges left by the palette knife. Although numerous intermediary colors result from the mixture of the pigment on the canvas, the artist began with a selection of black, white and the pure primaries red, blue and yellow.

When the painting is viewed from a slight distance, bright blue and black strips in the outermost layers of paint dominate the composition, spilling exuberantly across the canvas from the upper left corner. A sense of space is generated by dark pattern imposed over the matrix of yellow, green and red strips, some of which form radiating configurations. Viewed from a much closer range, these strips merge with the dense, multicolored layers beneath—and the complexity of individual strokes, modeled from rich, ample layers of mixed pigment, becomes apparent. The intricate, raised edges capture and reflect light in all directions, accentuating the luxuriant materiality of Riopelle's surface.

E.C.C.

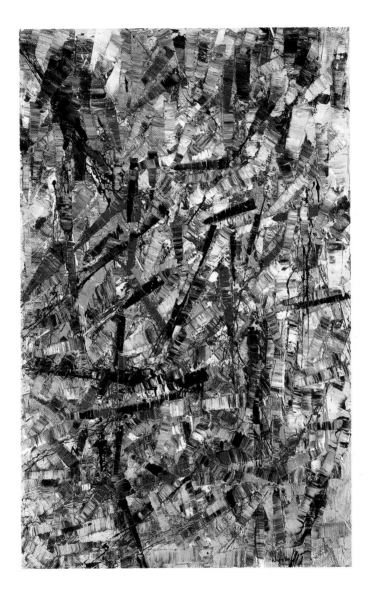

Tancredi 1927-1964

Tancredi Parmeggiani was born on September 25, 1927, in Feltre, Belluno, Italy. He became a friend of Vedova while studying at the Accademia di Belle Arti in Venice in 1946. The following year he visited Paris. From 1948 to 1949 he divided his time between Venice and Feltre. His first one-man show took place at the Galleria Sandri in Venice in 1949. Tancredi moved in 1950 to Rome, where he associated with the *Age d'Or* group, which sponsored exhibitions and publications of the international avant-garde. He participated in an exhibition of abstract Italian art at the Galleria Nazionale d'Arte Moderna in Rome in 1951. That year the artist settled in Venice, where he met Peggy Guggenheim, who gave him studio space and exhibited his work in her palazzo in 1954. He was awarded the Graziano Prize for painting in Venice in 1952.

In 1952 Tancredi and others signed the manifesto of the *Movimento Spaziale,* a group founded by Lucio Fontana in Milan about 1947 advocating a new "spatial" art appropriate to the postwar era. He was given solo exhibitions at the Galleria del Cavallino in Venice in 1952, 1953, 1956 and 1959 and at the Galleria del Naviglio in Milan in 1953. In 1954 he participated in *Tendances actuelles* with Pollock, Wols, Mathieu and others at the Kunsthalle Bern. His work was included in a group show in 1955 at the Galerie Stadler in Paris, a city he visited that year. In 1958 Tancredi was given solo exhibitions at the Saidenberg Gallery in New York and the Hanover Gallery in London, and he took part in the Carnegie International in Pittsburgh. In 1959 he settled in Milan, where he showed several times at the Galleria dell'Ariete. That same year Tancredi traveled again to Paris and in 1960 he visited Norway. Also in 1960 the painter participated in the exhibition *Anti-Procès* at the Galleria del Canale in Venice; the gallery gave him one-man shows this year and in 1962. He received the Marzotto Prize in Valdagno, Italy, in 1962 and exhibited at the Venice Biennale in 1964. Tancredi committed suicide in Rome on September 27, 1964.

143 Composition. 1955

Oil and tempera on canvas, 51 x 76¼" (129.5 x 195 cm.)
76.2553 PG 166

Where Mondrian used the square as a unit with which to express a notion of space and infinity, Tancredi, who saw his aims as parallel to those of Mondrian, seized on the point as his module. He was intrigued by the point's identity as the determinant sign of location, the smallest indication of presence. Tancredi's ideas about infinite space and the use of the point within it were developed by 1951, when he settled in Venice. This work typifies the crowded, architectonic compositions he painted before his visit to Paris in 1955.

Incomplete circles vibrant with undiluted pigment radiate from pivotal points and swirl throughout the canvas. These appear below, above and amid rectangular slabs, the whole comprising a multilayered scaffolding of light and color producing the illusion of extensive, textured depth. Density of form and color increases towards the center of the composition, which consequently appears to bulge forward from the corners, illustrating Tancredi's view of space as curved. The vitality of execution and tactile richness reflect the influence of Pollock. The choppy, animated repetition of color applied with a palette knife resembles that of the French-Canadian painter Riopelle (see cat. no. 142), with whom Tancredi exhibited in 1954.

L.F.

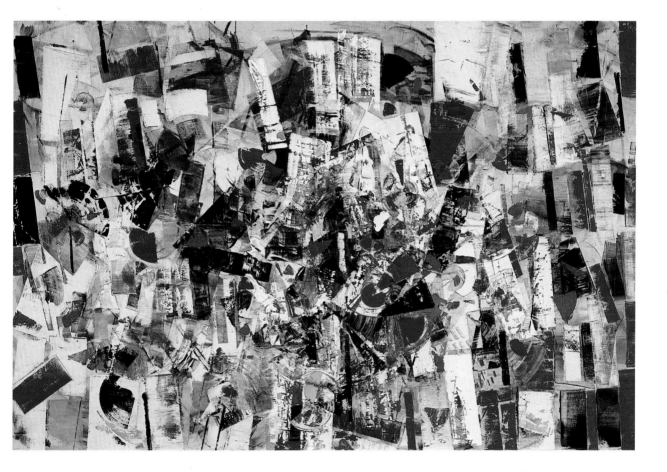

Giuseppe Santomaso b. 1907

Giuseppe Santomaso was born in Venice on September 26, 1907. He studied at the Accademia di Belle Arti there from 1932 to 1934. In 1938 he began his work in graphics, a medium that continues to interest him. In 1939 the artist traveled to Paris on the occasion of his first one-man exhibition at the Galerie Rive Gauche. Santomaso participated in the Quadriennale of Rome in 1943 and executed illustrations for Paul Eluard's *Grand Air* in 1945. In 1946 he was a founding member of the anti-fascist artists' organization *Nuova Secessione artistica italiana—Fronte nuovo delle arti* in Venice.

Since 1948 Santomaso has participated often in the Venice Biennale, where he was awarded the Prize of the Municipality of Venice in 1948 and First Prize for Italian Painting in 1954. He received the Graziano Prize from the Galleria del Naviglio in Milan in 1956 and the Marzotto Prize at the *Mostra Internazionale di Pittura Contemporanea* in Valdagno in 1958, among other awards. Santomaso taught at the Accademia di Belle Arti in Venice from 1957 to 1975. His first exhibition in the United States was held at the Grace Borgenicht Gallery in New York in 1957. The Stedelijk Museum in Amsterdam gave the artist a one-man exhibition in 1960. In 1961 he participated in the São Paulo Bienal and he traveled to Brazil the following year. A Santomaso retrospective toured from the Kunstverein in Hamburg to the Haus am Lützowplatz in Berlin and the Museum am Ostwall in Dortmund in 1965-66. He contributed lithographs to *On Angle*, a book of Ezra Pound's poetry published in 1971. His work appeared in the International Engraving Biennial in Cracow in 1972 and 1978. One-man exhibitions of his work were presented in 1979 by the Fondacio Joan Miró in Barcelona and the Staatsgalerie moderner Kunst in Munich. The Borgenicht Gallery organized a Santomaso show for the spring of 1983. The artist continues to live in Venice.

144 Secret Life. 1958

Oil on canvas, 28¹³⁄₁₆ x 19¹¹⁄₁₆″ (73.1 x 49.9 cm.)
76.2553 PG 161; PG coll. cat. 158

In resolving the problems of representing color and light, Santomaso relies on the daily experience of his native Venice, fortified by knowledge of classical culture. His development of a nonobjective mode of expression for his perceptions of nature was influenced by American abstract art, particularly after his visit in 1957 to New York, where he met Rothko, Motherwell, Newman, Kline, de Kooning and Hofmann. Santomaso uses nature as a "visual pretext" (to employ his own term), absorbing it and changing it into pictorial form; the resultant painting derives its impact not from the imitation of nature, but from the tension between art and nature. Life can be imparted to abstract form only through its disposition in an "abstract order." Santomaso refers to the eye's exploratory adventure as it perceives the "secret combination" of things in nature and their "fantastic equivalent" in painting.* The title of this work alludes to the encounter of life and art, and draws attention to the hint of a centralized human figure, the structural features of which appear and disappear, easily mistaken for the random patterns seen on a peeling Venetian wall. The romantic colors—rose, gray, smokey blue, warm browns and ochers—evoke gentle nostalgia.

* Conversation with the author, June 1981.

L.F.

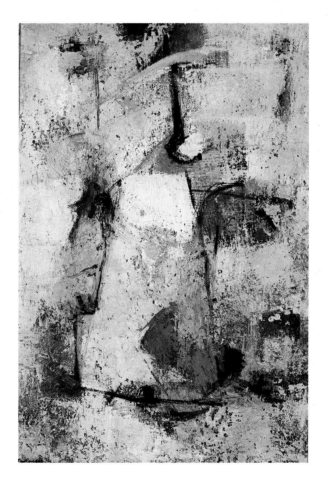

Emilio Vedova b. 1919

Emilio Vedova was born on August 9, 1919, in Venice. He is essentially self-taught as an artist. About 1942 Vedova joined the Milanese anti-fascist artists' association *Corrente,* which also included Renato Birolli, Umberto Vittorini, Renato Guttuso and Ennio Morlotti. Vedova participated in the Resistance movement throughout World War II. His first one-man show took place at the Galleria La Spiga e Corrente in Milan in 1943. In 1946 he collaborated with Morlotti on the manifesto *Oltre Guernica* in Milan and was a founding member of the *Nuova Secessione artistica italiana— Fronte nuovo delle arti* in Venice. Solo exhibitions of Vedova's work took place at the Art Club of Rome in 1946 and the Galleria Cavallino in Venice in 1947.

In 1948 the artist participated in *Arte astratta in Italia* at the Galleria di Roma and in a presentation of the *Fronte nuovo* group at the Venice Biennale. His first one-man show in the United States was held at the Catherine Viviano Gallery in New York in 1951. In 1952 he participated in the *Gruppo degli otto pittori italiani,* organized by Lionello Venturi, and traveled to France. He visited Brazil in 1954 when his one-man exhibition was presented at the Museu de Arte Moderna in Rio de Janeiro. Vedova was represented in the first *Documenta* in Kassel in 1955 and won a Guggenheim International Award in 1957. He executed his first lithographs in 1958, the year he went to Poland on the occasion of his retrospective at the Muzeum Narodowe in Poznań and the "Zachęta" in Warsaw. The artist traveled frequently during the 1960s and 1970s, visiting England, Scandinavia, Germany, Cuba, Yugoslavia and the United States, where he has lectured extensively. In 1965 a Vedova retrospective took place at the Institute of Contemporary Art in Chicago. That summer he succeeded Oskar Kokoschka as head of the Internationale Sommerakademie für bildende Kunst in Salzburg. In 1979 an exhibition of Vedova's graphics opened at the Art Gallery of Western Australia in Perth and toured Australia, and in 1982 he was given a one-man show at the Stedelijk Van Abbemuseum in Eindhoven. Vedova lives and works in Venice, where he has taught at the Accademia di Belle Arti since 1975.

145 **Image of Time (Barrier).** 1951

Egg tempera on canvas, 51⅜ x 67⅛"
(130.5 x 170.4 cm.)
76.2553 PG 162; PG coll. cat. 176

Vedova's work has antecedents in the long tradition of dynamic expression that has existed in Italian art since Tintoretto. Like the Futurists, Vedova sees his work as a response to contemporary social upheavals. Though he shares the emotional pitch of the Futurists, his political position is antithetical to theirs. While they romantically celebrated the aggressive energies of societal conflict, Vedova in his feverish, violent canvases conveys in abstract terms his horror and moral protestation in the face of man's assault on his own kind.

Vedova expressed a political consciousness in his work for the first time during the early 1940s, when his paintings were inspired by the Spanish Civil War. His continuing commitment to social issues gave rise to series such as *Cycle of Protest* and *Image of Time,* initiated during the first years of the 1950s. Though the generating impulse of this turbulent painting is political, its formal preoccupations parallel those of the American Abstract Expressionists Pollock and, above all, Franz Kline. The drama of the angular, graphic slashes of black on white is heightened with accents of orangered. Occupying a shallow space, pictorial elements are locked together in formal combat and emotional turmoil.

L.F.

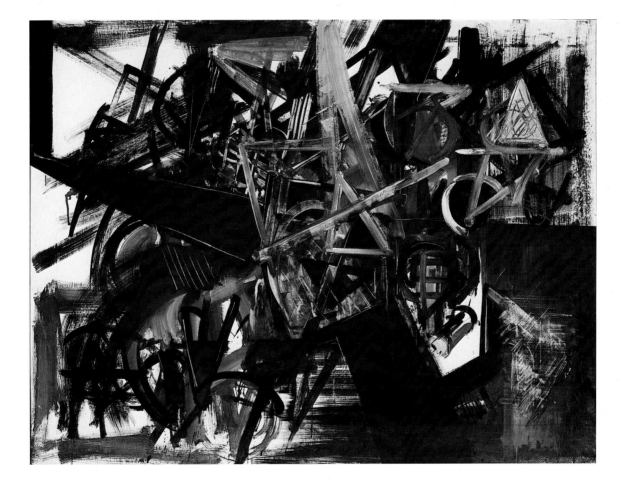

Edmondo Bacci 1913-1978

Edmondo Bacci was born on July 21, 1913, in Venice. He studied with Ettore Tito and Virgilio Guidi at the Accademia di Belle Arti of Venice from 1932 to 1937. His first one-man exhibition was held at the Galleria del Cavallino in Venice in 1945. In 1948 he participated in the Venice Biennale for the first of many times. Bacci was included in the first Genoa Biennale in 1951 and in an exhibition of the *Movimento Spaziale*, the group founded by Lucio Fontana, held in Venice in 1953. He contributed regularly to *Spazialismo* exhibitions thereafter, among them *Espacialismo* at the Galeria Bonino in Buenos Aires in 1966. From the mid-1950s Bacci received support from Peggy Guggenheim.

An important one-man exhibition of Bacci's work took place at the Galleria del Cavallino in 1955. His first one-man show in the United States occurred at the Seventy-Five Gallery in New York the following year. Solo exhibitions of his work were held also at the Galleria del Naviglio, Milan, the Galleria d'Arte Selecta, Rome, and the Galleria "La Cittadella" in Ascona, Switzerland, all in 1957. That same year he participated in *Between Space and Earth* at the Marlborough Gallery in London. Bacci was accorded a separate room at the Venice Biennale of 1958, and he received a Prize of the Municipality of Venice at the *Terza Biennale dell'Incisione Italiana Contemporanea* in Venice in 1959. He was given shows at the Drian Gallery in London in 1961 and at the Frank Perls Gallery in Beverly Hills the following year. In 1961 he also participated in *Neue italienische Kunst* at Galerie 59 in Aschaffenburg. He executed lithographs to accompany a poem by Guido Ballo, *Il ciè-lo Kàinos*, in 1972. Bacci died on October 16, 1978, in Venice.

146 Event #247. 1956

Oil with sand on canvas, 55³⁄₁₆ x 55⅛″ (140.2 x 140 cm.) 76.2553 PG 164; PG coll. cat. 11

Bacci has applied the physicality of action painting to the depiction of the origins of matter in extraterrestrial regions. Like the apocalyptic paintings of the years immediately preceding World War I by artists such as Kandinsky and Franz Marc, his work comingles themes of cosmic genesis and destruction expressed through swirling atmospheric color. The three primaries, red, blue and yellow, predominate, defining broad areas against which a wide range of other colors play. The painting is like a scenario in which light is separated from darkness and space from matter. Planetary forms seem to coalesce out of material produced by a cosmic eruption; they prepare to establish their orbits and generate life. The immediacy and drama of the event is conveyed through the tactility of the surface. The paint, mixed with sand, is encrusted on the canvas to form a kind of topographic ground evoking plains, ridges, lakes and peaks. The activity of the artist in ordering chaos is associated with elemental creational processes within the universe.

L.F.

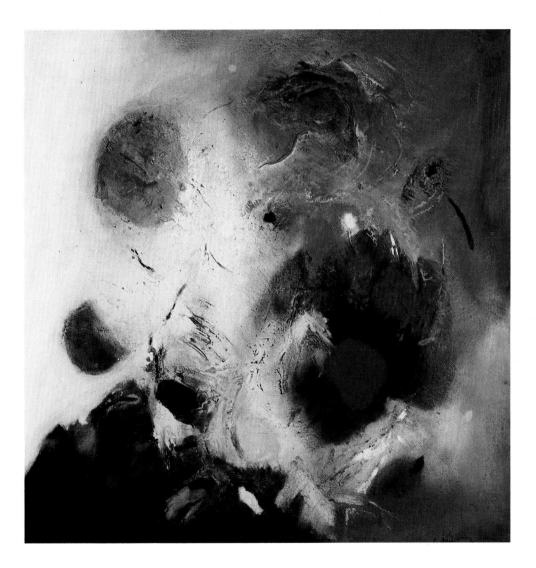

Piero Dorazio b. 1927

Piero Dorazio was born Piero D'Orazio on June 29, 1927, in Rome, where he undertook formal studies in architecture at the University of Rome from 1945 to 1951. About the same time he joined the *Arte Sociale* group, which published single issues of *Ariele* and *La Fabbrica*. In 1947 he co-founded the group *Forma 1*, which produced a *Manifesto del Formalismo—"FORMA I."* Also in 1947 Dorazio was awarded a scholarship to the Ecole des Beaux-Arts in Paris, where he spent a year and met Severini, Braque, Vantongerloo, Pevsner, Arp, Sonia Delaunay, Le Corbusier and other prominent artists. In 1950 he helped organize the cooperative gallery of the *Age d'Or* group in Rome and Florence and in 1952 promoted the international foundation *Origine* in Rome, which published the periodical *Arti Visive*. His friendship with Balla began in 1951.

Dorazio was invited to attend the Summer International Seminar at Harvard University in 1953, and he remained in the United States for a year afterwards. He met Motherwell, Rothko, Kiesler, Kline and Clement Greenberg in New York. His first one-man exhibitions were held at the Wittenborn One-Wall Gallery and the Rose Fried Gallery in New York in 1953. After returning to Rome in 1954, Dorazio periodically visited Paris, London and Berlin, where he became a friend of Will Grohmann and the dealer Rudolf Springer. His book *La fantasia dell'arte nella vita moderna* appeared in 1955. He traveled to Switzerland, Spain and Antibes in 1957, the year of his first one-man show in Rome, at the Galleria La Tartaruga. In 1960 the artist was given a one-man exhibition at the Venice Biennale. From 1960 to 1969 he taught at the Graduate School of Fine Arts at the University of Pennsylvania. Since then Dorazio has held many academic positions in the United States. He visited Greece, Africa and the Middle East in 1970 and in 1974 settled in Todi, Italy. On the occasion of his show at the André Emmerich Gallery in New York in 1977, Dorazio visited the United States; during the next few years he traveled extensively in Europe and Africa. Retrospectives of his work opened in 1979 at the Musée d'Art Moderne de la Ville de Paris and the Albright-Knox Art Gallery in Buffalo. The artist continues to live and work in Todi.

147 Unitas. 1965

Oil on canvas, 18⅟₁₆ x 30¼" (45.8 x 76.5 cm.)
76.2553 PG 168; PG coll. cat. 47

Dorazio has written that his conception of space and geometry was conceived in the spirit of both Mondrian and Malevich. He constructs his compositions of colored bands disposed horizontally, vertically and diagonally to form crisscross patterns. The palette here is limited to the primary colors, their complementaries, white and a pale flesh-color. Though the paint is applied thinly, the artist's gesture is still visible. The translucence of each chromatic strip allows colors to intermingle and produce new colors in the overlapping areas. By Dorazio's own testimony, his coloristic solutions were influenced in part by the work of Klee and Kandinsky, in part by that of Balla and Severini, whom he met during the late 1940s. Balla's abstract light studies of the early teens provided a specific inspiration. The even geometric simplicity and woven motifs of Dorazio's work from 1965 to the present also derive from Oriental and primitive art. In these paintings, as in North American Indian blankets, formal variations are elaborated within an apparently prescribed decorative patterning. The relationship with weaving is emphasized by the thinness of paint application, which leaves the canvas weave visible.

L.F.

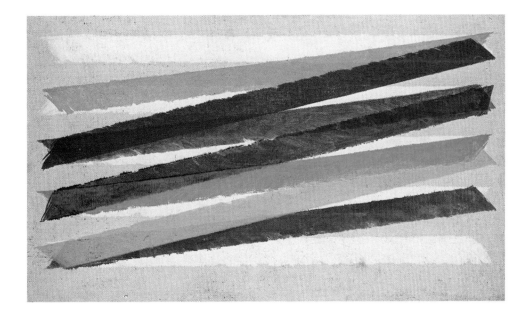

Pietro Consagra b. 1920

Pietro Consagra was born in Mazara del Vallo, Sicily, October 4, 1920. He attended the Accademia di Belle Arti in Palermo from 1938 to 1944, the year he moved to Rome. He first traveled to Paris in 1946 after participating in his first group exhibition in Rome at the Galleria del Cortile. In 1947 he was a founding member of the *Forma* group, which supported a socially oriented nonfigurative aesthetic. *Forma* held the first show of nonfigurative art in postwar Rome, *Mostra del Gruppo Forma I*, at the Art Club, and published a journal on contemporary aesthetics entitled *Forma I*. Consagra's first one-man show took place in 1947 at the Galleria Mola, Rome. In 1949 he contributed work to the exhibition *Scultura all'aperto* at the Peggy Guggenheim Collection in Venice.

Consagra was given one-man exhibitions at the Palais des Beaux-Arts, Brussels, in 1958, at the Galerie de France, Paris, in 1959, the Museum Boymans-van Beuningen, Rotterdam, in 1967, and at the Marlborough Gallery, Rome, in 1974. The artist received the Metallurgical Prize at the São Paulo Bienal in 1955. His first one-man show in New York was held at Staempfli Gallery in 1962. Consagra has participated frequently in the Venice Biennale, where he was awarded the Einaudi Prize in 1956 and a Grand Prize for Sculpture in 1960. In 1962 he participated in the exhibition *I Grandi Premi della Biennale 1948-1960* at Galleria Ca' Pesaro, Venice. In 1964 he executed a fountain in Mazara del Vallo.

Consagra has written at length on his art; many of his articles have been published, and his first book, *L'agguato c'è*, appeared in 1961, followed by *La città frontale* in 1969. His polemical pamphlet of 1952, *La necessità della scultura*, was an important refutation of Arturo Martini's *La scultura lingua morta*. Consagra was given retrospectives at the Galleria Civica d'Arte Moderna, Palermo, in 1973 and at the Marlborough Gallery, Rome, in 1976. The artist lives and works in Rome.

148 Mythical Conversation. 1959

Bronze, $33^{11}/_{16}$ x 28″ (85.5 x 71 cm.)
76.2553 PG 204a; PG coll. cat. 33

Mythical Conversation is one of a group of works Consagra executed in the 1950s and early 1960s that bear titles containing the word "conversation"; another is *Conversation Piece* of 1958 (Collection Solomon R. Guggenheim Museum, New York). These works were made in a variety of media, sometimes combined within a single piece.

Since the 1940s Consagra, as a member of the *Forma* group, has been preoccupied with the formulation of a nonobjective artistic vocabulary through which he could create a "rapport between the object and society."[*] This concern is reflected in the references to dialogue and myth in the title of the present sculpture. The perforated, overlapping formal elements "converse" with one another, while the work as a whole presents itself to the viewer in a frontal encounter. The tabular, two-dimensional nature of the sculpture draws attention to its surface dynamics—the interplay of solids and voids, planar superimpositions and recessions. Consagra expands the meaning of relief through his penetration of the surface, which releases forms that produce figurative associations and allows space to function as an active compositional element.

[*] N. Ponente, *Consagra*, exh. cat., Paris, 1960, n.p.

JANE SHARP

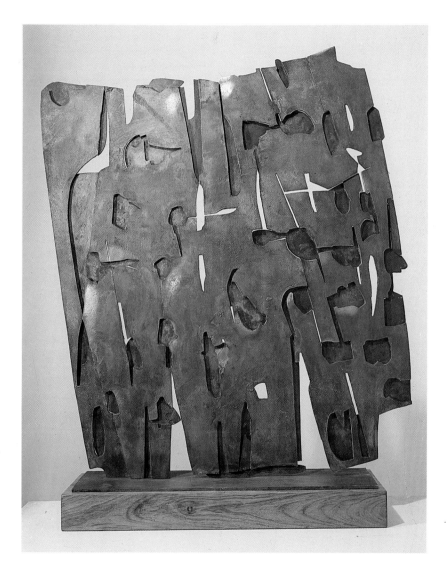

Arnaldo Pomodoro b. 1926

Arnaldo Pomodoro was born on June 23, 1926, in Morciano, Romagna, Italy. From the mid-1940s until 1957 he served as a consultant for the restoration of public buildings in Pesaro, while studying stage design and working as a goldsmith. In 1954 Pomodoro moved to Milan, where he met Fontana, Enrico Baj, Sergio Dangelo and other artists. His work was first exhibited that year at the Galleria Numero in Florence and at the Galleria Montenapoleone in Milan. In 1955 his sculpture was shown for the first time at the Galleria del Naviglio in Milan.

Pomodoro visited New York in 1956 and traveled in Europe in 1958. In Paris in 1959 he met Giacometti and Mathieu, before returning to the United States, where he organized exhibitions of contemporary Italian art at the Bolles Gallery in New York and San Francisco. In New York the following year Pomodoro met David Smith and Louise Nevelson. He helped found the *Continuità* group in Italy in 1961-62. The sculptor traveled to Brazil on the occasion of his participation in the 1963 São Paulo Bienal, where he was awarded the International Sculpture Prize. A one-man show of his work was included in the Venice Biennale of 1964. In 1965 he was given the first of many one-man exhibitions at the Marlborough galleries in New York and Rome.

The artist taught at Stanford University in California in 1966. In 1967 Pomodoro was represented in the Italian Pavilion at *Expo '67* in Montreal, and he received a prize at the Carnegie International in Pittsburgh. In 1968 he taught at the University of California at Berkeley; in 1970 he returned to Berkeley to attend the opening of an exhibition of his work that originated there and later traveled in the United States. During the late 1960s and early 1970s he executed commissions for outdoor sculpture in Darmstadt, New York and Milan. In 1975 a Pomodoro retrospective was sponsored by the Municipality of Milan at the Rotonda della Besana. Pomodoro lives and works in Milan.

149 Sphere No. 4. 1963-64 (cast 1964)

Bronze, 72⅞ (185 cm.) circumference
76.2553 PG 214; PG coll. cat. 154

Though the figurative tradition represented by Marini and Giacomo Manzù has flourished in postwar Italian sculpture, an equally energetic commitment to abstraction has been pursued by artists such as Consagra, Mirko and the Pomodoro brothers, Giò and Arnaldo. Trained in goldsmithing, Arnaldo Pomodoro combines the meticulous approach and skill of the craftsman with the techniques and aims of the caster of large-scale bronzes. His sculpture, cast from plasters of clay originals, contrasts the intricate detailing of jewelry with geometric breadth and clarity.

Using the basic shapes of cube, cylinder and sphere, he tears open their pristine, highly polished surfaces to reveal the internal structure of form. Underneath the gleaming skin and solid flesh of the bronze lies a regulating machinery of cogs and gears, which Pomodoro calls "sign systems," akin to the complex interlocking systems of language or of organic bodies. The sphere not only functions as a geometric shape and analogue of a living body or mineral form, but also suggests the globe of the earth. The equatorial rupture produces configurations suggesting land masses, and evokes the earth's core and dessicated ocean beds. By eliminating frontality, Pomodoro invites the viewer to circle the globe, conveying a sense of uninterrupted rotational movement imitating the orbit of planets.

L.F.

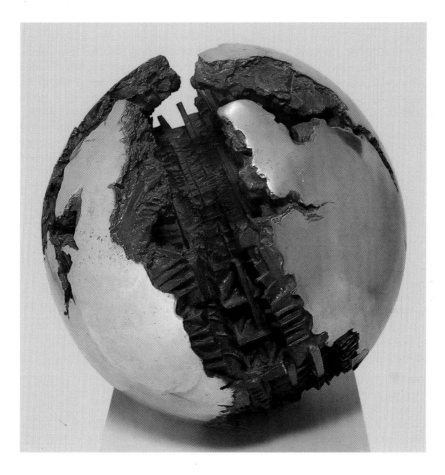

Marino Marini 1901-1980

Marino Marini was born in the Tuscan town of Pistoia on February 27, 1901. He attended the Accademia di Belle Arti in Florence in 1917. Though he never abandoned painting, Marini devoted himself primarily to sculpture from about 1922. From this time his work was influenced by Etruscan art and the sculpture of Arturo Martini. Marini succeeded Martini as professor at the Scuola d'Arte de Villa Reale in Monza, near Milan, in 1929, a position he retained until 1940. During this period Marini traveled frequently to Paris, where he associated with Campigli, de Chirico, Alberto Magnelli and de Pisis. In 1936 he moved to Tenero-Locarno, Canton Ticino in Switzerland; during the following few years the artist often visited Zürich and Basel, where he became a friend of Richier, Giacometti and Wotruba. In 1936 he received the Prize of the Quadriennale of Rome. He accepted a professorship in sculpture at the Accademia di Belle Arti di Brera, Milan, in 1940.

In 1946 the artist settled permanently in Milan. He participated in *Twentieth-Century Italian Art* at The Museum of Modern Art in New York in 1944. Curt Valentin began exhibiting Marini's work at his Buchholz Gallery in New York in 1950, on which occasion the sculptor visited the city and met Arp, Calder, Max Beckmann, Lipchitz and Feininger. On his return to Europe, he stopped in London, where the Hanover Gallery had organized a one-man show of his work, and there met Moore. In 1951 a Marini exhibition traveled from the Kestner-Gesellschaft Hannover to the Kunstverein in Hamburg and the Haus der Kunst of Munich. He was awarded the Grand Prize for Sculpture at the Venice Biennale in 1952 and the Feltrinelli Prize at the Accademia dei Lincei in Rome in 1954. One of his monumental sculptures was installed in The Hague in 1959.

Retrospectives of Marini's work took place at the Kunsthaus Zürich in 1962 and at the Palazzo Venezia in Rome in 1966. His paintings were exhibited for the first time at Toninelli Arte Moderna in Milan in 1963-64. In 1973 a permanent installation of his work opened at the Galleria d'Arte Moderna in Milan, and in 1978 a Marini show was presented at the National Museum of Modern Art in Tokyo. Marini died on August 6, 1980, in Viareggio.

150 The Angel of the City. 1948 (cast 1950?)

Bronze, including base 67¹¹⁄₁₆ x 41¾″ (172 x 106 cm.)
76.2553 PG 183; PG coll. cat. 109

Marini drew on the tradition of Etruscan and Northern European sculpture in developing his themes of the female nude, the portrait bust and the equestrian figure. By interpreting classical themes in light of modern concerns and with modern techniques, he sought to contribute a mythic image that would be applicable in a contemporary context.

The evolution of the subject of the horse and rider reflects Marini's personal response to that changing context. The theme first appears in his work in 1936, when the proportions of horse and rider are relatively slender and both figures are poised, formal and calm. By the following year the horse rears and the rider gestures. In 1940 the forms become simplified and more archaic in spirit, and the proportions become squatter. By the late 1940s the horse is planted immobile with its neck extended, strained, ears pinned back and mouth open, as in the present example, which conveys the qualities characteristic of this period of Marini's work—affirmation and charged strength associated explicitly with sexual potency. Later, the rider becomes increasingly oblivious of his mount, involved in his own visions or anxieties. Eventually he was to topple from the horse as it fell to the ground in an apocalyptic image of lost control, paralleling Marini's feelings of despair and uncertainty about the future of the world.

L.F.

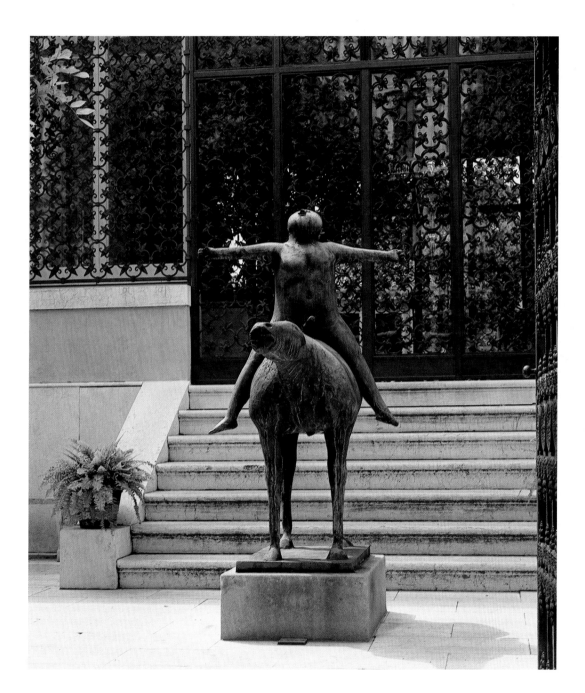

PEGGY GUGGENHEIM COLLECTION

The English-language title of each work is given first. Whenever applicable the title in its original language follows in parentheses.

Height precedes width followed by depth when relevant.

The first number given at the end of each entry is The Solomon R. Guggenheim Foundation number assigned to the work. The catalogue number that follows is the number in the present volume.

Pierre Alechinsky
Dressing Gown (Peignoir). 1972
Acrylic on paper mounted on canvas, 38³/₁₆ x 60⁷/₁₆″
(99.5 x 153.5 cm.)
76.2553 PG 176a; cat. no. 137

Marina Apollonio
Relief No. 505 (Rilievo, no. 505). ca. 1968
Aluminum and fluorescent paint on Masonite,
20 x 20″ (49.9 x 49.8 cm.)
76.2553 PG 230

Karel Appel
The Crying Crocodile Tries to Catch the Sun. 1956
Oil on canvas, 57¼ x 44½″ (145.5 x 113.1 cm.)
76.2553 PG 174; cat. no. 136

Alexander Archipenko
Boxing (La Boxe). 1935
Terra-cotta, 30⅛″ (76.6 cm.) high
76.2553 PG 26; cat. no. 19

Arman
Variable and Invariable (Variable et invariable). 1963
Metal and wood, 25½ x 33½″ (24.8 x 85.1 cm.)
76.2553 PG 219

Kenneth Armitage
People in a Wind. 1951
Bronze, 25⅝″ (65.2 cm.) high
76.2553 PG 196

Diarchy. 1957
Bronze, 11¾″ (29.8 cm.) high
76.2553 PG 197

Jean Arp
Large Collage (Grand Collage). 1955 reconstruction
of original of ca. 1918
Paper collage, watercolor, metallic and oil paint on
Masonite, 38⅜ x 30⅝″ (97.6 x 77.8 cm.)
76.2553 PG 52; cat. no. 64

*Overturned Blue Shoe with Two Heels Under a Black Vault
(Soulier bleu renversé à deux talons, sous une voûte noire).*
ca. 1925
Painted wood, 31¼ x 41⅛ x 2″ (79.3 x 104.6 x 5 cm.)
76.2553 PG 53; cat. no. 65

Head and Shell (Tête et coquille). ca. 1933
Polished brass, 2 pieces, total 7¾ x 8⅞″ (19.7 x 22.5 cm.)
76.2553 PG 54; cat. no. 66

Crown of Buds I (Couronne de bourgeons I). 1936
Limestone, 19⅜ x 14¾″ (49.1 x 37.5 cm.)
76.2553 PG 56; cat. no. 67

Maimed and Stateless (Mutilé et apatride). 1936
Newspaper and papier-mâché, 6¼ x 7³/₁₆ x 9¹³/₁₆″
(17.1 x 18.3 x 25 cm.)
76.2553 PG 55

Untitled. 1940
Pencil on paper, 10½ x 8³/₁₆″ (26.7 x 20.8 cm.)
76.2553 PG 57

Amphora-Fruit (Fruit-amphore). 1946(?) (cast 1951)
Bronze, 29⅜ x 38¹⁵/₁₆″ (74.5 x 99 cm.)
76.2553 PG 58; cat. no. 68

Edmondo Bacci
Event #247 (Avvenimento #247). 1956
Oil with sand on canvas, 55³/₁₆ x 55⅛″ (140.2 x 140 cm.)
76.2553 PG 164; cat. no. 146

Event #292 (Avvenimento #292). 1958
Oil on canvas, 32⅞ x 54⁵/₁₆″ (83.5 x 138 cm.)
76.2553 PG 165

Francis Bacon
Study for Chimpanzee. March 1957
Oil and pastel on canvas, 60 x 46¹/₁₆″ (152.4 x 117 cm.)
76.2553 PG 172; cat. no. 133

Enrico Baj
Lost (Perdu). 1967
Oil and collage on fabric, 23¾ x 28⅞″ (60.2 x 73.2 cm.)
76.2553 PG 184a

Giacomo Balla
Abstract Speed + Sound (Velocità astratta + rumore).
1913-14
Oil on board, including artist's painted frame
21½ x 30⅛" (54.5 x 76.5 cm.)
76.2553 PG 31; cat. no. 20

William Baziotes
Untitled. 1943
Gouache on paper mounted on cardboard, 9¹⁄₁₆ x 12"
(23 x 30.5 cm.)
76.2553 PG 157; cat. no. 118

The Room. 1945
Gouache on board, 17¹⁵⁄₁₆ x 24" (45.6 x 61 cm.)
76.2553 PG 156; cat. no. 119

Umberto Boccioni
*Dynamism of a Speeding Horse + Houses (Dinamismo di
un cavallo in corsa + case).* 1914-15
Gouache, oil, wood, cardboard, copper and coated iron,
44½ x 45¼" (112.9 x 115 cm.)
76.2553 PG 30; cat. no. 21

Martha Boto
Optical Structure (Structure optique). 1963
Plexiglass, 12½ x 12½ x 21¼" (31 x 31 x 53 cm.)
76.2553 PG 224

Constantin Brancusi
Maiastra. 1912(?)
Polished brass, including base 29" (73.1 cm.) high
76.2553 PG 50; cat. no. 43

Bird in Space (L'Oiseau dans l'espace). 1932-40
Polished brass, 53" (134.7 cm.) high
76.2553 PG 51; cat. no. 44

Georges Braque
The Clarinet (La Clarinette). Summer-fall 1912
Oil with sand on oval canvas, 36 x 25⅜" (91.4 x 64.5 cm.)
76.2553 PG 7; cat. no. 5

The Bowl of Grapes (Le Compotier de raisin). 1926
Oil with pebbles and sand on canvas, 39⅜ x 31¼"
(100 x 80.8 cm.)
76.2553 PG 8; cat. no. 6

Victor Brauner
Untitled. 1941
Gouache on paper, 3 works in 1 mat, 4¾ x 4¼"
(12 x 10.4 cm.); 5⁹⁄₁₆ x 4⅛" (14.2 x 10.7 cm.);
5 x 3³⁄₁₆" (12.8 x 8.2 cm)
76.2553 PG 114.1-.3

Untitled. 1945
Encaustic on board, sight, 9³⁄₁₆ x 5¹³⁄₁₆" (23.3 x 14.8 cm.)
76.2553 PG 115

The Surrealist (Le Surréaliste). January 1947
Oil on canvas, 23⅝ x 17¾" (60 x 45 cm.)
76.2553 PG 111; cat. no. 90

Téléventré. 1948
Encaustic on board, 28½ x 23⅝" (72.5 x 60 cm.)
76.2553 PG 112; cat. no. 91

Consciousness of Shock. April 1951
Encaustic on board, 25¼ x 31½" (64 x 80 cm.)
76.2553 PG 113; cat. no. 92

Untitled. 1954
Encaustic on board, 13⁹⁄₁₆ x 9¹⁵⁄₁₆" (34.5 x 25.2 cm.)
76.2553 PG 116

René Brô
Autumn at Courgeron (L'Automne à Courgeron). 1960
Oil on canvas, 73⅝ x 57¹¹⁄₁₆" (187 x 146.5 cm.)
76.2553 PG 188

Reg Butler
Woman Walking. 1951
Bronze, 19" (48.3 cm.) high
76.2553 PG 195

Alexander Calder
Mobile. ca. 1934
Glass, china, iron wire and thread, ca. 65¾ x 46¹⁄₁₆"
(ca. 167 x 117 cm.)
76.2553 PG 139; cat. no. 98

Mobile. 1941
Painted and unpainted aluminum and iron wire,
ca. 84¼" (214 cm.) high
76.2553 PG 137; cat. no. 99

Silver Bedhead. Winter 1945-46
Silver, 63 x 51⁹⁄₁₆" (160 x 131 cm.)
76.2553 PG 138; cat. no. 100

Le Grand Passage. 1974
Gouache on paper, 23⅞ x 30¾″ (58 x 78 cm.)
76.2553 PG 139a

Massimo Campigli
The Ball Game (Il gioco a palla). 1946
Tempera with gesso on canvas, 26¼ x 23⁷⁄₁₆″
(66.5 x 59.5 cm.)
76.2553 PG 160; cat. no. 126

Leonora Carrington
Oink (They Shall Behold Thine Eyes). 1959
Oil on canvas, 15¾ x 35¹³⁄₁₆″ (40 x 90.9 cm.)
76.2553 PG 117

César
Man in Spider's Web (L'Homme dans la toile d'araignée).
1955
Bronze, 13⁹⁄₁₆″ (34.4 cm.) high
76.2553 PG 206

Compression. 1969
Aluminum, 13¹⁵⁄₁₆ x 14³⁄₁₆ x 5½″ (35.4 x 36 x 14 cm.)
76.2553 PG 207

Lynn Chadwick
Maquette for *Teddyboy and Girl.* 1955
Iron and stolit, 15³⁄₁₆″ (38.6 cm.) high
76.2553 PG 198

Marc Chagall
Rain (La Pluie). 1911
Oil (and charcoal?) on canvas, 34⅛ x 42½″ (86.7 x 108 cm.)
76.2553 PG 63; cat. no. 47

Giorgio de Chirico
The Red Tower (La Tour rouge). 1913
Oil on canvas, 28¹⁵⁄₁₆ x 39⅝″ (73.5 x 100.5 cm.)
76.2553 PG 64; cat. no. 48

The Nostalgia of the Poet (La Nostalgie du poète). 1914
Oil and charcoal on canvas, 35⁵⁄₁₆ x 16″ (89.7 x 40.7 cm.)
76.2553 PG 65; cat. no. 49

The Gentle Afternoon (Le Doux Après-midi). Before
July 1916
Oil on canvas, 25¹¹⁄₁₆ x 22¹⁵⁄₁₆″ (65.3 x 58.3 cm.)
76.2553 PG 66; cat. no. 50

William Congdon
Piazza San Marco #15. 1957
Oil on board, 47⁷⁄₁₆ x 55¹⁄₁₆″ (120.5 x 139.8 cm.)
76.2553 PG 180

Venice #1. 1957
Oil on board, 19½ x 31⁷⁄₁₆″ (49.5 x 79.7 cm.)
76.2553 PG 179

Cambodia. 1960
Oil on board, 15¹³⁄₁₆ x 23¹⁵⁄₁₆″ (40.2 x 60.7 cm.)
76.2553 PG 181

Pietro Consagra
Mythical Conversation (Colloquio mitico). 1959
Bronze, 33¹¹⁄₁₆ x 28″ (85.5 x 71 cm.)
76.2553 PG 204a; cat. no. 148

Corneille
The Great Solar Symphony (La Grande Symphonie solaire).
1964
Oil on canvas, 51¹⁄₁₆ x 63¹³⁄₁₆″ (129.6 x 162 cm.)
76.2553 PG 176; cat. no. 139

Joseph Cornell
Fortune Telling Parrot. ca. 1937-38
Box construction, 16¹⁄₁₆ x 8¼ x 6¹¹⁄₁₆″ (40.8 x 22.2 x 17 cm.)
76.2553 PG 126; cat. no. 101

Swiss Shoot-the-Chutes. 1941
Box construction, 21¹⁄₁₆ x 13¹³⁄₁₆ x 4⅛″
(53.8 x 35.2 x 10.5 cm.)
76.2553 PG 127; cat. no. 102

Setting for a Fairy Tale. 1942
Box construction, 11⁹⁄₁₆ x 14⅜ x 3⅞″ (29.4 x 36.6 x 9.9 cm.)
76.2553 PG 125; cat. no. 104

Untitled (Pharmacy). ca. 1942
Box construction, 14 x 12¹⁄₁₆ x 4⅜″ (35.5 x 30.6 x 11.1 cm.)
76.2553 PG 128; cat. no. 103

Soap Bubble Set. 1942
Box construction, 15¾ x 18⅛ x 2⅝″ (40 x 46.7 x 6.7 cm.)
76.2553 PG 129

Toni Costa
Visual Dynamics (Dinamica visuale). 1964
Paper and plastic on wood frame, 19⅛ x 19⅛″
(48.6 x 48.6 cm.)
76.2553 PG 226

Franco Costalonga
Sphere (Sfera). 1969
Plexiglass and chrome, 49¹³⁄₁₆″ (126.5 cm.) circumference
76.2553 PG 231

Egidio Costantini
23 sculptures after sketches by Picasso. 1964
Poured glass, 3⁵⁄₁₆-12″ (10-30.5 cm.)
76.2553 PG 294.1-.23

Salvador Dalí
Untitled. 1931
Oil on canvas, 10¹¹⁄₁₆ x 13¾″ (27.2 x 35 cm.)
76.2553 PG 99; cat. no. 87

Birth of Liquid Desires (La Naissance des désirs liquides).
1931-32
Oil and collage on canvas, 37⅞ x 44¼″ (96.1 x 112.3 cm.)
76.2553 PG 100; cat. no. 88

Alan Davie
Peggy's Guessing Box. 1950
Collage and oil on Masonite, 47¹⁵⁄₁₆ x 59¹⁵⁄₁₆″
(121.7 x 152.2 cm.)
76.2553 PG 169; cat. no. 138

Orange Jumper. 1960
Oil on paper, 14 x 36″ (35 x 91 cm.)
76.2553 PG 170

The Golden Drummer Boy No. 2. 1962
Oil on canvas, 68 x 84″ (172.2 x 213.3 cm.)
76.2553 PG 171

Robert Delaunay
*Windows Open Simultaneously 1st Part, 3rd Motif
(Fenêtres ouvertes simultanément 1ère partie, 3e motif).* 1912
Oil on oval canvas, 22⅜ x 48⅜″ (57 x 123 cm.)
76.2553 PG 36; cat. no. 23

Paul Delvaux
The Break of Day (L'Aurore). July 1937
Oil on canvas, 47¼ x 59¼″ (120 x 150.5 cm.)
76.2553 PG 103; cat. no. 89

Theo van Doesburg
Composition in Gray (Rag-time). 1919
Oil on canvas, 38 x 23¼″ (96.5 x 59.1 cm.)
76.2553 PG 40; cat. no. 37

Counter-Composition XIII (Contra-Compositie XIII).
1925-26
Oil on canvas, 19⅝ x 19⅝″ (49.9 x 50 cm.)
76.2553 PG 41; cat. no. 38

Piero Dorazio
Unitas. 1965
Oil on canvas, 18¹⁄₁₆ x 30¼″ (45.8 x 76.5 cm.)
76.2553 PG 168; cat. no. 147

Jean Dubuffet
*Fleshy Face with Chestnut Hair (Châtaine aux hautes
chairs).* August 1951
Oil-based mixed media on board, 25⁹⁄₁₆ x 21¼″
(64.9 x 54 cm.)
76.2553 PG 121; cat. no. 134

Marcel Duchamp
*Nude (Study), Sad Young Man on a Train (Nu [esquisse],
Jeune Homme triste dans un train).* 1911-12
Oil on cardboard, 39⅜ x 28¾″ (100 x 73 cm.)
76.2553 PG 9; cat. no. 13

Box in a Valise (Boîte-en-valise). 1941
Leather valise containing miniature replicas, color reproductions and 1 photograph with graphite, watercolor and
ink additions of works by Duchamp, 16 x 14⅝ x 3¹⁵⁄₁₆″
(40.7 x 37.2 x 10.1 cm.)
76.2553 PG 10

Raymond Duchamp-Villon
The Horse (Le Cheval). 1914 (cast ca. 1930)
Bronze, 17³⁄₁₆ x 16⅛″ (43.6 x 41 cm.)
76.2553 PG 24; cat. no. 15

Dušan Džamonja
Totem. 1959
Wood, nails and glass, 38⁵⁄₁₆″ (97.3 cm.) high
76.2553 PG 217

Max Ernst
*Little Machine Constructed by Minimax Dadamax in Person
(Von minimax dadamax selbst konstruiertes maschinchen).*
1919-20
Hand printing (?), pencil and ink frottage, watercolor and
gouache on paper, 19½ x 12⅜″ (49.4 x 31.5 cm.)
76.2553 PG 70; cat. no. 55

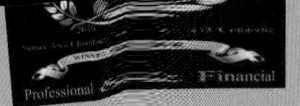

Call Anytime
(941) 483-1663

LOCATIONS TO SERVE YOU:

Island office
211 S. Tamiami Trail
Venice, Florida 34285

NEW ISLAND LOCATION
351 W. Venice Ave.,
Venice Florida 34285
and
981 Ridgewood Ave.
Venice, Florida 34285

Phone: (941) 483-1663
Fax: (941) 488-6640

Email: lueannewd@cs.com
Website: lueanne.com

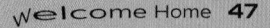

Welcome Home **47**

The Kiss (Le Baiser). 1927
Oil on canvas, 50¾ x 63½" (129 x 161.2 cm.)
76.2553 PG 71; cat. no. 56

The Forest (La Forêt). 1927-28
Oil on canvas, 37⅞ x 51" (96.3 x 129.5 cm.)
76.2553 PG 72; cat. no. 57

Sea, Sun, Earthquake (La Mer le soleil le tremblement de terre). 1931
Oil, gouache and collage on canvas, 17⅞ x 14⅞"
(45.4 x 37.8 cm.)
76.2553 PG 73

The Postman Cheval (Le Facteur cheval). 1932
Paper and fabric collage with pencil, ink and gouache on paper, 25⅜ x 19¼" (64.3 x 48.9 cm.)
76.2553 PG 74; cat. no. 58

Zoomorphic Couple (Couple zoomorphe). 1933
Oil on canvas, 36¼ x 28⅞" (91.9 x 73.3 cm.)
76.2553 PG 75; cat. no. 59

Garden Airplane-Trap (Jardin gobe-avions). 1935-36
Oil on canvas, 21¼ x 25½" (54 x 64.7 cm.)
76.2553 PG 76

The Entire City (La Ville entière). 1936-37
Oil on canvas, 38 x 63⅛" (96.5 x 160.4 cm.)
76.2553 PG 77; cat. no. 60

Attirement of the Bride (La Toilette de la mariée). 1940
Oil on canvas, 51 x 37⅞" (129.6 x 96.3 cm.)
76.2553 PG 78; cat. no. 61

"The Antipope." ca. 1941
Oil on cardboard mounted on board, 12¾ x 10⅜"
(32.5 x 26.5 cm.)
76.2553 PG 79

The Antipope. December 1941-March 1942
Oil on canvas, 63¼ x 50" (160.8 x 127.1 cm.)
76.2553 PG 80; cat. no. 62

Young Woman in the Form of a Flower (Jeune Femme en forme de fleur). 1944 (cast 1957)
Bronze, 13¾ x 14 x 8⁷⁄₁₆" (35 x 35.6 x 21.5 cm.)
76.2553 PG 81

In the Streets of Athens (Dans les rues d'Athènes).
1960 (cast January 1961)
Bronze, including base 38¾ x 19⁹⁄₁₆ x 7³⁄₁₆"
(98.4 x 49.7 x 18.3 cm.)
76.2553 PG 82; cat. no. 63

Claire Falkenstein
Entrance Gates to the Palazzo. 1961
Iron and colored glass, 2 parts, 109¹⁄₁₆ x 35⁷⁄₁₆"
(277 x 90 cm.); 109¹⁄₁₆ x 36" (277 x 91.2 cm.)
76.2553 PG 203

John Ferren
Tempora. 1937
Plaster print, ink and tempera, image 11¹³⁄₁₆ x 9⁷⁄₁₆"
(30 x 24 cm.); plaster 15 x 12⅝" (38.1 x 32.1 cm.)
76.2553 PG 49; cat. no. 106

Leonor Fini
The Shepherdess of the Sphinxes. 1941
Oil on canvas, 18³⁄₁₆ x 15¹⁄₁₆" (46.2 x 38.2 cm.)
76.2553 PG 118

Sam Francis
Untitled. March 1964
Acrylic on paper mounted on Masonite, 40⅞ x 27⅜"
(103.7 x 69.5 cm.)
76.2553 PG 185

Alberto Giacometti
Model for a Square (Projet pour une place). 1931-32
Wood, including base 7⅝ x 12⅛ x 8⅞"
(19.4 x 31.4 x 22.5 cm.)
76.2553 PG 130

Woman Walking (Femme qui marche). 1932
Plaster, including base 59¹⁄₁₆ x 10¹¹⁄₁₆" (150 x 27.2 cm.)
76.2553 PG 132; cat. no. 76

Woman Walking (Femme qui marche). 1932
Bronze, 56¹⁵⁄₁₆" (144.6 cm.) high
76.2553 PG 133

Woman with Her Throat Cut (Femme égorgée).
1932 (cast 1940)
Bronze, 9⅛ x 35¹⁄₁₆" (23.2 x 89 cm.)
76.2553 PG 131; cat. no. 77

Standing Woman ("Leoni") (Femme debout ["Leoni"]).
1947 (cast November 1957)
Bronze, including base 60¼" (153 cm.) high
76.2553 PG 134; cat. no. 78

Piazza. 1947-48 (cast 1948-49)
Bronze, 8¼ x 24⅝ x 16⅞" (21 x 62.5 x 42.8 cm.)
76.2553 PG 135; cat. no. 79

Rosalda Gilardi
Presence (Presenze). ca. 1967
Serpentine, 77⅝" (197.2 cm.) high
76.2553 PG 205a

Albert Gleizes
Woman with Animals (Madame Raymond Duchamp-Villon) (La Dame aux bêtes [Madame Raymond Duchamp-Villon]). Completed by February 1914
Oil on canvas, 77 5/16 x 45 15/16" (196.4 x 114.1 cm.)
76.2553 PG 17; cat. no. 11

Julio González
"Monsieur" Cactus (Cactus Man I) ("Monsieur" Cactus [L'Homme Cactus I]). 1939 (cast 1953-54)
Bronze, 23 5/16 x 9 13/16 x 6 11/16" (64.3 x 25 x 17 cm.)
76.2553 PG 136; cat. no. 75

Arshile Gorky
Untitled. Summer 1944
Oil on canvas, 65¾ x 70 3/16" (167 x 178.2 cm.)
76.2553 PG 152; cat. no. 107

Juan Gris
Bottle of Rum and Newspaper (Bouteille de rhum et journal). June 1914
Paper collage, gouache, conté crayon and pencil on newspaper mounted on canvas, 21⅝ x 18¼" (54.8 x 46.2 cm.)
76.2553 PG 11; cat. no. 9

Alberto Guzmán
Hammered Partition (Partizione percuitente). 1965
Bronze, 12⅜" (31.5 cm.) high
76.2553 PG 220

David Hare
Moon Cage. 1955
Welded steel, 30⅛" (76.5 cm.) high
76.2553 PG 201; cat. no. 125

Grace Hartigan
Ireland. 1958
Oil on canvas, 78¾ x 106¾" (200 x 271 cm.)
76.2553 PG 182

Raoul Hausmann
Untitled. 1919
Watercolor and gouache on paper, sight, 15¼ x 10 13/16" (38.8 x 27.5 cm.)
76.2553 PG 88

Stanley William Hayter
Defeat. 1938-39
Plaster print and ink, 9½ x 15" (24 x 38 cm.)
76.2553 PG 105

Jean Hélion
Equilibrium (Equilibre). 1933-34
Oil on canvas, 38⅜ x 51⅝" (97.4 x 131.2 cm.)
76.2553 PG 44; cat. no. 41

Composition. August-December 1935
Oil on canvas, 57⅛ x 78 13/16" (145 x 200.2 cm.)
76.2553 PG 45; cat. no. 42

Morris Hirshfield
Two Women in Front of a Mirror. 1943
Oil on canvas, 52⅜ x 59⅞" (133 x 152 cm.)
76.2553 PG 122; cat. no. 105

Hundertwasser
Shelter (Casa che protegge—Die Schutzhütte). May 1960
Watercolor on paper, 25 3/16 x 19⅜" (64 x 49.2 cm.)
76.2553 PG 186

Gwyther Irwin
Serendipity 2. 1957
Collage on canvas, sight, 47 x 33 15/16" (119.4 x 86.2 cm.)
76.2553 PG 173

Asger Jorn
Untitled. 1956-57
Oil on canvas, 55½ x 43⅜" (141 x 110.1 cm.)
76.2553 PG 175; cat. no. 135

Vasily Kandinsky
Landscape with Red Spots, No. 2 (Landschaft mit roten Flecken, No. 2). 1913
Oil on canvas, 46¼ x 55⅛" (117.5 x 140 cm.)
76.2553 PG 33; cat. no. 27

White Cross (Weisses Kreuz). January-June 1922
Oil on canvas, 39 9/16 x 43 9/16" (100.5 x 110.6 cm.)
76.2553 PG 34; cat. no. 28

Upward (Empor). October 1929
Oil on cardboard, 27 1/2 x 19 1/4" (70 x 49 cm.)
76.2553 PG 35; cat. no. 29

Zoltan Kemeny
Divided Movement (Mouvement partagé). 1957
Copper, copper and iron filings and wood, 31 1/8 x 20 1/8 x 1" (79 x 51 x 2.5 cm.)
76.2553 PG 208; cat. no. 130

Paul Klee
Portrait of Frau P. in the South (Bildnis der Frau P. im Süden). 1924
Watercolor and oil transfer drawing on paper mounted on gouache-painted board, including mount, 16 3/4 x 12 1/4" (42.5 x 31 cm.)
76.2553 PG 89; cat. no. 45

Magic Garden (Zaubergarten). March 1926
Oil on plaster-filled wire mesh, including artist's frame 20 7/8 x 17 3/4" (52.9 x 44.9 cm.)
76.2553 PG 90; cat. no. 46

Rosemarie Heber Koczÿ
Trees (Arbres). 1972
Hemp, sisal, linen, jute, raw silk, algae and wool, ca. 37 x 22 7/16" (94 x 57 cm.)
76.2553 PG 188a

Fritz Koenig
Chariot (Biga). 1957
Bronze, including base 20 1/16" (51 cm.) high
76.2553 PG 215

Willem de Kooning
Untitled. 1958
Pastel and charcoal, 22 7/16 x 30 1/2" (57 x 77.5 cm.)
76.2553 PG 159; cat. no. 109

Untitled. 1958
Oil on paper mounted on Masonite mounted on wood, 23 x 29 1/8" (58.5 x 74 cm.)
76.2553 PG 158; cat. no. 108

František Kupka
Untitled. ca. 1910(?)
Pastel on paper, 9 1/4 x 8 3/16" (23.5 x 20.8 cm.)
76.2553 PG 12

Study for *Amorpha, Warm Chromatics* and for *Fugue in Two Colors* (Study for *Amorpha, Chromatique chaude* and for *Fugue à deux couleurs*). ca. 1910-11
Pastel on paper, 18 15/16 x 19" (46.8 x 48.3 cm.)
76.2553 PG 13; cat. no. 24

Study for *Woman Picking Flowers* (Study for *Femme cueillant des fleurs*). ca. 1910(?)
Pastel on paper, 18 7/16 x 19 1/16" (46.8 x 48.3 cm.)
76.2553 PG 13a (reverse of 76.2553 PG 13)

Study for *Organization of Graphic Motifs I* (Study for *Localisations de mobiles graphiques I*). ca. 1911-12
Pastel on paper, 12 15/16 x 12 7/16" (32.9 x 31.6 cm.)
76.2553 PG 15; cat. no. 25

Around a Point (Autour d'un point). ca. 1920-25
Watercolor, gouache and graphite on paper, 7 15/16 x 9 3/8" (20.1 x 23.8 cm.)
76.2553 PG 16; cat. no. 26

Vertical Planes (Plans verticaux).
Gouache and watercolor on paper, 22 3/16 x 16" (56.3 x 40.6 cm.)
76.2553 PG 14

Berto Lardera
Dramatic Meeting (Rincontro drammatico). 1968
Iron and copper, including base 18 13/16" (47.8 cm.) high
76.2553 PG 204

Ibram Lassaw
Corax. December 1953
Chromium bronze and other metals, 19 1/2 x 23 x 10" (49.5 x 58.8 x 25.5 cm.)
76.2553 PG 202; cat. no. 124

Henri Laurens
Head of a Young Girl (Tête de jeune fillette). 1920 (cast 1959)
Terra-cotta, 13 1/2 x 6 1/2" (34.2 x 16.5 cm.)
76.2553 PG 27; cat. no. 16

Fernand Léger
Study of a Nude. Winter 1912-13
Oil on paper, 25 x 19 1/16" (63.6 x 48.5 cm.)
76.2553 PG 19; cat. no. 7

Men in the City (Les Hommes dans la ville). 1919
Oil on canvas, 57⅜ x 44 11/16" (145.7 x 113.5 cm.)
76.2553 PG 21; cat. no. 8

Leonid
Venetian Lagoon.
Oil on canvas, 32 5/16 x 50 1/16" (82 x 127.1 cm.)
76.2553 PG 221

Jacques Lipchitz
Seated Pierrot (Pierrot assis). 1922
Lead, including base 13 3/16" (33.5 cm.) high
76.2553 PG 28; cat. no. 17

Aurelia. 1946
Bronze, 25⅜" (64.5 cm.) high
76.2553 PG 29; cat. no. 18

El Lissitzky
Untitled. ca. 1919-20
Oil on canvas, 31 5/16 x 19½" (79.6 x 49.6 cm.)
76.2553 PG 43; cat. no. 31

Ludovico De Luigi
Parnassus, Apollo and Papileo Macaon. 1970
Oil on canvas, 39 9/16 x 59 3/16" (100.4 x 150.3 cm.)
76.2553 PG 181a

Heinz Mack
Cardiogram of an Angel (Cardiogram eines Engels). 1964
Aluminum mounted on Masonite, 68⅛ x 39 9/16"
(173 x 100.5 cm.)
76.2553 PG 228; cat. no. 140

René Magritte
Voice of Space (La Voix des airs). 1931
Oil on canvas, 28⅝ x 21⅜" (72.7 x 54.2 cm.)
76.2553 PG 101; cat. no. 85

Empire of Light (Empire des lumières). 1953-54
Oil on canvas, 76 15/16 x 51⅝" (195.4 x 131.2 cm.)
76.2553 PG 102; cat. no. 86

Kazimir Malevich
Untitled. ca. 1916
Oil on canvas, 20⅞ x 20⅞" (53 x 53 cm.)
76.2553 PG 42; cat. no. 30

Man Ray
Silhouette. 1916
India ink and charcoal (and gouache?) on board,
20 15/16 x 25¼" (51.6 x 64.1 cm.)
76.2553 PG 68; cat. no. 51

Untitled. 1923
Rayograph, gelatin silver print, 11⅜ x 9¼" (28.8 x 23.5 cm.)
76.2553 PG 69a; cat. no. 52

Untitled. 1927
Rayograph, gelatin silver print, 11 15/16 x 10" (30.4 x 25.4 cm.)
76.2553 PG 69b; cat. no. 53

Louis Marcoussis
The Regular (L'Habitué). 1920
Oil with sand and pebbles on canvas, 63¾ x 38 3/16"
(161.9 x 97 cm.)
76.2553 PG 22; cat. no. 12

Marino Marini
The Angel of the City (L'angelo della città). 1948 (cast 1950?)
Bronze, including base 67 11/16 x 41¾" (172 x 106 cm.)
76.2553 PG 183; cat. no. 150

Manfredo Massironi
Ipercubo Plexiglas. 1963
Plexiglass, 16⅛ x 14¾ x 14¾" (40.9 x 37.5 x 37.5 cm.)
76.2553 PG 227

André Masson
The Armor (L'Armure). January-April 1925
Oil on canvas, 31¾ x 21¼" (80.6 x 54 cm.)
76.2553 PG 106; cat. no. 93

Two Children. 1942
Bronze, 6 x 4¼" (15.3 x 10.7 cm.)
76.2553 PG 107

Bird Fascinated by a Snake (Oiseau fasciné par un serpent). 1942
Tempera on paper, 22¼ x 29¾" (56.5 x 75.5 cm.)
76.2553 PG 108; cat. no. 94

Matta
The Dryads. 1941
Pencil and crayon on paper, 22 15/16 x 28 15/16" (58.2 x 73.4 cm.)
76.2553 PG 109; cat. no. 95

*The Un-Nominator Renominated (Le Dénommeur
renommé).* 1952-53
Oil on canvas, 47⅜ x 68⅞″ (120.4 x 175 cm.)
76.2553 PG 110; cat. no. 96

Jean Metzinger
At the Cycle-Race Track (Au Vélodrome). ca. 1914(?)
Oil and collage on canvas, 51⅜ x 38¼″ (130.4 x 97.1 cm.)
76.2553 PG 18; cat. no. 10

Luciano Minguzzi
He-Goat. 1959
Bronze, 6⅝ x 13⅜″ (16.8 x 34 cm.)
76.2553 PG 212

Mirko
*Architectural Element—Lines of Force in Space (Elemento
architettonico—Linee forze nello spazio).* 1953
Copper, 78½ x 38⅜″ (199.3 x 97.5 cm.)
76.2553 PG 210

Little Chimera (Piccola chimera). 1956
Bronze, 6⅛″ (15.5 cm.) high
76.2553 PG 211

Joan Miró
Painting (Peinture). 1925
Oil on canvas, 45⅛ x 57⅜″ (114.5 x 145.7 cm.)
76.2553 PG 91; cat. no. 72

Dutch Interior II (Intérieur hollandais). Summer 1928
Oil on canvas, 36¼ x 28¾ (92 x 73 cm.)
76.2553 PG 92; cat. no. 73

Seated Woman II (Femme assise II). February 27, 1939
Oil on canvas, 63¾ x 51³⁄₁₆″ (162 x 130 cm.)
76.2553 PG 93; cat. no. 74

Piet Mondrian
Untitled (Oval Composition). 1914
Charcoal on paper mounted on panel, paper 60 x 39⅜″
(152.5 x 100 cm.)
76.2553 PG 37; cat. no. 35

The Sea. 1914
Charcoal and gouache on paper mounted on panel, paper
34½ x 47⅜″ (87.6 x 120.3 cm.)
76.2553 PG 38; cat no. 34

Composition. 1938-39
Oil on canvas mounted on wood support, canvas
41⁷⁄₁₆ x 40⁵⁄₁₆″ (105.2 x 102.3 cm.)
76.2553 PG 39; cat. no. 36

Henry Moore
Ideas for Sculpture. 1937
Chalk and crayon on paper mounted on cardboard, 15 x 22″
(38 x 56 cm.)
76.2553 PG 190

Untitled. 1937
Chalk, pastel and crayon on paper mounted on board,
15 x 22″ (38 x 56 cm.)
76.2553 PG 189

Stringed Object (Head). 1938 (cast 1956)
Bronze and string, 2¹⁵⁄₁₆ x 2¹⁄₁₆″ (7.5 x 5.2 cm.)
76.2553 PG 191

Reclining Figure. 1938 (cast 1946)
Polished bronze, 5⅛ x 12⅛″ (13.6 x 31.5 cm.)
76. 2553 PG 192

Family Group. ca. 1944 (cast 1956)
Bronze, 5⅝ x 4³⁄₁₆ x 2¹⁵⁄₁₆″ (14.2 x 13.8 x 7.5 cm.)
76.2553 PG 193

Three Standing Figures. 1953
Bronze, including base 28¾ x 26¼ x 11⅜″
(73.2 x 68 x 29 cm.)
76.2553 PG 194; cat. no. 80

Robert Motherwell
Personage (Autoportrait). December 9, 1943
Paper collage, gouache and ink on board, 40⅞ x 25¹⁵⁄₁₆″
(103.8 x 65.9 cm.)
76.2553 PG 155; cat. no. 120

E. R. Nele
Collective II (Kollektiv II). 1961
Bronze, 15¾″ (39.9 cm.) high
76.2553 PG 216

Ben Nicholson
February 1956 (menhir). 1956
Oil and ink(?) on board, 39⅛ x 11¹³⁄₁₆″ (99.4 x 30 cm.)
76.2553 PG 46; cat. no. 127

Richard Oelze
Untitled. ca. 1933
Pencil on paper, $10\frac{5}{16}$ x $7\frac{1}{4}$" (26.2 x 18.4 cm.)
76.2553 PG 104

Kenzo Okada
Above the White. 1960
Oil on canvas, $50\frac{1}{8}$ x $38\frac{1}{16}$" (127.3 x 96.7 cm.)
76.2553 PG 184; cat. no. 141

Amédée Ozenfant
Guitar and Bottles (Guitare et bouteilles). 1920
Oil on canvas, $31\frac{11}{16}$ x $39\frac{5}{16}$" (80.5 x 99.8 cm.)
76.2553 PG 24; cat. no. 40

Eduardo Paolozzi
Chinese Dog 2. May 1958
Bronze, $36\frac{3}{8}$ x $25\frac{3}{16}$" (92.3 x 64 cm.)
76.2553 PG 200; cat. no. 129

Pegeen
Girls in the Arches. ca. 1936
Gouache on paper, $15\frac{15}{16}$ x $21\frac{13}{16}$" (40.5 x 55.5 cm.)
76.2553 PG 178

At the Seaside. 1945
Oil on canvas, $31\frac{3}{4}$ x $42\frac{3}{4}$" (80.7 x 108.7 cm.)
76.2553 PG 267

The Exhibition. ca. 1945
Pastel on paper, $29\frac{5}{16}$ x $40\frac{7}{8}$" (74.5 x 103.7 cm.)
76.2553 PG 268

My Wedding. 1946
Oil on canvas, $29\frac{15}{16}$ x $35\frac{13}{16}$" (76.1 x 91 cm.)
76.2553 PG 177

Palazzo Venier dei Leoni. 1950s
Pastel on paper, sight, $9\frac{3}{8}$ x $25\frac{9}{16}$" (23.9 x 65 cm.)
76.2553 PG 269

Childbirth. ca. 1952
Crayon and gouache on paper, $8\frac{11}{16}$ x 11" (22.1 x 28 cm.)
76.2553 PG 270

On the Grand Canal. 1950s
Pastel, gouache and gold paint on paper, $9\frac{15}{16}$ x $15\frac{15}{16}$" (25.3 x 40.5 cm.)
76.2553 PG 271

In the Park. 1953
Oil on canvas, $21\frac{5}{8}$ x $43\frac{3}{4}$" (55 x 111.1 cm.)
76.2553 PG 177a

Family Portrait. Late 1950s
Pastel on paper, sight, $20\frac{5}{16}$ x $29\frac{5}{16}$" (51.7 x 74.7 cm.)
76.2553 PG 272

In the Bath. Late 1950s
Pastel on paper, sight, $19\frac{1}{4}$ x $25\frac{1}{4}$" (48.9 x 64.2 cm.)
76.2553 PG 273

Palazzo Venier—Grand Canal. 1960s
Pastel on paper, $12\frac{5}{8}$ x $19\frac{1}{4}$" (32 x 49 cm.)
76.2553 PG 274

The Sunshade. 1960s
Pastel on paper, $18\frac{5}{16}$ x $12\frac{3}{8}$" (46.6 x 31.5 cm.)
76.2553 PG 275

Intimate Conversation. 1960s
Pastel on paper, $12\frac{9}{16}$ x $19\frac{5}{16}$" (31.9 x 49 cm.)
76.2553 PG 276

Girls in a Room. 1964
Pastel on paper, sight, $19\frac{7}{8}$ x $26\frac{7}{16}$" (49.3 x 67.1 cm.)
76.2553 PG 277

Pegeen with Egidio Costantini
Clementine. 1966
12 poured glass sculptures in vitrine
Vitrine, $55\frac{1}{2}$ x 37" (141 x 94 cm.)
76.2553 PG 278

Antoine Pevsner
Anchored Cross (La Croix anchrée). 1933
Glass, marble and brass, $33\frac{5}{16}$" (84.6 cm.) long (diagonally)
76.2553 PG 60; cat. no. 32

Developable Surface (Surface développable). 1938-August 1939
Bronze and copper, including base, $20\frac{1}{2}$ x $12\frac{3}{16}$" (52.1 x 31 cm.)
76.2553 PG 61

Developable Surface (Surface développable). 1941
Bronze and silver plate, $21\frac{5}{8}$ x $14\frac{1}{4}$ x $19\frac{5}{16}$" (55 x 36.3 x 49.1 cm.)
76.2553 PG 62; cat. no. 33

Francis Picabia
Very Rare Picture on the Earth (Très rare tableau sur la terre). 1915
Oil and metallic paint on board, and silver and gold leaf on wood, including artist's painted frame 49½ x 38½″ (125.7 x 97.8 cm.)
76.2553 PG 67; cat. no. 54

Pablo Picasso
The Poet (Le Poète). August 1911
Oil on canvas, 51⅝ x 35¼″ (131.2 x 89.5 cm.)
76.2553 PG 1; cat. no. 1

Pipe, Glass, Bottle of Vieux Marc (Pipe, verre, bouteille de Vieux Marc). Spring 1914
Paper collage, charcoal, India ink, printer's ink, graphite and gouache on canvas, 28¹³⁄₁₆ x 23⅜″ (73.2 x 59.4 cm.)
76.2553 PG 2; cat. no. 2

The Studio (L'Atelier). 1928
Oil and crayon on canvas, 63⅝ x 51⅛″ (161.6 x 129.9 cm.)
76.2553 PG 3; cat. no. 3

On the Beach (La Baignade). February 12, 1937
Oil, conté crayon and chalk on canvas, 50¹³⁄₁₆ x 76⅜″ (129.1 x 194 cm.)
76.2553 PG 5; cat. no. 4

The Dream and Lie of Franco (Sueño y mentira de Franco). 1937
56/150
Etching and aquatint, 2 parts, each 15¹⁄₁₆ x 22⁷⁄₁₆″ (38.2 x 54.5 cm.)
76.2553 PG 4a-b

Half-length Portrait of a Man in a Striped Jersey (Buste d'homme en tricot rayé). September 14, 1939
Gouache on paper, 24⅞ x 17¹⁵⁄₁₆″ (63.1 x 45.6 cm.)
76.2553 PG 6

Jackson Pollock
The Moon Woman. 1942
Oil on canvas, 69 x 43¹⁄₁₆″ (175.2 x 109.3 cm.)
76.2553 PG 141; cat. no. 110

Untitled. 1944
Oil on canvas, 28¹³⁄₁₆ x 17¹⁵⁄₁₆″ (73.2 x 45.6 cm.)
76.2553 PG 142

Two. 1943-45
Oil on canvas, 76 x 43¼″ (193 x 110 cm.)
76.2553 PG 143; cat. no. 111

Direction. October 1945
Oil on canvas, 31¾ x 21¹⁵⁄₁₆″ (80.6 x 55.7 cm.)
76.2553 PG 144; cat. no. 112

Circumcision. January 1946
Oil on canvas, 56¹⁄₁₆ x 66⅛″ (142.3 x 168 cm.)
76.2553 PG 145; cat. no. 113

Untitled. ca. 1946
Gouache and pastel on paper, 22⅞ x 31½″ (58 x 80 cm.)
76.2553 PG 147

Bird Effort. 1946
Oil on canvas, 24 x 20¹⁄₁₆″ (61 x 51 cm.)
76.2553 PG 146

Croaking Movement. 1946
Oil on canvas, 54 x 44⅛″ (137 x 112 cm.)
76.2553 PG 148; cat. no. 115

Eyes in the Heat. 1946
Oil (and enamel?) on canvas, 54 x 43″ (137.2 x 109.2 cm.)
76.2553 PG 149; cat. no. 114

Enchanted Forest. 1947
Oil on canvas, 45⅛ x 87⅛″ (114.6 x 221.3 cm.)
76.2553 PG 151; cat. no. 117

Alchemy. 1947
Oil, aluminum (and enamel?) paint and string on canvas, 45⅛ x 87⅛″ (114.6 x 221.3 cm.)
76.2553 PG 150; cat. no. 116

Arnaldo Pomodoro
Study No. 1 (Tablet of Signs) (Studio no. 1 [Tavola dei segni]). 1961
Bronze, including base, 22¾ x 13¹⁄₁₆″ (57.8 x 33.2 cm.)
76.2553 PG 213

Sphere No. 4 (Sfera no. 4). 1963-64 (cast 1964)
Bronze, 72⅞″ (185 cm.) circumference
76.2553 PG 214; cat. no. 149

Germaine Richier
Tauromachy (Tauromachie). 1953
Bronze, figure 43⅞″ (111.5 cm.) high; base 37¹¹⁄₁₆ x 20⅝″ (95.7 x 52.5 cm.)
76.2553 PG 205; cat. no. 128

Hans Richter
Dadahead (Dadakopf). 1918
Ink on paper, 10¹¹⁄₁₆ x 6³⁄₁₆″ (27.2 x 15.7 cm.)
76.2553 PG 83

Dadahead (Dadakopf). 1923
Oil on canvas mounted on wood, ca. 11 x 6½"
(28 x 16.6 cm.)
76.2553 PG 84

Jean-Paul Riopelle
Painting (Peinture). 1955
Oil on canvas, 45⅜ x 28⁹⁄₁₆" (115.2 x 72.5 cm.)
76.2553 PG 187; cat. no. 142

Mark Rothko
Sacrifice. April 1946
Watercolor, gouache and India ink on paper, 39⁷⁄₁₆ x 25⅞"
(100.2 x 65.8 cm.)
76.2553 PG 154; cat. no. 121

Giuseppe Santomaso
Secret Life (Vita segreta). 1958
Oil on canvas, 28¹³⁄₁₆ x 19¹¹⁄₁₆" (73.1 x 49.9 cm.)
76.2553 PG 161; cat. no. 144

Kurt Schwitters
Merz Drawing 75 (Merzzeichnung 75). 1920
Collage, gouache, ink and graphite on papers and fabric,
including artist's mat 5¾ x 3¹⁵⁄₁₆" (14.6 x 10 cm.)
76.2553 PG 85; cat. no. 69

Blue in Blue (Blau in Blau). 1926-29
Collage and lithographic crayon on paper, 14⁷⁄₁₆ x 11¾"
(36.7 x 29.9 cm.)
76.2553 PG 86; cat. no. 70

Maraak, Variation I. 1930
Oil and assemblage of objects on board, 18⅛ x 14⁹⁄₁₆"
(46 x 37 cm.)
76.2553 PG 87; cat. no. 71

Gino Severini
Sea=Dancer (Mare=Ballerina). January 1914
Oil on canvas, including artist's painted frame
41½ x 33¹³⁄₁₆" (105.3 x 85.9 cm.)
76.2553 PG 32; cat. no. 22

Francisco Sobrino
*Unstable Transformation—Superposition—Juxtaposition
(Transformation instable—Superposition—Juxtaposition).*
1963
Plexiglass, 32⁷⁄₁₆ x 16¾ x 16¾" (82.3 x 42.5 x 42.5 cm.)
76.2553 PG 255

Clyfford Still
Jamais. May 1944
Oil on canvas, 65¹⁄₁₆ x 32¼" (165.2 x 82 cm.)
76.2553 PG 153; cat. no. 122

Graham Sutherland
Organic Form. 1962-68
Oil on canvas, 51¼ x 38⅜" (130.2 x 97.4 cm.)
76.2553 PG 120; cat. no. 132

Takis
Signal. 1958
Iron, ca. 141¾" (360 cm.) high
76.2553 PG 209

Rufino Tamayo
Heavenly Bodies. 1946
Oil with sand on canvas, 34⅛ x 66¹⁵⁄₁₆" (86.6 x 170 cm.)
76.2553 PG 119; cat. no. 131

Tancredi
Untitled. ca. 1951-52
Gouache on paper, 27⅜ x 39¼" (69.6 x 99.7 cm.)
76.2553 PG 279

Paesaggio di spazio. ca. 1951-52
Gouache on paper, 27⅝ x 39³⁄₁₆" (70.2 x 99.6 cm.)
76.2553 PG 280

Untitled. ca. 1952
Gouache and crayon on paper, 27⁹⁄₁₆ x 39¼" (70 x 99.8 cm.)
76.2553 PG 281

Untitled. ca. 1953
Gouache, graphite and pastel on paper, 27⁹⁄₁₆ x 39¼"
(70 x 99.8 cm.)
76.2553 PG 282

Untitled. ca. 1953
Gouache and pastel on paper, 27⁹⁄₁₆ x 39¼" (70.1 x 99.8 cm.)
76.2553 PG 283

Untitled. ca. 1953
Gouache and pastel on paper, 27¼ x 39⅛" (69.2 x 99.5 cm.)
76.2553 PG 284

Untitled. ca. 1954
Gouache on paper, 29⅜ x 41¼" (74.6 x 104.8 cm.)
76.2553 PG 285

Untitled. ca. 1954
Gouache on paper, 27½ x 39¼" (69.9 x 99.8 cm.)
76.2553 PG 286

Composition. 1955
Oil and tempera on canvas, 51 x 76¼″ (129.5 x 195 cm.)
76.2553 PG 166; cat. no. 143

Trasparenze degli elementi. 1957
Wax crayon and gouache on paper, 27 x 39⅟₁₆″
(68.7 x 99.2 cm.)
76.2553 PG 287

Composition. 1957
Tempera on canvas, 51⅝₁₆ x 66¹¹⁄₁₆″ (130.4 x 169.4 cm.)
76.2553 PG 167

Yves Tanguy
Promontory Palace (Palais promontoire). 1931
Oil on canvas, 28¾ x 23⅜″ (73 x 60 cm.)
76.2553 PG 94; cat. no. 81

The Sun in Its Jewel Case (Le Soleil dans son écrin). 1937
Oil on canvas, 45⁷⁄₁₆ x 34¹¹⁄₁₆″ (115.4 x 88.1 cm.)
76.2553 PG 95; cat. no. 82

Untitled. 1938
Gouache on paper, 3¹¹⁄₁₆ x 9³⁄₁₆″ (9.3 x 23.3 cm.)
76.2553 PG 96; cat. no. 83

Untitled. July 20, 1938
Pencil and feather on paper, 21⁷⁄₁₆ x 7³⁄₁₆″ (54.5 x 18.2 cm.)
76.2553 PG 97

In an Indeterminate Place (En lieu oblique). March 1941
Oil on canvas, 16¹⁵⁄₁₆ x 28⅛″ (43 x 71.4 cm.)
76.2553 PG 98; cat. no. 84

Leslie Thornton
Roundabout. 1955
Bronze, 27⅞″ (70.8 cm.) high
76.2553 PG 199

Mark Tobey
Advance of History. 1964
Gouache and watercolor on paper, 25⅝ x 19¹¹⁄₁₆″
(65.2 x 50.1 cm.)
76.2553 PG 140; cat. no. 123

Tomonori Toyofuku
Drifting No. 2. 1959
Wood, 69½ x 119½″ (176.5 x 303.5 cm.)
76.2553 PG 218

John Tunnard
Psi. 1938
Oil, gesso, gouache, pastel(?) and wax crayon on board,
31⁷⁄₁₆ x 47³⁄₁₆″ (79.9 x 119.8 cm.)
76.2553 PG 47; cat. no. 97

Pi. Spring 1941
Gouache, wash, conté crayon, graphite, pastel and
paint or ink on paper, 15⅜ x 22″ (39 x 56 cm.)
76.2553 PG 48

Günther Uecker
Tactile Rotating Structure (Taktile Struktur rotierend). 1961
Wood, burlap, aluminum, iron nails and silver paint,
24 x 20¼″ (61 x 52.7 cm.)
76.2553 PG 229

Laurence Vail
Screen. 1940
Gouache and paper collage on canvas mounted on wood
screen, 3 panels, total ca. 67 x 65″ (170 x 165 cm.)
76.2553 PG 123

Untitled. ca. 1962
Assemblage of objects, 19¾″ (50 cm.) high
76.2553 PG 124

Untitled
Assemblage of objects and fabric, 13⁹⁄₁₆″ (34.5 cm.) high
76.2553 PG 288

Untitled
Glass bottle and collage, 8¼″ (21 cm.) high
76.2553 PG 289

Untitled
Glass bottle and collage, 16¹⁵⁄₁₆″ (43 cm.) high
76.2553 PG 290

Untitled
Glass bottle, light fixture and collage, 11⅜″ (29 cm.) high
76.2553 PG 291

Untitled
Glass bottles, 17⅛″ (43.5 cm.) high
76.2553 PG 292

Untitled. n.d.
Glass bottle with paper, fabric and sequin collage,
11″ (28 cm.) high
76.2553 PG 293

Georges Vantongerloo
*Construction of Volumetric Interrelationships Derived from
the Inscribed Square and the Square Circumscribed by a
Circle (Construction des rapports des volumes émanante du
carré inscrit et le carré circonscrit d'une cercle).* 1924
Cast cement with paint, 11¹³⁄₁₆ x 10¹⁄₁₆″ (30 x 25.5 cm.)
76.2553 PG 59; cat. no. 39

Victor Vasarely
JAK. 1965
Metallic and acrylic paint on wood, 32⁷⁄₁₆ x 32⁷⁄₁₆″
(82.3 x 82.3 cm.)
76.2553 PG 223

Emilio Vedova
*Image of Time (Barrier) (Immagine del tempo
[Sbarramento]).* 1951
Egg tempera on canvas, 51³⁄₈ x 67¹⁄₈″ (130.5 x 170.4 cm.)
76.2553 PG 162; cat. no. 145

Hostage City (Città ostaggio). 1954
Tempera, India ink, sand and enamel on paper,
27⁵⁄₈ x 39⁷⁄₁₆″ (70.2 x 100.1 cm.)
76.2553 PG 163

Jacques Villon
Spaces (Espaces). 1920
Oil on canvas, 28³⁄₄ x 36¹⁄₁₆″ (73 x 91.6 cm.)
76.2553 PG 23; cat. no. 14

SCULPTURE FROM AFRICA, OCEANIA, THE AMERICAS, JAPAN AND CORFU

Africa
Reliquary Figure
Gabon, Kota
Wood and brass, 22¹⁄₂″ (57 cm.) high
76.2553 PG 245

Mask
Guinea, Toma
Wood, 33¹⁄₂″ (85 cm.) high
76.2553 PG 246

Yoka Mask (Nimba)
Guinea, Baga
Wood, 55″ (138 cm.) high
76.2553 PG 243

Mask (Gelede)
Nigeria, Yoruba
Polychrome wood, 29″ (72 cm.) high
76.2553 PG 247

Bird (Porpianong)
Ivory Coast, Senufo
Polychrome wood, 55″ (140 cm.) high
76.2553 PG 242

Pair of Male and Female Figures (Rhythm Pounders)
Ivory Coast, Senufo
Wood, 52″ (130 cm.) high
76.2553 PG 250a-b

Horse and Rider
Ivory Coast, Senufo
Wood, 20″ (50 cm.) long
76.2553 PG 251

Seat
Ivory Coast, Senufo
Wood, 30 x 7″ (74 x 18 cm.)
76.2553 PG 255

Standing Male Figure
Ivory Coast, Senufo
Wood, 24¹⁄₂″ (72 cm.) high
76.2553 PG 257

Helmet Mask
Ivory Coast, Senufo
Wood, 18 x 13 x 27″ (46 x 33 x 68.5 cm.)
76.2553 PG 244

Mask
Zaire, Salampasu
Wood, copper, paint and vegetable fiber, 24″ (62 cm.) high
76.2553 PG 258

Wall Panel with Sculptured Face of Owl
Zaire, Yaka
Polychrome wood, 19½″ (48 cm.) high
76.2553 PG 252

Wall Panel with Sculptured Face of Animal
Zaire, Yaka
Polychrome wood, 19½″ (48 cm.) high
76.2553 PG 253

Initiation Mask
Zaire, Yaka
Polychrome wood, woven raffia and raffia,
20½″ (50 cm.) high
76.2553 PG 254

Male Antelope Headdress (Chi Wara)
Mali, Bamana
Wood, 39″ (98 cm.) high
76.2553 PG 256a

Female Antelope Headdress (Chi Wara)
Mali, Bamana
Wood, 33″ (84 cm.) high
76.2553 PG 256b

Seated Figure
Mali, Dogon
Wood, 27¼″ (69 cm.) high
76.2553 PG 241

Lidded Container
Mali, Dogon
Wood, 44″ (110 cm.) high
76.2553 PG 249

Coffer
Mali, Dogon
Wood, 47½″ (118 cm.) long
76.2553 PG 248

Oceania
Tatanua Mask
Northern New Ireland
Polychrome wood with fringe, 14¼″ (37.5 cm.) high
76.2553 PG 232

Funerary Carving (Malanggan)
Northern New Ireland
Polychrome wood, 63″ (158 cm.) long
76.2553 PG 233

Soul Ship
Irian Jaya (West New Guinea), Asmat
Polychrome wood, 88⅛″ (223.9 cm.) long
76.2553 PG 236

Ancestral Carving
Papua, New Guinea, East Sepik Province, Southern Abelam
Polychrome wood, 58″ (144 cm.) high
76.2553 PG 240

Ancestral Figure
Papua, New Guinea, East Sepik Province, Southern Abelam
Polychrome wood, 65″ (164 cm.) high
76.2553 PG 234

Suspension Hook
Papua, New Guinea, East Sepik Province, Western Iatmul
Wood, 26″ (65 cm.) high
76.2553 PG 235

Figure
Papua, New Guinea, East Sepik Province, Yamok
Village, Sawos
Wood, 54″ (134 cm.) high
76.2553 PG 237

Male Figure
Papua, New Guinea, East Sepik Province, Murik
Wood, 31½″ (78 cm.) high
76.2553 PG 238

Flute Figure
Papua, New Guinea, East Sepik Province, Chambri
Polychrome wood and dog's teeth, 20″ (50 cm.) high
76.2553 PG 239

The Americas
Bark Mask
Amazon River, Brazil
Fabric and straw, 50″ (123 cm.) high
76.2553 PG 261

Three Panels, One with Mask
North Peru, Chimu
Wood, 20 x 21″ (50 x 52 cm.)
76.2553 PG 262

Poncho with Llamas
North Peru, Chimu
Feathers and cotton, 32 x 32″ (80 x 80 cm.)
76.2553 PG 263

Female Figure
Mexico, Nayarit
Terra-cotta, 17″ (42 cm.) high
76.2553 PG 264

Male Figure
Mexico, Nayarit
Terra-cotta, 19″ (47 cm.) high
76.2553 PG 265

Embracing Couple with Baby
Mexico, Nayarit
Terra-cotta, 12″ (32 cm.) high
76.2553 PG 266

Japan
Wagōjin
Wood, 28 x 15″ (71 x 38 cm.)
76.2553 PG 260

Corfu
Two Horses
Stone, 45¼ x 49¼ x 22″ (115 x 125 x 56 cm.)
76.2553 PG 259a-b

INDEX

Photographic Credits

Cover photograph by Carmelo Guadagno

All photographs in the catalogue are by Carmelo Guadagno and David Heald with the following exceptions:

cat. nos. 11, 19, 22, 32, 39, 43, 49, 77, 99, 114 by Julian Kayne

cat. nos. 15, 20, 23, 44, 71, 75, 148, 149 by Mirko Lion

cat. nos. 10, 11, 13, 14, 16, 22-29, 41-44, 47, 51-53, 64-68, 72-79, 85, 86, 95, 96, 98-100, 123, 128, 134, 137, 139, 142 © A.D.A.G.P., Paris/V.A.G.A., New York, 1986

cat. nos. 34-36, 136 © BEELDRECHT, Amsterdam/V.A.G.A., New York, 1986

cat. nos. 45, 46, 69-71, 132 © COSMOPRESS, Geneva/ A.D.A.G.P., Paris/V.A.G.A., New York, 1986

cat. no. 130 © HUNGART, Hungary/V.A.G.A., New York, 1986

cat. no. 120 © Robert Motherwell, 1986/V.A.G.A., New York, 1986

cat. nos. 48-50, 126, 147, 150 © S.I.A.E., Italy/V.A.G.A., New York, 1986

cat. nos. 1-4, 7-9, 12, 40, 55-63, 81-84, 87-94 © S.P.A.D.E.M., Paris/V.A.G.A., New York, 1986

cat. nos. 5, 6, 54 © S.P.A.D.E.M.-A.D.A.G.P., Paris/V.A.G.A., New York, 1986

15,000 softcover copies of this English-language catalogue and 13,000 softcover copies of the Italian translation, designed by Malcolm Grear Designers and typeset by Schooley Graphics/Craftsman Type Inc., have been printed by Arnoldo Mondadori Editore in February 1986 for the Trustees of The Solomon R. Guggenheim Foundation. 2,000 hardcover copies of the Italian edition have been printed for Arnoldo Mondadori Editore.

The extended season of the Peggy Guggenheim Collection is made possible through a grant from **United Technologies Corporation.**

The free Saturday evening opening of the Peggy Guggenheim Collection is financed by a grant from the **Montedison Group.**

The Solomon R. Guggenheim Foundation gratefully acknowledges the generous support of **Alitalia** on an annual basis.

The climate control and surveillance system "Sentinel" for the Peggy Guggenheim Collection have been provided by **Jacorossi S.p.A.**